EXPLORING MICROSOFT® WORD FOR WINDOWS™ 95

VERSION 7.0

EXPLORING MICROSOFT® WORD FOR WINDOWS™ 95

VERSION 7.0

Robert T. Grauer / Maryann Barber

University of Miami

Prentice Hall, Upper Saddle River, New Jersey 07458

Library of Congress Cataloging-in-Publication Data

Grauer, Robert T. [date]
   Exploring Microsoft Word for Windows 95 Version 7.0 / Robert T. Grauer, Maryann Barber.
      p. cm.
   Includes index.
   ISBN 0-13-504044-2
   1. Microsoft Word for Windows. 2. Word processing. I. Barber. Maryann M. II. Title.
   Z52.5.M523G74 1994
   652.5' 536—dc20   95-30344
                                                                     CIP

Acquisitions editor: Carolyn Henderson
Editorial/production supervisor: Greg Hubit Bookworks
Interior and cover design: Suzanne Behnke
Manufacturing buyer: Paul Smolenski
Managing editor: Nicholas Radhuber
Editorial assistant: Audrey Regan
Production coordinator: Renée Pelletier

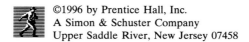©1996 by Prentice Hall, Inc.
A Simon & Schuster Company
Upper Saddle River, New Jersey 07458

All rights reserved. No part of this book may be
reproduced, in any form or by any means,
without permission in writing from the publisher.

Printed in the United States of America
10 9 8 7 6 5 4 3 2 1

ISBN 0-13-504044-2

Prentice Hall International (UK) Limited, *London*
Prentice Hall of Australia Pty. Limited, *Sydney*
Prentice Hall of Canada Inc., *Toronto*
Prentice Hall Hispanoamericano, S.A., *Mexico*
Prentice Hall of India Private Limited, *New Delhi*
Prentice Hall of Japan, Inc., *Tokyo*
Simon & Schuster Asia Pte. Ltd., *Singapore*
Editora Prentice Hall do Brasil, Ltda., *Rio de Janeiro*

Contents

PREFACE ix

Microsoft Office for Windows 95: Four Applications in One xv

1

Microsoft Word 7.0: What Will Word Processing Do for Me? 1

CHAPTER OBJECTIVES 1
OVERVIEW 1
The Basics of Word Processing 2
    Word Wrap 2   The Insertion Point 2   Toggle Switches 3
    Insertion versus Overtype 4   Deleting Text 5
Introduction to Microsoft Word 5
The File Menu 8
Learning by Doing 8
HANDS-ON EXERCISE 1: MY FIRST DOCUMENT 10
Troubleshooting 16
The TipWizard 17
HANDS-ON EXERCISE 2: MODIFYING AN EXISTING DOCUMENT 18
The Spell Check 26
    AutoCorrect 28
Save Command 28
    Backup Options 30
HANDS-ON EXERCISE 3: THE SPELL CHECK 31
Summary 35
Key Words and Concepts 36

Multiple Choice 37
Exploring Microsoft Word 38
Practice with Microsoft Word 42
Case Studies 45

2

Gaining Proficiency: Editing and Formatting 47

CHAPTER OBJECTIVES 47
OVERVIEW 47
Select-Then-Do 48
Moving and Copying Text 49
Undo and Redo Commands 49
Find and Replace Commands 50
Scrolling 51
View Menu 53
HANDS-ON EXERCISE 1: EDITING A DOCUMENT 55
Typography 63
    Typeface 63 Type Size 65 Format Font Command 65
Page Setup Command 67
    Page Breaks 67
An Exercise in Design 68
HANDS-ON EXERCISE 2: CHARACTER FORMATTING 69
Paragraph Formatting 76
    Alignment 76 Indents 76 Tabs 79 Line Spacing 79
    Format Paragraph Command 80 Borders and Shading 82
HANDS-ON EXERCISE 3: PARAGRAPH FORMATTING 84
Summary 90
Key Words and Concepts 91
Multiple Choice 92
Exploring Microsoft Word 94
Practice with Microsoft Word 97
Case Studies 101

3

Enhancing a Document: Proofing, Wizards, ClipArt, and WordArt 103

CHAPTER OBJECTIVES 103
OVERVIEW 103

Thesaurus 104
Grammar Check 104
A Résumé and Cover Letter 107
    The Insert Date and Time Command 110   The Insert Symbol Command 110   Creating an Envelope 111
HANDS-ON EXERCISE 1: PROOFING A DOCUMENT 111
Wizards and Templates 120
HANDS-ON EXERCISE 2: WIZARDS AND TEMPLATES 123
The Insert Object Command 129
    Microsoft ClipArt Gallery 129   Microsoft WordArt 131
HANDS-ON EXERCISE 3: THE CLIPART GALLERY AND WORDART 133
Summary 140
Key Words and Concepts 141
Multiple Choice 141
Exploring Microsoft Word 144
Practice with Microsoft Word 146
Case Studies 151

4

The Professional Document: Footnotes, Tables, and Styles 153

CHAPTER OBJECTIVES 153
OVERVIEW 153
Bullets and Lists 154
Footnotes and Endnotes 154
HANDS-ON EXERCISE 1: PRESIDENTIAL ANECDOTES 156
Tables 163
HANDS-ON EXERCISE 2: TABLES 165
Styles 172
    The AutoFormat Command 173
HANDS-ON EXERCISE 3: STYLES 174
Working in Long Documents 180
    Page Numbers 181   Headers and Footers 181   Sections 182   Table of Contents 184   The Go To Command 184
HANDS-ON EXERCISE 4: WORKING IN LONG DOCUMENTS 184
Summary 193
Key Words and Concepts 194
Multiple Choice 194
Exploring Microsoft Word 196
Practice with Microsoft Word 200
Case Studies 203

5

Desktop Publishing: Creating a Newsletter 205

CHAPTER OBJECTIVES 205
OVERVIEW 205
The Newsletter 206
    Typography 206   Columns 208
The Newsletter Wizard 209
HANDS-ON EXERCISE 1: NEWSPAPER COLUMNS 211
Graphics 217
    Frames 220
HANDS-ON EXERCISE 2: GRAPHICS 221
Elements of Graphic Design 229
    The Grid 229   White Space 230   Emphasis 230
    Facing Pages 233
Summary 234
Key Words and Concepts 234
Multiple Choice 234
Exploring Microsoft Word 236
Practice with Microsoft Word 240
Case Studies 243

APPENDIX A: OBJECT LINKING AND EMBEDDING 245
APPENDIX B: MAIL MERGE 265
APPENDIX C: TOOLBARS 279

Prerequisites: Essentials of Windows 95®
INDEX 11

Preface

Exploring Microsoft Word Version 7.0 is one of several books in the *Exploring Windows 95* series. Other series titles include: *Exploring Windows 95 and Essential Computing Concepts, Exploring Microsoft Excel Version 7.0, Exploring Microsoft PowerPoint Version 7.0, Exploring Microsoft Access Version 7.0, Exploring Microsoft Office 95* (a combination of selected chapters from the individual books), *Exploring Lotus 95, Exploring WordPerfect 95,* and *Exploring the Internet.* Each book in the series is suitable on a stand-alone basis for any course that teaches a specific application; alternatively, several modules can be packaged together for a single course that teaches multiple applications.

The *Exploring Windows* series is different from other texts, both in its scope as well as in the way in which material is presented. Students learn by doing. Concepts are stressed and memorization is minimized. Shortcuts and other important information are consistently highlighted in the many tips that appear throughout the series. Every chapter contains an average of three guided exercises to be completed at the computer.

Each book in the *Exploring Windows* series is accompanied by a comprehensive Instructor's Resource Manual with tests, transparency masters, and student/instructor resource disks. Instructors can also use the Prentice Hall Computerized Online Testing System to prepare customized tests for their courses and may obtain Interactive Multimedia courseware as a further supplement. The *Exploring Windows* series is part of the Prentice Hall custom binding program.

What's New

Exploring Microsoft Word Version 7.0 is a revision of our existing text, *Exploring Microsoft Word 6.0.* There were several goals in the revision, the most obvious being to update the existing book to reflect all changes in the new release of Microsoft Word. We also sought to add topics that were previously omitted and have added exercises on the Microsoft ClipArt Gallery, Microsoft WordArt, and footnotes and endnotes. The Windows 3.1 material was removed from Chapter 1 and placed in an appendix on the Essentials of Windows 95. An introductory section to the Microsoft Office has also been added to emphasize the benefits of the common user interface.

We believe, however, that our most significant improvement is the expanded end-of-chapter material, which provides a wide variety of student assignments. Every chapter contains 15 *multiple-choice questions* (with answers) so that students can test themselves quickly and objectively. Every chapter has four *conceptual problems* that do not require participation at the computer. Every chapter also has four *computer-based practice exercises* to build student proficiency. And finally, every chapter ends with four less structured *case studies* in which the student is given little guidance in the means of solution. This unique *15-four-by-four-by-four* format provides substantial opportunity for students to master the material while simultaneously giving instructors considerable flexibility in student assignments. Instructors may also assign the hands-on exercises within each chapter to ensure further practice on the part of their students.

FEATURES AND BENEFITS

Exploring Microsoft Word Version 7.0 is written for the computer novice and assumes no previous knowledge about Windows 95. A detailed supplement introduces the reader to the operating system and emphasizes the file operations he or she will need.

An introductory section on the Microsoft Office emphasizes the benefits of the common user interface. Although the text assumes no previous knowledge, some users may already be acquainted with another Office application, in which case they can take advantage of what they already know.

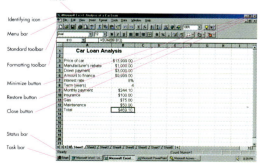

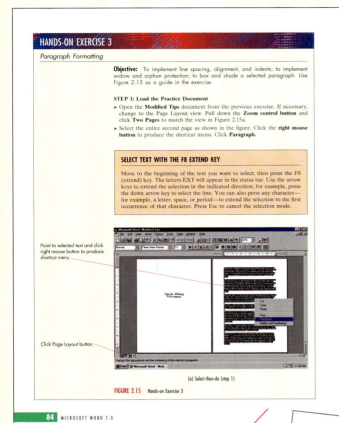

FIGURE 2.15 Hands-on Exercise 3

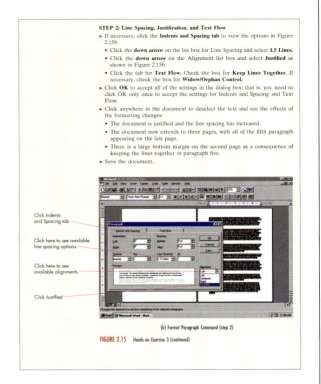

(b) Format Paragraph Command (step 2)

FIGURE 2.15 Hands-on Exercise 3 (continued)

A total of 18 in-depth tutorials (hands-on exercises) guide the reader at the computer. Each tutorial is illustrated with large, full-color, screen captures that are clear and easy to read. Each tutorial is accompanied by numerous tips that present different ways to accomplish a given task, but in a logical and relaxed fashion.

Object Linking and Embedding is stressed throughout the series, beginning in the introductory section on Microsoft Office, where the reader is shown the power of this all-important technology. Examples of OLE appear throughout the book and are distinguished by an OLE icon. Appendix A, on pages 245–263, provides additional information.

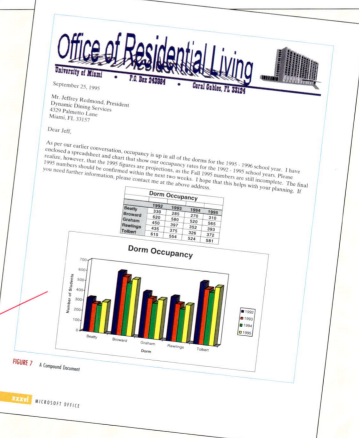

FIGURE 7 A Compound Document

PRACTICE WITH MICROSOFT WORD

1. Retrieve the *Chapter1 Practice 1* document shown in Figure 1.17 from the Exploring Word folder, then make the following changes:
   a. Select the text *Your name* and replace it with your name.
   b. Replace *May 31, 1995* with the current date.
   c. Insert the phrase *one or* in line 2 so that the text reads *... one or more characters than currently exist.*
   d. Delete the word *And* from sentence four in line 5, then change the w in *when* to a capital letter to begin the sentence.
   e. Change the phrase *most efficient to best.*
   f. Place the insertion point at the end of sentence 2, make sure you are in the insert mode, then add the following sentence: *The insert mode adds characters at the insertion point while moving existing text to the right in order to make room for the new text.*
   g. Place the insertion point at the end of the last sentence, press the enter key twice in a row, then enter the following text: *There are several keys that function as toggle switches of which you should be aware. The Ins key switches between the insert and overtype modes, the Caps Lock key toggles between upper- and lowercase letters, and the Num Lock key alternates between typing numbers and using the arrow keys.*
   h. Save the revised document, then print it and submit it to your instructor.

2. Select-then-do: Formatting is not covered until Chapter 2, but we think you are ready to try your hand at basic formatting now. Most formatting operations are done in the context of select-then-do as described in the document in Figure 1.18. You select the text you want to format, then you execute the appropriate formatting command, most easily by clicking the appropriate button on the Formatting toolbar. The function of each button should be apparent from its icon, but you can simply point to a button to display a ToolTip that is indicative of the button's function.

   An unformatted version of the document in Figure 1.18 exists on the data disk as *Chapter1 Practice 2*. Open the document, then format it to match the completed version in Figure 1.18. Just select the text to format, then click the appropriate button. We changed type size in the original document to 24 points for the title and 12 points for text in the document itself. Be sure to add your name and date as shown in the figure, then submit the completed document to your instructor.

3. Your background: Write a short description of your computer background similar to the document in Figure 1.19. The document should be in the form of a note from student to instructor that describes your background and should mention any previous knowledge of computers you have, prior computer courses you have taken, your objectives for this course, and so on. Indicate whether you own a PC, whether you have access to one at work, and/or whether you are considering purchase. Include any other information about yourself and/or your computer-related background.

   Place your name somewhere in the document in boldface italics. We would also like you to use boldface and italics to emphasize the components of any computer system you describe. Use any font or point size you like. Note, too, the last paragraph, which asks you to print the summary statistics for the document when you submit the assignment to your instructor.

FIGURE 1.17 Document for Practice with Word Exercise 1

FIGURE 1.18 Document for Practice with Word Exercise 2

At the end of every chapter are abundant and thought-provoking exercises that review and extend the material in different ways. There are objective multiple-choice questions, conceptual problems that do not require interaction with the computer, guided computer exercises, and less structured case studies that encourage the reader to further exploration and independent study.

(a) UM Jazz Band

(b) CIS 120 Study Sessions

FIGURE 5.14 Flyers for Practice with Word Exercise 1

Chapter 5 on Desktop Publishing covers the basics of graphic design and its implementation in Microsoft Word. Students learn how to merge text with graphics to create professional-looking documents without reliance on external sources.

Concepts are emphasized so that the reader appreciates the theory behind the applications. Students are not just taught what to do, but are provided with the rationale for why they are doing it, and are thus able to extend the information to additional learning on their own.

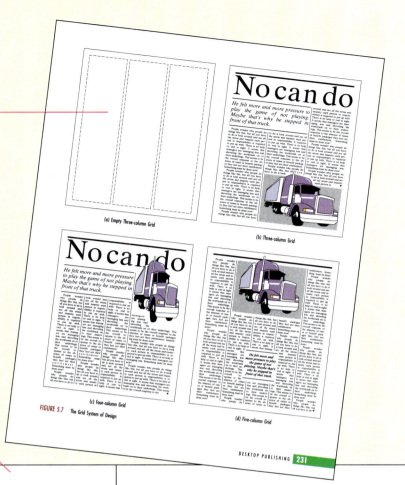

Acknowledgments

We want to thank the many individuals who helped bring this project to fruition. We are especially grateful to our editors at Prentice Hall, Carolyn Henderson and P. J. Boardman, without whom the series would not have been possible. Cecil Yarbrough did an outstanding job in checking the manuscript for technical accuracy. Suzanne Behnke created the innovative and attractive design. Gretchen Marx of Saint Joseph College and Carlotta Eaton of Radford University produced an outstanding set of Instructor Manuals. Greg Hubit was in charge of production. Nancy Evans and Deborah Emry, our marketing managers at Prentice Hall, developed the innovative campaigns which helped make the series a success. We also want to acknowledge our reviewers who, through their comments and constructive criticism, greatly improved the *Exploring Windows* series.

Lynne Band, Middlesex Community College
Stuart P. Brian, Holy Family College
Carl M. Briggs, Indiana University School of Business
Kimberly Chambers, Scottsdale Community College
Alok Charturvedi, Purdue University
Jerry Chin, Southwest Missouri State University
Dean Combellick, Scottsdale Community College
Cody Copeland, Johnson County Community College
Larry S. Corman, Fort Lewis College
Janis Cox, Tri-County Technical College
Martin Crossland, Southwest Missouri State
Paul E. Daurelle, Western Piedmont Community College
David Douglas, University of Arkansas
Carlotta Eaton, Radford University
Raymond Frost, Central Connecticut State University
James Gips, Boston College
Vernon Griffin, Austin Community College
Michael Hassett, Fort Hays State University
Wanda D. Heller, Seminole Community College
Bonnie Homan, San Francisco State University
Ernie Ivey, Polk Community College
Mike Kelly, Community College of Rhode Island
Jane King, Everett Community College
John Lesson, University of Central Florida
David B. Meinert, Southwest Missouri State University
Alan Moltz, Naugatuck Valley Technical Community College
Kim Montney, Kellogg Community College
Kevin Pauli, University of Nebraska
Mary McKenry Percival, University of Miami
Delores Pusins, Hillsborough Community College
Gale E. Rand, College Misericordia
Judith Rice, Santa Fe Community College
David Rinehard, Lansing Community College
Marilyn Salas, Scottsdale Community College
John Shepherd, Duquesne University
Helen Stoloff, Hudson Valley Community College
Mike Thomas, Indiana University School of Business
Suzanne Tomlinson, Iowa State University
Karen Tracey, Central Connecticut State University
Sally Visci, Lorain County Community College
David Weiner, University of San Francisco
Connie Wells, Georgia State University
Wallace John Whistance-Smith, Ryerson Polytechnic University
Jack Zeller, Kirkwood Community College

A final word of thanks to the unnamed students at the University of Miami who make it all worthwhile. And most of all, thanks to you, our readers, for choosing this book. Please feel free to contact us with any comments and suggestions.

Robert T. Grauer
RGRAUER@UMIAMI.MIAMI.EDU

Maryann Barber
MBARBER@UMIAMI.MIAMI.EDU

MICROSOFT OFFICE FOR WINDOWS 95: FOUR APPLICATIONS IN ONE

OVERVIEW

Word processing, spreadsheets, and data management have always been significant microcomputer applications. The early days of the PC saw these applications emerge from different vendors with radically different user interfaces. WordPerfect, Lotus, and dBASE, for example, were dominant applications in their respective areas, and each was developed by a different company. The applications were totally dissimilar, and knowledge of one application did not help in learning another.

The widespread acceptance of Windows 3.1 promoted the concept of a common user interface, which required all applications to follow a consistent set of conventions. This meant that all applications worked essentially the same way, and it provided a sense of familiarity when you learned a new application, since every application presented the same user interface. The development of a suite of applications from a single vendor extended this concept by imposing additional similarities on all applications within the suite.

This introduction will acquaint you with the ***Microsoft Office for Windows 95*** and its four major applications—Word, Excel, PowerPoint, and Access. Our primary purpose is to emphasize the similarities between these applications and to help you extend your knowledge from one application to the next. You will find the same commands in the same menus. You will also recognize familiar toolbars and will be able to take advantage of similar keyboard shortcuts. Our goal is to show you how much you already know and to get you up and running as quickly as possible.

The introduction also introduces you to Schedule+, and to shared applications and utilities such as the ClipArt Gallery and WordArt, which are included within Microsoft Office. We discuss the Office Shortcut Bar and describe how to start an application and open a new or existing document. We introduce you to Object Linking and Embedding, which enables you to combine data from multiple applications into a single document. And finally, we include a hands-on exercise that lets you sit down at the computer and apply what you have learned.

> **TRY THE COLLEGE BOOKSTORE**
>
> Any machine you buy will come with Windows 95, but that is only the beginning since you must also obtain the application software you intend to run. Many first-time buyers are surprised that they have to pay extra for software, so you had better allow for software in your budget. Some hardware vendors will bundle (at no additional cost) Microsoft Office as an inducement to buy from them. If you have already purchased your system and you need software, the best place to buy Microsoft Office is the college bookstore, where it can be obtained at a substantial educational discount.

MICROSOFT OFFICE FOR WINDOWS 95

All Office applications share the common user interface for Windows 95 with which you may already be familiar. (If you are new to Windows 95, then read the appendix on the "Essentials of Windows 95," which appears at the end of this book.) Figure 1 displays a screen from each application in the Microsoft Office—Word, Excel, PowerPoint, and Access, in Figures 1a, 1b, 1c, and 1d, respectively. Look closely at Figure 1, and realize that each screen contains both an application window and a document window, and that each document window has been maximized within the application window. The title bars of the application and document windows have been merged into a single title bar that appears at the top of the application window. The title bar displays the application (e.g., Microsoft Word in Figure 1a) as well as the name of the document (Letter to My Instructor in Figure 1a) on which you are working.

All four screens in Figure 1 are similar in appearance despite the fact that the applications accomplish very different tasks. Each application window has an identifying icon, a menu bar, a title bar, and a minimize, maximize or restore, and a close button. Each document window has its own identifying icon, and its own minimize, maximize or restore, and close button. The Windows 95 taskbar appears at the bottom of each application window and shows the open applications. The status bar appears above the taskbar and displays information relevant to the window or selected object.

Each application in Microsoft Office uses a consistent command structure in which the same basic menus are found in all applications. The File, Edit, View, Insert, Tools, Window, and Help menus are present in all four applications. The same commands are found in the same menus. The Save, Open, Print, and Exit commands, for example, are contained in the File menu. The Cut, Copy, Paste, and Undo commands are found in the Edit menu.

The means for accessing the pull-down menus are consistent from one application to the next. Click the menu name on the menu bar, or press the Alt key plus the underlined letter of the menu name; for example, press Alt+F to pull down the File menu. If you already know some keyboard shortcuts in one application, there is a good chance that the shortcuts will work in another application. Ctrl+Home and Ctrl+End, for example, move to the beginning and end of a document, respectively. Ctrl+B, Ctrl+I, and Ctrl+U boldface, italicize, and underline text. Ctrl+X (the "X" is supposed to remind you of a pair of scissors), Ctrl+C, and Ctrl+V will cut, copy, and paste, respectively. You may not know what these

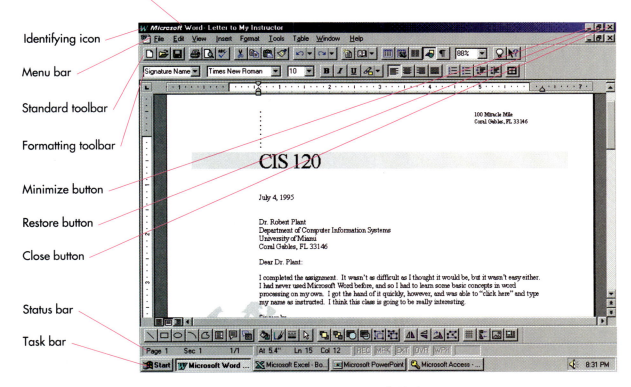

FIGURE 1 The Common User Interface

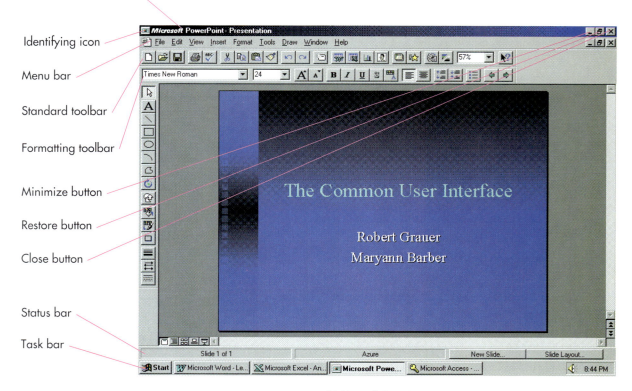

(c) Microsoft PowerPoint

(d) Microsoft Access

FIGURE 1 The Common User Interface (continued)

commands do now, but once you learn how they work in one application, you will intuitively know how they work in the others.

All four applications use consistent (and often identical) dialog boxes. The dialog boxes to open and close a file, for example, are identical in every application. All four applications also share a common dictionary. The AutoCorrect feature (to correct common spelling mistakes) works identically in all four applications. The help feature also functions identically.

There are, of course, differences between the applications. Each application has its own unique menus and associated toolbars. Nevertheless, the Standard and Formatting toolbars in all applications contain many of the same tools (especially the first several tools on the left of each toolbar). The ***Standard toolbar*** contains buttons for basic commands such as Open, Save, or Print. It also contains buttons to cut, copy, and paste, and all of these buttons are identical in all four applications. The ***Formatting toolbar*** provides access to common formatting operations such as boldface, italics, or underlining, or changing the font or point size, and again, these buttons are identical in all four applications. ToolTips are present in all applications. Suffice it to say, therefore, that once you know one Office application, you have a tremendous head start in learning another.

MICROSOFT OFFICE VERSUS OFFICE PROFESSIONAL

Microsoft distributes two versions of the Office Suite: Standard Office and Office Professional. Both versions include Word, Excel, and PowerPoint. The Office Professional also has Microsoft Access. The difference is important when you are shopping and comparing prices from different sources. Be sure to purchase the version that is appropriate for your needs.

Online Help

Each application in the Microsoft Office has the extensive ***online help*** facility as shown in Figure 2. Help is available at any time, and is accessed from the application's Help menu. (The Help screens in Figure 2 pertain to Microsoft Office, as opposed to a specific application, and were accessed through the Answer Wizard button on the Office Shortcut Bar.)

The ***Contents tab*** in Figure 2a is similar to the table of contents in an ordinary book. The major topics are represented by books, each of which can be opened to display additional topics. Each open book displays one or more topics, which may be viewed and/or printed to provide the indicated information.

The ***Index tab*** in Figure 2b is analogous to the index of an ordinary book. Type the first several letters of the topic to look up, such as "he" in Figure 2b. Help then returns all of the topics beginning with the letters you entered. Select the topic you want, then display the topic for immediate viewing, or print it for later reference.

The ***Answer Wizard*** in Figure 2c lets you ask questions in your own words, then it returns the relevant help topics. The Help screen in Figure 2d was accessed from the selections provided by the Answer Wizard, and it, in turn, will lead you to new features in the individual applications.

Office Shortcut Bar

The ***Microsoft Office Shortcut Bar*** provides immediate access to each application within Microsoft Office. It consists of a row of buttons and can be placed anywhere

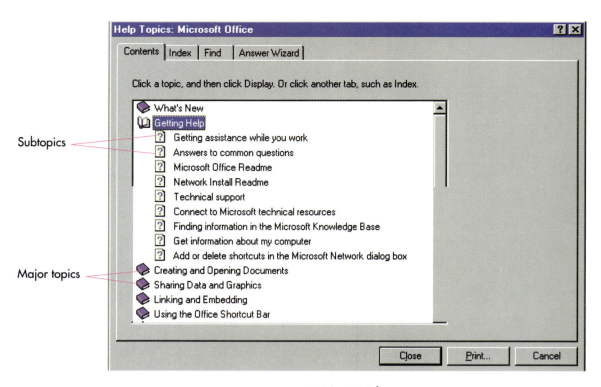

(a) Contents Tab

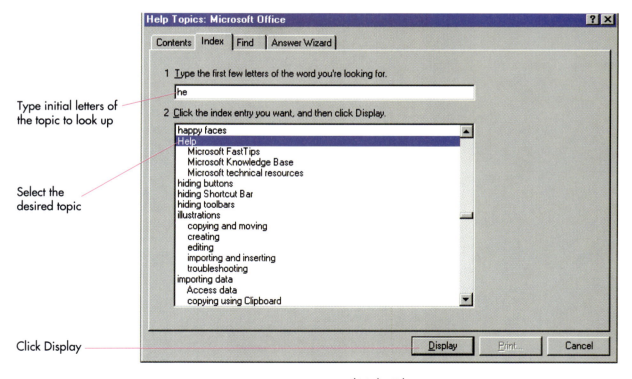

(b) Index Tab

FIGURE 2 Online Help

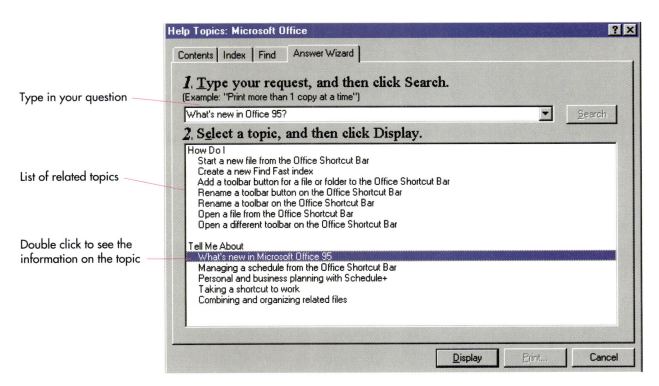

(c) Answer Wizard

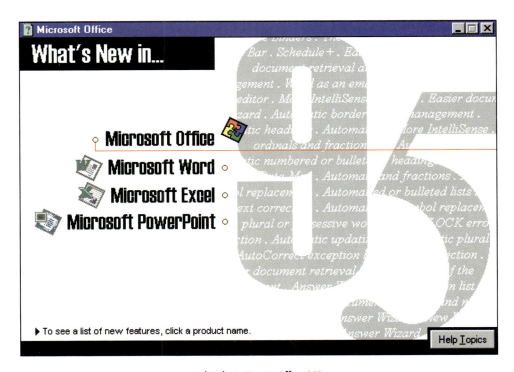

(d) What's New in Office 95?

FIGURE 2   Online Help (continued)

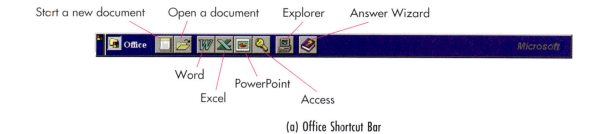

(a) Office Shortcut Bar

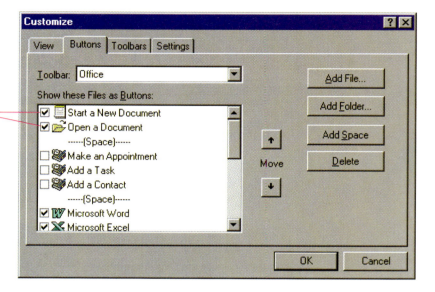

(b) Customize Dialog Box

FIGURE 3 Office Shortcut Bar

on the screen. The Shortcut Bar is anchored by default on the right side of the desktop, but you can position it along any edge, or have it "float" in the middle of the desktop. You can even hide it from view when it is not in use.

Figure 3a displays the Shortcut Bar as it appears on our desktop. The buttons that are displayed (and the order in which they appear) are established through the Customize dialog box in Figure 3b. (We show you how to customize the Shortcut Bar in the hands-on exercise that follows shortly.) Our Shortcut Bar contains a button for each Office application, a button for the Windows Explorer, and a button to access help.

Docucentric Orientation

Our Shortcut Bar contains two additional buttons: to open an existing document and to start a new document. These buttons are very useful and take advantage of the "docucentric" orientation of Microsoft Office, which lets you think in terms of a document rather than the associated application. You can still open a document in traditional fashion, by starting the application (e.g., clicking its button on the Shortcut Bar), then using the File Open command to open the document. It's easier, however, to locate the document, then double click its icon, which automatically loads the associated program.

Consider, for example, the Open dialog box in Figure 4a, which is displayed by clicking the Open a Document button on the Shortcut Bar. The Open dialog

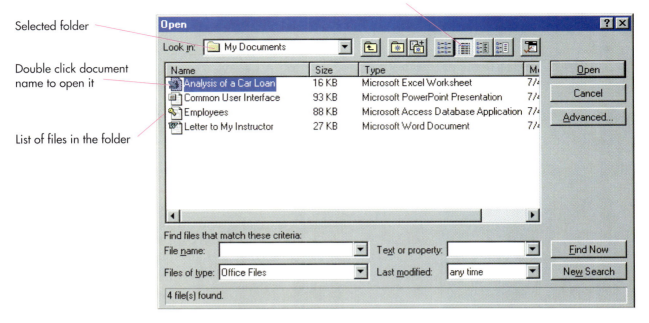

(a) Open an Existing Document

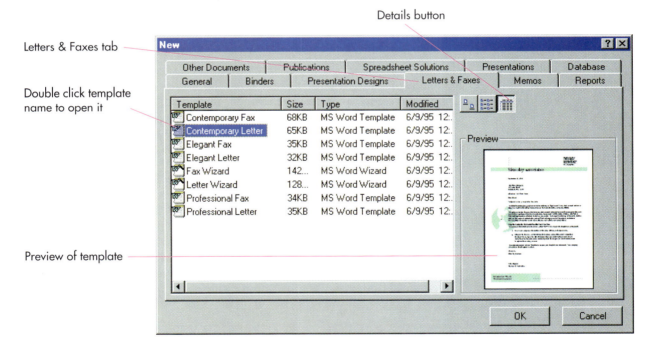

(b) Start a New Document

FIGURE 4 Document Orientation

box is common to all Office applications, and it works identically in each application. The My Documents folder is selected in Figure 4a, and it contains four documents of various file types. The documents are displayed in the Details view, which shows the document name, size, file type, and date and time the document was last modified. To open any document—for example, "Analysis of a Car

Loan"—just double click its name or icon. The associated application (Microsoft Excel in this example) will be started automatically; and it, in turn, will open the selected workbook.

The "docucentric" orientation also applies to new documents. Click the Start a New Document button on the Office Shortcut Bar, and you display the New dialog box in Figure 4b. Click the tab corresponding to the type of document you want to create, such as Letters & Faxes in Figure 4b. Change to the Preview view, then click (select) various templates so that you can choose the one most appropriate for your purpose. Double click the desired template to start the application, which opens the template and enables you to create the document.

> **CHANGE THE VIEW**
>
> The toolbar in the Open dialog box displays the documents within the selected folder in one of several views. Click the Details button to switch to the Details view and see the date and time the file was last modified, as well as its size and type. Click the List button to display an icon representing the associated application, enabling you to see many more files than in the Details view. The Preview button lets you see a document before you open it. The Properties button displays information about the document, including the number of revisions.

LEARNING BY DOING

Learning is best accomplished by doing, and so we come now to the first of many hands-on exercises that appear throughout the book. The exercises enable you to apply the concepts you have learned, then extend those concepts to further exploration on your own. This exercise focuses on the Office Shortcut Bar and assumes a basic knowledge of the Windows 95 desktop and associated mouse operations. (See the supplement on "Essentials of Windows 95" at the end of the book if you need to brush up on this material.)

The exercise has you display the Office Shortcut Bar, then customize its appearance. It also guides you in creating a new document based on an existing template that is accessed through the Start a New Document button. At the end of the exercise you will have created a letter to introduce yourself to your instructor. We are confident you will be able to do the exercise, even if you have never used Microsoft Word, because of your knowledge of the common user interface. Should you get stuck (and you won't), try the online help facility that functions identically in every Windows application.

HANDS-ON EXERCISE 1

Introduction to Microsoft Office

Objective: To load and customize the Microsoft Office Shortcut Bar; to create and print a Word document. Use Figure 5 as a guide in the exercise.

STEP 1: Welcome to Windows 95

➤ Turn on the computer and all of its peripherals. The floppy drive should be empty prior to starting your machine. This ensures that the system starts by reading files from the hard disk (which contains the Windows files), as opposed to a floppy disk (which does not).

➤ Your system will take a minute or so to get started, after which you should see the desktop in Figure 5a. Do not be concerned if the appearance of your desktop is different from ours.

➤ If you are new to Windows 95 and you want a quick introduction, click the **What's New** or **Windows Tour command buttons.** Follow the instructions in the boxed tip to display the dialog box if it does not appear on the system.

➤ Click the **Close button** to close the Welcome window and continue with the exercise.

> ### TAKE THE WINDOWS 95 TOUR
>
> Windows 95 greets you with a Welcome window that contains a command button to take you on a 10-minute tour of Windows 95. Click the command button and enjoy the show. You might also try the What's New command button for a quick overview of changes from Windows 3.1. If you do not see the Welcome window when you start Windows 95, click the Start button, click Run, type C:\WINDOWS\WELCOME in the Open text box, and press enter.

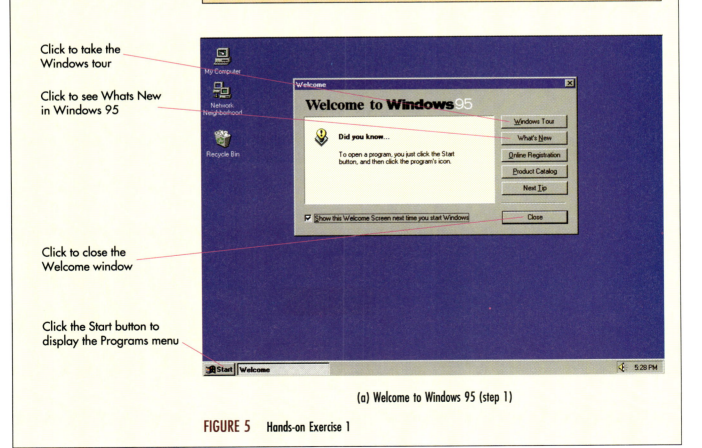

Click to take the Windows tour

Click to see Whats New in Windows 95

Click to close the Welcome window

Click the Start button to display the Programs menu

(a) Welcome to Windows 95 (step 1)

FIGURE 5 Hands-on Exercise 1

STEP 2: The Office Shortcut Bar

➤ Click the **Start button** to display the Start menu. Click (or point to) the **Programs menu,** click (or point to) the **Microsoft office submenu,** then click the **Microsoft Office Shortcut Bar** to display the Shortcut Bar.

➤ The default position of the Shortcut Bar is on the right side of the desktop, but you can drag it anywhere on the desktop. Just point to an empty area on the bar, then click and drag the bar to a new location on the desktop. If you drag the bar to an edge of the desktop, the bar will be docked along that edge when you release the mouse.

> ### TOOLTIPS
>
> Point to any button on any toolbar in any application, and you will see a ToolTip containing the name of the button to indicate its function. If ToolTips are not visible when you point to the Office Shortcut Bar, point to an empty space on the bar, click the right mouse button to display a menu, click Customize, click the View tab, then click the box to Show ToolTips. If ToolTips are not visible in an Office application, pull down the View menu, click Toolbars, then check the box to Show ToolTips.

STEP 3: Customize the Shortcut Bar

➤ Do not be concerned if your Shortcut Bar is different from Figure 5b since its appearance or content is easily changed.

➤ Point to an empty area of the Shortcut Bar, then click the **right mouse button** to display a Shortcut menu. Click **Customize** to display the Customize dialog box.

➤ If necessary, click the **View tab,** then check (or clear) the various option buttons according to the options you prefer. The settings do not take effect until you click the **OK command button** to close the dialog box.

➤ Clear the check box to Use the Standard Toolbar color, then click the **Change Color command button** to display the Color dialog box in Figure 5b.

➤ Click (select) a color, then click **OK** to accept the color change and close the Color dialog box. Click **OK** a second time to close the Customize dialog box and implement the changes.

> ### AUTO HIDE THE SHORTCUT BAR
>
> The Auto Hide option hides the Shortcut Bar between uses, giving you additional space on the desktop when you are in another application. Point to an empty space on the Shortcut Bar, click the right mouse button to display a menu, then check the Auto Hide command. (Clicking the command a second time removes the check and toggles the command off). To use the Shortcut Bar when it's hidden, point to the edge of the screen where the Shortcut Bar is docked, and the bar will appear. Click the appropriate button on the Shortcut Bar, then move the mouse back into the window containing your document to return to work.

(b) Customize the Toolbar (step 3)

FIGURE 5 Hands-on Exercise 1 (continued)

STEP 4: Add/Remove Buttons

➤ Point to an empty area of the Shortcut Bar, then click the **right mouse button** to display a shortcut menu. Click **Customize** to display the Customize dialog box, then click the **Buttons tab** to display the dialog box in Figure 5c.

➤ Check (clear) the buttons you wish to display or hide. The effects of checking (or clearing) a button are visible immediately, without having to exit the dialog box; for example, checking the button for Microsoft Word displays the associated button immediately on the Shortcut Bar.

➤ Click **OK** to close the Customize dialog box.

ADD THE EXPLORER

The Windows Explorer is the primary means of file management within Windows 95, and thus, it is convenient to have it readily available. To add the Explorer to the Shortcut Bar, right click the Shortcut Bar, click the Customize command, click the Buttons tab, then scroll until you can check the box to add the Windows Explorer. Click OK to close the Customize dialog box. The Explorer has been added to the Shortcut Bar and is now a mouse click away.

Click to select buttons to be displayed on Shortcut Bar

Clear check box to remove buttons from Shortcut Bar

(c) Add/Remove Buttons (step 4)

FIGURE 5 Hands-on Exercise 1 (continued)

STEP 5: Start a New Document

➤ Click the **Start a New Document button** to display the New dialog box in Figure 5d. Click the **Letters & Faxes tab** as shown in Figure 5d.

➤ Click the **Details button** to change the view within the New dialog box. Click and drag the border separating the Template and Size columns so that you can read the title of the template.

➤ Select (click) the **Contemporary Letter template** as shown in Figure 5d. The preview for the selected document appears in the right of the dialog box. Click the **OK command button** to open the template.

ONLINE HELP

Online help is available for Microsoft Office just as it is for any other Windows application. Click the Answer Wizard button on the Office Shortcut Bar to display the dialog box containing Help Topics for Microsoft Office. The help facility is intuitive and easy to use and functions identically in every Windows application. The help displays are task specific and fit in a single screen to keep you from having to scroll through large amounts of information.

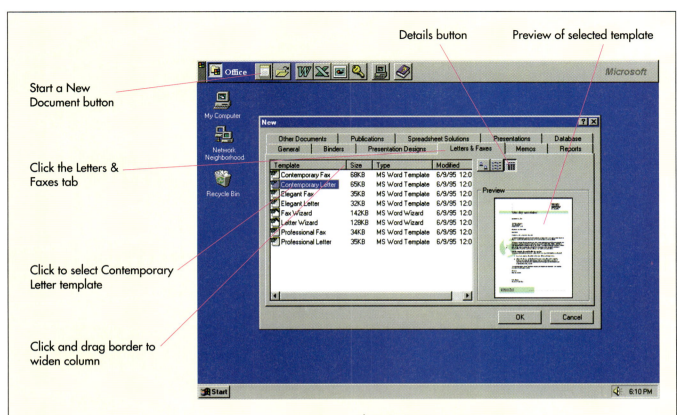

(d) Start a New Document (step 5)

FIGURE 5   Hands-on Exercise 1 (continued)

STEP 6: Click Here

➤ You should see the contemporary letter template open as a Word document as shown in Figure 5e. Do not be concerned if the appearance of your screen is different from ours.

➤ Follow the indicated instructions within the template, but do not enter the company name or the body of the letter at this time. Simply click where indicated at various points in the letter, then enter the appropriate text:

- Click on the message **[Click here and type return address]** as shown in Figure 5e. Type your street address (which replaces the existing text), press **enter,** then type your city, state, and zip code.

THE AUTOMATIC SPELL CHECK

A red wavy line under an entry indicates that the underlined word is misspelled or that the word is spelled correctly but not found in the Office dictionary. In either event, point to the underlined word, then click the right mouse button to display a shortcut menu. Select (click) the corrected spelling from the list of suggestions. You can also click the Add command to add the word to an auxiliary dictionary or the Ignore command to accept the word as it is.

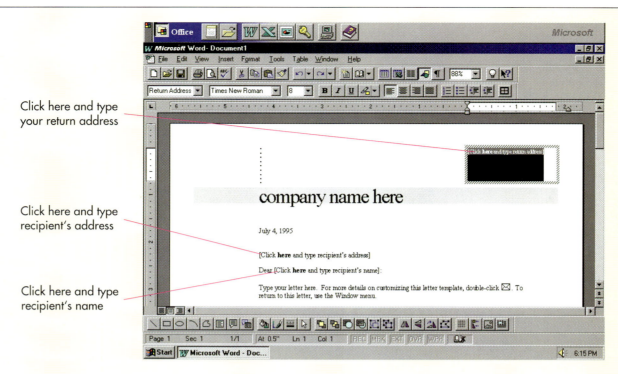

(e) Write the Letter (step 6)

FIGURE 5 Hands-on Exercise 1 (continued)

- Click beneath the date on the message **[Click here and type recipient's address]** and type your instructor's name and address. Press **enter** at the end of each line of the address.
- Click beneath your professor's address on the message **[Click here and type recipient's name]** and enter an appropriate salutation.

STEP 7: Select-then-do

➤ Click and drag to select the text "Company Name Here" as shown in Figure 5f. Type the name of your course, which replaces the selected text.

➤ You have just taken advantage of the select-then-do methodology in which you select the text to which a command is to apply, then you execute the command:

- The most basic way to select text is by dragging the mouse; that is, click at the beginning of the selection, press and hold the left mouse button as you move to the end of the selection, then release the mouse.
- To delete and replace text in one operation, select the text to be replaced, then just type the new text (as you did to replace the entry "Company Name Here").
- To boldface or italicize text, select the text, then click the Bold or Italic button on the Formatting toolbar.
- To left, center, right align, or justify text, select the text, then click the appropriate button on the Formatting toolbar.
- Selected text is affected by any subsequent operation. The text continues to be selected until you click elsewhere in the document.

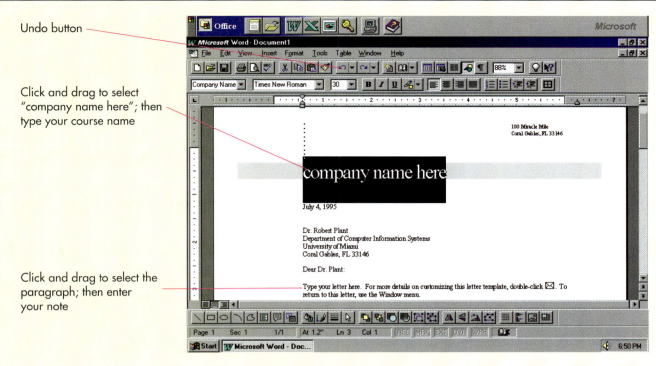

(f) Select-then-do (step 7)

FIGURE 5 Hands-on Exercise 1 (continued)

➤ Click and drag to select the paragraph beginning "Type your letter here", then enter a note to your instructor. Type just as you would on a typewriter with one exception; do *not* press the enter key at the end of a line because Word will automatically wrap text from one line to the next. Press the **enter key** at the end of the paragraph.

➤ Click the **Undo button** to reverse the last command or whenever something happens in your document that differs from what you expected.

100 LEVELS OF UNDO

The Undo command is present in Microsoft Word as it is in every other Office application. Incredible as it sounds, however, Word enables you to undo the last 100 changes to a document. Click the arrow next to the Undo button to produce a reverse-order list of your previous actions, then click the action you want to undo, which also undoes all of the preceding commands in the list. Undoing the fifth command in the list, for example, will also undo the preceding four commands.

STEP 8: Complete the Letter

➤ If necessary, click the **down arrow** on the vertical scroll bar to bring the signature portion of the document into view as shown in Figure 5g.

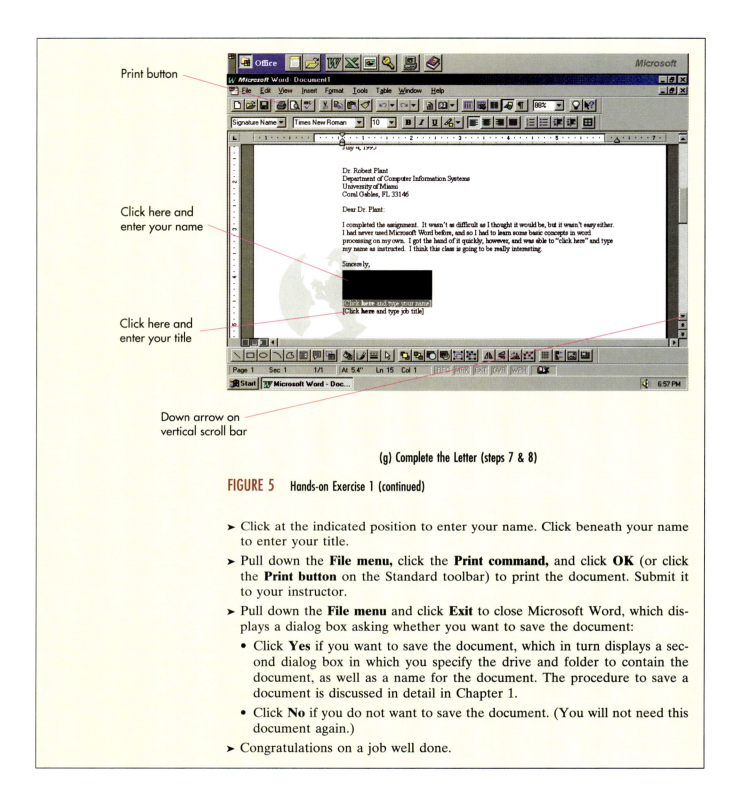

(g) Complete the Letter (steps 7 & 8)

FIGURE 5   Hands-on Exercise 1 (continued)

➤ Click at the indicated position to enter your name. Click beneath your name to enter your title.
➤ Pull down the **File menu,** click the **Print command,** and click **OK** (or click the **Print button** on the Standard toolbar) to print the document. Submit it to your instructor.
➤ Pull down the **File menu** and click **Exit** to close Microsoft Word, which displays a dialog box asking whether you want to save the document:
  • Click **Yes** if you want to save the document, which in turn displays a second dialog box in which you specify the drive and folder to contain the document, as well as a name for the document. The procedure to save a document is discussed in detail in Chapter 1.
  • Click **No** if you do not want to save the document. (You will not need this document again.)
➤ Congratulations on a job well done.

SHARED APPLICATIONS AND UTILITIES

Microsoft Office includes a fifth application, Schedule+, as well as several smaller applications and shared utilities. ***Schedule+*** can be started from the Office Shortcut Bar or from the submenu for Microsoft Office, which is accessed through the Programs command on the Start button. Figure 6a displays one screen from Schedule+, providing some indication of what the application can do.

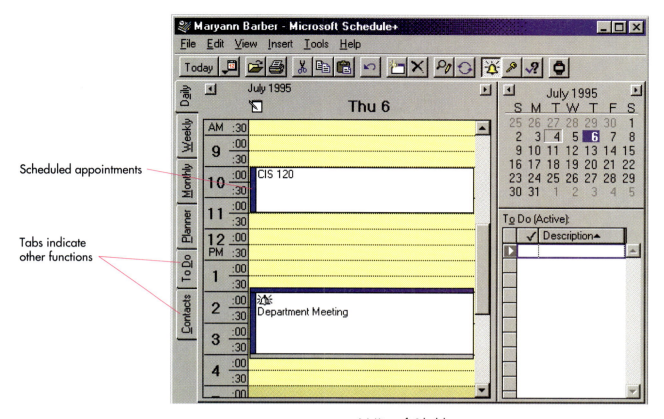

(a) Microsoft Schedule+

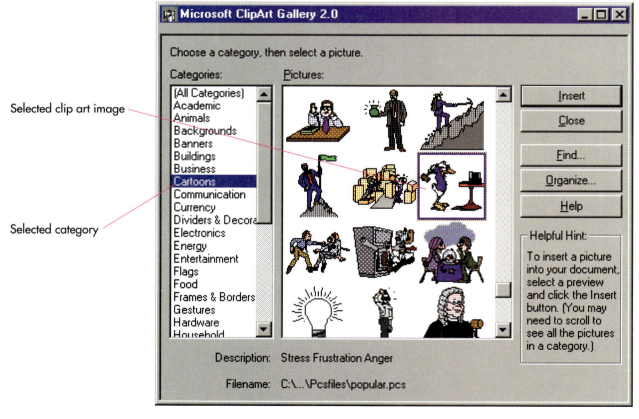

(b) ClipArt Gallery

FIGURE 6   Shared Applications

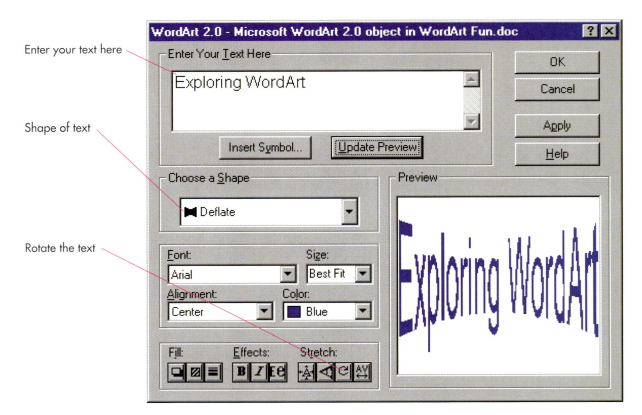

(c) WordArt

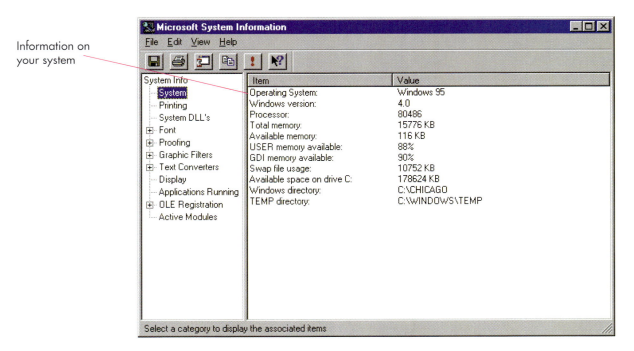

(d) Microsoft System Information

FIGURE 6 Shared Applications (continued)

In essence, Schedule+ is a personal information manager that helps you schedule (and keep) appointments. It will display your schedule on a daily, weekly, or monthly basis. It will beep to remind you of appointments. It will also maintain a list of important phone numbers and contacts. Schedule+ is beyond the scope of our text, but it is an easy application to learn since it follows the common user interface and has a detailed help facility.

The other applications (or applets as they are sometimes known) are easy to miss because they do not appear as buttons on the Shortcut Bar. Nor do they appear as options on any menu. Instead, these applications are loaded from within one of the major applications, typically through the Insert Object command. Two of the more popular applications, the ***ClipArt Gallery*** and ***WordArt,*** are illustrated in Figures 6b and 6c, respectively.

The ClipArt Gallery contains more than 1,100 clip art images in 26 different categories. Select a category such as Cartoons, select an image such as the duck smashing a computer, then click the Insert command button to insert the clip art into a document. Once an object is inserted into a document (regardless of whether it is a Word document, an Excel worksheet, a PowerPoint presentation, or an Access form or report), it can be moved and sized like any other Windows object.

WordArt enables you to create special effects with text. It lets you rotate and/or flip text, shade it, slant it, arch it, or even print it upside down. WordArt is intuitively easy to use. In essence, you enter the text in the dialog box of Figure 6c, choose a shape from the drop-down list box, then choose a font and point size. You can boldface or italicize the text or add special effects such as stretching or shadows.

The ***System Information Utility*** in Figure 6d is accessed from any major application by pulling down the Help menu, clicking the About button, then clicking the System Info command button. The utility provides detailed information about all aspects of your system. The information may prove to be invaluable should problems arise on your system and you need to supply technical details to support personnel.

THE OTHER SHARED APPLICATIONS

Microsoft Office includes several additional applications whose functions can be inferred from their names. The Equation Editor, Organization Chart, Data Map, and Graph utilities are accessed through the Insert Object command. All of these applications are straightforward and easy to use as they follow the common user interface and provide online help.

OBJECT LINKING AND EMBEDDING

The applications in Microsoft Office are thoroughly integrated with one another. They look alike and they work in consistent fashion. Equally important, they share information through a technology known as ***Object Linking and Embedding*** (OLE), which enables you to create a ***compound document*** containing data (objects) from multiple applications.

The compound document in Figure 7 was created in Word, and it contains objects (a worksheet and a chart) that were created in Excel. The letterhead uses a logo that was taken from the ClipArt Gallery, while the name and address of the recipient were drawn from an Access database. The various objects were inserted into the compound document through linking or embedding, which are

Office of Residential Living

University of Miami • **P.O. Box 243984** • **Coral Gables, FL 33124**

September 25, 1995

Mr. Jeffrey Redmond, President
Dynamic Dining Services
4329 Palmetto Lane
Miami, FL 33157

Dear Jeff,

As per our earlier conversation, occupancy is up in all of the dorms for the 1995 - 1996 school year. I have enclosed a spreadsheet and chart that show our occupancy rates for the 1992 - 1995 school years. Please realize, however, that the 1995 figures are projections, as the Fall 1995 numbers are still incomplete. The final 1995 numbers should be confirmed within the next two weeks. I hope that this helps with your planning. If you need further information, please contact me at the above address.

Dorm Occupancy				
	1992	1993	1994	1995
Beatty	330	285	270	310
Broward	620	580	520	565
Graham	450	397	352	393
Rawlings	435	375	326	372
Tolbert	615	554	524	581

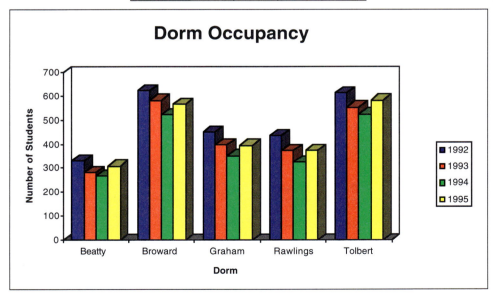

FIGURE 7 A Compound Document

actually two very different techniques. Both operations, however, are much more sophisticated than simply pasting an object, because with either linking or embedding, you can edit the object by using the tools of the original application.

The difference between linking and embedding depends on whether the object is stored within the compound document (***embedding***) or in its own file (***linking***). An *embedded object* is stored in the compound document, which in turn becomes the only user (client) of that object. A *linked object* is stored in its own file, and the compound document is one of many potential clients of that object. The compound document does not contain the linked object per se, but only a representation of the object as well as a pointer (link) to the file containing the object. The advantage of linking is that the document is updated automatically if the object changes.

The choice between linking and embedding depends on how the object will be used. Linking is preferable if the object is likely to change and the compound document requires the latest version. Linking should also be used when the same object is placed in many documents so that any change to the object has to be made in only one place. Embedding should be used if you need to take the object with you—for example, if you intend to edit the document on a different computer.

OBJECT LINKING AND EMBEDDING

Object Linking and Embedding (OLE) enables you to create a compound document containing objects (data) from multiple Windows applications. OLE is one of the major benefits of working in the Windows environment, but it would be impossible to illustrate all of the techniques in a single exercise. Accordingly, we have created the icon at the left to help you identify the many examples of object linking and embedding that appear throughout the Exploring Windows series.

SUMMARY

The common user interface requires every Windows application to follow a consistent set of conventions and ensures that all applications work basically the same way. The development of a suite of applications from a single vendor extends this concept by imposing additional similarities on all applications within the suite.

Microsoft distributes two versions of the Office Suite: Standard Office and Office Professional. Both versions include Word, Excel, and PowerPoint. The Office Professional also has Microsoft Access. Both versions also include a fifth application, Schedule+, as well as several smaller applications and shared utilities.

The Microsoft Office Shortcut Bar provides immediate access to each application in Microsoft Office. The Shortcut Bar is fully customizable with respect to the buttons it displays, its appearance, and its position on the desktop. The Open a Document and Start a New Document buttons enable you to think in terms of a document rather than the associated application.

Object Linking and Embedding (OLE) enables you to create a compound document containing data (objects) from multiple applications. Linking and embedding are different operations. The difference between the two depends on whether the object is stored within the compound document (embedding) or in its own file (linking).

KEY WORDS AND CONCEPTS

- Answer Wizard
- ClipArt Gallery
- Compound document
- Common user interface
- Contents tab
- Embedding
- Formatting toolbar
- Index tab
- Linking
- Microsoft Access
- Microsoft Excel
- Microsoft Office Professional
- Microsoft PowerPoint
- Microsoft Standard Office
- Microsoft Word
- Object Linking and Embedding (OLE)
- Microsoft Office Shortcut Bar
- Online help
- Schedule+
- Standard toolbar
- System Information Utility
- WordArt

MICROSOFT WORD 7.0: WHAT WILL WORD PROCESSING DO FOR ME?

OBJECTIVES

After reading this chapter you will be able to:

1. Define word wrap; differentiate between a hard and a soft return.
2. Distinguish between the insert and overtype modes; explain how to switch from one mode to the other.
3. Describe the elements on the Microsoft Word screen.
4. Create, save, retrieve, edit, and print a simple document.
5. Check a document for spelling; describe the function of the custom dictionary.
6. Describe the AutoCorrect feature; explain how it can be used to create your own shorthand.
7. Differentiate between the Save and Save As commands; describe various backup options that can be selected.

OVERVIEW

Have you ever produced what you thought was the perfect term paper only to discover that you omitted a sentence or misspelled a word, or that the paper was three pages too short or one page too long? Wouldn't it be nice to make the necessary changes, and then be able to reprint the entire paper with the touch of a key? Welcome to the world of word processing, where you are no longer stuck with having to retype anything. Instead, you retrieve your work from disk, display it on the monitor and revise it as necessary, then print it at any time, in draft or final form.

This chapter provides a broad-based introduction to word processing in general and Microsoft Word in particular. We begin by presenting (or perhaps reviewing) the essential concepts of a word processor, then show you how these concepts are implemented in Word. We show you how to create a document, how to save it on disk, then retrieve the document you just created. We also introduce you to the spell check, an essential tool in any word processor.

The chapter contains three hands-on exercises that enable you to apply the material at the computer. The exercises are indispensable to the learn-by-doing philosophy we follow throughout the text. The exercises also assume a basic knowledge of Windows 95. (See the appendix on Windows essentials if you need to review this material.)

THE BASICS OF WORD PROCESSING

All word processors adhere to certain basic concepts that must be understood if you are to use the program effectively. The next several pages introduce ideas that are applicable to any word processor (and which you may already know). We follow the conceptual material with a hands-on exercise that gives you the opportunity to practice all that you have learned.

Word Wrap

A newcomer to word processing has one major transition to make from a typewriter, and it is an absolutely critical adjustment. Whereas a typist returns the carriage at the end of every line, just the opposite is true of a word processor. One types continually *without* pressing the enter key at the end of a line because the word processor automatically wraps text from one line to the next. This concept is known as ***word wrap*** and is illustrated in Figure 1.1.

The word *primitive* does not fit on the current line in Figure 1.1a, and is automatically shifted to the next line, *without* the user having to press the enter key. The user continues to enter the document, with additional words being wrapped to subsequent lines as necessary. The only time you use the enter key is at the end of a paragraph, or when you want the insertion point to move to the next line and the end of the current line doesn't reach the right margin.

Word wrap is closely associated with another concept, that of hard and soft returns. A ***hard return*** is created by the user when he or she presses the enter key at the end of a paragraph; a ***soft return*** is created by the word processor as it wraps text from one line to the next. The locations of the soft returns change automatically as a document is edited (e.g., as text is inserted or deleted, or as margins or fonts are changed). The locations of the hard returns can be changed only by the user, who must intentionally insert or delete each hard return.

There are two hard returns in Figure 1.1b, one at the end of each paragraph. There are also six soft returns in the first paragraph (one at the end of every line except the last) and four soft returns in the second paragraph. Now suppose the margins in the document are made smaller (that is, the line is made longer) as shown in Figure 1.1c. The number of soft returns drops to four and two (in the first and second paragraph, respectively) as more text fits on a line and fewer lines are needed. The revised document still contains the two original hard returns, one at the end of each paragraph.

The Insertion Point

The ***insertion point*** is a flashing vertical line that marks the place where text will be entered. The insertion point is always at the beginning of a new document, but it can be moved anywhere within an existing document. If, for example, you wanted to add text to the end of a document, you would move the insertion point to the end of the document, then begin typing.

The original IBM PC was extremely pr

primitive cannot fit on current line

The original IBM PC was extremely primitive

primitive is automatically moved to the next line

(a) Entering the Document

The original IBM PC was extremely primitive (not to mention expensive) by current standards. The basic machine came equipped with only 16Kb RAM and was sold without a monitor or disk (a TV and tape cassette were suggested instead). The price of this powerhouse was $1565. ¶
　　　You could, however, purchase an expanded business system with 256Kb RAM, two 160Kb floppy drives, monochrome monitor, and 80-cps printer for $4425. ¶

Hard returns are created by pressing the enter key at the end of a paragraph.

(b) Completed Document

The original IBM PC was extremely primitive (not to mention expensive) by current standards. The basic machine came equipped with only 16Kb RAM and was sold without a monitor or disk (a TV and tape cassette were suggested instead). The price of this powerhouse was $1565. ¶
　　　You could, however, purchase an expanded business system with 256Kb RAM, two 160Kb floppy drives, monochrome monitor, and 80-cps printer for $4425. ¶

Revised document still contains two hard returns, one at the end of each paragraph.

(c) Completed Document

FIGURE 1.1   Word Wrap

Toggle Switches

Suppose you sat down at the keyboard and typed an entire sentence without pressing the Shift key; the sentence would be in all lowercase letters. Then you pressed the Caps Lock key and retyped the sentence, again without pressing the Shift key. This time the sentence would be in all uppercase letters. You could repeat the process as often as you like. Each time you pressed the Caps Lock key, the sentence would switch from lowercase to uppercase and vice versa.

　　　The point of this exercise is to introduce the concept of a ***toggle switch,*** a device that causes the computer to alternate between two states. The Caps Lock key is an example of a toggle switch. Each time you press it, newly typed text will change from uppercase to lowercase and back again. We will see several other examples of toggle switches as we proceed in our discussion of word processing.

Insert versus Overtype

Microsoft Word is always in one of two modes, *insert* or *overtype,* and uses a toggle switch (the Ins key) to alternate between the two. Press the Ins key once and you switch from insert to overtype. Press the Ins key a second time and you go from overtype back to insert.

Text that is entered into a document during the insert mode moves existing text to the right to accommodate the characters being added. Text entered from the overtype mode replaces (overtypes) existing text. Text is always entered or replaced immediately to the right of the insertion point.

The insert mode is best when you enter text for the first time, but either mode can be used to make corrections. The insert mode is the better choice when the correction requires you to add new text; the overtype mode is easier when you are substituting one or more character(s) for another. The difference is illustrated in Figure 1.2.

Figure 1.2a displays the text as it was originally entered, with two misspellings. The letters *se* have been omitted from the word *insert*, whereas an *x* has been erroneously typed instead of an *r* in the word *overtype*. The insert mode is used in Figure 1.2b to add the missing letters, which in turn moves the rest of the line to the right. The overtype mode is used in Figure 1.2c to replace the *x* with an *r*.

Misspelled words

The inrt mode is better when adding text that has been omitted; the ovextype mode is easier when you are substituting one (or more) characters for another.

(a) Text to Be Corrected

"se" has been inserted and existing text moved to the right

The insert mode is better when adding text that has been omitted; the ovextype mode is easier when you are substituting one (or more) characters for another.

(b) Insert Mode

"r" replaces the "x"

The insert mode is better when adding text that has been omitted; the overtype mode is easier when you are substituting one (or more) characters for another.

(c) Overtype Mode

FIGURE 1.2   Insert and Overtype Modes

Deleting Text

The backspace and Del keys delete one character immediately to the left or right of the insertion point, respectively. The choice between them depends on when you need to erase a character(s). The backspace key is easier if you want to delete a character immediately after typing it. The Del key is preferable during subsequent editing.

You can delete several characters at one time by selecting (dragging the mouse over) the characters to be deleted, then pressing the Del key. And finally, you can delete and replace text in one operation by selecting the text to be replaced and then typing the new text in its place.

> **LEARN TO TYPE**
>
> The ultimate limitation of any word processor is the speed at which you enter data; hence the ability to type quickly is invaluable. Learning how to type is easy, especially with the availability of computer-based typing programs. As little as a half hour a day for a couple of weeks will have you up to speed, and if you do any significant amount of writing at all, the investment will pay off many times.

INTRODUCTION TO MICROSOFT WORD

We used Microsoft Word to write this book, as can be inferred from the screen in Figure 1.3. Your screen will be different from ours in many ways. You will not have the same document nor is it likely that you will customize Word in exactly the same way. You should, however, be able to recognize the basic elements that are found in the Microsoft Word window that is open on the desktop.

There are actually two open windows in Figure 1.3—an application window for Microsoft Word and a document window for the specific document on which you are working. Each window has its own Minimize, Maximize (or Restore), and Close buttons. Both windows have been maximized, and thus the title bars have been merged into a single title bar that appears at the top of the application window and reflects the application (Microsoft Word) as well as the document name (Exploring Word Chapter 1). A menu bar appears immediately below the title bar. Vertical and horizontal scroll bars appear at the right and bottom of the document window. The Windows taskbar appears at the bottom of the screen and shows the open applications.

Microsoft Word is also part of the Microsoft Office suite of applications, and thus shares additional features with Excel, Access, and PowerPoint, that are also part of the Office suite. **Toolbars** provide immediate access to common commands and appear immediately below the menu bar. The toolbars can be displayed or hidden using the View menu as described on page 17 later in the chapter.

The **Standard toolbar** contains buttons corresponding to the most basic commands in Word—for example, opening and closing a file or printing a document. The icon on the button is intended to be indicative of its function (e.g., a printer to indicate the Print command). You can also point to the button to display a **ToolTip** showing the name of the button. The **Formatting toolbar** appears under the Standard toolbar and provides access to common formatting operations such as boldface, italics, or underlining.

The toolbars may appear overwhelming at first, but there is absolutely no need to memorize what the individual buttons do. That will come with time. We

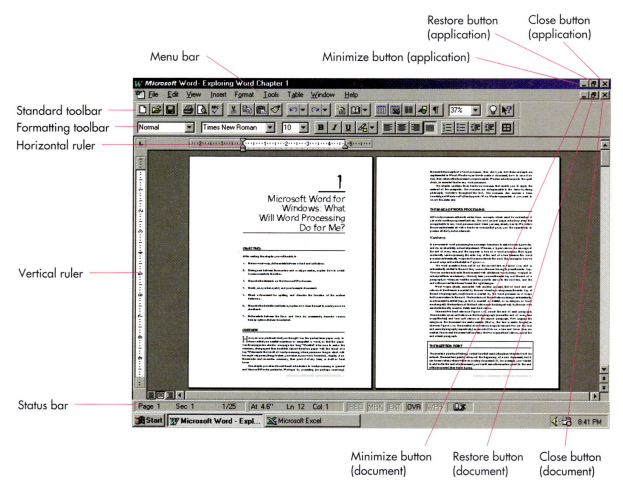

FIGURE 1.3 Microsoft Word

suggest, however, that you will have a better appreciation for the various buttons if you consider them in groups according to their general function as shown in Figure 1.4a.

The ***horizontal ruler*** is displayed underneath the toolbars and enables you to change margins, tabs, and/or indents for all or part of a document. A ***vertical ruler*** shows the vertical position of text on the page and can be used to change the top or bottom margins.

The ***status bar*** at the bottom of the document window displays the location of the insertion point (or information about the command being executed.) The status bar also shows the status (settings) of various indicators—for example, OVR to show that Word is in the overtype, as opposed to the insert, mode.

USE ONLINE HELP

The answer to almost anything you need to know about Microsoft Word is available through online help if only you take the trouble to look. The Help facility is intuitive and easy to use. The help displays are task-specific and fit in a single screen to keep you from having to scroll through large amounts of information.

	Starts a new document, opens an existing document, or saves the document in memory
	Prints the document or previews the document prior to printing
	Checks spelling
	Cuts, copies, or pastes the selected text; copies formatting of selected text
	Undoes or redoes a previously executed command
	AutoFormats the document or inserts an address
	Creates a table, inserts an Excel spreadsheet, or creates columns; creates a drawing or chart
	Shows (hides) nonprinting characters within a document
	Changes the zoom percentage
	Toggles the Tip Wizard on (off); displays formatting information

(a) Standard Toolbar

	Applies a specific style to the selected text
	Changes the font (typeface) and point size
	Toggles boldface, italics, underline; applies highlighting
	Aligns left, center, right, or full
	Creates a numbered or bulleted list
	Decreases or increases indentation
	Shows (hides) the Borders toolbar

(b) Formatting Toolbar

FIGURE 1.4 Toolbars

THE FILE MENU

The *File menu* is a critically important menu in virtually every Windows application. It contains the Save and Open commands to save a document on disk, then subsequently retrieve (open) that document at a later time. The File menu also contains the Print command to print a document, the Close command to close the current document but continue working in the application, and the Exit command to quit the application altogether.

The *Save command* copies the document that is currently being edited (the document in memory) to disk. The Save As dialog box appears the first time that the document is saved so that you can specify the file name and other required information. All subsequent executions of the Save command save the document under the assigned name, replacing the previously saved version with the new version.

The Save As dialog box requires a file name (e.g., My First Document in Figure 1.5a), which can be up to 255 characters in length. The file name may contain spaces but cannot contain commas. (Periods are permitted, but discouraged, since they are too easily confused with DOS extensions.)

The dialog box also requires the specification of the drive and folder in which the file is to be saved as well as the file type that determines which application the file is associated with. (Long-time DOS users will remember the three-character extension at the end of a file name—for example, DOC—to indicate the associated application. The extension may be hidden in Windows 95 according to options set through the View menu in My Computer. Refer to page 30 in the Windows appendix.)

The *Open command* brings a copy of a previously saved document into memory enabling you to work with that document. The Open command displays the Open dialog box in which you specify the file to retrieve. You indicate the drive (and optionally the folder) that contains the file, as well as the type of file you want to retrieve. Word will then list all files of that type on the designated drive (and folder), enabling you to open the file you want.

The Save and Open commands work in conjunction with one another. The Save As dialog box in Figure 1.5a, for example, saves the file *My First Document* onto the disk in drive A. The Open dialog box in Figure 1.5b brings that file back into memory so that you can work with the file, after which you can save the revised file for use at a later time.

A VERY USEFUL TOOLBAR

The Open and Save As dialog boxes share a common toolbar with several very useful buttons. Click the Details button to switch to the Details view and see the date and time the file was last modified as well as its size. Click the List button to display an icon for each file enabling you to see many more files than in the Details view. The Preview button lets you see a document before you open it. The Properties button displays information about the document, including the number of revisions.

LEARNING BY DOING

Every chapter contains a series of hands-on exercises that enable you to apply what you learn at the computer. The exercises in this chapter are linked to one another in that you create a simple document in exercise one, then open and edit

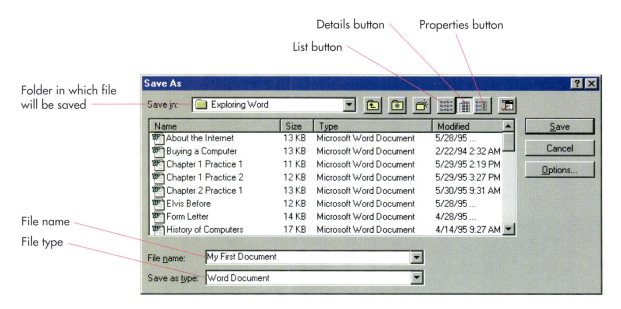

(a) Save As Dialog Box

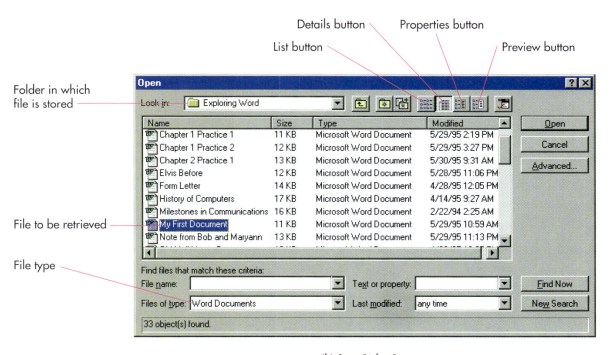

(b) Open Dialog Box

FIGURE 1.5   The Save and Open Commands

that document in exercise two. The ability to save and open a document is critical, and you do not want to spend an inordinate amount of time entering text unless you are confident in your ability to retrieve it later.

The following exercise also introduces you to the data disk that is referenced throughout this text. You can obtain a copy of the data disk from your instructor, or you can download the files on the data disk as described in step 2. The data disk contains a series of documents that are used in various exercises throughout the text. It can also be used to store the documents you create (or you can store the documents on a hard disk if you have access to your own computer).

THERE'S ALWAYS A REASON

We would love to tell you that everything will go perfectly, that you will never be frustrated, and that the computer will always perform exactly as you expect. Unfortunately, that is not going to happen, because a computer does what you tell it to do, which is not necessarily what you want it to do. There can be a tremendous difference! There is, however, a logical reason for everything the computer does or does not do; sooner or later you will discover that reason, at which point everything will fall into place.

HANDS-ON EXERCISE 1

My First Document

Objective: To start Microsoft Word in order to create, save, and print a simple document. To execute commands via the toolbar or from pull-down menus. Use Figure 1.6 as a guide in doing the exercise.

STEP 1: Welcome to Windows 95

➤ Turn on the computer and all of its peripherals. The floppy drive should be empty prior to starting your machine. This ensures that the system starts from the hard disk, which contains the Windows files, as opposed to a floppy disk, which does not.

➤ Your system will take a minute or so to get started, after which you should see the Windows desktop in Figure 1.6a. Do not be concerned if the appearance of your desktop is different from ours, or if you do not see the Welcome message.

➤ If you are new to Windows 95 and you want a quick introduction, click the **What's New** or **Windows Tour command buttons.** Follow the instructions in the boxed tip to display the Welcome window if it does not appear on your system.

➤ Click the **Close button** if you see the Welcome message in Figure 1.6a.

TAKE THE WINDOWS 95 TOUR

Windows 95 greets you with a Welcome window that contains a command button to take you on a 10-minute tour of Windows 95. Click the command button and enjoy the show. You might also try the What's New command button for a quick overview of changes from Windows 3.1. If you do not see the Welcome window when you start Windows 95, click the Start button, click Run, type C:\WINDOWS\WELCOME in the Open *text box,* and press enter.

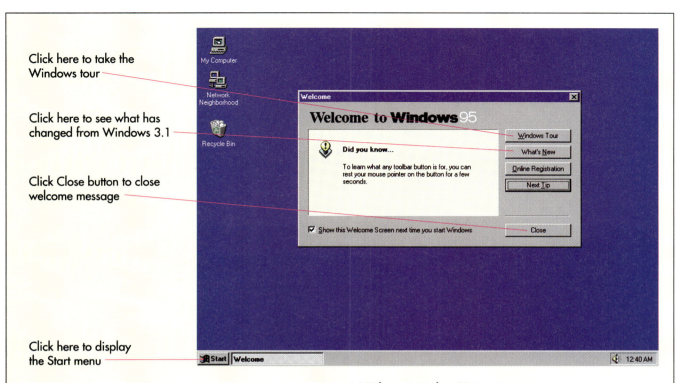

(a) Welcome to Windows 95 (step 1)

FIGURE 1.6 Hands-on Exercise 1

STEP 2: Install the Data Disk

➤ Do this step *only* if you have your own computer and you want to install (copy) the files from the data disk to the hard drive. Place the data disk in drive A.

➤ Click the **Start button** to display the Start menu. Click the **Run command** to display the Run dialog box.

➤ Type **A:\Install C** in the text box. (The drive letter, drive C in the example, is variable and indicates the drive on which to install the data disk.) Click **OK** or press the **enter key.**

DOWNLOAD THE DATA DISK

The data disk for all books in the Exploring Windows series can be downloaded from the Prentice Hall Web site (http:/www.prenhall.com). Use any Web browser to log on to the site, select Business and Economics, then move to the Exploring Windows page. To download the files for a single application, go to the page for that book, then click the icon to download the data disk. To download the files for all Office applications simultaneously, go to the Exploring Microsoft Office page.

STEP 3: Start Microsoft Word

➤ Click the **Start button** to display the Start menu. Click (or point to) the **Programs menu,** then click **Microsoft Word** to open the program.

➤ If necessary, click the **Maximize button** in the application window so that Word takes the entire desktop as shown in Figure 1.6b. Click the **Maximize button** in the document window (if necessary) so that the document window is as large as possible.

➤ Do not be concerned if your screen is different from ours as we include a troubleshooting section immediately following this exercise.

> **POINT AND SLIDE**
>
> Click the Start button, then slowly slide the mouse pointer over the various menu options. Notice that each time you point to a submenu, its items are displayed. Point to (don't click) the Programs menu, then click Microsoft Word to open the application. In other words, you don't have to click a submenu—you can just point and slide!

STEP 4: Create the Document

➤ Create the document in Figure 1.6c. Type just as you would on a typewriter with one exception; do *not* press the enter key at the end of a line because Word will automatically wrap text from one line to the next. Press the **enter key** at the end of the paragraph.

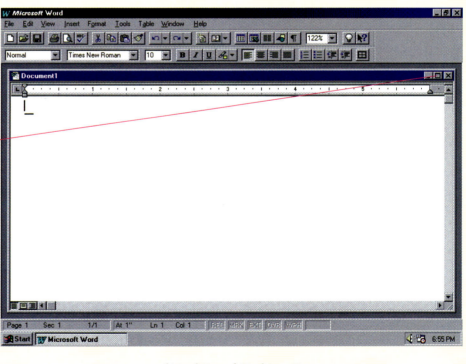

Click here to maximize the document window

(b) Load Microsoft Word (step 3)

FIGURE 1.6 Hands-on Exercise 1 (continued)

Show/Hide button (displays/hides nonprinting characters)

Press the enter key at the end of the paragraph

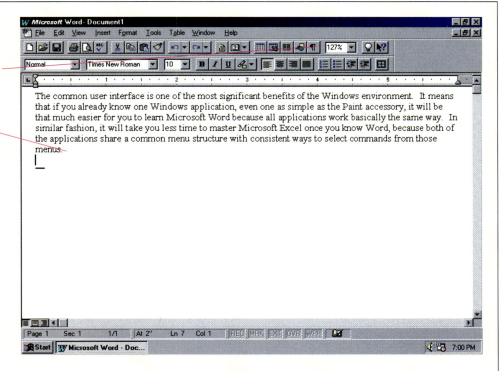

(c) Create the Document (step 4)

FIGURE 1.6 Hands-on Exercise 1 (continued)

➤ Proofread the document and correct any errors. Use the **Ins key** to toggle between the insert and overtype modes as appropriate.

➤ You may (or may not) see a red wavy underline beneath misspelled words, depending on whether (or not) the automatic spell check is in effect. If a misspelling is indicated, point to the misspelled word, click the right mouse button, then select (click) the correct spelling from the list of suggestions.

DISPLAY THE HARD RETURNS

Click the Show/Hide ¶ button on the Standard toolbar to display the hard returns (paragraph marks) and other nonprinting characters (such as tab characters or blank spaces) contained within a document. The Show/Hide ¶ button (denoted by the ¶ symbol indicating a hard return) functions as a toggle switch: the first time you click it, the hard returns are displayed; the second time you press it, the returns are hidden; and so on.

STEP 5: Save the Document

➤ Pull down the **File menu** and click **Save** (or click the **Save button** on the Standard toolbar). You should see the Save As dialog box in Figure 1.6d. If necessary, click the **List button** so that the display on your monitor more closely matches our figure.

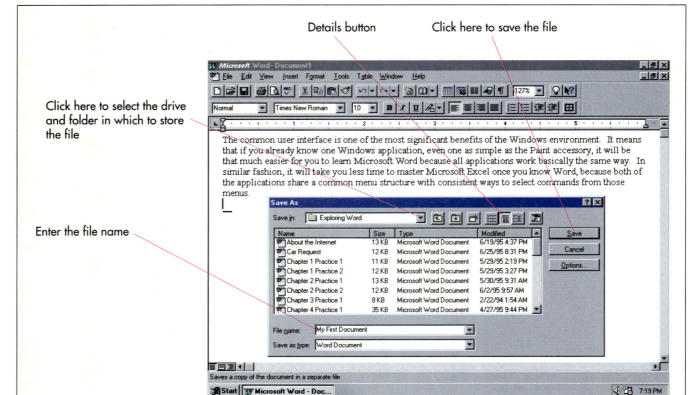

(d) Save the Document (step 5)

FIGURE 1.6 Hands-on Exercise 1 (continued)

➤ To save the file:
- Click the **drop-down arrow** on the Save In list box.
- Click the appropriate drive, drive C or drive A, depending on whether or not you installed the data disk on your hard drive.
- Double click the **Exploring Word folder,** to make it the active folder (the folder in which you will save the document).
- Click and drag over the default entry in the File name text box. Type **My First Document** as the name of your document. (A DOC extension will be added automatically when the file is saved to indicate that this is a Word document.)
- Click **Save** or press the **enter key.** The title bar changes to reflect the document name.

DOUBLE CLICKING FOR BEGINNERS

If you are having trouble double clicking, it is because you are not clicking quickly enough, or more likely, because you are moving the mouse (however slightly) between clicks. Relax, hold the mouse firmly in place, and try again.

➤ Add your name at the end of the document, then click the **Save button** on the Standard toolbar to save the document with the revision. This time the Save As dialog box does not appear, since Word already knows the name of the document.

STEP 6: Print the Document

➤ You can print the document in one of two ways:
- Pull down the **File menu.** Click **Print** to display the dialog box of Figure 1.6e. Click the **OK command button** to print the document.
- Click the **Print button** on the Standard toolbar to print the document immediately without displaying the Print dialog box.

ABOUT MICROSOFT WORD

Pull down the Help menu and click About Microsoft Word to display the specific release number and other licensing information, including the product serial number. This help screen also contains two very useful command buttons, System Information and Technical Support. The first button displays information about the hardware installed on your system, including the amount of memory and available space on the hard drive. The Technical Support button provides telephone numbers for technical assistance.

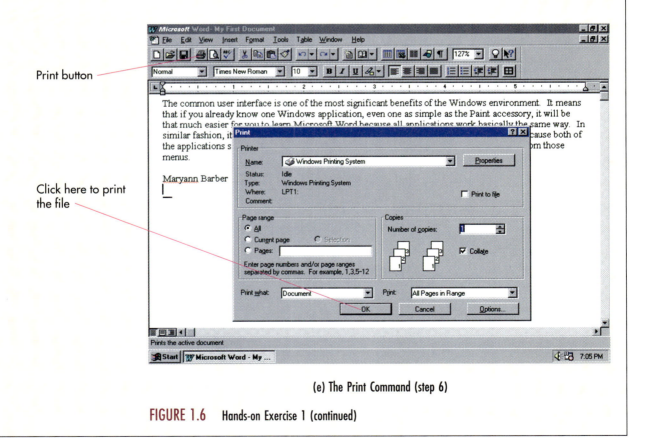

(e) The Print Command (step 6)

FIGURE 1.6 Hands-on Exercise 1 (continued)

STEP 7: Close the Document

➤ Pull down the **File menu.** Click **Close** to close this document but remain in Word. (Click **Yes** if prompted to save the document.) The document disappears from the screen, but Word is still open.

➤ Pull down the **File menu** a second time. Click **Exit** to close Word and return to Windows.

➤ Submit the printed document from step 6 to your instructor as proof that you did the exercise.

TROUBLESHOOTING

We trust that you completed the hands-on exercise without difficulty, and that you were able to create, save, and print the document in Figure 1.6. There is, however, one area of potential confusion in that Word offers different views of the same document, depending on the preferences of the individual user. Your screen will not match ours exactly, and, indeed, there is no requirement that it should. The *contents* of the document, however, should be identical to ours.

Figure 1.6 displayed the document in the ***Normal view.*** Figure 1.7 displays an entirely different view called the ***Page Layout view.*** Each view has its advantages. The Normal view is generally faster, but the Page Layout view more closely

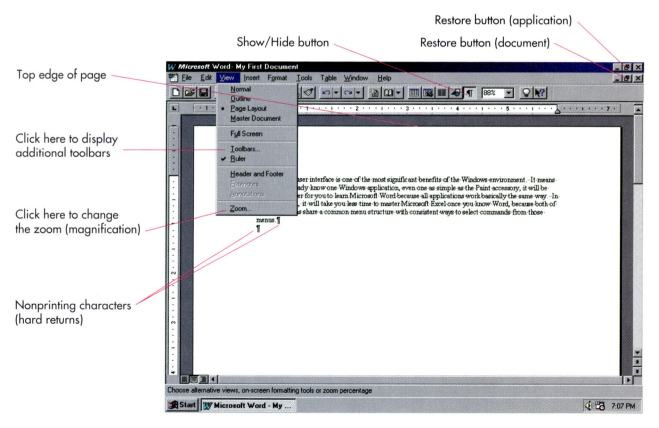

FIGURE 1.7 Troubleshooting

resembles the printed page as it displays top and bottom margins, headers and footers, graphic elements in their exact position, a vertical ruler, and other elements not seen in the Normal view. The Normal view is preferable only when entering text and editing. The Page Layout view is used to apply the finishing touches and check a document prior to printing.

Your screen may or may not match either figure, and you will undoubtedly develop preferences of your own. The following suggestions will help you match the screens of Figure 1.6:

- If the application window for Word does not take the entire screen, and/or the document does not take the entire window within Word, click the Maximize button in the application and/or the document window. There are two Restore buttons in Figure 1.6b to indicate that the application window and its associated document window have been maximized.
- If the text does not come up to the top of the screen—that is, you see the top edge of the page (as in Figure 1.7)—it means that you are in the Page Layout view instead of the Normal view. Pull down the View menu and click Normal to match the document in Figure 1.6c.
- If the text seems unusually large or small, it means that you or a previous user elected to zoom in or out to get a different perspective on the document. Pull down the View menu, click Zoom, then click Page Width so that the text takes the entire line as in Figure 1.6b.
- If you see the ¶ and other nonprinting symbols, it means that you or a previous user elected to display these characters. Click the Show/Hide ¶ button on the Standard toolbar to make the symbols disappear.
- If the Standard or Formatting toolbar is missing and/or a different toolbar is displayed, pull down the View menu, click Toolbars, then click the appropriate toolbars on or off. If the ruler is missing, pull down the View menu and click Ruler.
- The automatic spell check may (or may not) be implemented as indicated by the appearance (absence) of the open book icon on the status bar. If you do not see the icon, pull down the Tools menu, click Options, click the Spelling tab, then check the box for Automatic Spell Checking.

THE WRONG KEYBOARD

Microsoft Word facilitates conversion from WordPerfect by providing an alternative (software-controlled) keyboard that implements WordPerfect conventions. If you are sharing your machine with others, and if various keyboard shortcuts do not work as expected, it could be because someone else has implemented the WordPerfect keyboard. Pull down the Tools menu, click Options, then click the General tab in the dialog box. Clear the check box next to Navigation keys for WordPerfect users to return to the normal Word keyboard.

THE TIPWIZARD

The ***TipWizard*** has a different ***Tip of the Day*** every time you start Word, but that is only one of its capabilities. The true purpose of the TipWizard is to introduce you to new features by suggesting more efficient ways to accomplish the tasks you are doing.

The TipWizard monitors your work and offers advice throughout a session. The TipWizard button on the Standard toolbar "lights up" whenever there is a suggestion. (Click the button to display the TipWizard; click the button a second time to close it.) You can read the suggestions as they occur and/or review them at the end of a session. You needn't always follow the advice of the TipWizard (at first you may not even understand all of its suggestions), but over time it will make you much more proficient.

HANDS-ON EXERCISE 2

Modifying an Existing Document

Objective: To open an existing document, revise it, and save the revision; to demonstrate the Undo command and online help. Use Figure 1.8 as a guide in doing the exercise.

STEP 1: Open an Existing Document
- Start Microsoft Word as described in step 3 of the previous exercise.
- Pull down the **File menu** and click **Open** (or click the **Open button** on the Standard toolbar). You should see a dialog box similar to the one in Figure 1.8a. (The Exploring Word folder is not yet selected.)

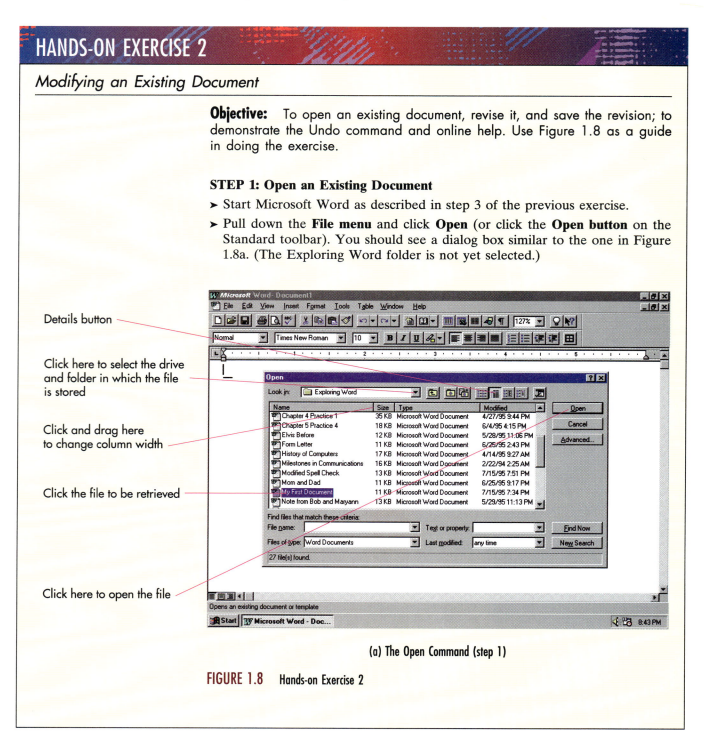

(a) The Open Command (step 1)

FIGURE 1.8 Hands-on Exercise 2

18 MICROSOFT WORD 7.0

➤ To open a file:
- Click the **Details button** to change to the Details view. Click and drag the vertical border between columns to increase (or decrease) the size of a column.
- Click the **drop-down arrow** on the Look In list box.
- Click the appropriate drive, drive C or drive A, depending on the location of your data.
- Double click the **Exploring Word folder** to make it the active folder (the folder in which you will save the document).
- Click the **down arrow** in the Name list box, then scroll until you can select **My First Document** from the first exercise. Click the **Open command button** to open the file.

➤ Your document should appear on the screen.

THE MOST RECENTLY OPENED FILE LIST

The easiest way to open a recently used document is to select the document directly from the File menu. Pull down the File menu, but instead of clicking the Open command, check to see if the document appears on the list of the most recently opened documents at the bottom of the menu. If so, you can click the document name rather than having to make the appropriate selections through the Open dialog box.

STEP 2: The View Menu (Troubleshooting)

➤ Modify the settings within Word so that your settings correspond to ours.
- To change to the Normal view, pull down the **View menu** and click **Normal** (or click the **Normal View** button at the bottom of the window).
- To change the amount of text that is visible on the screen, click the **drop-down arrow** on the Zoom Control box on the Standard toolbar and select **Page Width.**
- To display (hide) the ruler, pull down the **View menu** and toggle the **Ruler command** on or off. End with the ruler on.

➤ There may still be subtle differences between your screen and ours, depending on the resolution of your monitor. These variations, if any, need not concern you at all as long as you are able to complete the exercise.

DISPLAY (HIDE) TOOLBARS WITH THE RIGHT MOUSE BUTTON

Point to any visible toolbar, then click the right mouse button to display a shortcut menu listing the available toolbars. Click the individual toolbars on or off as appropriate. If no toolbars are visible, pull down the View menu, click Toolbars, then display or hide the desired toolbars.

STEP 3: The Tip of the Day

➤ Click the **TipWizard button** to display the Tip of the Day as shown in Figure 1.8b. (You will probably see a different tip than the one in the figure.)

➤ Click the **TipWizard button** a second time to close the TipWizard dialog box.

> ### RESET THE TIPWIZARD
>
> The TipWizard will not repeat a tip from one session to the next unless it is specifically reset each time you start Microsoft Word. Press and hold the Ctrl key as you click the TipWizard button (the light bulb) to reset the TipWizard. You will see a tip indicating that you have reset the TipWizard and that it may display tips you have already seen. This is especially important in a laboratory situation when you are sharing the same computer with other students.

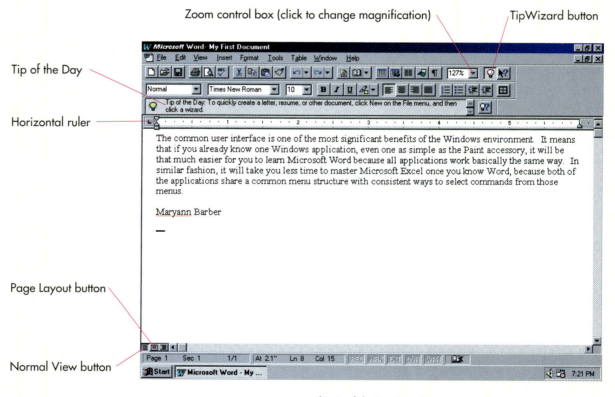

(b) Tip of the Day (step 3)

FIGURE 1.8 Hands-on Exercise 2 (continued)

STEP 4: Display the Hard Returns

➤ The **Show/Hide ¶** button on the Standard toolbar functions as a toggle switch to display (hide) the hard returns (and other nonprinting characters) in a document.

➤ Click the **Show/Hide ¶ button** to display the hard returns as in Figure 1.8c. Click the **Show/Hide ¶ button** a second time to hide the nonprinting characters.

➤ Display or hide the paragraph markers as you see fit.

> ### TOOLTIPS
>
> Point to any button on any toolbar and Word displays a ToolTip, containing the name of the button to indicate its function. If pointing to a button has no effect, pull down the View menu, click Toolbars, and check the box to Show ToolTips.

STEP 5: Modify the Document

➤ Press **Ctrl+End** to move to the end of the document. Press the **up arrow key** once or twice until the insertion point is on a blank line above your name. If necessary, press the **enter key** once (or twice) to add additional blank line(s).

➤ Add the sentence, **Success, I can save and retrieve a document!,** as shown in Figure 1.8c.

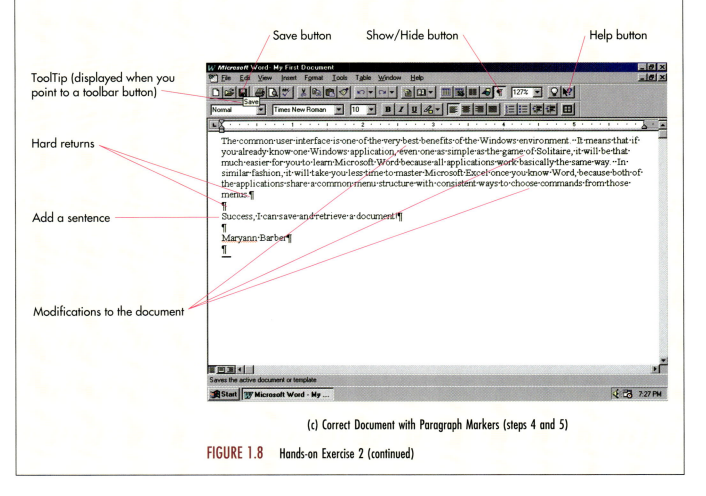

(c) Correct Document with Paragraph Markers (steps 4 and 5)

FIGURE 1.8 Hands-on Exercise 2 (continued)

➤ Make the following additional modifications to practice editing:
  - Change the phrase *most significant* to **very best.**
  - Change *Paint accessory* to **game of Solitaire.**
  - Change the word *select* to **choose.**
➤ Switch between the insert and overtype modes as necessary. Press the **Ins key** or double click the **OVR indicator** on the status bar to toggle between the insert and overtype modes.

> ### MOVING WITHIN A DOCUMENT
>
> Press Ctrl+Home and Ctrl+End to move to the beginning and end of a document, respectively. These shortcuts work not just in Word, but in any other Windows application, and are worth remembering as they allow your hands to remain on the keyboard as you type.

STEP 6: Save the Changes
➤ It is very, very important to save your work repeatedly during a session.
➤ Pull down the **File menu** and click **Save,** or click the **Save button** on the Standard toolbar. You will not see the Save As dialog box because the document is saved automatically under the existing name (My First Document).

> ### THE HELP BUTTON
>
> Click the Help button on the Standard toolbar (the mouse pointer changes to include a large question mark), then click any other toolbar button to display a help screen with information about that button. Double click the Help button as a shortcut to the help facility, then click the Answer Wizard tab to ask a question in your own words.

STEP 7: Deleting Text
➤ Point to the first letter in the first sentence. Press and hold the left mouse button as you drag the mouse over the first sentence. Release the mouse.
➤ The sentence should remain selected as shown in Figure 1.8d. The selected text is the text that will be affected by the next command. Click anywhere else in the document to deselect the text.
➤ Point to any word in the first sentence, then press and hold the **Ctrl key** as you click the mouse, to select the entire sentence. Press the **Del key** to delete the selected text (the first sentence) from the document.

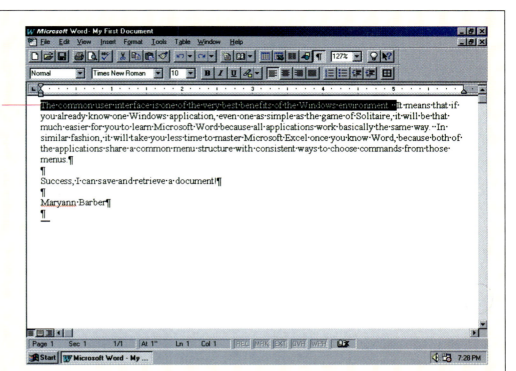

Click and drag over the first sentence to select it

(d) Selecting Text (step 6)

FIGURE 1.8 Hands-on Exercise 2 (continued)

PICK UP THE MOUSE

It seems that you always run out of room on your real desk, just when you need to move the mouse a little further. The solution is to pick up the mouse and move it closer to you—the pointer will stay in its present position on the screen, but when you put the mouse down, you will have more room on your desk in which to work.

STEP 8: The Undo Command

➤ Pull down the **Edit menu** as shown in Figure 1.8e. Click **Undo** to reverse (undo) the last command.

100 LEVELS OF UNDO

The ***Undo command*** is present in Word as it is in every Windows application. Incredible as it sounds, however, Word enables you to undo the last 100 changes to a document. Click the drop-down arrow next to the Undo button to produce a list of your previous actions. (The most recent command is listed first.) Click the action you want to undo, which also undoes all of the preceding commands. Undoing the fifth command in the list, for example, will also undo the preceding four commands.

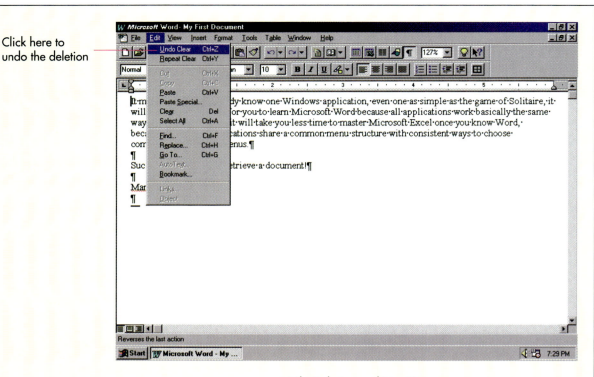

(e) The Undo Command (step 7)

FIGURE 1.8 Hands-on Exercise 2 (continued)

➤ The deleted text should be returned to your document. The Undo command is a tremendous safety net and can be used at almost any time.
➤ Click anywhere outside the selected text to deselect the sentence.

STEP 9: Online Help
➤ Pull down the **Help menu.** Click **Microsoft Word Help Topics** to display the Help topics window in Figure 1.8f.
➤ Click the **Index tab.** Type **Undo** (the topic you wish to look up). The Undoing actions topic is automatically selected. Click **Display** to show a second help screen.
➤ Click **Undo mistakes** to select this topic. Click the **Display command button** to show the detailed instructions.
➤ Click the **Close button** to close the Help window.

THE ANSWER WIZARD

The *Answer Wizard* enables you to request help by posing a question in English. Pull down the Help menu, click Microsoft Word Help Topics, then click the Answer Wizard tab. Type your question in the text box—for example, "How do I request help?"—then click the Search command button. The wizard will return a list of help topics that answer your question, together with a list of related topics that may be of interest to you.

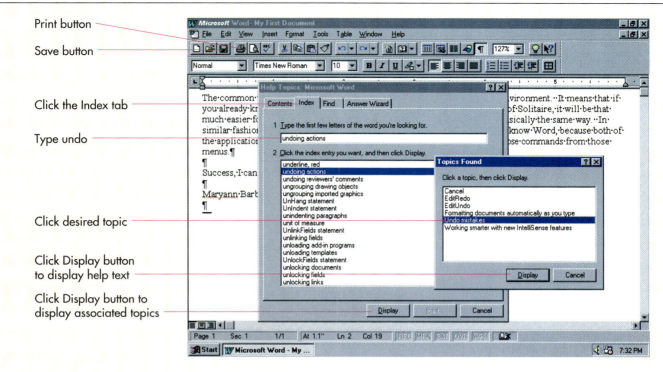

(f) Online Help (step 8)

FIGURE 1.8 Hands-on Exercise 2 (continued)

STEP 10: Print the Revised Document

➤ Click the **Save button** on the Standard toolbar to save the revised document a final time.

➤ Click the **Print button** to print the document.

➤ Pull down the **File menu.** Click **Close** to close the document and remain in Word. Click **Exit** if you do not want to continue with the next exercise at this time.

SUMMARY INFORMATION

Word maintains summary statistics about a document that include the number of pages, words, and characters; the date and time of the last revision; and the total editing time. You can view this ***summary information*** from both the Open and Save As dialog boxes by clicking the Properties button on the toolbar. You can also print the statistics with your document and show your instructor how much time you spent on the assignment. Pull down the Tools menu, click Options, click the Print tab, then check the box to print summary information. Click OK. The summary statistics will appear on a separate page the next time you print a document.

THE SPELL CHECK

There is simply no excuse to misspell a word, since the **spell check** is an integral part of Microsoft Word. (The spell check is also available for every other application in the Microsoft Office.) Spelling errors make your work look sloppy and discourage the reader before he or she has read what you had to say. They can cost you a job, a grade, a lucrative contract, or an award you deserve.

The spell check can be set to automatically check a document as text is entered (see page 34), or it can be called explicitly by clicking the Spelling button on the Standard toolbar. The spell check compares each word in a document to the entries in a built-in dictionary, then flags any word that is in the document, but not in the built-in dictionary, as an error.

The dictionary included with Microsoft Office is limited to standard English and does not include many proper names, acronyms, abbreviations, or specialized terms, and hence, the use of any such item is considered a misspelling. You can, however, add such words to a **custom dictionary** so that they will not be flagged in the future. You can also purchase specialized dictionaries containing medical or legal terminology or even a foreign language dictionary. The spell check will inform you of repeated words and irregular capitalization. It cannot, however, flag properly spelled words that are used improperly, and thus cannot tell you that *Two bee or knot too be* is not the answer.

The capabilities of the spell check are illustrated in conjunction with Figure 1.9a. The spell check goes through the document and returns the errors one at a time, offering several options for each mistake. You can change the misspelled word to one of the alternatives suggested by Word, leave the word as is, or add the word to a custom dictionary.

The first error is *embarassing* with Word's suggestion(s) for correction displayed in the list box in Figure 1.9b. To accept the highlighted suggestion, click the Change command button and the substitution will be made automatically in the document. To accept an alternative suggestion, click the desired word, then click the Change command button. Alternatively, you can click the AutoCorrect button to correct the mistake in the current document, and, in addition, automatically correct the same mistake in any future document.

The spell check detects both irregular capitalization and duplicated words as shown in Figures 1.9c and 1.9d, respectively. The error in Figure 1.9e, *Grauer,* is not a misspelling per se, but a proper noun not found in the standard dictionary. No correction is required and the appropriate action is to ignore the word (taking no further action)—or better yet, add it to the custom dictionary so that it will not be flagged in future sessions. And finally, we could not resist including the example in Figure 1.9f, which shows another use of the spell check.

HELP IN CROSSWORDS

Quick, what is a five-letter word, meaning severe or firm, with the pattern S _ _ RN? If you answered stern, you don't need our help. But if not, you might want to use the spell check to come up with the answer. Type the pattern using a question mark for each unknown character; for example, S??RN. Click anywhere within the word, then click the Spelling button on the Standard toolbar. Word will return all of the matching words in the dictionary (scorn, shorn, spurn, stern, and sworn). It's then a simple matter to pick out the word that fits.

Flagged errors

A spelling checker will catch embarassing mistakes, iRregular capitalization, and duplicate words words. It will also flag proper nouns, for example, Robert Grauer, but you can add these terms to an auxiliary dictionary so that they will not be flagged in the future. It will not, however, notice properly spelled words that are used incorrectly; for example, Two bee or knot too be is not the answer.

(a) The Text

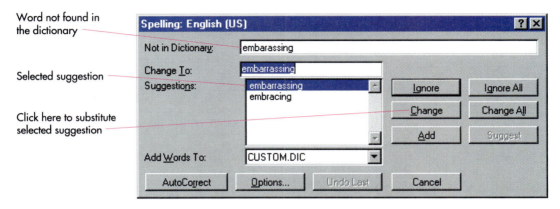

(b) Ordinary Misspelling

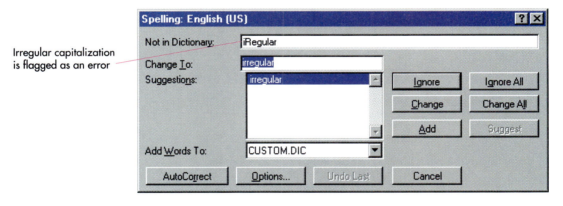

(c) Irregular Capitalization

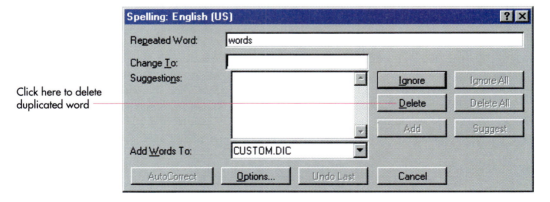

(d) Duplicated Word

FIGURE 1.9 The Spell Check

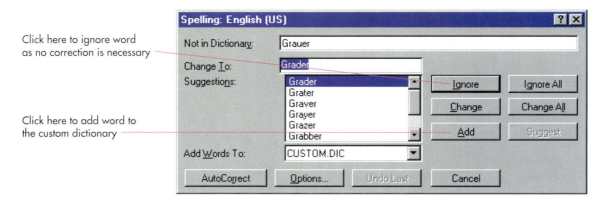

(e) Proper Noun

(f) Help with Crosswords

FIGURE 1.9 The Spell Check (continued)

AutoCorrect

The *AutoCorrect* feature corrects mistakes as they are made without any effort on your part. It makes you a better typist. If, for example, you typed *teh* instead of *the,* Word would change the spelling without even telling you. Word will also change *adn* to *and, i* to *I,* and *occurence* to *occurrence.*

Microsoft Word includes a predefined table of common mistakes and uses that table to make substitutions whenever it encounters an error it recognizes. You can add additional items to the table to include the frequent errors you make. You can also use the feature to define your own shorthand—for example, cis for Computer Information Systems as shown in Figure 1.10.

The AutoCorrect will also correct mistakes in capitalization; for example, it will capitalize the first letter in a sentence, recognize that MIami should be Miami, and capitalize the days of the week. It's even smart enough to correct the accidental use of the Caps Lock key, and it will toggle the key off!

SAVE COMMAND

The Save command was used in the first two exercises. The Save As command will be introduced in the next exercise as a very useful alternative. We also introduce you to different backup options. We believe that now, when you are first

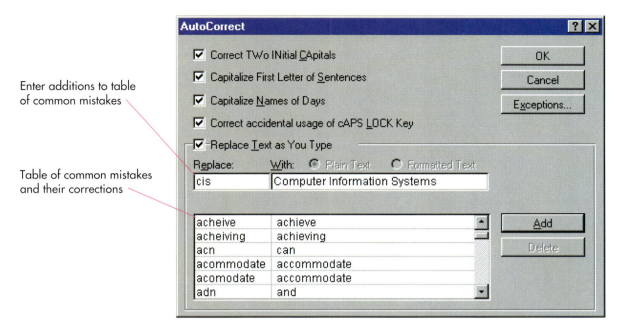

FIGURE 1.10   AutoCorrect

starting to learn about word processing, is the time to develop good working habits.

You already know that the Save command copies the document currently being edited (the document in memory) to disk. The initial execution of the command requires you to assign a file name and to specify the drive and folder in which the file is to be stored. All subsequent executions of the Save command save the document under the original name, replacing the previously saved version with the new one.

The **Save As command** saves another copy of a document under a different name, and is useful when you want to retain a copy of the original document. The Save As command provides you with two copies of a document. The original document is kept on disk under its original name. A copy of the document is saved on disk under a new name and remains in memory. All subsequent editing is done on the new document.

We cannot overemphasize the importance of periodically saving a document, so that if something does go wrong, you won't lose all of your work. Nothing is more frustrating than to lose two hours of effort, due to an unexpected problem in Windows or to a temporary loss of power. Save your work frequently, at least once every 15 minutes. Pull down the File menu and click Save, or click the Save button on the Standard toolbar. Do it!

QUIT WITHOUT SAVING

There will be times when you do not want to save the changes to a document, such as when you have edited it beyond recognition and wish you had never started. Pull down the File menu and click the Close command, then click No in response to the message asking whether you want to save the changes to the document. Pull down the File menu and reopen the file (it should be the first file in the list of most recently edited documents), then start over from the beginning.

Backup Options

Microsoft Word offers several different *backup* options. We believe the two most important options are to create a backup copy in conjunction with every save command, and to periodically (and automatically) save a document. Both options are implemented in step 3 in the next hands-on exercise.

Figure 1.11 illustrates the option to create a backup copy of the document every time a Save command is executed. Assume, for example, that you have created the simple document, *The fox jumped over the fence* and saved it under the name "Fox". Assume further that you edit the document to read, *The quick brown fox jumped over the fence,* and that you saved it a second time. The second save command changes the name of the original document from "Fox" to "Backup of Fox", then saves the current contents of memory as "Fox". In other words, the disk now contains two versions of the document: the current version "Fox" and the most recent previous version "Backup of Fox".

The cycle goes on indefinitely, with "Fox" always containing the current version, and "Backup of Fox" the most recent previous version. Thus if you revise and save the document a third time, "Fox" will contain the latest revision while "Backup of Fox" would contain the previous version alluding to the quick brown fox. The original (first) version of the document disappears entirely since only two versions are kept.

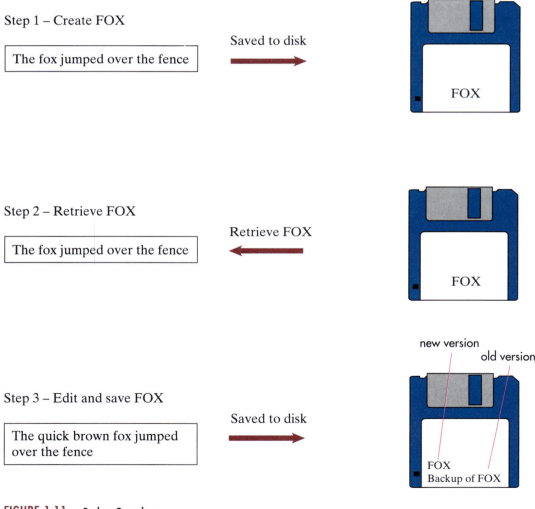

FIGURE 1.11 Backup Procedures

The contents of "Fox" and "Backup of Fox" are different, but the existence of the latter enables you to retrieve the previous version if you inadvertently edit beyond repair or accidentally erase the current "Fox" version. Should this occur (and it will), you can always retrieve its predecessor and at least salvage your work prior to the last save operation.

> **KEEP DUPLICATE COPIES OF IMPORTANT FILES**
>
> It is absolutely critical to maintain duplicate copies of important files on a separate disk stored away from the computer. In addition, you should print each new document at the end of every session, saving it before printing (power failures happen when least expected—for example, during the print operation). Hard copy is not as good as a duplicate disk, but it is better than nothing.

HANDS-ON EXERCISE 3

The Spell Check

Objective: To open an existing document, check it for spelling, then use the Save As command to save the document under a different file name. Use Figure 1.12 as a guide in the exercise.

STEP 1: Preview a Document

- Start Microsoft Word. Pull down the **File menu** and click **Open** (or click the **Open button** on the Standard toolbar). You should see the dialog box similar to the one in Figure 1.12a.
- Select the appropriate drive, drive C or drive A, depending on the location of your data. Double click the **Exploring Word folder** to make it the active folder (the folder in which you will save the document).
- Scroll in the Name list box until you can select (click) the **Try the Spell Check** document. Click the **Preview button** on the toolbar to preview the document as shown in Figure 1.12a.
- Click the **Open command button** to open the file. Your document should appear on the screen.

> **CHANGE THE DEFAULT FOLDER**
>
> The default folder is the folder where Word opens (saves) documents unless it is otherwise instructed. To change the default folder, pull down the Tools menu, click Options, click the File Locations tab, click Documents, and click the Modify command button. Enter the name of the new folder (for example, C:\Exploring Word), click OK, then click the Close button. The next time you access the File menu, the default folder will reflect these changes.

MICROSOFT WORD 7.0

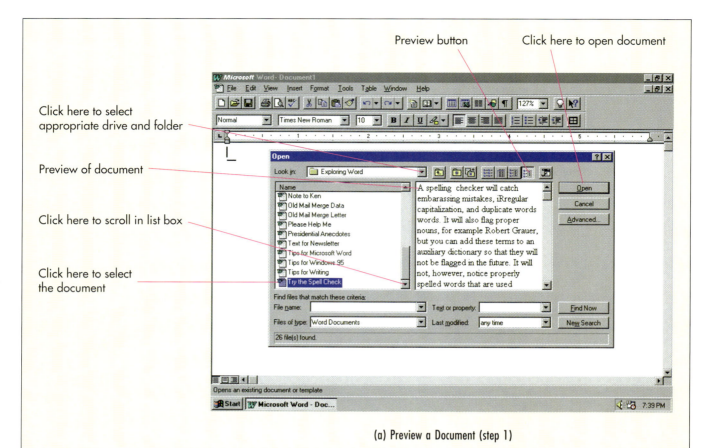

(a) Preview a Document (step 1)

FIGURE 1.12 Hands-on Exercise 3

STEP 2: The Save As Command

➤ Pull down the **File menu.** Click **Save As** to produce a dialog box in Figure 1.12b.

➤ Enter **Modified Spell Check** as the name of the new document. (A file name may contain up to 255 characters, and blanks are permitted.) Click the **Save command button.**

➤ There are now two identical copies of the file on disk: Try the Spell Check, which we supplied, and Modified Spell Check, which you just created. The title bar of the document window shows the latter name.

STEP 3: Establish Automatic Backup

➤ Pull down the **Tools menu.** Click **Options.** Click the **Save tab** to display the dialog box of Figure 1.12c.

➤ Click the first check box to choose **Always Create Backup Copy.**

➤ Set the other options as you see fit; for example, you can specify that the document be saved automatically every 10–15 minutes. Click **OK.**

STEP 4: The Spell Check

➤ If necessary, press **Ctrl+Home** to move to the beginning of the document. Click the Spelling button on the Standard toolbar to initiate the spell check.

➤ "Embarassing" is flagged as the first misspelling as shown in Figure 1.12d. Click the **Change button** to accept the suggested spelling.

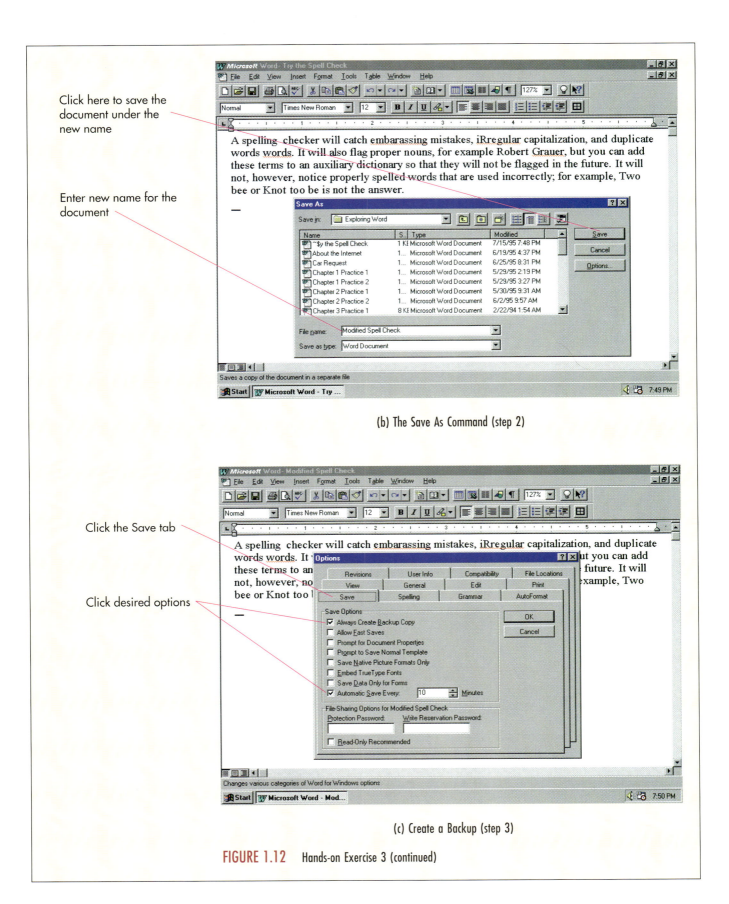

(b) The Save As Command (step 2)

(c) Create a Backup (step 3)

FIGURE 1.12 Hands-on Exercise 3 (continued)

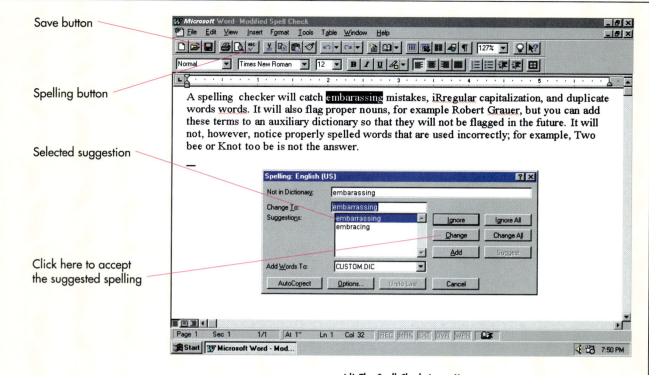

(d) The Spell Check (step 4)

FIGURE 1.12 Hands-on Exercise 3 (continued)

➤ "iRregular" is flagged as an example of irregular capitalization. Click the **Change button** to accept the suggested correction.
➤ Continue checking the document, which displays misspellings and other irregularities one at a time. Click the appropriate command button as each mistake is found.
  • Click the **Delete button** to remove the duplicated word.
  • Click the **Ignore button** to accept Grauer (or click the **Add button** to add Grauer to the supplementary dictionary).
➤ Click **OK** when the spell check has finished checking the document.

CHECK SPELLING AUTOMATICALLY

The spell check can be set to automatically check a document as text is entered, which in turn displays a red wavy line under any misspelled word. To correct a misspelling, right click the wavy line, then choose the appropriate correction from the suggested list or choose the option to add the word to the custom dictionary. To set the option, pull down the Tools menu, click Options, click the Spelling tab, then check (clear) the box for Automatic Spell Checking. An open book icon will appear on the status bar to indicate that the automatic spell check is in effect.

STEP 5: AutoCorrect

- Check to be sure that you are positioned at the beginning of the document and be sure you are in the Insert mode.
- Type the *misspelled* phrase **Teh Spelling Check will be used to check this document.** Try to look at the monitor as you type the word *Teh* to see the Auto-Correct feature in action; Word will correct the misspelling and change *Teh* to *The*.
- If you did not see the correction being made, click the arrow next to the Undo command on the Standard toolbar and undo the last several actions. Click the arrow next to the Redo command and redo the corrections in order to see the typing and auto correction.
- Save the file.

CREATE YOUR OWN SHORTHAND

Use AutoCorrect to expand abbreviations such as "usa" for United States of America. Pull down the Tools menu, click AutoCorrect, type the abbreviation in the Replace text box and the expanded entry in the With text box. Click the Add command button, then click OK to exit the dialog box and return to the document. The next time you type usa in a document, it will automatically be expanded to United States of America.

STEP 6: Exit Word

- Pull down the **File menu.** Click **Exit** to exit Word.

SUMMARY

The chapter provided a broad-based introduction to word processing in general and Microsoft Word in particular. Microsoft Word is always in one of two modes, insert or overtype, and uses a toggle switch (the Ins key) to alternate between the two. The insertion point marks the place within a document where text is added or replaced.

The enter key is pressed at the end of a paragraph, but not at the end of a line because Word automatically wraps text from one line to the next. A hard return is created by the user when he or she presses the enter key; a soft return is created by Word as it wraps text and begins a new line.

The Save and Open commands work in conjunction with one another. The Save command copies the document in memory to disk under its existing name. The Open command retrieves a previously saved document. The Save As command saves the document under a different name and is useful when you want to retain a copy of the current document prior to all changes.

A spell check compares the words in a document to those in a standard and/or custom dictionary and offers suggestions to correct the mistakes it finds. It will detect misspellings, duplicated phrases, and/or irregular capitalization, but will not flag properly spelled words that are used incorrectly.

The AutoCorrect feature corrects predefined spelling errors and/or mistakes in capitalization, automatically, as the words are entered. The feature can also be used to create a personal shorthand as it will expand abbreviations as they are typed.

KEY WORDS AND CONCEPTS

Answer Wizard	Open command	Text box
AutoCorrect	Overtype mode	Tip of the Day
Backup	Page Layout view	TipWizard
Custom dictionary	Save As command	Toggle switch
File menu	Save command	Toolbar
Formatting toolbar	Show/Hide ¶ button	ToolTip
Hard return	Soft return	Undo command
Horizontal ruler	Spell check	Vertical ruler
Insert mode	Standard toolbar	View menu
Insertion point	Status bar	Word wrap
Normal view	Summary Information	

MULTIPLE CHOICE

1. When entering text within a document, the enter key is normally pressed at the end of every:
   (a) Line
   (b) Sentence
   (c) Paragraph
   (d) All of the above

2. Which menu contains the commands to save the current document, or to open a previously saved document?
   (a) The Tools menu
   (b) The File menu
   (c) The View menu
   (d) The Edit menu

3. How do you execute the Print command?
   (a) Click the Print button on the standard toolbar
   (b) Pull down the File, then click the Print command
   (c) Use the appropriate keyboard shortcut
   (d) All of the above

4. The Open command:
   (a) Brings a document from disk into memory
   (b) Brings a document from disk into memory, then erases the document on disk

(c) Stores the document in memory on disk
(d) Stores the document in memory on disk, then erases the document from memory

5. The Save command:
    (a) Brings a document from disk into memory
    (b) Brings a document from disk into memory, then erases the document on disk
    (c) Stores the document in memory on disk
    (d) Stores the document in memory on disk, then erases the document from memory

6. What is the easiest way to change the phrase, *revenues, profits, gross margin,* to read *revenues, profits, and gross margin?*
    (a) Use the insert mode, position the cursor before the *g* in *gross,* then type the word *and* followed by a space
    (b) Use the insert mode, position the cursor after the *g* in *gross,* then type the word *and* followed by a space
    (c) Use the overtype mode, position the cursor before the *g* in *gross,* then type the word *and* followed by a space
    (d) Use the overtype mode, position the cursor after the *g* in *gross,* then type the word *and* followed by a space

7. What happens if you press the Ins key *twice in a row* from within Word?
    (a) You will be in the insert mode
    (b) You will be in the overtype mode
    (c) You will be in the same mode you were in before pressing the key at all
    (d) You will be in the opposite mode you were in before pressing the key at all

8. A document has been entered into Word with a given set of margins, which are subsequently changed. What can you say about the number of hard and soft returns before and after the change in margins?
    (a) The number of hard returns is the same, but the number and/or position of the soft returns is different
    (b) The number of soft returns is the same, but the number and/or position of the hard returns is different
    (c) The number and position of both hard and soft returns is unchanged
    (d) The number and position of both hard and soft returns is different

9. Which of the following is an example of a toggle switch within Word?
    (a) The Ins key
    (b) The Caps Lock key
    (c) The Show/Hide ¶ button on the Standard toolbar
    (d) All of the above

10. Which of the following will be detected by the spell check?
    (a) Duplicate words
    (b) Irregular capitalization
    (c) Both (a) and (b)
    (d) Neither (a) nor (b)

11. Which of the following is likely to be found in a custom dictionary?
    (a) Proper names
    (b) Words related to the user's particular application

(c) Acronyms created by the user for his or her application
(d) All of the above

12. Ted and Sally both use Word but on different computers. Both have written a letter to Dr. Joel Stutz and have run a spell check on their respective documents. Ted's program flags *Stutz* as a misspelling, whereas Sally's accepts it as written. Why?
    (a) The situation is impossible; that is, if they use identical word processing programs they should get identical results
    (b) Ted has added *Stutz* to his custom dictionary
    (c) Sally has added *Stutz* to her custom dictionary
    (d) All of the above reasons are equally likely as a cause of the problem

13. The spell check will do all of the following *except:*
    (a) Flag properly spelled words used incorrectly
    (b) Identify misspelled words
    (c) Accept (as correctly spelled) words found in the custom dictionary
    (d) Suggest alternatives to misspellings it identifies

14. The AutoCorrect feature will:
    (a) Correct errors in capitalization as they occur during typing
    (b) Expand user-defined abbreviations as the entries are typed
    (c) Both (a) and (b)
    (d) Neither (a) nor (b)

15. When does the Save As dialog box appear?
    (a) The first time a file is saved using either the Save or Save As commands
    (b) Every time a file is saved by clicking the Save button on the Standard toolbar
    (c) Both (a) and (b)
    (d) Neither (a) nor (b)

ANSWERS

1. c	**6.** a	**11.** d
2. b	**7.** c	**12.** c
3. d	**8.** a	**13.** a
4. a	**9.** d	**14.** c
5. c	**10.** c	**15.** a

EXPLORING MICROSOFT WORD

1. Use Figure 1.13 to match each action with its result; a given action may be used more than once or not at all.

Action	Result
a. Click at 1	____ Save the document
b. Click at 2	____ Hide the paragraph markers
c. Click at 3	____ Toggle the overtype mode off

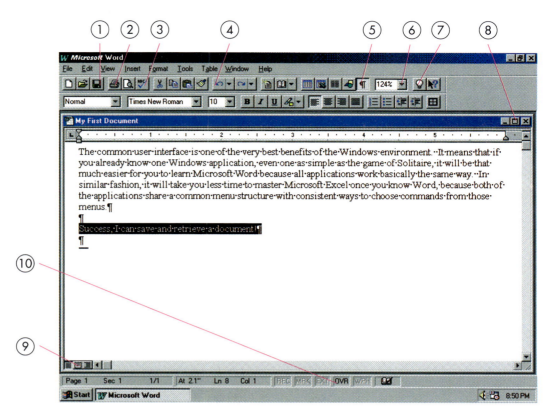

FIGURE 1.13 Screen for Problem 1

    d. Click at 4   ____ Print the document
    e. Click at 5   ____ Maximize the document window
    f. Click at 6   ____ Display the TipWizard
    g. Click at 7   ____ Change the magnification
    h. Click at 8   ____ Switch to the Page Layout view
    i. Click at 9   ____ Correct the spelling in the document
    j. Double click at 10   ____ Undo the previous action

2. Troubleshooting: The informational messages in Figure 1.14 appeared (or could have appeared) in response to various commands issued during the chapter.

    a. Which command produced the message in Figure 1.14a? What action is necessary to correct the indicated problem?

    b. Which command produced the message in Figure 1.14b? When would No be an appropriate response to this message?

    c. The message in Figure 1.14c appeared in response to a File Open command in which the user typed the name of the file to open. What is the most likely corrective action?

    d. What is the effect of pressing the enter key in response to any of the error messages? What is the effect of pressing the Esc key?

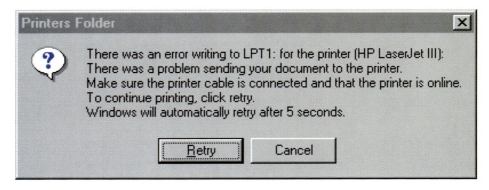

(a) Informational Message 1

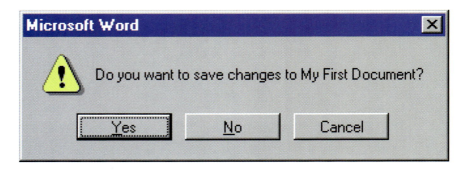

(b) Informational Message 2

(c) Informational Message 3

FIGURE 1.14   Scrrens for Problem 2

3. Answer the following with respect to Figure 1.15:
   a. What is the name of the document currently being edited?
   b. Which view is selected, Page View or Normal?
   c. Is the ruler present? The Formatting toolbar? The Standard toolbar? How do you cause the missing elements to reappear?
   d. Which mode is active, insert or overtype? How do you switch from one mode to the other?
   e. How do you display (hide) the hard returns? Are the hard returns displayed in the figure?

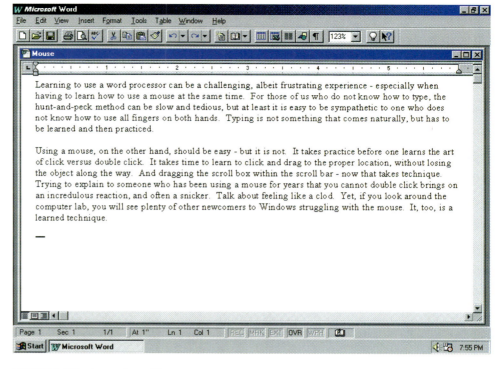

FIGURE 1.15 Screen for Problem 3

4. Answer the following with respect to Figure 1.16:
   a. Which command produced the dialog box shown in the figure?
   b. Which view is selected? How do you change to the List view?
   c. Which document is selected? In which folder is the document located?
   d. How do you preview the selected document? How do you view the properties of that document?
   e. What happens if you double click the selected document? If you right click the selected document?

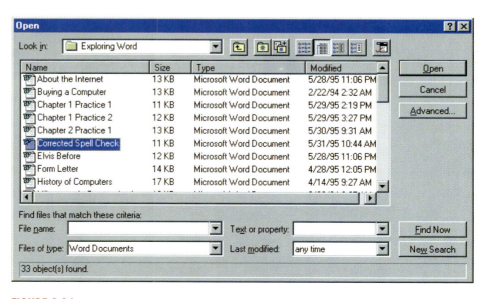

FIGURE 1.16 Screen for Problem 4

PRACTICE WITH MICROSOFT WORD

1. Retrieve the *Chapter1 Practice 1* document shown in Figure 1.17 from the Exploring Word folder, then make the following changes:
   a. Select the text *Your name* and replace it with your name.
   b. Replace *May 31, 1995* with the current date.
   c. Insert the phrase *one or* in line 2 so that the text reads ... *one or more characters than currently exist.*
   d. Delete the word *And* from sentence four in line 5, then change the w in *when* to a capital letter to begin the sentence.
   e. Change the phrase *most efficient to best.*
   f. Place the insertion point at the end of sentence 2, make sure you are in the insert mode, then add the following sentence: *The insert mode adds characters at the insertion point while moving existing text to the right in order to make room for the new text.*
   g. Place the insertion point at the end of the last sentence, press the enter key twice in a row, then enter the following text: *There are several keys that function as toggle switches of which you should be aware. The Ins key switches between the insert and overtype modes, the Caps Lock key toggles between upper- and lowercase letters, and the Num Lock key alternates between typing numbers and using the arrow keys.*
   h. Save the revised document, then print it and submit it to your instructor.

2. Select-then-do: Formatting is not covered until Chapter 2, but we think you are ready to try your hand at basic formatting now. Most formatting operations are done in the context of select-then-do as described in the document in Figure 1.18. You select the text you want to format, then you execute the appropriate formatting command, most easily by clicking the appropriate button on the Formatting toolbar. The function of each button should be apparent from its icon, but you can simply point to a button to display a ToolTip that is indicative of the button's function.

   An unformatted version of the document in Figure 1.18 exists on the data disk as *Chapter1 Practice 2.* Open the document, then format it to match the completed version in Figure 1.18. Just select the text to format, then click the appropriate button. We changed type size in the original document to 24 points for the title and 12 points for text in the document itself. Be sure to add your name and date as shown in the figure, then submit the completed document to your instructor.

3. Your background: Write a short description of your computer background similar to the document in Figure 1.19. The document should be in the form of a note from student to instructor that describes your background and should mention any previous knowledge of computers you have, prior computer courses you have taken, your objectives for this course, and so on. Indicate whether you own a PC, whether you have access to one at work, and/or whether you are considering purchase. Include any other information about yourself and/or your computer-related background.

   Place your name somewhere in the document in boldface italics. We would also like you to use boldface and italics to emphasize the components of any computer system you describe. Use any font or point size you like. Note, too, the last paragraph, which asks you to print the summary statistics for the document when you submit the assignment to your instructor.

To: Your Name

From: Robert Grauer and Maryann Barber

Subject: Microsoft Word for Windows

Date: May 31, 1995

This is just a short note to help you get acquainted with the insertion and replacement modes in Word for Windows. When the editing to be done results in more characters than currently exist, you want to be in the insertion mode when making the change. On the other hand, when the editing to be done contains the same or fewer characters, the replacement mode is best. And when replacing characters, it is most efficient to use the mouse to select the characters to be deleted and then just type the new characters; the selected characters are automatically deleted and the new characters typed take their place.

FIGURE 1.17   Document for Practice with Word Exercise 1

Select-Then-Do

Many operations in Word are executed as select-then-do operations. You first select a block of text, then you issue a command that will affect the selected text. You may select the text in many different ways, the most basic of which is to click and drag over the desired characters. You may also take one of many shortcuts, which include double clicking on a word, pressing Ctrl as you click a sentence, and triple clicking on a paragraph.

Once text is selected, you may then delete it, **boldface** or *italicize* it, or even change its color. You may move it or copy it to another location, in the same or a different document. You can highlight it, underline, or even check its spelling. Then, depending on whether or not you like what you have done, you may undo it, redo it, and/or repeat it on subsequently selected text.

Jessica Kinzer
September 1, 1995

FIGURE 1.18   Document for Practice with Word Exercise 2

The Computer and Me

My name is Jessica Kinzer and I am a complete novice when it comes to computers. I did not take a computer course in high school and this is my first semester at the University of Miami. My family does not own a computer, nor have I had the opportunity to use one at work. So when it comes to beginners, I am a beginner's beginner. I am looking forward to taking this course, as I have heard that it will truly make me computer literate. I know that I desperately need computer skills not only when I enter the job market, but to survive my four years here as well. I am looking forward to learning Word, Excel, and PowerPoint, and I hope that I can pick up some Internet skills as well.

I did not buy a computer before I came to school as I wanted to see what type of system I would be using for my classes. After my first few weeks in class, I think that I would like to buy a ***100 Mz Pentium*** machine with ***16Mb RAM*** and a ***1 Gb hard drive***. I would like a ***quad speed CD-ROM*** and a ***sound card*** (with ***speakers***, of course). I also would like to get a laser printer. Now, if only I had the money.

This document did not take long at all to create as you can see by the summary statistics that are printed on the next page. I think I will enjoy this class.

Jessica Kinzer
September 1, 1995

FIGURE 1.19 Document for Practice with Word Exercise 3

Exploring Word Assignment

Jessica Kinzer
CIS 120
September 1, 1995

FIGURE 1.20 Document for Practice with Word Exercise 4

4. The cover page: Create a cover page that you can use for your assignments this semester. Your cover page should be similar to the one in Figure 1.20 with respect to content and should include the title of the assignment, your name, course information, and date. The formatting is up to you. Print the completed cover page and submit it to your instructor for inclusion in a class contest to judge the most innovative design.

Case Studies

It's a Mess

Newcomers to word processing quickly learn the concept of word wrap and the distinction between hard and soft returns. This lesson was lost, however, on your friend who created the *Please Help Me* document on the data disk. The first several sentences were entered without any hard returns at all, whereas the opposite problem exists toward the end of the document. This is a good friend, and her paper is due in one hour. Please help.

Planning for Disaster

Do you have a backup strategy? Do you even know what a backup strategy is? You should learn, because sooner or later you will wish you had one. You will erase a file, be unable to read from a floppy disk, or worse yet suffer a hardware failure in which you are unable to access the hard drive. The problem always seems to occur the night before an assignment is due. The ultimate disaster is the disappearance of your computer, by theft or natural disaster (e.g., Hurricane Andrew). Describe in 250 words or less the backup strategy you plan to implement in conjunction with your work in this class.

A Letter Home

You really like this course and want very much to have your own computer, but you're strapped for cash and have decided to ask your parents for help. Write a one-page letter describing the advantages of having your own system and how it will help you in school. Tell your parents what the system will cost, and that you can save money by buying through the mail. Describe the configuration you intend to buy (don't forget to include the price of software) and then provide prices from at least three different companies. Cut out the advertisements and include them in your letter. Bring your material to class and compare your research with that of your classmates.

Computer Magazines

A subscription to a computer magazine should be given serious consideration if you intend to stay abreast in a rapidly changing field. The reviews on new products are especially helpful and you will appreciate the advertisements should you need to buy. Go to the library or a newsstand and obtain a magazine that appeals to you, then write a brief review of the magazine for class. Devote at least one paragraph to an article or other item you found useful.

GAINING PROFICIENCY: EDITING AND FORMATTING

OBJECTIVES

After reading this chapter you will be able to:

1. Define the select-then-do methodology; describe several shortcuts with the mouse and/or the keyboard to select text.
2. Use the clipboard and/or the drag-and-drop capability to move and copy text within a document.
3. Use the Find and Replace commands to substitute one character string for another.
4. Define scrolling; scroll to the beginning and end of a document.
5. Distinguish between the Normal and Page Layout views; state how to change the view and/or magnification of a document.
6. Define typography; distinguish between a serif and a sans serif typeface; use the Format Font command to change the font and/or type size.
7. Use the Format Paragraph command to change line spacing, alignment, tabs, and indents, and to control pagination.
8. Use the Borders and Shading command to box and shade text.
9. Describe the Undo and Redo commands and how they are related to one another.
10. Use the Page Setup command to change the margins and/or orientation; differentiate between a soft and a hard page break.

OVERVIEW

The previous chapter taught you the basics of Microsoft Word and enabled you to create and print a simple document. The present chapter significantly extends your capabilities, by presenting a variety of commands to change the contents and appearance of a document. These operations are known as editing and formatting, respectively.

You will learn how to move and copy text within a document and how to find and replace one character string with another. You will also learn the basics of typography and be able to switch between the different fonts included within Windows. You will be able to change alignment, indentation, line spacing, margins, and page orientation. All of these commands are used in three hands-on exercises, which require your participation at the computer, and which are the very essence of the chapter.

As you read the chapter, realize that there are many different ways to accomplish the same task and that it would be impossible to cover them all. Our approach is to present the overall concepts and suggest the ways we think are most appropriate at the time we introduce the material. We also offer numerous shortcuts in the form of boxed tips that appear throughout the chapter and urge you to explore further on your own. It is not necessary for you to memorize anything as online help is always available. Be flexible and willing to experiment.

> **WRITE NOW, EDIT LATER**
>
> You write a sentence, then change it, and change it again, and one hour later you've produced a single paragraph. It happens to every writer—you stare at a blank screen and flashing cursor and are unable to write. The best solution is to brainstorm and write down anything that pops into your head, and to keep on writing. Don't worry about typos or spelling errors because you can fix them later. Above all, resist the temptation to continually edit the few words you've written because overediting will drain the life out of what you are writing. The important thing is to get your ideas on paper.

SELECT-THEN-DO

Many operations in Word take place within the context of a *select-then-do* methodology; that is, you select a block of text, then you execute the command to operate on that text. The most basic way to select text is by dragging the mouse; that is, click at the beginning of the selection, press and hold the left mouse button as you move to the end of the selection, then release the mouse.

There are, however, a variety of shortcuts to facilitate the process; for example, double click anywhere within a word to select the word, or press the Ctrl key and click the mouse anywhere within a sentence to select the sentence. Additional shortcuts are presented in each of the hands-on exercises, at which point you will have many opportunities to practice selecting text.

Selected text is affected by any subsequent operation; for example, clicking the Bold or Italic button changes the selected text to boldface or italics, respectively. You can also drag the selected text to a new location, press the Del key to erase the selected text, or execute any other editing or formatting command. The text continues to be selected until you click elsewhere in the document.

> **THE RIGHT MOUSE BUTTON**
>
> Point anywhere within a document, then click the right mouse button to display a shortcut menu. Shortcut menus contain commands appropriate to the item you have selected. Click in the menu to execute a command, or click outside the menu to close the menu without executing a command.

MOVING AND COPYING TEXT

The ability to move and/or copy text is essential in order to develop any degree of proficiency in editing. A move operation removes the text from its current location and places it elsewhere in the same (or even a different) document; a copy operation retains the text in its present location and places a duplicate elsewhere. Either operation can be accomplished using the Windows clipboard and a combination of the ***Cut, Copy,*** and ***Paste commands.*** (A shortcut, using the mouse to ***drag-and-drop*** text from one location to another, is described in step 8 in the first hands-on exercise.)

The ***clipboard*** is a temporary storage area available to any Windows application. Selected text is cut or copied from a document and placed onto the clipboard from where it can be pasted to a new location(s). A move requires that you select the text and execute a Cut command to remove the text from the document and place it on the clipboard. You then move the insertion point to the new location and paste the text from the clipboard into that location. A copy operation necessitates the same steps except that a Copy command is executed rather than a cut, leaving the selected text in its original location as well as placing a copy on the clipboard.

The Cut, Copy, and Paste commands are found in the Edit menu, or alternatively, can be executed by clicking the appropriate buttons on the Standard toolbar. The contents of the clipboard are replaced by each subsequent Cut or Copy command, but are unaffected by the Paste command; that is, the contents of the clipboard can be pasted into multiple locations in the same or different documents.

DELETE WITH CAUTION

You work too hard developing your thoughts to see them disappear in a flash. Hence, instead of deleting large blocks of text, try moving them to the end of your document (or even a new document) from where they can be recalled later if you change your mind. A related practice is to remain in the insert mode (as opposed to overtype) to prevent the inadvertent deletion of existing text as new ideas are added.

UNDO AND REDO COMMANDS

The ***Undo command*** was introduced in Chapter 1, but it is repeated here because it is so valuable. The command is executed from the Edit menu or by clicking the Undo button on the Standard toolbar. Word enables you to undo up to the last 100 changes to a document. You just click the arrow next to the Undo button on the Standard toolbar to display a reverse-order list of your previous commands, then you click the command you want to undo, which also undoes all of the preceding commands. Undoing the fifth command in the list, for example, will also undo the preceding four commands.

The ***Redo command*** redoes (reverses) the last command that was undone. As with the Undo command, the Redo command redoes all of the previous commands prior to the command you select. Redoing the fifth command in the list, for example, will also redo the preceding four commands. The Undo and Redo commands work in conjunction with one another; that is, every time a command is undone it can be redone at a later time.

FIND AND REPLACE COMMANDS

The ***Find command*** enables you to locate a specific occurrence of a character string in order to perform a subsequent editing or formatting operation. The ***Replace command*** incorporates the Find command and allows you to locate and optionally replace (one or more occurrences of) a designated character string with a different character string.

The two strings are known as the find and replacement strings, respectively, and may consist of a single letter, a word, a sentence, or any combination of text and/or formatting. The two strings do *not* have to be the same length; for example, you could replace *16* with *sixteen.* The commands are illustrated in Figure 2.1.

The search may or may not be ***case-sensitive.*** A case-sensitive search (where Match Case is selected as in Figure 2.1a) matches not only the characters, but the use of upper- and lowercase letters. Thus, *There* is different from *there,* and a search on one will not identify the other. A ***case-insensitive*** search (where Match Case is *not* selected) is just the opposite and finds both *There* and *there.* The search may also specify a match on ***whole words only,*** which will identify *there,* but not *therefore* or *thereby.*

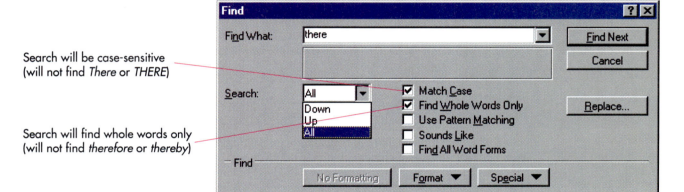

(a) Find Command

FIGURE 2.1 Find and Replace Commands

The Replace command in Figure 2.1b implements either ***selective replacement,*** which lets you examine each occurrence of the character string in context and decide whether to replace it, or ***automatic replacement,*** where the substitution is made automatically. The latter often produces unintended consequences and is not recommended; for example, if you substitute the word *text* for *book,* the phrase *text book* would become *text text,* which is not what you had in mind.

Selective replacement is implemented in Figure 2.1b by clicking the Find Next command button, then clicking (or not clicking) the Replace button to make the substitution. Automatic replacement (through the entire document) is implemented by clicking the Replace All button.

The Find and Replace commands can include formatting and/or special characters. You can change all italicized text to boldface, or you can change five consecutive spaces to a tab character. You can also use pattern matching to introduce a wild card into the search string. For example, to find all four-letter words that begin with "f" and end with "l" (such as fall, fill, or fail), enter f??l as the find string and select the option for pattern matching. You can even search for a word based on how it sounds. When searching for Marion, for example, check the Sounds Like check box, and the search will find both Marion and Marian.

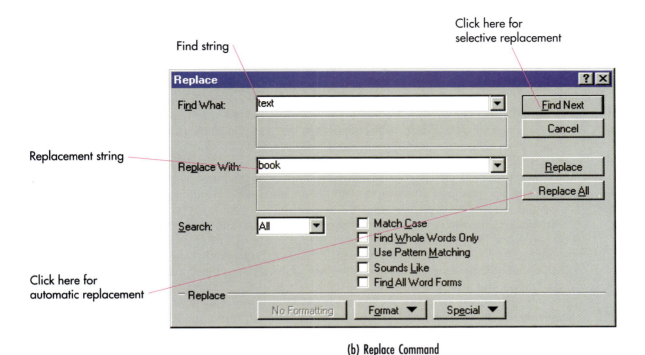

(b) Replace Command

FIGURE 2.1 Find and Replace Commands (continued)

SCROLLING

Scrolling occurs when a document is too large to be seen in its entirety. Figure 2.2a displays a large printed document, only part of which is visible on the screen as illustrated in Figure 2.2b. In order to see a different portion of the document, you need to scroll, whereby new lines will be brought into view as the old lines disappear.

Scrolling comes about automatically as you reach the bottom of the screen. Entering a new line of text, clicking on the down arrow within the scroll bar, or pressing the down arrow key brings a new line into view at the bottom of the screen and simultaneously removes a line at the top. (The process is reversed at the top of the screen.)

Scrolling can be done with either the mouse or the keyboard. Scrolling with the mouse (e.g., clicking the down arrow in the scroll bar) changes what is displayed on the screen, but does not move the insertion point, so that you must click the mouse after scrolling prior to entering the text at the new location. Scrolling with the keyboard, however (e.g., pressing Ctrl+End to move to the end of a document), changes what is displayed on the screen as well as the location of the insertion point, and you can begin typing immediately.

Scrolling occurs most often in a vertical direction as shown in Figure 2.2. It can also occur horizontally, when the length of a line in a document exceeds the number of characters that can be displayed horizontally on the screen.

GAINING PROFICIENCY

To: Our Students
From: Robert Grauer and Mary Ann Barber

Welcome to the wonderful world of word processing. Over the next several chapters we will build a foundation in the basics of Word for Windows, then teach you to format specialized documents, create professional looking tables and charts, and produce well-designed newsletters. Before you know it, you will be a word processing wizard!

The first chapter presented the basics of Windows as they apply to Word for Windows, then showed you how to create a simple document. You learned how to insert, replace, and/or delete text. This chapter will teach you about fonts and special effects (such as boldfacing and italicizing) and how to use them effectively -- how too little is better than too much.

You will go on to experiment with margins, tab stops, line spacing, and justification, learning first to format simple documents and then going on to longer, more complex ones. It is with the latter that we explore headers and footers, page numbering, widows and orphans (yes, we really did mean widows and orphans). It is here that we bring in graphics, working with newspaper-type columns, and the elements of a good page design. And without question, we will introduce the tools that make life so much easier (and your writing so much more impressive) -- the Speller, Grammar Checker, Thesaurus, Glossaries, and Styles.

If you are wondering what all these things are, read on in the text and proceed with the hands-on exercises. Create a simple newsletter, then really knock their socks off by adding graphics, fonts, and WordArt. Create a simple calendar and then create more intricate forms that no one will believe were done by little old you. Create a resume with your beginner's skills, and then make it look like so much more with your intermediate (even advanced) skills. Last, but not least, run a mail merge to produce the cover letters that will accompany your resume as it is mailed to companies across the United States (and even the world).

It is up to you to practice for it is only through working at the computer that you will learn what you need to know. Experiment and don't be afraid to make mistakes. Practice and practice some more.

Our goal is for you to learn and to enjoy what you are learning. We have great confidence in you, and in our ability to help you discover what you can do. And to prove us right, we'd love to have you mail us copies of documents that you have created. Write to us at the following address:

>   Dr. Robert Grauer/Ms. Mary Ann Barber
>   University of Miami
>   421 Jenkins Building
>   Coral Gables, Florida 33124

We look forward to hearing from you and hope that you will like our textbook. You are about to embark on a wonderful journey toward computer literacy. Be patient, be inquisitive, and enjoy.

(a) Printed Document

FIGURE 2.2   Scrolling

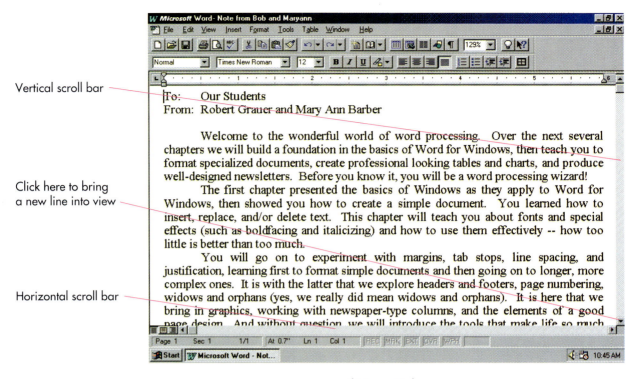

(b) Screen Display

FIGURE 2.2 Scrolling (continued)

VIEW MENU

The *View menu* provides different views of a document. Each view can be displayed at different magnifications, which in turn determine the amount of scrolling necessary to see remote parts of a document.

The *Normal view* is the default view and the one you use most of the time. The *Page Layout* view more closely resembles the printed document and displays the top and bottom margins, headers and footers, page numbers, and other features that do not appear in the Normal view. The Normal view tends to be faster because Word spends less time formatting the display.

The *Zoom command* displays the document on the screen at different magnifications; for example, 75%, 100%, or 200%. (The Zoom command does not affect the size of the text on the printed page.) A Zoom percentage (magnification) of 100% displays the document in the approximate size of the text on the printed page. You can increase the percentage to 200% to make the characters appear larger. You can also decrease the magnification to 75% to see more of the document at one time.

You can let Word determine the magnification for you, by selecting one of three additional Zoom options—Page Width, Whole Page, or Many Pages (Whole Page and Many Pages are available only in the Page Layout view). Figure 2.3a, for example, displays a two-page document in Page Layout view. Figure 2.3b shows the corresponding settings in the Zoom command. (The 37% magnification is determined automatically once you specify the number of pages as shown in the figure.)

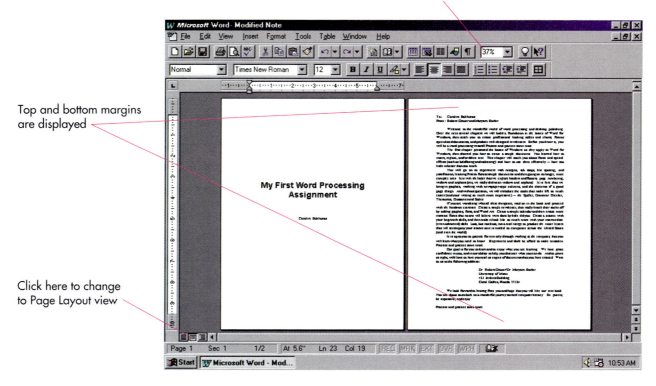

(a) Page Layout View (Zoom to Many Pages)

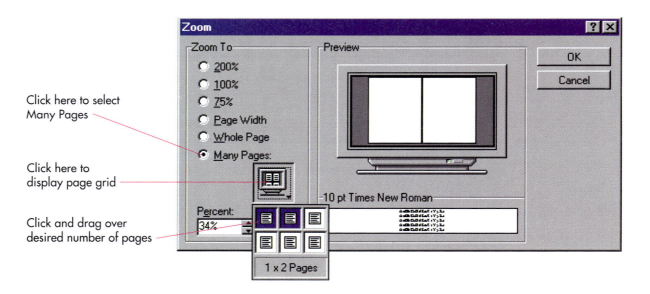

(b) Zoom Command

FIGURE 2.3   View Menu and Zoom Command

HANDS-ON EXERCISE 1

Editing a Document

Objective: To edit an existing document; to change the view and magnification of a document; to scroll through a document. To use the Find and Replace commands; to move and copy text using the clipboard and the drag-and-drop facility. Use Figure 2.4 as a guide in the exercise.

STEP 1: Open the Existing Document

➤ Start Word as described in the hands-on exercises from Chapter 1. Pull down the **File menu** and click **Open** (or click the **Open button** on the toolbar).
- Click the **drop-down arrow** on the Look In list box. Click the appropriate drive, drive C or drive A, depending on the location of your data.
- Double click the **Exploring Word folder** to make it the active folder (the folder in which you will save the document).
- Scroll in the Name list box (if necessary) until you can click the **Note from Bob and Maryann** to select this document. Double click the **document icon** or click the **Open command button** to open the file.

➤ The document should appear on the screen as shown in Figure 2.4a.

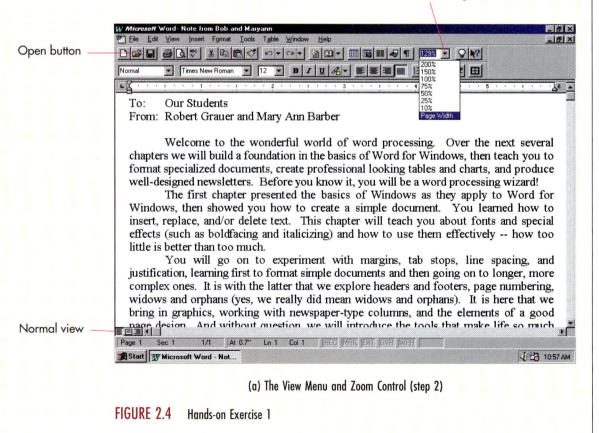

(a) The View Menu and Zoom Control (step 2)

FIGURE 2.4 Hands-on Exercise 1

STEP 2: The View Menu

➤ Change the view:
  - Pull down the **View menu.** Click **Normal.** *Or*
  - Click the **Normal view button** above the status bar.

➤ Change the zoom percentage:
  - Pull down the **View menu.** Click **Zoom.** Click **Page Width.** Click **OK.** *Or*
  - Click the **drop-down arrow** on the Zoom control box and click **Page Width.**

STEP 3: The Save As Command

➤ Pull down the **File menu.** Click the **Save As** command to produce the dialog box in Figure 2.4b.

➤ Enter **Modified Note** as the name of the new document. Click **Save.**

➤ There are now two identical copies of the file on disk: A Note from Bob and Maryann, which we supplied, and Modified Note, which you just created. The title bar of the document window shows the latter name.

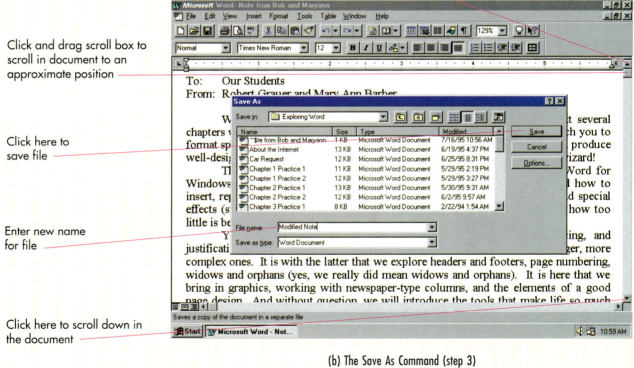

(b) The Save As Command (step 3)

FIGURE 2.4 Hands-on Exercise 1 (continued)

CREATE A BACKUP COPY

The Options button in the Save As dialog box enables you to specify the backup options in effect. Click the Options command button, then check the box to Always Create Backup Copy. The next time you save the document, the previous version on disk becomes a backup copy while the document in memory becomes the current version on disk. See the discussion on page 30 for additional information.

STEP 4: Scrolling

- Click the **down arrow** at the bottom of the vertical scroll bar to move down in the document, causing the top line to disappear and be replaced with a new line at the bottom.
- Click the **down arrow** several times to move through the document, then click the **up arrow key** to scroll in the other direction.
- Drag the **scroll box** to the bottom of the scroll bar, to the top of the scroll bar, then to the middle of the scroll bar, noting that in every instance the insertion point does *not* follow the scrolling; that is, you must click the mouse to move the insertion point to the new location after scrolling with the mouse.

THE MOUSE AND THE SCROLL BAR

Scroll quickly through a document by clicking above or below the scroll box to scroll up or down an entire screen. Move to the top, bottom, or an approximate position within a document by dragging the scroll box to the corresponding position in the scroll bar; for example, dragging the scroll box to the middle of the bar moves the mouse pointer to the middle of the document. Scrolling with the mouse does not change the location of the insertion point, however, and thus you must click the mouse at the new location prior to entering text at that location.

STEP 5: Insert versus Overtype

- Press the **Ins key** once or twice until you clearly see OVR in one of the status boxes at the bottom of the screen. Press the **Ins key** once more so that OVR becomes dim. You are now in the insert mode.
- Use the mouse to scroll to the top of the document, click immediately before the period ending the first sentence, press the **space bar,** then add the phrase **and desktop publishing.**
- Drag the **scroll box** to scroll to the bottom of the document, and click immediately before the first M in Ms. Mary Ann Barber.
- Press the **Ins key** (OVR should appear in the status bar) to toggle to the replacement mode, then type **Dr** to replace Ms. Press the **Ins key** a second time to toggle back to the insert mode.

GAINING PROFICIENCY

➤ Press **Ctrl+Home** to move to the beginning of the document. Click and drag the mouse to select the phrase **Our Students.** Type your name to replace the selected text.

➤ Pull down the **File menu** and click **Save** (or click the **Save button**) to save the changes.

> ### SCROLLING WITH THE KEYBOARD
>
> Scrolling with the mouse or keyboard changes the text that you see displayed on the screen, but only the keyboard changes the location of the insertion point in conjunction with scrolling. Press Ctrl+Home and Ctrl+End to move to the beginning and end of a document. Press Home and End to move to the beginning and end of a line. Press PgUp or PgDn to scroll one screen in the indicated direction. The advantage to scrolling via the keyboard (instead of the mouse) is that the location of the insertion point changes automatically and you can begin typing immediately.

STEP 6: Find and Replace

➤ Press **Ctrl+Home** to move to the beginning of the document. Pull down the **Edit menu.** Click **Replace** to produce the dialog box of Figure 2.4c.

Save button

First occurrence of Find string is selected (not an appropriate substitution)

Click here to find next occurrence of Find string

Find string

Replacement string

Click here to make a replacement (when appropriate)

(c) Replace Command (step 6)

FIGURE 2.4   Hands-on Exercise 1 (continued)

MICROSOFT WORD 7.0

- Type **text** in the Find What text box.
- Press the **Tab key.** Type **book** in the Replace With text box.

➤ Click the **Find Next button** to find the first occurrence of the word "text". The dialog box remains on the screen and the first occurrence of "text" is selected. This is *not* an appropriate substitution; that is, you should not substitute book for text at this point.

➤ Click the **Find Next button** to move to the next occurrence without making the replacement. This time the substitution is appropriate.

➤ Click **Replace** to make the change and automatically move to the next occurrence where the substitution is again inappropriate. Click **Find Next** a final time. Word will indicate that it has finished searching the document. Click **OK.**

➤ Change the Find and Replace strings to **Mary Ann** and **Maryann,** respectively. Click the **Replace All** button to make the substitution globally without confirmation. Word will indicate that it has finished searching and that two replacements were made. Click **OK.**

➤ Click the **Close command button** to close the dialog box. Click the **Save button** to save the document. Scroll through the document to review your changes.

SEARCH THE ENTIRE DOCUMENT

The Find command searches from the insertion point *down* to the end of the document, or *up* to the beginning of the document, then asks whether you want to continue searching from the end or beginning of the document (according to the direction you specified). To search the entire document automatically, click the down arrow in the Search list box, and select All (instead of down or up), which will search the document from the beginning to the end.

STEP 7: The Clipboard

➤ Press **PgDn** to scroll toward the end of the document until you come to the paragraph beginning **It is up to you.** Select the sentence **Practice and practice some more** by dragging the mouse over the sentence. (Be sure to include the period.) The sentence will be selected as shown in Figure 2.4d.

➤ Pull down the **Edit menu** and click the **Copy command** or click the **Copy button** on the Standard toolbar.

➤ Press **Ctrl+End** to scroll to the end of the document. Press the **enter key** twice. Pull down the **Edit menu** and click the **Paste command** (or click the **Paste button** on the Standard toolbar). The contents of the clipboard (the copied sentence) are pasted into the document.

➤ Move the insertion point to the end of the first paragraph (following the exclamation point after the word *Wizard*). Press the **space bar** twice. Click the **Paste button** on the Standard toolbar to paste the sentence a second time.

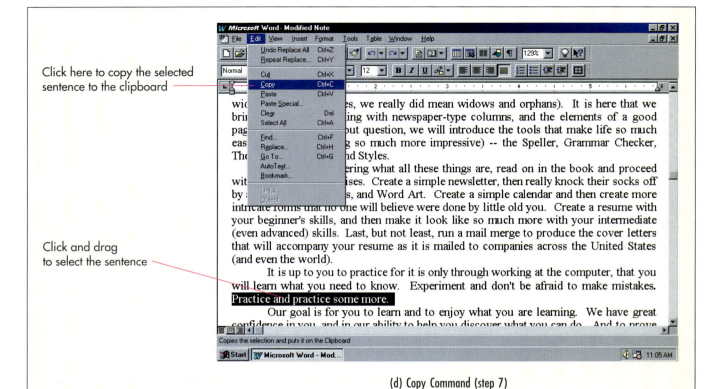

(d) Copy Command (step 7)

FIGURE 2.4 Hands-on Exercise 1 (continued)

> ### CUT, COPY, AND PASTE
>
> **Ctrl+X, Ctrl+C,** and **Ctrl+V** are shortcuts to cut, copy, and paste, respectively, and apply to all applications in the Office suite as well as to Windows applications in general. (The shortcuts are easier to remember when you realize that the operative letters X, C, and V are next to each other at the bottom left side of the keyboard.) You can also use the Cut, Copy, and Paste buttons on the Standard toolbar.

STEP 8: Undo and Redo

➤ Click the **drop-down arrow** next to the Undo button to display the previously executed actions as in Figure 2.4e.

➤ The list of actions corresponds to the editing commands you have issued since the start of the exercise. (Your list will be different from ours if you deviated from any instructions in the hands-on exercise.)

➤ Click the **drop-down arrow** for the Redo command. You will hear a beep indicating that there are no actions to be redone; that is, the Undo command has not yet been issued and so there is nothing to redo.

➤ Click the **drop-down arrow** for the Undo command. Click **Paste** (the first command on the list) to undo the last editing command; the sentence, Practice and practice some more, disappears from the end of the first paragraph.

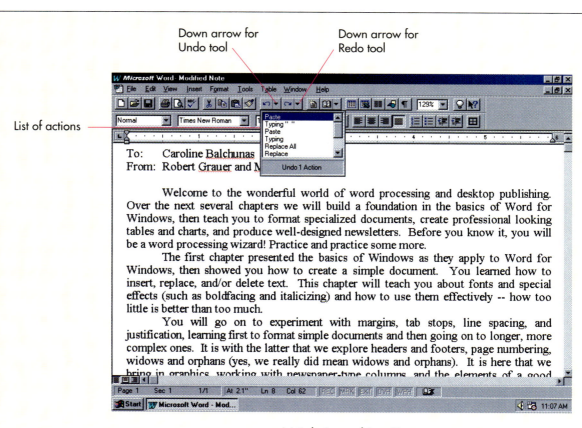

(e) Undo Command (step 8)

FIGURE 2.4 Hands-on Exercise 1 (continued)

➤ Click the remaining steps on the undo list to retrace your steps through the exercise one command at a time. Alternatively, you can scroll to the bottom of the list and click the last command, which automatically undoes all of the preceding commands. Either way, when the undo list is empty, you will have the document as it existed at the start of the exercise.

➤ Click the **down arrow** for the Redo command. This time you will see the list of commands you have undone; click each command in sequence (or click the command at the bottom of the list) and you will restore the document.

STEP 9: Drag and Drop

➤ This step takes a little practice, but it is well worth it. Use the Find command to locate and select the phrase **format specialized documents,** as shown in Figure 2.4f. (Be sure to search the entire document and to include the comma and the space after the comma in the search string.)

➤ Drag the phrase to its new location immediately before the word "and", then release the mouse button to complete the move. (A dotted vertical bar appears as you drag the text, to indicate its new location.)

➤ Click the **drop-down list box** for the Undo command; click **Move** to undo the move.

➤ To copy the selected text to the same location (instead of moving it), press and hold the **Ctrl key** as you drag the text to its new location. (A plus sign appears as you drag the text, to indicate it is being copied rather than moved.)

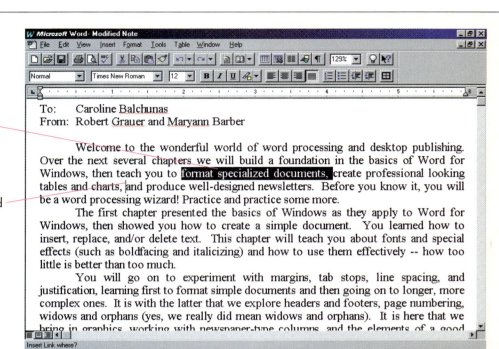

(f) Drag and Drop (step 9)

FIGURE 2.4 Hands-on Exercise 1 (continued)

➤ Practice the drag-and-drop procedure several times until you are confident you can move and copy with precision.
➤ Click anywhere in the document to deselect the text. Save the document.

STEP 10: Print the Completed Document
➤ Pull down the **View menu** and click the **Page Layout command** (or click the **Page Layout button** above the status bar).
➤ Pull down the **View menu,** click **Zoom,** select **Whole Page,** and click **OK** (or use the **Zoom control box** on the Standard toolbar). Your screen should match Figure 2.4g, which shows the completed document.
➤ Pull down the **File menu,** click **Print,** and click **OK** (or click the **Print button** on the Standard toolbar) to print the completed document. Submit the document to your instructor as proof you did the exercise.
➤ Pull down the **File menu.** Click **Close** to close the document and remain in Word.
➤ Pull down the **File menu** a second time. Click **Exit** if you do not want to continue with the next exercise at this time.

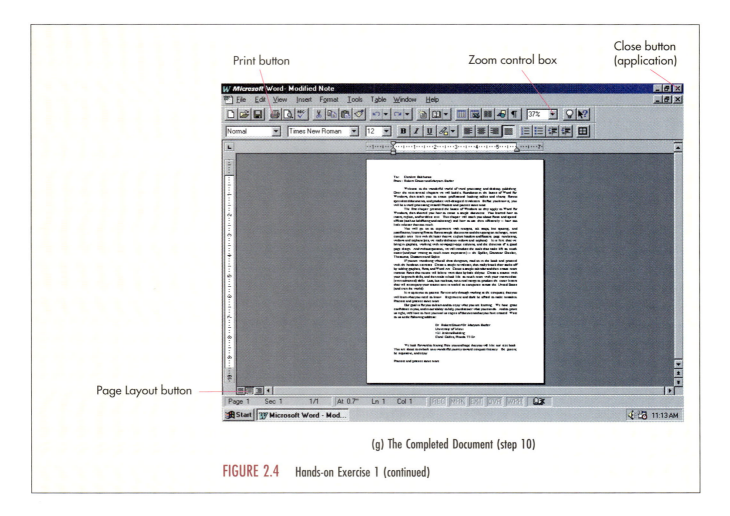

(g) The Completed Document (step 10)

FIGURE 2.4   Hands-on Exercise 1 (continued)

TYPOGRAPHY

Typography is the process of selecting typefaces, type styles, and type sizes. The importance of these decisions is obvious, for the ultimate success of any document depends greatly on its appearance. Type should reinforce the message without calling attention to itself and should be consistent with the information you want to convey.

Typeface

A *typeface* is a complete set of characters (upper- and lowercase letters, numbers, punctuation marks, and special symbols). Figure 2.5 illustrates three typefaces—***Times New Roman, Arial,*** and ***Courier New***—that are supplied with Windows, and which in turn are accessible from any Windows application.

One definitive characteristic of any typeface is the presence or absence of tiny cross lines that end the main strokes of each letter. A ***serif*** typeface has these lines. A ***sans serif*** typeface (*sans* from the French for *without*) does not. Times New Roman and Courier New are examples of a serif typeface. Arial is a sans serif typeface.

Serifs help the eye to connect one letter with the next and are generally used with large amounts of text. This book, for example, is set in a serif typeface. A sans serif typeface is more effective with smaller amounts of text and appears in headlines, corporate logos, airport signs, and so on.

Typography is the process of selecting typefaces, type styles, and type sizes. A serif typeface has tiny cross strokes that end the main strokes of each letter; a sans serif typeface does not. A monospaced typeface uses the same amount of space for every character. A proportional typeface allocates space in accordance with the width of the character. The ultimate success of any document depends on its appearance and underlying typography.

(a) Times New Roman (serif and proportional)

Typography is the process of selecting typefaces, type styles, and type sizes. A serif typeface has tiny cross strokes that end the main strokes of each letter; a sans serif typeface does not. A monospaced typeface uses the same amount of space for every character. A proportional typeface allocates space in accordance with the width of the character. The ultimate success of any document depends on its appearance and underlying typography.

(b) Arial (sans serif and proportional)

```
Typography is the process of selecting typefaces, type styles
and type sizes.  A serif typeface has tiny cross strokes that end
the main strokes of each letter; a sans serif typeface does not.
A monospaced typeface uses the same amount of space for every
character.  A proportional typeface allocates space in accordance
with the width of the character.  The ultimate success of any
document depends on its appearance and underlying typography.
```

(c) Courier New (serif and monospaced)

FIGURE 2.5   Typefaces

A second characteristic of a typeface is whether it is monospaced or proportional. A ***monospaced typeface*** (e.g., Courier New) uses the same amount of space for every character regardless of its width. A ***proportional typeface*** (e.g., Times New Roman or Arial) allocates space according to the width of the character. Monospaced fonts are used in tables and financial projections where items must be precisely lined up, one beneath the other. Proportional typefaces create a more professional appearance and are appropriate for most documents.

Any typeface can be set in different ***type styles*** (e.g., regular, bold, or italic). A ***font*** (as the term is used in Windows) is a specific typeface in a specific style; for example, *Times New Roman Italic,* Arial Bold, or `Courier New Bold Italic.`

> ### TYPOGRAPHY TIP—USE RESTRAINT
>
> More is not better, especially in the case of too many typefaces and styles, which produce cluttered documents that impress no one. Try to limit yourself to a maximum of two typefaces per document, but choose multiple sizes and/or styles within those typefaces. Use boldface or italics for emphasis; but do so in moderation, because if you emphasize too many elements, the effect is lost.

Type Size

Type size is a vertical measurement and is specified in points, where one ***point*** is equal to ¹⁄₇₂ of an inch; that is, there are 72 points to the inch. The measurement is made from the top of the tallest letter in a character set (for example, an uppercase T) to the bottom of the lowest letter (for example, a lowercase y). Most documents are set in 10 or 12 point type; newspaper columns may be set as small as 8 point type. Type sizes of 14 points or higher are ineffective for large amounts of text. Figure 2.6 shows the same phrase set in varying type sizes.

Some typefaces appear larger (smaller) than others even though they may be set in the same point size. The type in Figure 2.6a, for example, looks smaller than the corresponding type in Figure 2.6b even though both are set in the same point size. This is because the letters in the Arial typeface have a taller body than the letters in the Times New Roman design.

Format Font Command

The ***Format Font command*** gives you complete control over the typeface, size, and style of the text in a document. Executing the command before entering text will set the format of the text you type from that point on. You can also use the command to change the font of existing text by selecting the text, then executing the command. Either way, you will see the dialog box in Figure 2.7, in which you specify the font (typeface), style, and point size.

You can choose any of the special effects (e.g., ~~strikethrough~~ or SMALL CAPS) and/or change the underline options (whether or not spaces are to be underlined). You can even change the color of the text on the monitor, but you need a color printer for the printed document. (The Character Spacing tab produces a different set of options in which you control the spacing of the characters and is beyond our discussion.)

The Preview box shows the text as it will appear in the document. The message at the bottom of the dialog box indicates that Times New Roman is a

This is Arial 8 point type

This is Arial 10 point type

This is Arial 12 point type

This is Arial 18 point type

This is Arial 24 point type

(a) Sans Serif Typeface

This is Times New Roman 8 point type

This is Times New Roman 10 point type

This is Times New Roman 12 point type

This is Times New Roman 18 point type

This is Times New Roman 24 point type

(b) Serif Typeface

FIGURE 2.6 Type Size

TrueType font and that the same font will be used on both the screen and the monitor. TrueType fonts ensure that your document is truly WYSIWYG (What You See Is What You Get) because the fonts you see on the monitor will be identical to those in the printed document. Equally important, TrueType fonts are scaleable, so that you can select any font in any (reasonable) size.

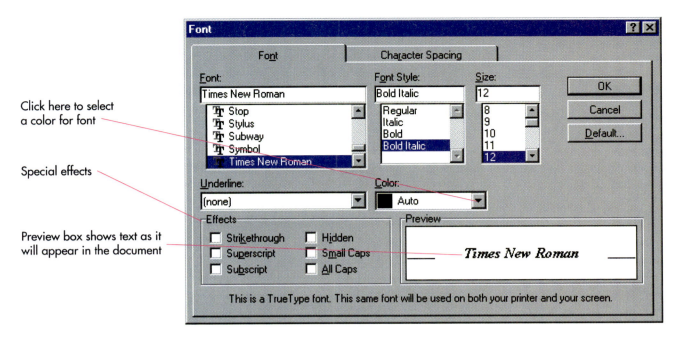

FIGURE 2.7 Format Font Command

PAGE SETUP COMMAND

The ***Page Setup command*** in the File menu lets you change margins, paper size, orientation, paper source, and/or layout. All parameters are accessed from the dialog box in Figure 2.8 by clicking the appropriate tab within the dialog box.

The default margins are indicated in Figure 2.8a and are one inch on the top and bottom of the page, and one and a quarter inches on the left and right. You can change any (or all) of these settings by entering a new value in the appropriate text box, either by typing it explicitly or clicking the up/down arrow. All of the settings in the Page Setup command apply to the whole document regardless of the position of the insertion point. (Different settings can be established for different parts of a document by creating sections, which is beyond the scope of our present discussion.)

The Paper Size tab within the Page Setup command enables you to change the orientation of a page as shown in Figure 2.8b. ***Portrait orientation*** is the default. ***Landscape orientation*** flips the page 90 degrees so that its dimensions are 11 × 8½ rather than the other way around. Note, too, the Preview box in the figure, which shows how the document will appear with the selected parameters.

The Paper Source tab is used to specify which tray should be used on printers with multiple trays, and is helpful when you want to load different types of paper simultaneously. The Layout tab is used to specify options for headers and footers (text that appears at the top or bottom of each page in a document).

Page Breaks

One of the first concepts you learned was that of word wrap, whereby Word inserts a soft return at the end of a line in order to begin a new line. The number and/or location of the soft returns change automatically as you add or delete text within a document. Soft returns are very different from the hard returns inserted by the user, whose number and location remain constant.

GAINING PROFICIENCY

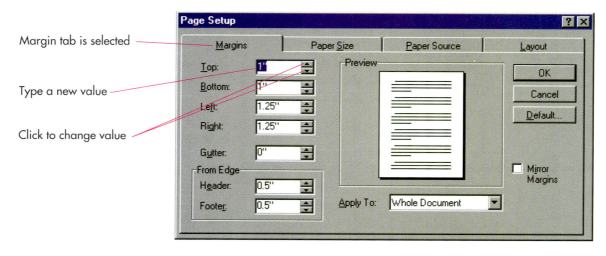

(a) Margins

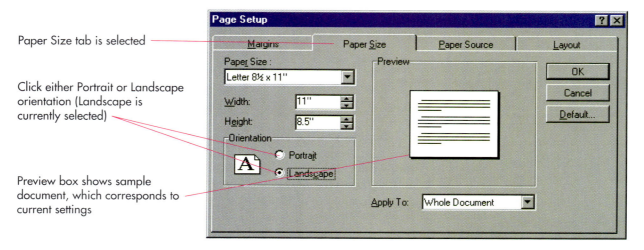

(b) Size and Orientation

FIGURE 2.8   Page Setup Command

In much the same way, Word creates a ***soft page break*** to go to the top of a new page when text no longer fits on the current page. And just as you can insert a hard return to start a new paragraph, you can insert a ***hard page break*** to force any part of a document to begin on a new page. A hard page break is inserted into a document using the Break command in the Insert menu or through the Ctrl+enter keyboard shortcut. (You can prevent the occurrence of awkward page breaks through the Format Paragraph command as described later in the chapter on page 81.)

AN EXERCISE IN DESIGN

The following exercise has you retrieve an existing document from the data disk, then experiment with various typefaces, type styles, and point sizes. The original document uses a monospaced (typewriter style) font, without boldface or italics, and you are asked to improve its appearance. The first step directs you to save the document under a new name so that you can always return to the original if necessary.

There is no right and wrong with respect to design, and you are free to choose any combination of fonts that appeals to you. The exercise takes you through various formatting options but lets you make the final decision. It does, however, ask you to print the final document and submit it to your instructor.

> **IMPOSE A TIME LIMIT**
>
> A word processor is supposed to save time and make you more productive. It will do exactly that, provided you use the word processor for its primary purpose—writing and editing. It is all too easy, however, to lose sight of that objective and spend too much time formatting the document. Concentrate on the content of your document rather than its appearance. Impose a time limit on the amount of time you will spend on formatting. End the session when the limit is reached.

HANDS-ON EXERCISE 2

Character Formatting

Objective: To experiment with character formatting; to change fonts and to use boldface and italics; to copy formatting with the format painter; to insert a page break and see different views of a document. Use Figure 2.9 as a guide in the exercise.

STEP 1: Open the Existing Document

➤ Start Word. Pull down the **File menu** and click **Open** (or click the **Open button** on the toolbar). To open a file:
- Click the **drop-down arrow** on the Look In list box. Click the appropriate drive, drive C or drive A, depending on the location of your data.
- Double click the **Exploring Word folder** to make it the active folder (the folder in which you will open and save the document).
- Scroll in the **Name list box** (if necessary) until you can click **Tips for Writing** to select this document. Double click the **document icon** or click the **Open command button** to open the file.

> **SELECTING TEXT**
>
> The *selection bar,* a blank column at the far left of the document window, makes it easy to select a line, paragraph, or the entire document. To select a line, move the mouse pointer to the selection bar, point to the line and click the left mouse button. To select a paragraph, move the mouse pointer to the selection bar, point to any line in the paragraph, and double click the mouse. To select the entire document, move the mouse pointer to the selection bar and press the Ctrl key while you click the mouse.

➤ Pull down the **File menu.** Click the **Save As command** to save the document as **Modified Tips.**

➤ Pull down the **View menu** and click **Normal** (or click the **Normal View button** above the status bar).

➤ Set the magnification (zoom) to **Page Width.**

STEP 2: The Right Mouse Button

➤ Select the first tip as shown in Figure 2.9a. Click the **right mouse button** to produce the shortcut menu shown in the figure. The shortcut menu contains selected commands from both the Edit and Format menus.

➤ Click outside the menu to close the menu without executing a command.

➤ Press the **Ctrl key** as you click the selection bar to select the entire document, then click the **right mouse button** to display the shortcut menu.

➤ Click **Font** to execute the Format Font command.

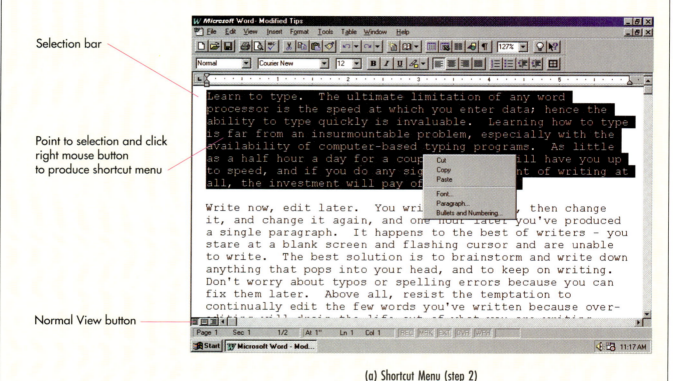

(a) Shortcut Menu (step 2)

FIGURE 2.9 Hands-on Exercise 2

STEP 3: Changing Fonts

➤ Click the **drop-down arrow** on the Font list box of Figure 2.9b to scroll through the available fonts. Select a different font, such as Times New Roman.

➤ Click the **drop-down arrow** in the Font Size list box to choose a point size.

➤ Click **OK** to change the font and point size for the selected text.

➤ Pull down the **Edit menu** and click **Undo** (or click the **Undo button** on the Standard toolbar) to return to the original font.

➤ Experiment with different fonts and/or different point sizes until you are satisfied with the selection; we chose 12 point Times New Roman.

➤ Save the document.

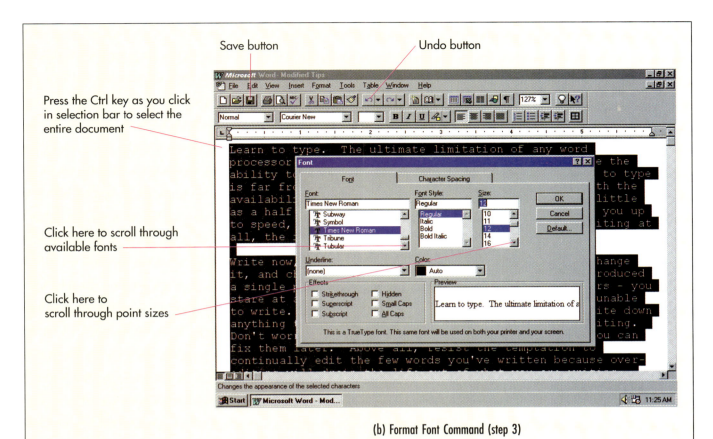

(b) Format Font Command (step 3)

FIGURE 2.9 Hands-on Exercise 2 (continued)

STEP 4: Boldface and Italics

➤ Drag the mouse over the sentence **Learn to type** at the beginning of the document.

➤ Click the **Italic button** on the Formatting toolbar to italicize the selected phrase, which will remain selected after the italics take effect.

➤ Click the **Bold button** to boldface the selected text. The text is now in bold italic.

FIND AND REPLACE FORMATTING

The Replace command enables you to replace formatting as well as text. For example, to replace any text set in bold with the same text in italics, pull down the Edit menu, and click the Replace command to display the Replace dialog box. Click the Find What text box, but do *not* enter any text. Click the Format command button, click Font, click Bold in the Font Style list, and click OK. Click the Replace With text box and again do *not* enter any text. Click the Format command button, click Font, click Italic in the Font Style list, and click OK. Click the Find Next or Replace All command button to do selective or automatic replacement. Use a similar technique to replace one font with another—for example, to replace Times New Roman with Arial.

➤ Experiment with different styles (bold, italics, underlining, or bold italic) until you are satisfied. The Italic, Bold, and Underline buttons function as toggle switches; that is, clicking the Italic button when text is already italicized returns the text to normal.

➤ Save the document.

STEP 5: The Format Painter

➤ Click anywhere within the sentence Learn to Type. **Double click** the **Format Painter button** on the Standard toolbar. The mouse pointer changes to a paintbrush as shown in Figure 2.9c.

➤ Drag the mouse pointer over the next title, **Write now, edit later,** and release the mouse. The formatting from the original sentence (bold italic as shown in Figure 2.9c) has been applied to this sentence as well.

➤ Drag the mouse pointer (in the shape of a paintbrush) over the remaining titles (the first sentence in each paragraph) to copy the formatting.

➤ Click the **Format Painter button** after you have painted the title of the last tip to turn the feature off.

➤ Save the document.

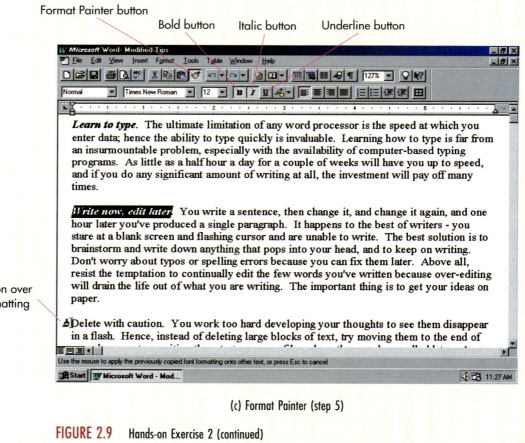

(c) Format Painter (step 5)

FIGURE 2.9 Hands-on Exercise 2 (continued)

THE FORMAT PAINTER

The *Format Painter* copies the formatting of the selected text to other places in a document. Select the text with the formatting you want to copy, then click or double click the Format Painter button on the Standard toolbar. Clicking the button will paint only one selection. Double clicking the button will paint multiple selections until the feature is turned off by again clicking the Format Painter button. Either way, the mouse pointer changes to a paintbrush to indicate that you can paint other selections in the document with the current formatting. Just drag the paintbrush over selected text, which will assume the identical formatting characteristics as the original selection.

STEP 6: Change Margins

➤ Press **Ctrl+End** to move to the end of the document as shown in Figure 2.9d. You will see a dotted line indicating a soft page break. (If you do not see the page break, it means that your document fits on one page because you used a different font and/or a smaller point size; we used 12 point Times New Roman.)

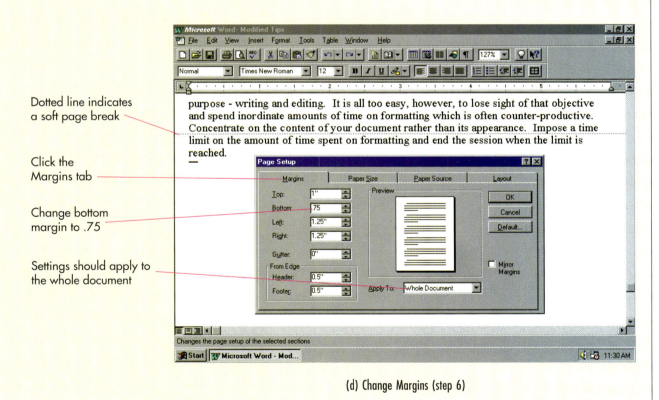

(d) Change Margins (step 6)

FIGURE 2.9 Hands-on Exercise 2 (continued)

GAINING PROFICIENCY

➤ Pull down the **File menu.** Click **Page Setup.** Click the **Margins tab** if necessary. Change the bottom margin to **.75** inch. Check that these settings apply to the **Whole Document.** Click **OK.** The page break disappears because more text fits on the page.

> ### DIALOG BOX SHORTCUTS
>
> You can use the mouse to click an option button, to mark a check box on or off, or to select an option from a list. You can also use a keyboard shortcut for each of these actions. Press Tab (Shift+Tab) to move forward (backward) from one field or command button to the next. Press Alt plus the underlined letter to move directly to a field or command button. Press enter to activate the selected command button. Press Esc to exit the dialog box without taking action. Press the space bar to toggle check boxes on or off. Press the down arrow to open a drop-down list box once the list has been accessed, then press the up or down arrow to move between options in a list box

STEP 7: Create a Title Page

➤ Press **Ctrl+Home** to move to the beginning of the document. Press **enter** three or four times to add a few blank lines.

➤ Press **Ctrl+enter** to insert a hard page break. You will see the words "Page Break" in the middle of a dotted line as shown in Figure 2.9e.

➤ Press the **up arrow key** three times. Enter the title **Tips for Writing.** Select the title, and format it in a larger point size, such as 24 points.

➤ Enter your name on the next line and format it in a different point size, such as 14 points. Select both the title and your name as shown in the figure. Click the **Center button** on the Formatting toolbar. Save the document.

> ### THE SPELL CHECK
>
> Use the spell check prior to saving a document for the last time, even if the document is just a sentence or two. Spelling errors make your work look sloppy and discourage the reader before he or she has read what you had to say. Spelling errors can cost you a job, a grade, or a lucrative contract. The spell check requires but a single click, so why not use it?

STEP 8: The Completed Document

➤ Pull down the **View menu** and click **Page Layout** (or click the **Page Layout button** above the status bar).

➤ Click the **Zoom Control arrow** on the Standard toolbar and select **Two Pages.** Release the mouse to view the completed document in Figure 2.9f. You may want to add additional blank lines on the title page to move the title further down on the page.

➤ Save the document a final time. Exit Word if you do not want to continue with the next exercise at this time.

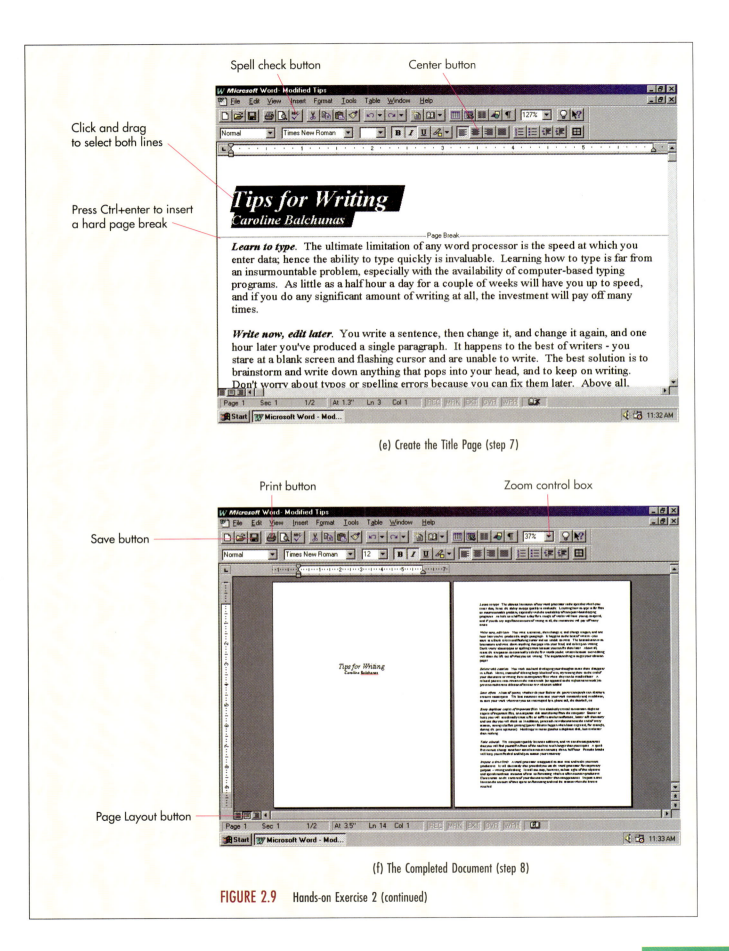

(e) Create the Title Page (step 7)

(f) The Completed Document (step 8)

FIGURE 2.9 Hands-on Exercise 2 (continued)

PARAGRAPH FORMATTING

A change in typography is only one way to alter the appearance of a document. You can also change the alignment, indentation, tab stops, or line spacing for any paragraph(s) within the document. You can control the pagination (text flow) and prevent the occurrence of awkward page breaks by specifying that an entire paragraph has to appear on the same page, or that a one-line paragraph (e.g., a heading) should appear on the same page as the next paragraph. You can include borders or shading for added emphasis around selected paragraphs.

All of these features are implemented at the paragraph level and affect all selected paragraphs. If no paragraphs are selected, the commands affect the entire current paragraph (the paragraph containing the insertion point), regardless of the position of the insertion point when the command is executed.

Alignment

Text can be aligned in four different ways as shown in Figure 2.10. It may be justified (flush left/flush right), left aligned (flush left with a ragged right margin), right aligned (flush right with a ragged left margin), or centered within the margins (ragged left and right).

Left aligned text is perhaps the easiest to read. The first letters of each line align with each other, helping the eye to find the beginning of each line. The lines themselves are of irregular length. There is uniform spacing between words, and the ragged margin on the right adds white space to the text, giving it a lighter and more informal look.

Justified text produces lines of equal length, with the spacing between words adjusted to align at the margins. It may be more difficult to read than text that is left aligned because of the uneven (sometimes excessive) word spacing and/or the greater number of hyphenated words needed to justify the lines.

Type that is centered or right aligned is restricted to limited amounts of text where the effect is more important than the ease of reading. Centered text, for example, appears frequently on wedding invitations, poems, or formal announcements. Right aligned text is used with figure captions and short headlines.

Indents

Individual paragraphs can be indented so that they appear to have different margins from the rest of a document. Indentation is established at the paragraph level; thus different indentation can be in effect for different paragraphs. One paragraph may be indented from the left margin only, another from the right margin only, and a third from both the left and right margins. The first line of any paragraph may be indented differently from the rest of the paragraph. And finally, a paragraph may be set with no indentation at all, so that it aligns on the left and right margins.

The indentation of a paragraph is determined by three settings: the ***left indent,*** the ***right indent,*** and a special indent (if any). There are two types of special indentation, first line and hanging, as will be explained shortly. The left and right indents are set to zero by default and produce a paragraph with no indentation at all as shown in Figure 2.11a. Positive values for the left and right indents offset the paragraph from both margins as shown in Figure 2.11b.

We, the people of the United States, in order to form a more perfect Union, establish justice, insure domestic tranquillity, provide for the common defense, promote the general welfare, and secure the blessings of liberty to ourselves and our posterity, do ordain and establish this Constitution for the United States of America.

(a) Justified (flush left/flush right)

We, the people of the United States, in order to form a more perfect Union, establish justice, insure domestic tranquillity, provide for the common defense, promote the general welfare, and secure the blessings of liberty to ourselves and our posterity, do ordain and establish this Constitution for the United States of America.

(b) Left Aligned (flush left/ragged right)

We, the people of the United States, in order to form a more perfect Union, establish justice, insure domestic tranquillity, provide for the common defense, promote the general welfare, and secure the blessings of liberty to ourselves and our posterity, do ordain and establish this Constitution for the United States of America.

(c) Right Aligned (ragged left/flush right)

We, the people of the United States, in order to form a more perfect Union, establish justice, insure domestic tranquillity, provide for the common defense, promote the general welfare, and secure the blessings of liberty to ourselves and our posterity, do ordain and establish this Constitution for the United States of America.

(d) Centered (ragged left/ragged right)

FIGURE 2.10   Alignment

The ***first line indent*** (Figure 2.11c) affects only the first line in the paragraph and is implemented by pressing the Tab key at the beginning of the paragraph. A ***hanging indent*** (Figure 2.11d) sets the first line of a paragraph at the left indent and indents the remaining lines according to the amount specified. Hanging indents are often used with bulleted or numbered lists.

The left and right indents are defined as the distance between the text and the left and right margins, respectively. Both parameters are set to zero in this paragraph and so the text aligns on both margins.

(a) No Indents

Positive values for the left and right indents offset a paragraph from the rest of a document and are often used for long quotations. This paragraph has left and right indents of one-half inch each.

(b) Left and Right Indents

A first line indent affects only the first line in the paragraph and is implemented by pressing the Tab key at the beginning of the paragraph. The remainder of the paragraph is aligned at the left margin (or the left indent if it differs from the left margin) as can be seen from this example.

(c) First Line Indent

A hanging indent sets the first line of a paragraph at the left indent and indents the remaining lines according to the amount specified. Hanging indents are often used with bulleted or numbered lists.

(d) Hanging Indent

FIGURE 2.11 Indents

> ### INDENTS VERSUS MARGINS
>
> ***Indents*** measure the distance between the text and the margins. ***Margins*** mark the distance from the text to the edge of the page. Indents are determined at the paragraph level, whereas margins are established at the section (document) level. The left and right margins are set (by default) to 1.25 inches each; the left and right indents default to zero. The first line indent is measured from the setting of the left indent.

Tabs

Anyone who has used a typewriter is familiar with the function of the Tab key; that is, press Tab and the insertion point moves to the next ***tab stop*** (a measured position to align text at a specific place.) The Tab key is much more powerful in Word as you can choose from four different types of tab stops (left, center, right, and decimal). You can also specify a ***leader character,*** typically dots or hyphens, to draw the reader's eye across the page. Tabs are often used to create tables within a document.

The default tab stops are set every ½ inch and are left aligned, but you can change the ***alignment*** and/or position with the Format Tabs command in Figure 2.12. Four types of alignment are possible:

- Left alignment, where the text *begins* at the tab stop, corresponds to the Tab key on a typewriter.
- Right alignment, where the text *ends* at the tab stop, is used to align page numbers in a table of contents or to align text at the right margin.
- Center alignment, where text centers over the tab stop, is used infrequently for special effect.
- Decimal alignment, which lines up numeric values in a column on the decimal point, is helpful with statistical text.

Figure 2.12 illustrates a dot leader in combination with a right tab to produce a Table of Contents. The default tab stops have been cleared in Figure 2.12a, in favor of a single right tab at 5.5 inches. The option button for a dot leader has also been checked. The resulting document is shown in Figure 2.12b.

Line Spacing

Line spacing determines the space between the lines in a paragraph. Word provides complete flexibility and enables you to select any multiple of line spacing (single, double, line and a half, and so on). You can also specify line spacing in terms of points (there are 72 points per inch).

Line spacing is set at the paragraph level through the Format Paragraph command, which sets the spacing within a paragraph. The command also enables you to add extra spacing before the first line in a paragraph or after the last line. (Either technique is preferable to the common practice of single spacing the paragraphs within a document, then adding a blank line between paragraphs.)

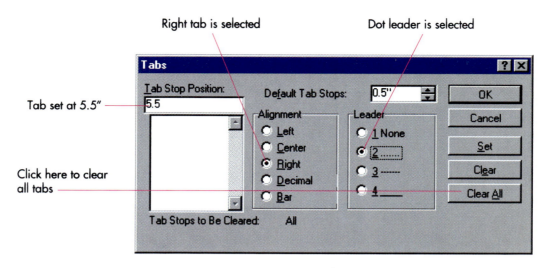

(a) Tab Stops

(b) Table of Contents

FIGURE 2.12 Tabs

FORMAT PARAGRAPH COMMAND

The **Format Paragraph command** is where you specify the alignment, indentation, line spacing, and pagination (text flow) for the selected paragraph(s). As indicated, all of these features are implemented at the paragraph level and affect all selected paragraphs. If no paragraphs are selected, the command affects the entire current paragraph (the paragraph containing the insertion point), regardless of the position of the insertion point when the command is executed.

The Format Paragraph command is illustrated in Figure 2.13. The Indents and Spacing tab in Figure 2.13a calls for a hanging indent, line spacing of 1.5 lines, and justified alignment. The preview within the dialog box enables you to see how the paragraph will appear within the document.

The Text Flow tab in Figure 2.13b illustrates an entirely different set of parameters in which you control the pagination within a document. You are

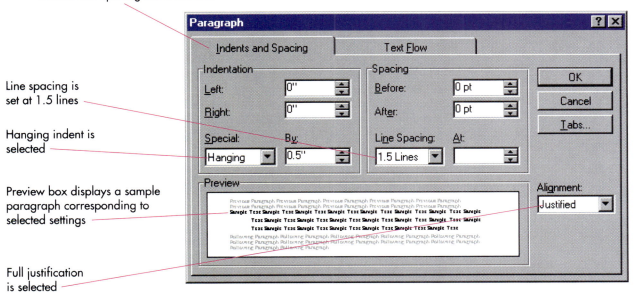

(a) Indents and Spacing

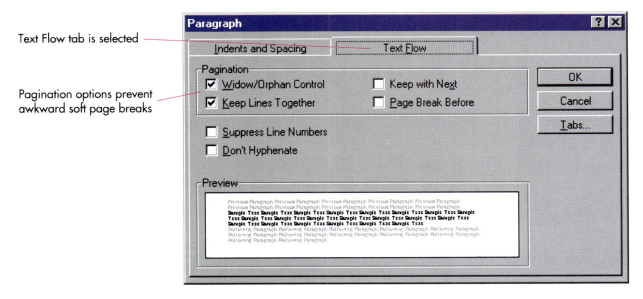

(b) Text Flow

FIGURE 2.13 Format Paragraph Command

already familiar with the concept of page breaks, and the distinction between soft page breaks (inserted by Word) versus hard page breaks (inserted by the user). The check boxes in Figure 2.13b enable you to prevent the occurrence of awkward soft page breaks that detract from the appearance of a document.

You might, for example, want to prevent widows and orphans, terms used to describe isolated lines that seem out of place. A *widow* refers to the last line of a paragraph appearing by itself at the top of a page. An **orphan** is the first line of a paragraph appearing by itself at the bottom of a page.

You can also impose additional controls by clicking one or more check boxes. Use the Keep Lines Together option to prevent a soft page break from occurring within a paragraph and ensure that the entire paragraph appears on the same page. (The paragraph is moved to the top of the next page if it doesn't fit on the bottom of the current page.) Use the Keep with Next option to prevent a soft page break between the two paragraphs. This option is typically used to keep a heading (a one-line paragraph) with its associated text in the next paragraph.

FORMATTING AND THE PARAGRAPH MARK

The paragraph mark ¶ at the end of a paragraph does more than just indicate the presence of a hard return. It also stores all of the formatting in effect for the paragraph. Hence in order to preserve the formatting when you move or copy a paragraph, you must include the paragraph mark in the selected text. Click the Show/Hide ¶ button on the toolbar to display the paragraph mark and make sure it has been selected.

Borders and Shading

The ***Borders and Shading command*** puts the finishing touches on a document and is illustrated in Figure 2.14. It lets you create boxed and/or shaded text as well as

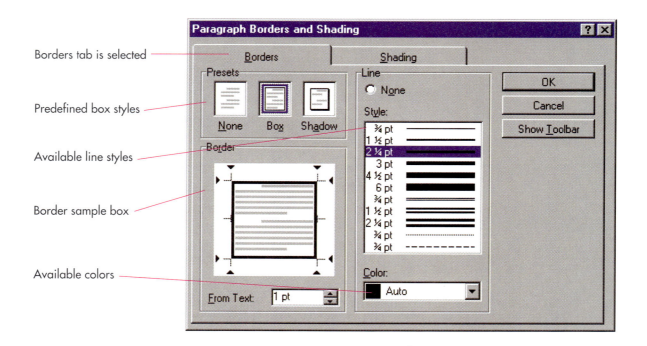

(a) Borders

FIGURE 2.14 Paragraph Borders and Shading

place horizontal or vertical lines around a paragraph. You can choose from several different line styles in any color (assuming you have a color printer). You can place a uniform border around a paragraph (choose Box), or you can create a ***drop shadow*** effect with thicker lines at the right and bottom. You can also apply lines to selected sides of a paragraph(s) by selecting a line style, then clicking the desired sides within the Border sample box.

Shading is implemented independently of the border. Clear (no shading) is the default. Solid (100%) shading creates a solid box where the text is turned white so you can read it. Shading of 10 or 20 percent is generally most effective to add emphasis to the selected paragraph. The Borders and Shading command is implemented on the paragraph level and affects the entire paragraph—either the current or selected paragraph(s).

PARAGRAPH FORMATTING AND THE INSERTION POINT

Indents, tab stops, line spacing, alignment, text flow, borders, and shading are all set at the paragraph level and affect all selected paragraphs and/or the current paragraph (the paragraph containing the insertion point). The position of the insertion point within the paragraph does not matter as the insertion point can be anywhere within the paragraph when the Format Paragraph command is executed. Keep the concept of paragraph formatting in mind as you do the following hands-on exercise.

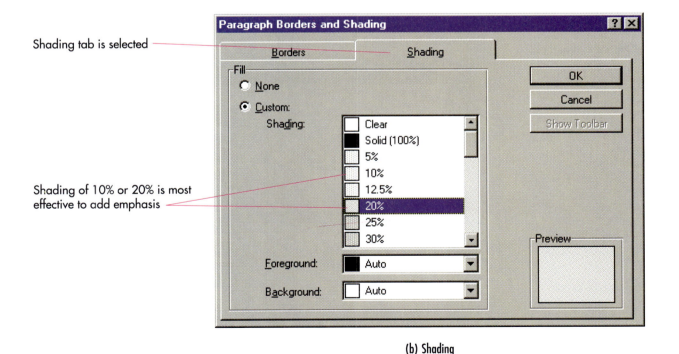

(b) Shading

FIGURE 2.14   Paragraph Borders and Shading (continued)

HANDS-ON EXERCISE 3

Paragraph Formatting

Objective: To implement line spacing, alignment, and indents; to implement widow and orphan protection; to box and shade a selected paragraph. Use Figure 2.15 as a guide in the exercise.

STEP 1: Load the Practice Document

➤ Open the **Modified Tips** document from the previous exercise. If necessary, change to the Page Layout view. Pull down the **Zoom control button** and click **Two Pages** to match the view in Figure 2.15a.

➤ Select the entire second page as shown in the figure. Click the **right mouse button** to produce the shortcut menu. Click **Paragraph.**

SELECT TEXT WITH THE F8 EXTEND KEY

Move to the beginning of the text you want to select, then press the F8 (extend) key. The letters EXT will appear in the status bar. Use the arrow keys to extend the selection in the indicated direction; for example, press the down arrow key to select the line. You can also press any character— for example, a letter, space, or period—to extend the selection to the first occurrence of that character. Press Esc to cancel the selection mode.

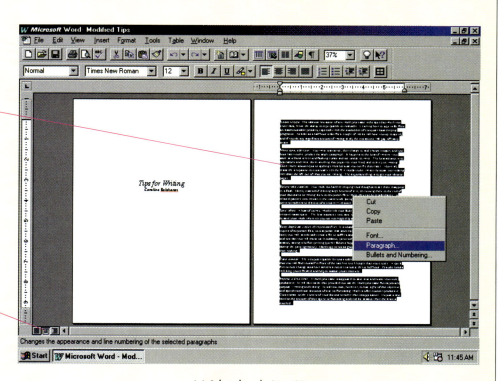

Point to selected text and click right mouse button to produce shortcut menu

Click Page Layout button

(a) Select-then-do (step 1)

FIGURE 2.15 Hands-on Exercise 3

STEP 2: Line Spacing, Justification, and Text Flow

➤ If necessary, click the **Indents and Spacing tab** to view the options in Figure 2.15b.
  - Click the **down arrow** on the list box for Line Spacing and select **1.5 Lines.**
  - Click the **down arrow** on the Alignment list box and select **Justified** as shown in Figure 2.15b.
  - Click the tab for **Text Flow.** Check the box for **Keep Lines Together.** If necessary, check the box for **Widow/Orphan Control.**

➤ Click **OK** to accept all of the settings in the dialog box; that is, you need to click OK only once to accept the settings for Indents and Spacing and Text Flow.

➤ Click anywhere in the document to deselect the text and see the effects of the formatting changes:
  - The document is justified and the line spacing has increased.
  - The document now extends to three pages, with all of the fifth paragraph appearing on the last page.
  - There is a large bottom margin on the second page as a consequence of keeping the lines together in paragraph five.

➤ Save the document.

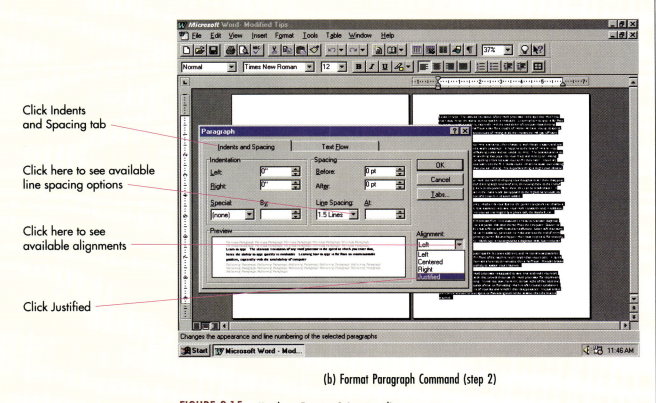

(b) Format Paragraph Command (step 2)

FIGURE 2.15   Hands-on Exercise 3 (continued)

LINE SPACING

Place the insertion point anywhere within a paragraph(s), then press Ctrl+1, Ctrl+2, or Ctrl+5 to set the line spacing at one line (single space), two lines (double space), or 1.5 lines, respectively. You can also customize the Formatting toolbar to display buttons for different line spacing. Point to any toolbar, click the right mouse button to display a shortcut menu, then click Customize to display the Customize dialog box. Select Format from the categories list box, then click and drag the line spacing buttons from the Customize dialog box to the desired position on the toolbar. Click the Close command button to close the dialog box and continue working.

STEP 3: Indents

➤ Select the second paragraph as shown in Figure 2.15c. (The second paragraph will not yet be indented.)

➤ Pull down the **Format menu** and click **Paragraph** (or press the **right mouse button** to produce the shortcut menu and click **Paragraph**).

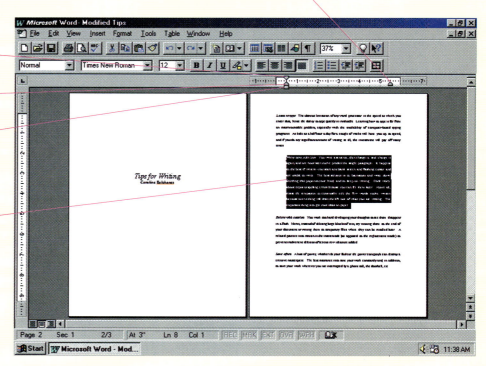

(c) Indents and the Ruler (step 3)

FIGURE 2.15   Hands-on Exercise 3 (continued)

- ➤ If necessary, click the **Indents and Spacing tab** in the Paragraph dialog box. Click the **up arrow** on the Left Indentation text box to set the **Left Indent** to **.5** inch. Set the **Right indent** to **.5** inch. Click **OK.** Your document should match Figure 2.15c.
- ➤ Save the document.

> ### INDENTS AND THE RULER
>
> Use the ruler to change the first line, left, and/or right indents. Select the paragraph (or paragraphs) in which you want to change indents, then drag the appropriate indent markers to the new location(s).
>
> | | |
> |---|---|
> | First line indent only | Drag the top triangle |
> | Left indent only | Drag the bottom triangle |
> | First line *and* left indents | Drag the box (both triangles move) |
> | Right indent | Drag the triangle at the right margin |
>
> If you get a hanging indent when you wanted to change the left indent, it means you dragged the bottom triangle instead of the box. Click the Undo button and try again. (You can always use the Format Paragraph command rather than the ruler if you continue to have difficulty.)

STEP 4: Borders and Shading

- ➤ Pull down the **Format menu.** Click **Borders and Shading** to produce the dialog box in Figure 2.15d.
- ➤ If necessary, click the **Borders tab.** Click a style for the line around the box. Click the rectangle labeled **Box** under Presets.
- ➤ Click the **Shading Tab.** Click **10%** within the Shading list box.
- ➤ Click **OK** to accept the settings for both Borders and Shading.
- ➤ Save the document.

> ### THE BORDERS TOOLBAR
>
> Click the Borders button on the Formatting toolbar to display (hide) the Borders toolbar, which contains buttons for many capabilities within the Borders and Shading command. The Borders toolbar contains a list box for the line width, buttons for the border types, and a second list box for shadings.

STEP 5: Help with Formatting

- ➤ Click outside the selected text to see the effects of the Borders and Shading command.

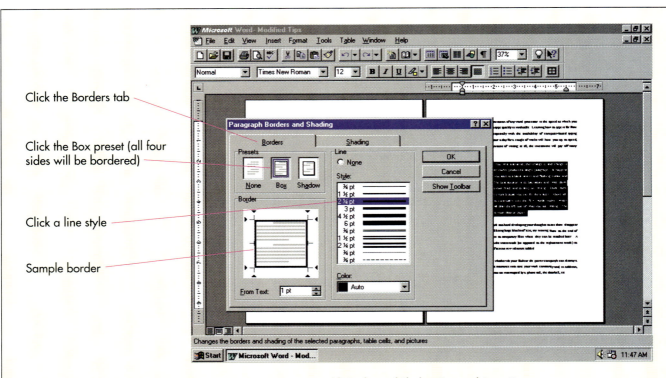

(d) Borders and Shading Command (step 4)

FIGURE 2.15 Hands-on Exercise 3 (continued)

➤ Click the **Help button** on the Standard toolbar. The mouse pointer changes to include a large question mark. Click inside the boxed paragraph to see the formatting in effect for this paragraph as shown in Figure 2.15e.

➤ Click the **Help button** a second time to exit help. The mouse pointer returns to normal.

THE INCREASE AND DECREASE INDENT BUTTONS

The Formatting toolbar provides yet another way to indent (unindent) a paragraph(s). The Increase Indent button increases the left indent, which moves the paragraph to the right; that is, it indents the paragraph to the next tab stop and wraps the text to fit the new indentation. The Decrease Indent button moves the paragraph one tab stop back (to the left).

STEP 6: The Zoom Command

➤ Pull down the **View menu.** Click **Zoom** to produce the dialog box in Figure 2.15f.

➤ Click the **Many Pages** option button. Click the **monitor icon** to display a sample selection box, then click and drag to display three pages across as shown in the figure. Release the mouse. Click **OK.**

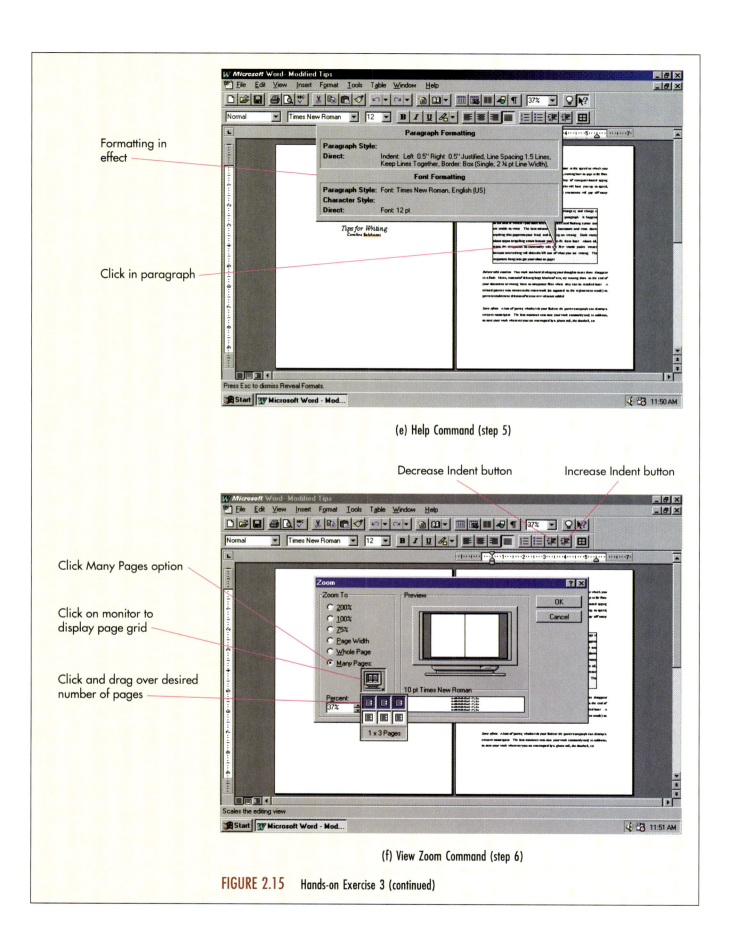

FIGURE 2.15 Hands-on Exercise 3 (continued)

STEP 7: The Completed Document

➤ Your screen should match the one in Figure 2.15g, which displays all three pages of the document.

➤ The Page Layout view displays both a vertical and a horizontal ruler. The boxed and indented paragraph is clearly shown in the second page.

➤ The soft page break between pages two and three occurs between tips rather than within a tip; that is, the text of each tip is kept together on the same page.

➤ Save the document a final time. Print the completed document and submit it to your instructor. Exit Word.

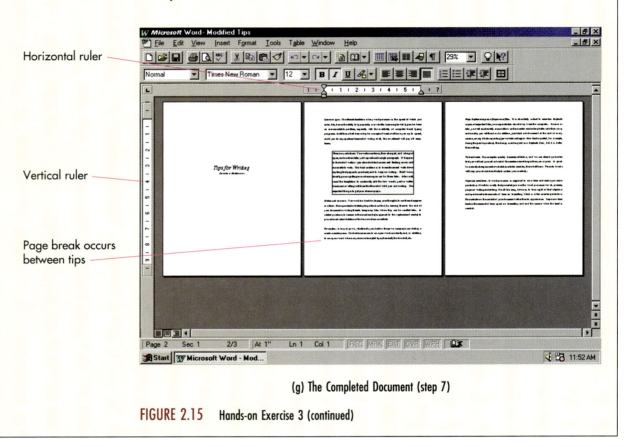

(g) The Completed Document (step 7)

FIGURE 2.15 Hands-on Exercise 3 (continued)

SUMMARY

Many operations in Word are done within the context of select-then-do; that is, select the text, then execute the necessary command. Text may be selected by dragging the mouse, by using the selection bar to the left of the document, or by using the keyboard. Text is deselected by clicking anywhere within the document.

The Find and Replace commands locate a designated character string and optionally replace one or more occurrences of that string with a different character string. The search may be case-sensitive and/or restricted to whole words as necessary.

Text is moved or copied through a combination of the Cut, Copy, and Paste commands and/or the drag-and-drop facility. The contents of the clipboard are replaced by any subsequent Cut or Copy command, but are unaffected by the Paste command; that is, the same text can be pasted into multiple locations.

The Undo command reverses the effect of previous commands. The Undo and Redo commands work in conjunction with one another; that is, every command that is undone can be redone at a later time.

Scrolling occurs when a document is too large to be seen in its entirety. Scrolling with the mouse changes what is displayed on the screen, but does not move the insertion point; that is, you must click the mouse to move the insertion point. Scrolling via the keyboard (for example, PgUp and PgDn) changes what is seen on the screen as well as the location of the insertion point.

The Page Layout view displays top and bottom margins, headers and footers, and other elements not seen in the Normal view. The Normal view is faster because Word spends less time formatting the display. Both views can be seen at different magnifications.

TrueType fonts are scaleable and accessible from any Windows application. The Format Font command enables you to choose the typeface (e.g., Times New Roman or Arial), style (e.g., bold or italic), point size, and color of text.

The Format Paragraph command determines the line spacing, alignment, indents, and text flow, all of which are set at the paragraph level. Borders and shading are also set at the paragraph level. Margins, page size, and orientation, are set in the Page Setup command and affect the entire document (or section).

KEY WORDS AND CONCEPTS

Alignment
Arial
Automatic replacement
Borders and Shading command
Case-insensitive replacement
Case-sensitive replacement
Clipboard
Copy command
Courier New
Cut command
Drag and drop
Drop shadow
Find command
First line indent
Font
Format Font command
Format Painter
Format Paragraph command

Hanging indent
Hard page break
Indents
Landscape orientation
Leader character
Left indent
Line spacing
Margins
Monospaced typeface
Normal view
Page break
Page Layout view
Page Setup command
Paste command
Point size
Portrait orientation
Proportional typeface
Redo command
Replace command
Right indent
Sans serif typeface

Scrolling
Select-then-do
Selection bar
Selective replacement
Serif typeface
Shortcut menu
Soft page break
Tab stop
Times New Roman
Typeface
Type size
Type style
Typography
Undo command
View menu
Whole word replacement
Widows and orphans
Zoom command

Multiple Choice

1. Which of the following commands does *not* place data onto the clipboard?
   (a) Cut
   (b) Copy
   (c) Paste
   (d) All of the above

2. What happens if you select a block of text, copy it, move to the beginning of the document, paste it, move to the end of the document, and paste the text again?
   (a) The selected text will appear in three places: at the original location, and at the beginning and end of the document
   (b) The selected text will appear in two places: at the beginning and end of the document
   (c) The selected text will appear in just the original location
   (d) The situation is not possible; that is, you cannot paste twice in a row without an intervening cut or copy operation

3. What happens if you select a block of text, cut it, move to the beginning of the document, paste it, move to the end of the document, and paste the text again?
   (a) The selected text will appear in three places: at the original location and at the beginning and end of the document
   (b) The selected text will appear in two places: at the beginning and end of the document
   (c) The selected text will appear in just the original location
   (d) The situation is not possible; that is, you cannot paste twice in a row without an intervening cut or copy operation

4. Which of the following are set at the paragraph level?
   (a) Borders and shading
   (b) Tabs and indents
   (c) Line spacing and alignment
   (d) All of the above

5. How do you change the font for *existing* text within a document?
   (a) Select the text, then choose the new font
   (b) Choose the new font, then select the text
   (c) Either (a) or (b)
   (d) Neither (a) nor (b)

6. The Page Setup command can be used to change:
   (a) The margins in a document
   (b) The orientation of a document
   (c) Both (a) and (b)
   (d) Neither (a) nor (b)

7. Which of the following is a true statement regarding indents?
   (a) Indents are measured from the edge of the page rather than from the margin
   (b) The left, right, and first line indents must be set to the same value
   (c) The insertion point can be anywhere in the paragraph when indents are set
   (d) Indents must be set with the Format Paragraph command

8. The spacing in an existing multipage document is changed from single spacing to double spacing throughout the document. What can you say about the number of hard and soft page breaks before and after the formatting change?
   (a) The number of soft page breaks is the same, but the number and/or position of the hard page breaks is different
   (b) The number of hard page breaks is the same, but the number and/or position of the soft page breaks is different
   (c) The number and position of both hard and soft page breaks is the same
   (d) The number and position of both hard and soft page breaks is different

9. The default tab stops are set to:
   (a) Left indents every ½ inch
   (b) Left indents every ¼ inch
   (c) Right indents every ½ inch
   (d) Right indents every ¼ inch

10. Which of the following describes the Arial and Times New Roman fonts?
    (a) Arial is a sans serif font, Times New Roman is a serif font
    (b) Arial is a serif font, Times New Roman is a sans serif font
    (c) Both are serif fonts
    (d) Both are sans serif fonts

11. The find and replacement strings must be
    (a) The same length
    (b) The same case, either upper or lower
    (c) The same length and the same case
    (d) None of the above

12. Assume that you are in the middle of a multipage document. How do you scroll to the beginning of the document and simultaneously change the insertion point?
    (a) Press Ctrl+Home
    (b) Drag the scroll bar to the top of the scroll box
    (c) Both (a) and (b)
    (d) Neither (a) nor (b)

13. Which of the following substitutions can be accomplished by the Find and Replace command?
    (a) All occurrences of the words "Times New Roman" can be replaced with the word "Arial"
    (b) All text set in the Times New Roman font can be replaced by the Arial font
    (c) Both (a) and (b)
    (d) Neither (a) nor (b)

14. Which of the following deselects a selected block of text?
    (a) Clicking anywhere outside the selected text
    (b) Clicking any alignment button on the toolbar
    (c) Clicking the Bold, Italic, or Underline button
    (d) All of the above

15. Which view, and which magnification, lets you see the whole page, including top and bottom margins?
    (a) Page Layout view at 100% magnification
    (b) Page Layout view at Whole Page magnification
    (c) Normal view at 100% magnification
    (d) Normal view at Whole Page magnification

ANSWERS

1. c	**6.** c	**11.** d
2. a	**7.** c	**12.** a
3. b	**8.** b	**13.** c
4. d	**9.** a	**14.** a
5. a	**10.** a	**15.** b

Exploring Microsoft Word

1. Use Figure 2.16 to match each action with its result; a given action may be used more than once or not at all.

   Action
   a. Click at 1
   b. Click at 2
   c. Click at 3
   d. Click at 4
   e. Click at 5
   f. Click at 6
   g. Click at 7
   h. Click at 8
   i. Click at 9
   j. Click at 10

   Result
   ____ Undo the previous two commands
   ____ Cut the selected text from the document
   ____ Change the alignment of the current paragraph to justified
   ____ Change the font of the selected text to Arial
   ____ Change the left and right indents to .5 inch
   ____ Change the size of the selected text to 16 point
   ____ Remove the boldface from the selected text
   ____ Change to the Page Layout view
   ____ Paint another phrase with the same format as the currently selected phrase
   ____ Change the magnification to Whole Page

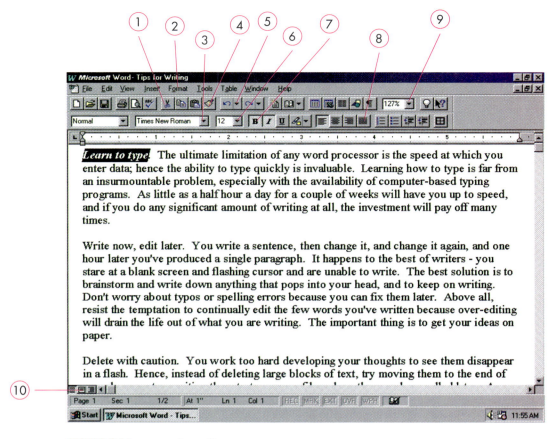

FIGURE 2.16 Screen for Problem 1

2. Describe at least one way, using the mouse or keyboard, to do each of the following. (The answers are found in the boxed tips throughout the chapter. Alternatively, you can access the online help facility to find the information.) How do you:
   a. Scroll to the beginning or end of a document? Does the action you describe also change the insertion point?
   b. Select a sentence? a paragraph? the entire document?
   c. Set the left and right indents?
   d. Insert an additional tab stop?
   e. Copy the formatting in a block of text to multiple places in the same document?
   f. Change selected text to bold, italic, or underlining?
   g. Change the line spacing and alignment for a selected paragraph?
   h. Save the document under a different name?
   i. Box and shade a selected paragraph?

3. The dialog box in Figure 2.17 is intended to replace all occurrences of IT (set in uppercase) with the words Information Technology, with the latter set in italics.
   a. Which options (if any) should be changed so that the command works as intended?
   b. What is the difference between clicking the Find Next and Replace command buttons? Between the Replace and Replace All buttons?

GAINING PROFICIENCY

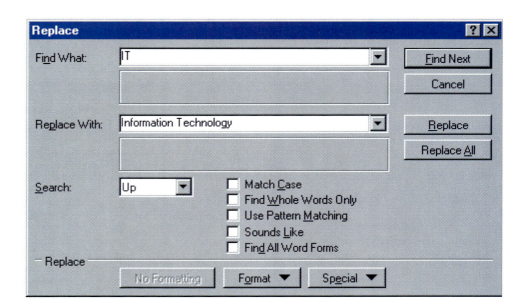

FIGURE 2.17   Screen for Problem 3

4. Exploring Fonts: The fonts available to Microsoft Word (and to every other Windows application) are located in a special Fonts folder as shown in Figure 2.18.
   a. How do you open the Fonts folder? (Hint: Look at the buttons displayed on the taskbar, which indicate the open applications and/or folders on the desktop.)

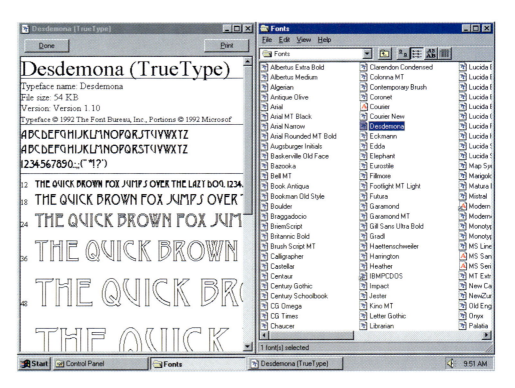

FIGURE 2.18   Screen for Problem 4

b. Which view is displayed in the Fonts folder? How do you change the view?

c. Is a toolbar displayed in the window containing the Fonts folder? How do you display (hide) the toolbar?

d. How do you print a sample of the Desdemona font? How would you print a sample of a different font?

e. How do you minimize the Fonts folder? Would this action remove the Fonts folder from the taskbar?

f. How do you close the Fonts folder? Would this action remove the Fonts folder from the taskbar?

PRACTICE WITH MICROSOFT WORD

1. Open the *Chapter 2 Practice 1* document that is displayed in Figure 2.19 and make the following changes.
   a. Copy the sentence *Discretion is the better part of valor* to the beginning of the first paragraph.
   b. Move the second paragraph to the end of the document.
   c. Change the typeface of the entire document to 12 point Arial.
   d. Change all whole word occurrences of *feel* to *think*.
   e. Change the spacing of the entire document from single spacing to 1.5. Change the alignment of the entire document to justified.

It is not difficult, especially with practice, to learn to format a document. It is not long before the mouse goes automatically to the Format Font command to change the selected text to a sans-serif font, to increase the font size, or to apply a boldface or italic style. Nor is it long before you go directly to the Format Paragraph command to change the alignment or line spacing for selected paragraphs.

What is not easy, however, is to teach discretion in applying formats. Too many different formats on one page can be distracting, and in almost all cases, less is better. Be conservative and never feel that you have to demonstrate everything you know how to do in each and every document that you create. Discretion is the better part of valor. No more than two different typefaces should be used in a single document, although each can be used in a variety of different styles and sizes.

It is always a good idea to stay on the lookout for what you feel are good designs and then determine exactly what you like and don't like about each. In that way, you are constantly building ideas for your own future designs.

FIGURE 2.19 Document for Practice with Word Exercise 1

f. Set the phrases *Format Font command* and *Format Paragraph command* in italics.
g. Indent the second paragraph .25 inch on both the left and right.
h. Box and shade the last paragraph.
i. Create a title page that precedes the document. Set the title, *Discretion in Design,* in 24 point Arial bold and center it approximately two inches from the top of the page. Right align your name toward the bottom of the title page in 12 point Arial regular.
j. Print the revised document and submit it to your instructor.

2. Figure 2.20 displays a completed version of the *Chapter 2 Practice 2* document that exists on the data disk. We want you to retrieve the original document from the data disk, then change the document so that it matches Figure 2.20. No editing is required as the text in the original document is identical to the finished document. The only changes are in formatting, but you will have to compare the documents in order to determine the nature of the changes. Color is a nice touch (which depends on the availability of a color printer) and is not required. Add your name somewhere in the document, then print the revised document and submit it to your instructor.

TYPOGRAPHY

The art of formatting a document is more than just knowing definitions, but knowing the definitions is definitely a starting point. A ***typeface*** is a complete set of characters with the same general appearance, and can be *serif* (cross lines at the end of the main strokes of each letter) or *sans serif* (without the cross lines). A ***type size*** is a vertical measurement, made from the top of the tallest letter in the character set to the bottom of the lowest letter in the character set. ***Type style*** refers to variations in the typeface, such as boldface and italics.

Several typefaces are shipped with Windows, including **Times New Roman,** a serif typeface, and **Arial**, a sans serif typeface. Times New Roman should be used for large amounts of text, whereas Arial is best used for titles and subtitles. It is best not to use too many different typefaces in the same document, but rather to use only one or two and then make the document interesting by varying their size and style.

FIGURE 2.20 Document for Practice with Word Exercise 2

3. Create a simple document containing the text of the Preamble to the Constitution as shown in Figure 2.21.
    a. Set the Preamble in 12 point Times New Roman. Use single spacing and left alignment.
    b. Copy the Preamble to a new page, then change to a larger point size and more interesting typeface.
    c. Create a title page for your assignment, containing your name, course name, and appropriate title. Use a different typeface for the title page than in the rest of the document, and set the title in at least 24 points. Submit all three pages (the title page and both versions of the Preamble) to your instructor.

> We, the people of the United States, in order to form a more perfect Union, establish justice, insure domestic tranquillity, provide for the common defense, promote the general welfare, and secure the blessings of liberty to ourselves and our posterity, do ordain and establish this Constitution for the United States of America.

FIGURE 2.21 Document for Practice with Word Exercise 3

4. As indicated in the chapter, anyone who has used a typewriter is familiar with the function of the Tab key; that is, press Tab and the insertion point moves to the next tab stop (a measured position to align text at a specific place.) The Tab key is more powerful in Word because you can choose from four different types of tab stops (left, center, right, and decimal). You can also specify a leader character, typically dots or hyphens, to draw the reader's eye across the page.

    Create the document in Figure 2.22 (on the next page) and add your name in the indicated position. (Use the Help facility to discover how to work with tab stops.) Submit the completed document to your instructor as proof that you have mastered the Tab key.

EXAMPLES OF TAB STOPS

Example 1 - Right tab at 6":

CIS 120   **Maryann Barber**
FALL 1995   **September 21, 1995**

Example 2 - Right tab with a dot leader at 6":

Chapter 1 1
Chapter 2 31
Chapter 3 56

Example 3 - Right tab at 1" and left tab at 1.25":

           To: Maryann Barber
     From: Joel Stutz
Department: Computer Information Systems
  Subject: Exams

Example 4 - Left tab at 2" and a decimal tab at 3.5":

                      Rent $375.38
                      Utilities $125.59
                      Phone $56.92
                      Cable $42.45

FIGURE 2.22 Document for Practice with Word Exercise 4

Case Studies

Computers Past and Present

The ENIAC was the scientific marvel of its day and the world's first operational electronic computer. It could perform 5,000 additions per second, weighed 30 tons, and took 1,500 square feet of floor space. The price was a modest $486,000 in 1946 dollars. The story of the ENIAC and other influential computers of the author's choosing is found in the file *History of Computers,* which we forgot to format, so we are asking you to do it for us. Be sure to use appropriate emphasis for the names of the various computers. Create a title page in front of the document, then submit the completed assignment to your instructor.

Your First Consultant's Job

Go to a real installation, such as a doctor's or an attorney's office, the company where you work, or the computer lab at school. Determine the backup procedures that are in effect, then write a one-page report indicating whether the policy is adequate and, if necessary, offering suggestions for improvement. Your report should be addressed to the individual in charge of the business, and it should cover all aspects of the backup strategy—that is, which files are backed up and how often, and what software is used for the backup operation. Use appropriate emphasis (for example, bold italics) to identify any potential problems. This is a professional document (it is your first consultant's job), and its appearance must be perfect in every way.

Paper Makes a Difference

Most of us take paper for granted, but the right paper can make a significant difference in the effectiveness of the document. Reports and formal correspondence are usually printed on white paper, but you would be surprised how many different shades of white there are. Other types of documents lend themselves to colored paper for additional impact. In short, which paper you use is far from an automatic decision. Walk into a local copy store and see if they have any specialty papers available. Our favorite source for paper is a company called PAPER DIRECT (1-800-APAPERS). Ask for a catalog, then consider the use of a specialty paper the next time you have an important project.

The Invitation

Choose an event and produce the perfect invitation. The possibilities are endless and limited only by your imagination. You can invite people to your wedding or to a fraternity party. Your laser printer and abundance of fancy fonts enable you to do anything a professional printer can do. Clip art and/or special paper will add the finishing touch. Go to it—this assignment is a lot of fun.

ENHANCING A DOCUMENT: PROOFING, WIZARDS, CLIPART, AND WORDART

OBJECTIVES

After reading this chapter you will be able to:

1. Use the thesaurus to look up synonyms and antonyms.
2. Explain the objectives and limitations of the grammar check; customize the grammar check for business or casual writing.
3. Use the Insert Symbol command to insert special characters into a document.
4. Use the Insert Date command to insert a date into a document; explain the advantage of inserting the date as a field rather than as text.
5. Create an envelope.
6. Use wizards and templates to create a document; list several wizards provided with Microsoft Word.
7. Use the ClipArt Gallery to insert clip art into a document; explain how frames are used to move and size a graphic object.
8. Use WordArt to insert decorative text into a document.

OVERVIEW

This chapter describes how to add the finishing touches to a document and make it as error free as possible. In it, we review the spell check and introduce the thesaurus as a means of adding precision to your writing. We present the grammar check as a convenient way of finding a variety of errors, but remind you there is no substitute for carefully proofreading the final document. We also show you how to add the date to a document, how to insert special symbols, and how to create and print an envelope.

The second half of the chapter introduces the wizards and templates that are built into Microsoft Word to help you create professionally formatted documents quickly and easily. A template is a partially completed document that contains formatting, text, and/or graphics to which you add additional information to personalize the document. A wizard makes the process even easier as it asks you questions about the document you wish to create, then creates a custom template for you.

The last portion of the chapter introduces the Microsoft ClipArt Gallery, a collection of 1,100 clip art images that can be added to any document. It also introduces Microsoft WordArt, an application included with Microsoft Word that enables you to create decorative text. We believe this to be a very enjoyable chapter that will add significantly to your capability in Microsoft Word. As always, learning is best accomplished by doing, and the hands-on exercises are essential to master the material.

THESAURUS

Mark Twain said the difference between the right word and almost the right word is the difference between a lightning bug and lightning. The *thesaurus* is an important tool in any word processor and is both fun and educational. It helps you to avoid repetition, and it will polish your writing.

The thesaurus is called from the Tools menu. You position the cursor at the appropriate word within the document, then invoke the thesaurus and follow your instincts. The thesaurus recognizes multiple meanings and forms of a word (for example, adjective, noun, and verb) as in Figure 3.1a, and (by double clicking) allows you to look up any listed meaning to produce additional choices as in Figure 3.1b.

Substitutions in the document are made automatically by selecting the desired synonym and clicking the Replace button. You can explore further alternatives by selecting a synonym and clicking on the Look Up button. The thesaurus also provides a list of antonyms for most entries, as in Figure 3.1c.

GRAMMAR CHECK

The *grammar check* attempts to catch mistakes in punctuation, writing style, and word usage by comparing strings of text within a document to a series of predefined rules. As with the spell check, errors are brought to the screen where you can accept the suggested correction and make the replacement automatically, or more often, edit the selected text and make your own changes.

You can also ask the grammar check to explain the rule it is attempting to enforce. Unlike a spell check, the grammar check is subjective, and what seems appropriate to you may be objectionable to someone else. The English language is also too complex for the grammar check to detect every error, although it will find many errors.

CASUAL OR BUSINESS WRITING

Word enables you to change almost every aspect of its environment to suit your personal preference. One option you may want to change is the rules in effect within the grammar check—for example, whether Word should check for business or casual writing. Pull down the Tools menu, click Options, then click the Grammar tab. Choose the option(s) you want, then click OK.

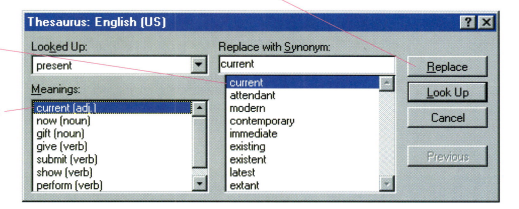

(a) Initial Word

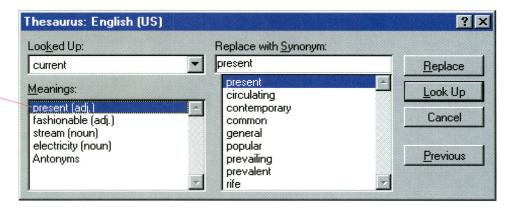

(b) Additional Choices

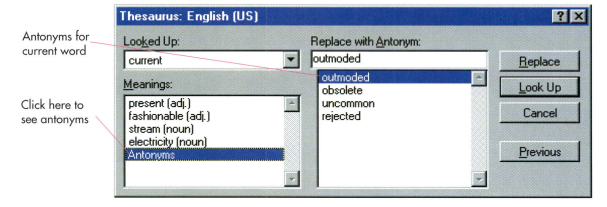

(c) Antonyms

FIGURE 3.1   The Thesaurus

ENHANCING A DOCUMENT

The grammar check caught the inconsistency between subject and verb in Figure 3.2a and suggested the appropriate correction (catch instead of catches). In Figure 3.2b, it suggested the elimination of the superfluous comma. These examples show the grammar check at its best, but much of the time it is more subjective and less capable.

It objects, for example, to the phrase *all men are created equal* in Figure 3.2c, citing excessive use of the passive voice and (in a second message) indicating that the phrase is gender specific. Whether or not you accept the suggestion is entirely up to you. Even with the most stringent options in effect, the entire paragraph in Figure 3.2d went through without error, showing that there is no substitute for carefully proofreading every document.

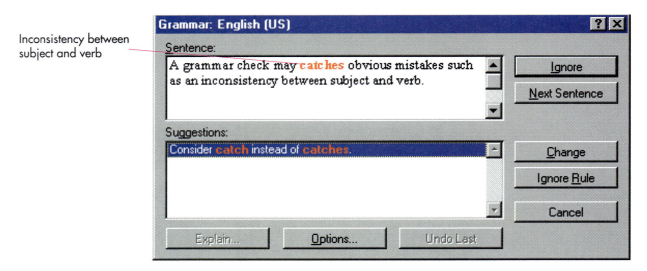

(a) Inconsistent Verb

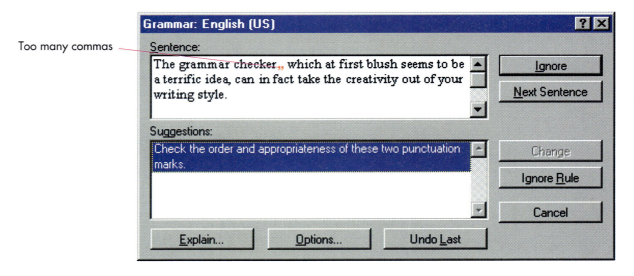

(b) Doubled Punctuation

FIGURE 3.2 The Grammar Check

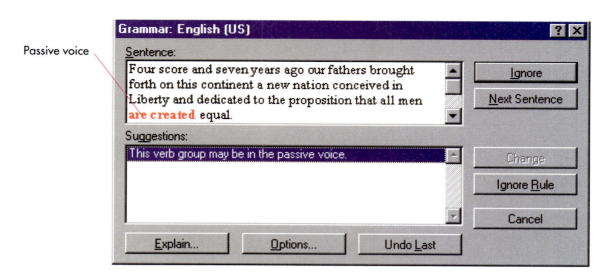

(c) Subjective Rules

Most items are not notice because English is just to complicated. The grammar program will accept this entire paragraph even though it contains many errors and this sentence is very long and the paragraph does not make any cents. It did not find any mistakes in the previous sentences that used notice rather than noticed, to instead of too, and cents instead of sense. It does not object to misplaced tenses such as yesterday I will go to the store or tomorrow I went to the store.

(d) Limitations

FIGURE 3.2 The Grammar Check (continued)

A RÉSUMÉ AND COVER LETTER

The hands-on exercise that follows shortly is based on the cover letter and accompanying résumé shown in Figure 3.3. The résumé was created using the Résumé Wizard supplied with Microsoft Word as described later in the chapter. The cover letter includes the date and requires an envelope in which it can be mailed. The cover letter also illustrates the use of special symbols such as the accented e's in the word résumé.

THIRTY SECONDS IS ALL YOU HAVE

Thirty seconds is the average amount of time a personnel manager spends skimming your résumé and deciding whether or not to call you for an interview. It doesn't matter how much training you've had or how good you are if your résumé and cover letter fail to project a professional image. Know your audience and use the vocabulary of your targeted field. Be positive and describe your experience from an accomplishment point of view. Maintain a separate list of references and have it available on request. Be sure all information is accurate. Be conscientious about the design of your résumé and proofread the final documents very carefully.

1 Graceland Mansion
Memphis, Tennessee
(901) 332-3322

ELVIS AARON PRESLEY

Objective	To emerge from hiding and perform once more before live audiences at major Las Vegas night clubs
Education	1953 - Graduated from Humes High School, Memphis, Tennessee
Employment	1954 - 1977 **Featured Singer - Concert Circuit**

- Traveled extensively on the concert circuit, including 22 club appearances in Las Vegas and Lake Tahoe

1956 - 1977
Recording Artist

- Recorded 72 albums, including *Loving You*, *Elvis' Christmas Album*, *Elvis Is Back*, *G.I. Blues*, *Blue Hawaii*, *Elvis for Everyone*, *How Great Thou Art*, *Worldwide 50 Gold Award Hits*, and *Moody Blues*

1956 - 1972
Recording Artist

- Recorded 38 Top Ten hits, 18 of which climbed to #1 on the chart, including *Heartbreak Hotel*, *Hound Dog*, *Don't Be Cruel*, *Love Me Tender*, *All Shook Up*, *Teddy Bear*, *Jailhouse Rock*, *Hard Headed Woman*, *Stuck on You*, *It's Now or Never*, *Are You Lonesome Tonight*, *Good Luck Charm*, and *Suspicious Minds*

1956 - 1972
Movie and Television Star

- Performed in 38 feature length movies, including *Love Me Tender*, *Jailhouse Rock*, *Blue Hawaii*, *Viva Las Vegas*, *The Trouble with Girls*, and *Elvis On Tour*

- Featured on 15 television shows, including *The Milton Berle Show*, *The Steve Allen Show*, *Ed Sullivan's Toast of the Town*, and the *Today Show*

1958 - 1960
Soldier, United States Army

- Served in the United States Army as a tank crewman with the Third Armored Division. Stationed in Germany

Awards received	Picture placed on United States Postage Stamp 3 Grammy Awards Male Entertainer of the Year
References	Colonel Thomas Andrew Parker, Manager John Q. Public, Elvis Impersonator's Association Priscilla Presley, Actress

(a) Résumé

FIGURE 3.3   The Presley Comeback

ELVIS PRESLEY

Graceland Mansion
Memphis, TN 38116
(901) 332-3322

June 1, 1995

Mr. David Letterman
1697 Broadway
New York, NY 10019

Dear Mr. Letterman,

I am seeking an engagement at a Las Vegas night club. I have extensive experience both in private clubs and road tours throughout the United States, and have enclosed my résumé for your review.

It has been some time since I have been in the public eye, but I have never stopped singing or living my music. I am well aware of current trends and have many new songs that will, without question, catch the public's imagination. Everyone needs a gimmick in today's market and I have several extraordinary ideas in mind.

I would welcome the opportunity to meet you to discuss my ideas and audition my new act. Please contact me at the above address or call me at 1-800-HOUND-DOG. I look forward to hearing from you.

Sincerely,

Elvis

(b) Cover Letter

FIGURE 3.3   The Presley Comeback (continued)

The Insert Date and Time Command

The *Insert Date and Time command* puts the date (and/or time) into a document. The information can be inserted as either a specific value (the date and time on which the command is executed) or as a *field.* The latter is updated automatically from the computer's internal clock whenever the document is opened in the Page Layout view or when the document is printed. You can also update a field manually by selecting the appropriate command from a shortcut menu.

The date may be printed in a variety of formats as shown in Figure 3.4. Note that the Insert as Field box is checked, so that the date is inserted as a field. If the box were not checked, the date would be inserted as text and remain constant.

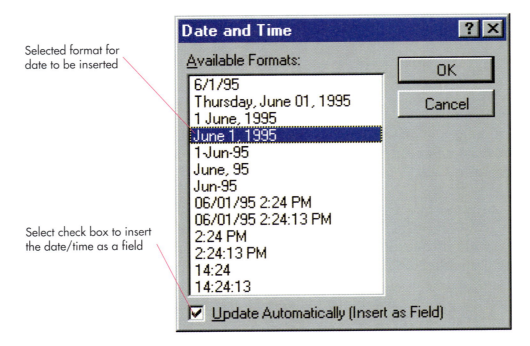

FIGURE 3.4   Insert Date and Time Command

The Insert Symbol Command

One quality that distinguishes the professional document is the use of typographic characters or foreign language symbols; for example, ™ rather than TM, © rather than (C), or ½ and ¼ rather than 1/2 and 1/4. Many of these symbols are contained within the Wingdings or Symbol fonts that are supplied with Windows.

> **AUTOCORRECT AND AUTOFORMAT**
>
> The AutoCorrect feature corrects mistakes as you type by substituting one character string for another—for example "the" for "teh". It will also substitute symbols for typewritten equivalents such as © for (c), provided the entries are included in the table of substitutions. The AutoFormat feature is similar in concept and replaces common fractions such as 1/2 or 1/4 with ½ or ¼. It also converts ordinal numbers such as 1st or 2nd to 1st or 2nd. See practice exercise 4 on page 147 for additional examples.

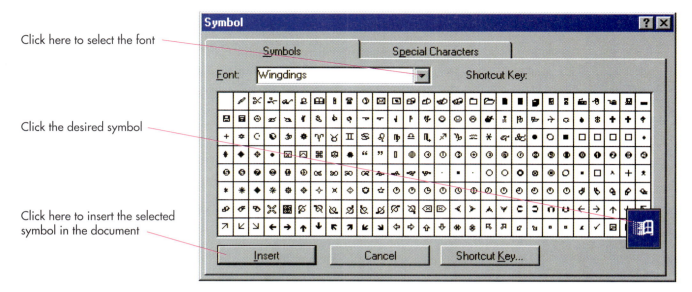

FIGURE 3.5 Insert Symbol Command

The *Insert Symbol command* provides easy access to all of the fonts installed on your system. Choose the font containing the desired symbol—for example, Wingdings in Figure 3.5—then click the Insert command button to place the character into the document. Remember, too, that TrueType fonts are scaleable, enabling you to create some truly unusual documents. (See practice exercise 3 at the end of the chapter.)

Creating an Envelope

An envelope is based on a different physical document from the letter it will contain. Microsoft Word saves you the trouble of having to change margins and orientation by providing the *Envelopes and Labels command* in the Tools menu. Execution of the command produces a dialog box where you supply or edit the necessary addresses. Word takes care of the rest.

The addressee's information can be taken directly from the cover letter as described in step 8 of the following exercise. The return address can be entered directly into the dialog box, or it can be selected from a set of previously stored return addresses. Word also lets you choose from different size envelopes; it will even supply the postal bar code if you request that option.

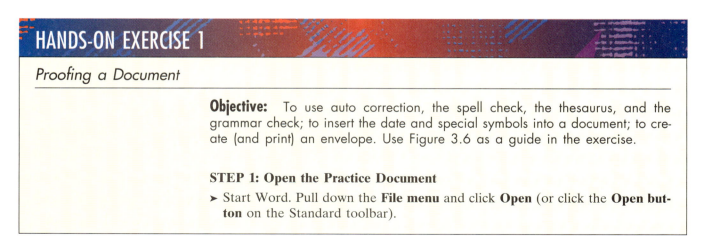

HANDS-ON EXERCISE 1

Proofing a Document

Objective: To use auto correction, the spell check, the thesaurus, and the grammar check; to insert the date and special symbols into a document; to create (and print) an envelope. Use Figure 3.6 as a guide in the exercise.

STEP 1: Open the Practice Document
> Start Word. Pull down the **File menu** and click **Open** (or click the **Open button** on the Standard toolbar).

➤ If you have not yet changed the default folder:
  • Select the appropriate drive, drive C or drive A, from the Look in list.
  • Double click the **Exploring Word folder** to make it the active folder.
  • Double click the **Elvis Before** document to open the document.
➤ The document opens in the Page Layout view (the view in which it was last saved). The date displayed on your monitor should reflect today's date rather than the date in our document, because the date field is updated automatically.
➤ Click the **Normal button** above the status bar to change to the Normal view as shown in Figure 3.6a.
➤ Pull down the **File menu.** Click the **Save As command** to save the document as **Elvis After.** Click **Save.** The title bar reflects the new document **Elvis After,** but you can always return to the original document if you edit the duplicated file beyond redemption.

> ### DATES AND VIEWS
> Any document that is opened in the Page Layout view will have all of its fields updated automatically. This is not true in the Normal view, however, and date fields must be updated manually. Point to the field, click the right mouse button to display a shortcut menu, then click the Update Field command.

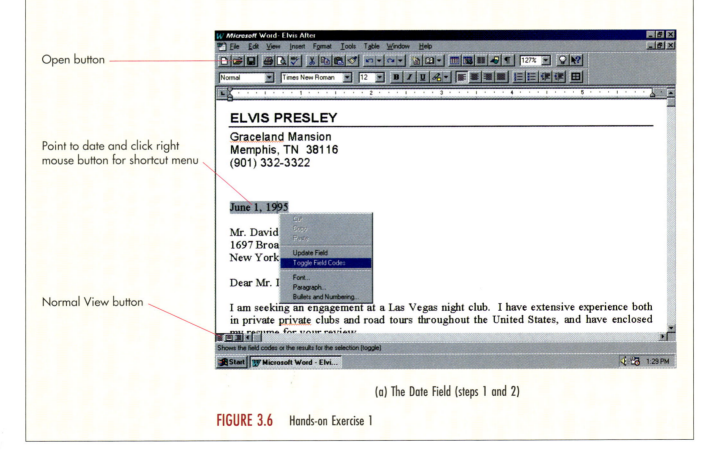

(a) The Date Field (steps 1 and 2)

FIGURE 3.6 Hands-on Exercise 1

STEP 2: The Date Field

➤ Click anywhere in the date, which is then displayed in gray as shown in Figure 3.6a, to indicate the date is a field rather than text.

➤ Press **Shift+F9** to display the date as a field (code). Press **Shift+F9** a second time to toggle back to the formatted date.

➤ Point to the date, then click the **right mouse button** to display the shortcut menu in Figure 3.6a, which contains commands relevant to the date field (Update Field and Toggle Field Codes). This is an alternate way to update the date and toggle between displaying a field code or field result.

➤ Press **Esc** to close the shortcut menu without executing a command.

FIELD CODES VERSUS FIELD RESULTS

All fields are displayed in a document in one of two formats, as a *field code* or as a *field result.* A field code appears in braces and indicates instructions to insert variable data when the document is printed; a field result displays the information as it will appear in the printed document. You can toggle the display between the field code and field result by pressing Shift+F9 during editing.

STEP 3: Customize the Spell Check

➤ Pull down the **Tools menu,** click **Options** to display the Options dialog box, then click the **Spelling tab** to display the dialog box in Figure 3.6b.

➤ Set the spelling options to match those in the figure so that the results of the spell check in step 4 will match the instructions in our exercise.

➤ Click **OK** to accept the settings and close the dialog box.

STEP 4: The Spell Check

➤ A red wavy underline appears under misspelled words because the automatic spell check is in effect according to the options set in the previous step. Regardless, it's faster to use the Spelling button to automatically go from one misspelling to another, rather than moving through the document manually.

➤ Press **Ctrl+Home** to move to the beginning of the document. Click the **Spelling button** on the Standard toolbar to initiate the spell check.

➤ Graceland is flagged as the first misspelling as shown in Figure 3.6c. Click the **Ignore command button** to accept Graceland as written (or click the **Add command button** to add Graceland to the custom dictionary).

➤ Continue checking the document, which returns misspellings and other irregularities one at a time.

- Click **Delete** to delete the second occurrence of the repeated word (*private*).
- Click **Change** to correct the irregular capitalization in *everyone.*
- Click **Change** to accept the correct spelling for *gimmick.*
- Click **Change** to accept the correct spelling for *Sincerely.*

➤ Click **OK** when the spell check is complete.

➤ Save the document.

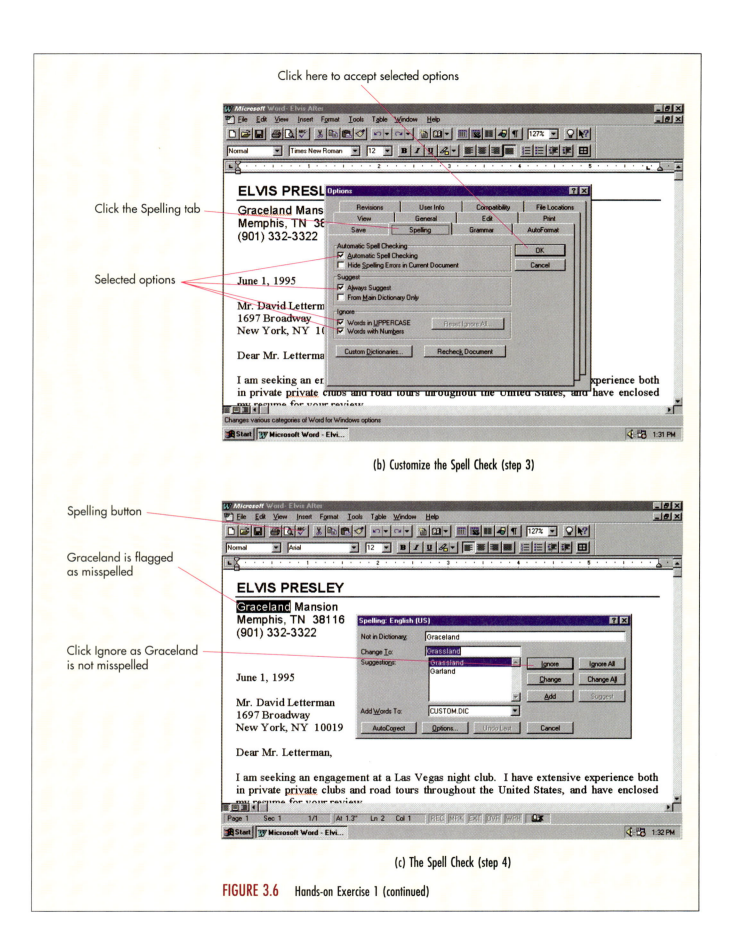

FIGURE 3.6 Hands-on Exercise 1 (continued)

THE CUSTOM DICTIONARY

It's easy to add a word to the custom dictionary, but how do you delete a word if you've added it incorrectly? Word anticipates the problem and allows you to edit the custom dictionary as an ordinary Word document. Pull down the Tools menu, click Options, and select the Spelling tab. Click the Custom Dictionaries command button, select the custom dictionary (if there is more than one) and click Edit. The custom dictionary opens as a Word document. Make and save the necessary changes, close the custom dictionary, and continue working in your regular document. Editing the custom dictionary turns off the automatic spell check, which must be reset if you want the option in effect. Pull down the Tools menu, click the Spelling tab, and check the box for Automatic Spell Checking.

STEP 5: The Thesaurus

➤ Click anywhere within a word you wish to change—for example, the word **magnificent** in Figure 3.6d.

➤ Pull down the **Tools menu.** Click **Thesaurus** to display synonyms for the selected word (magnificent) as shown in the figure.

➤ Double click **grand** (in either list box) to display synonyms for this word.

➤ Click the **Previous command button** to return to the original synonyms for magnificent.

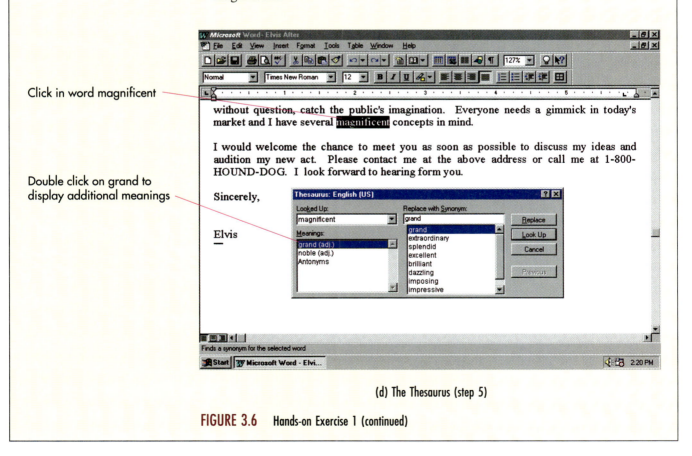

(d) The Thesaurus (step 5)

FIGURE 3.6   Hands-on Exercise 1 (continued)

➤ Click **extraordinary** in the list of synonyms. Click **Replace**.
➤ Change other words as you see fit; for example, we changed **chance** to opportunity.
➤ Save the document.

> ### TO CLICK OR DOUBLE CLICK
>
> The thesaurus displays the different meanings and forms of the selected word. Click any meaning, and its synonyms appear in the synonym list box in the right of the window. Double click any meaning or synonym, and Word will look up the selected word and provide additional meanings and synonyms

STEP 6: Customize the Grammar Check
➤ Pull down the **Tools menu.** Click **Options** to display the Options dialog box in Figure 3.6e.
➤ Click the **Grammar tab** and select **For Business Writing** from the list box of available styles. Be sure there is a check next to the box to Show Readability Statistics.
➤ Click the **Customize Settings command button** to customize the grammar check in order to use all possible rules so that you can see it at its potential best.

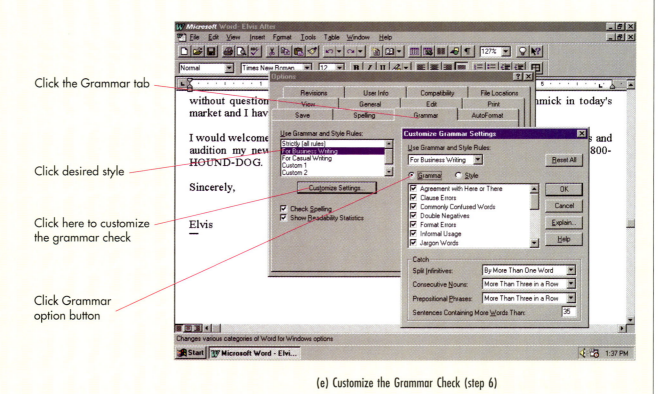

(e) Customize the Grammar Check (step 6)

FIGURE 3.6   Hands-on Exercise 1 (continued)

- Click the **Grammar option button,** then scroll through the list box in order to place a check next to every option as shown in Figure 3.6d.
- Click the **Style option button,** then scroll through its list box in order to place a check next to every option.

➤ Click **OK** to accept the settings for the Grammar Check. Click **OK** a second time to exit the Options dialog box and return to your document.

STEP 7: Check the Document

➤ Press **Ctrl+Home** to move to the beginning of the document. Pull down the **Tools menu** a second time. Click **Grammar** to begin checking the document. Suggestions for correction will be returned one at a time; you can accept or reject the suggestions as you see fit.

➤ Click the **Explain button** at any time to display an explanation of the rule as shown in Figure 3.6f. Click the **Close button** (or press Esc) to close the explanation window.
- We elected to keep the phrase *in the public eye* by clicking the **Ignore button,** but we accepted the next suggestion to change *concepts* to ideas.
- We deleted the phrase *as soon as possible,* by selecting the phrase in the Sentence box, pressing the **Del key,** then clicking the **Change button.**
- The grammar check is not perfect, but it does detect one very significant error: the incorrect use of *form* rather than *from* in the last sentence.

➤ Click **OK** after viewing the readability statistics to return to the document. Save the document.

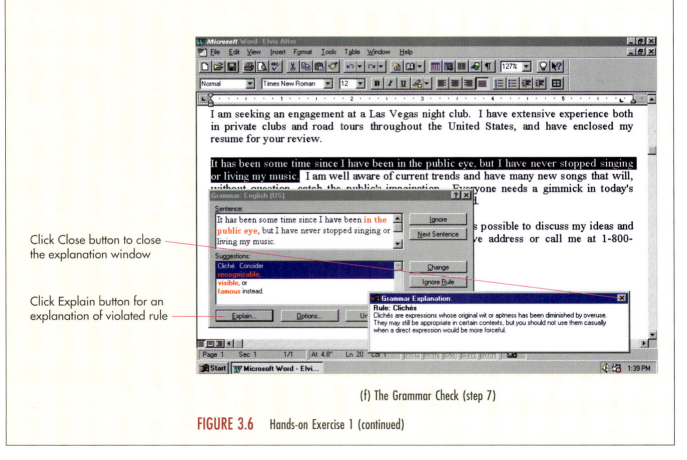

(f) The Grammar Check (step 7)

FIGURE 3.6 Hands-on Exercise 1 (continued)

ENHANCING A DOCUMENT 117

STEP 8: Special Characters

➤ The proper spelling of résumé places accents over both e's. Click before the first e in resume (in the first paragraph of the letter).

➤ Pull down the **Insert menu,** click **Symbol,** and choose **normal text** from the Font list box.

➤ Click the **é** as shown in Figure 3.6g. Click the **Insert button** to insert the character into the document.

➤ Click in the document window and delete the unaccented e. Click before the second e. Click **Insert.** Click **Close.** Delete the second unaccented e.

➤ Save the document.

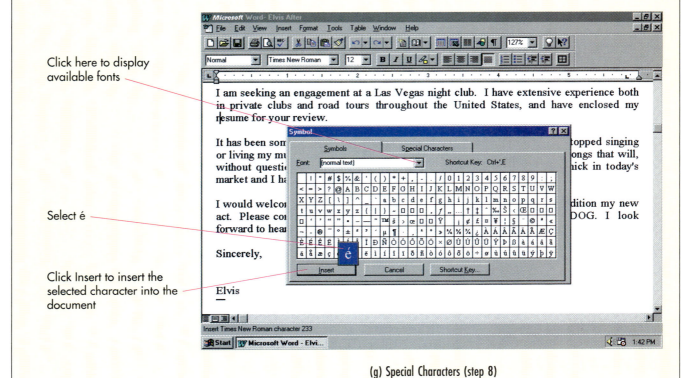

(g) Special Characters (step 8)

FIGURE 3.6   Hands-on Exercise 1 (continued)

STEP 9: Create an Envelope

➤ Click and drag to select the three lines in David Letterman's address. Pull down the **Tools menu.** Click **Envelopes and Labels** to produce the dialog box in Figure 3.6h.

➤ David Letterman's address should be in the Delivery address box because you selected the address prior to executing the Envelopes and Labels command. If this is not the case, you can enter (or edit) the address in the Envelopes and Labels dialog box. You can also enter (or edit) the return address.

➤ Click the **Add to document command button.** Click **Yes** or **No,** depending on whether you want to change the default return address.

➤ Save the document.

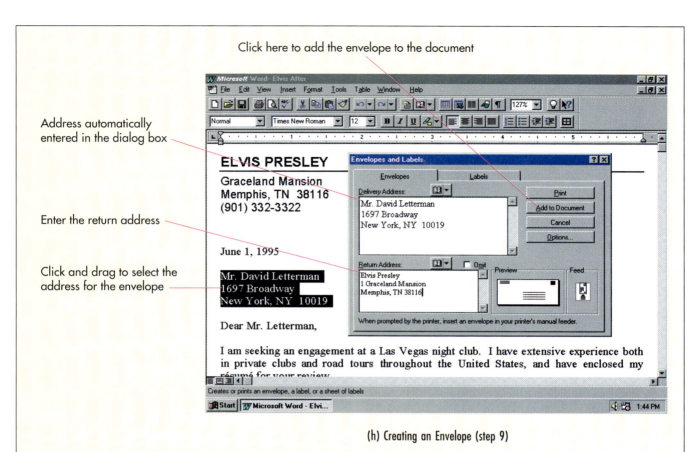

(h) Creating an Envelope (step 9)

FIGURE 3.6 Hands-on Exercise 1 (continued)

CUSTOMIZE THE TOOLBAR

The Create Envelope button is a perfect addition to the Standard toolbar if you print envelopes frequently. Pull down the Tools menu, click Customize, then click the Toolbars tab in the dialog box. If necessary, click the arrow in the Categories list box, select Tools, then drag the Create Envelope button to the Standard toolbar. Close the Customize dialog box. The Create Envelope button appears on the Standard toolbar and can be used the next time you need to create an envelope or label.

STEP 10: The Completed Document

➤ Click the **Page Layout icon** on the status bar. Click the **Zoom Control arrow** on the Standard toolbar and select **Two Pages.** You should see the completed letter and envelope as shown in Figure 3.6i.

➤ Do *not* print the envelope unless you can manually feed an envelope to the printer. Click the page containing the letter (page two in our document).

➤ Pull down the **File menu.** Click **Print.** Click the **Current Page option button.** Click **OK** to print only the letter. Exit Word if you do not want to continue with the next exercise at this time.

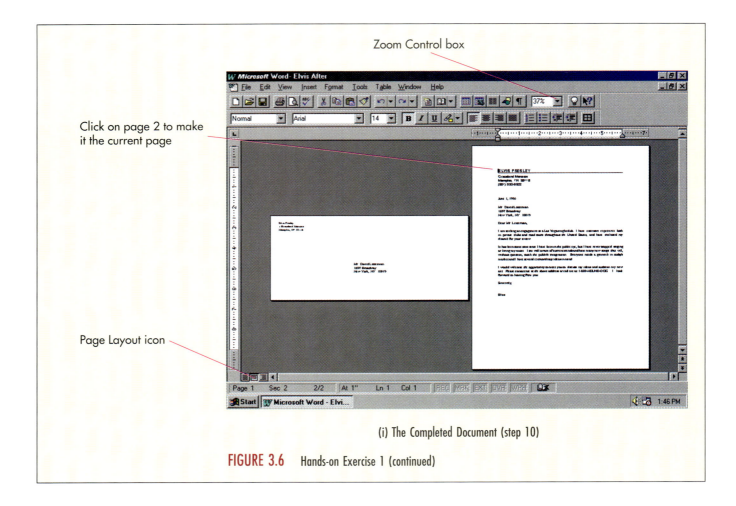

(i) The Completed Document (step 10)

FIGURE 3.6 Hands-on Exercise 1 (continued)

WIZARDS AND TEMPLATES

A ***template*** is a partially completed document that contains formatting, text, and/or graphics. It may be as simple as a memo or as complex as a résumé or newsletter. Word provides a variety of templates for common documents including a résumé, letter, memo, report, or fax cover sheet. You can design your own templates, or you can use the ones built into Word. A ***wizard*** attempts to make the process even easier by asking questions, then creating the template for you.

Figure 3.7 illustrates the use of wizards and templates in conjunction with a résumé. You can choose from one of three existing templates (contemporary, elegant, and professional) as shown in Figure 3.7a. Each of these templates is a partially completed résumé to which you add personal information to create your own résumé according to the formatting stored within the template.

We prefer, however, to use the ***Résumé Wizard*** to create a custom template. This is accomplished by selecting the wizard in Figure 3.7a, then answering the questions posed by the Wizard. We specify the type of résumé in Figure 3.7b, enter some personal information in Figure 3.7c, and choose the categories in Figure 3.7d. (The wizard continues to ask additional questions not shown in Figure 3.7.)

The end product of the Résumé Wizard is the template in Figure 3.7e. You save the finished product as a regular document, then you complete the résumé by entering the specifics of your employment. You can copy and paste information within the résumé, just as you would with a regular document. It takes a little practice, but the end result is a professional résumé.

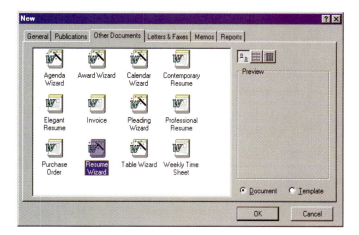

(a) Résumé Wizards and Templates

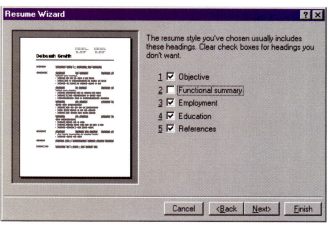

(d) Choose the Categories

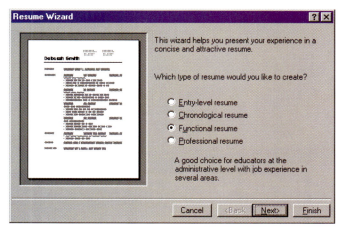

(b) Résumé Wizard

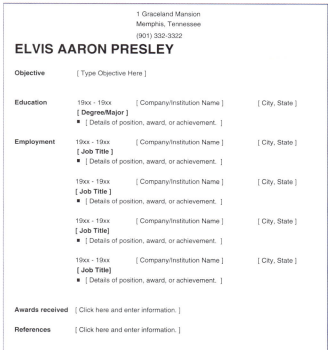

(e) The Template

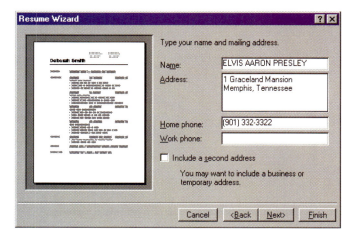

(c) Supply the Information

FIGURE 3.7 Creating a Résumé

ENHANCING A DOCUMENT

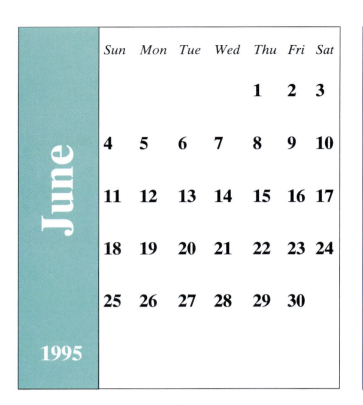

(a) Calendar

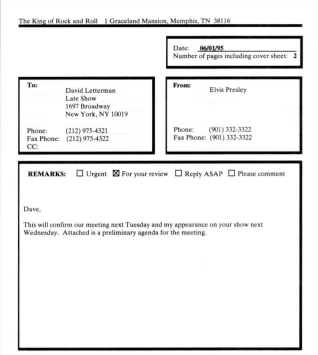

(b) Fax Cover Sheet

(c) Agenda

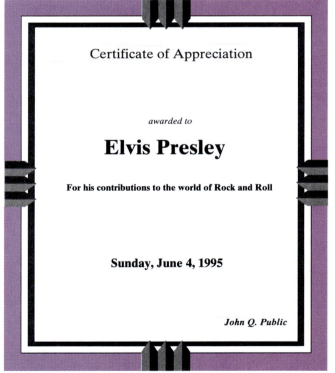

(d) Award

FIGURE 3.8   What You Can Do with Wizards

The Résumé Wizard is one of several different wizards available within Microsoft Word. Look carefully at the tabs within the dialog box of Figure 3.7a, and you can infer that Word supplies both templates and wizards for reports, memos, letters, and faxes. The Other Documents tab provides access to the Agenda, Award, and Calendar wizards as well as several other documents. Figure 3.8 shows four attractive documents that were created by using the respective wizards.

Wizards and templates help you to create professionally designed documents, but they are only a beginning. The content is still up to you. Some wizards are easier to use than others. The *Calendar Wizard,* for example, asks you for the month, year, and type of calendar, then completes the document for you. The *Fax Cover Sheet, Agenda,* and *Award Wizards* create a template, but require you to enter additional information.

Any document that is created with a wizard or template can be saved under its own name, then edited like any other document. Wizards and templates are illustrated in the following exercise.

HANDS-ON EXERCISE 2

Wizards and Templates

Objective: To use wizards and templates to create two documents based on existing templates. To view multiple documents at the same time. Use Figure 3.9 as a guide in the exercise.

STEP 1: The File New Command

➤ Start Word. Pull down the **File menu.** Click **New** to produce the New dialog box shown in Figure 3.9a.

➤ Click the **Letters & Faxes tab** to display the indicated wizards and templates. Check that the **Document option button** is selected.

➤ Double click the **Fax Wizard** to begin creating a fax cover sheet.

STEP 2: The Fax Wizard

➤ The Fax Wizard asks a series of questions in order to build a template:

- Click **Portrait** as shown in Figure 3.9b. Click **Next.**
- Choose a style for the cover sheet. (We chose **Jazzy.**) Click **Next.**
- Click the text box(es) to enter (or change) your name, company name, and address. Click **Next.**
- Click the text box(es) to enter (or change) your telephone number and your fax number. Click **Next.**
- Click the text box(es) to enter the recipient's name, company name, and address. Click **Next.**
- Click the text box(es) to enter the recipient's phone and fax number. Click **Next.**

➤ The final screen of the Fax Wizard indicates that the wizard has all the information it needs and asks whether you want help in completing the fax cover sheet. Click **No,** then click the **Finish command button.**

➤ Save the document as **Elvis Fax Cover Sheet.**

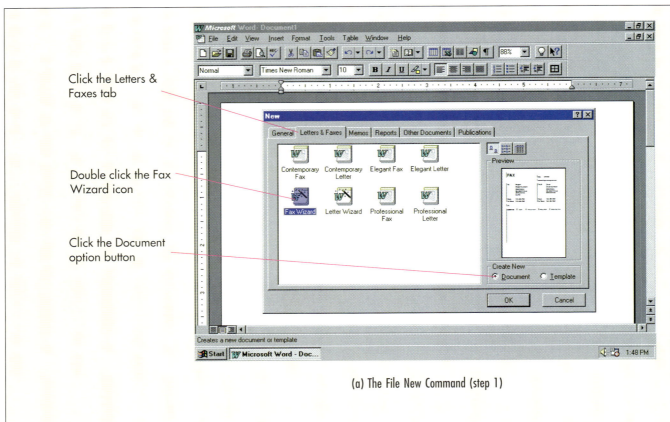

(a) The File New Command (step 1)

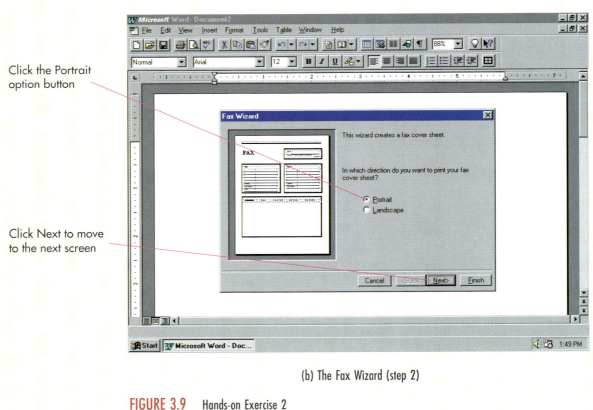

(b) The Fax Wizard (step 2)

FIGURE 3.9 Hands-on Exercise 2

RETRACE YOUR STEPS

The *Fax Wizard* guides you every step of the way, but what if you make a mistake or change your mind? Click the Back command button at any time to return to a previous screen in order to enter different information, then continue working with the wizard.

STEP 3: Complete the Fax

- If necessary, zoom to **Page Width.** Figure 3.9c displays the Fax cover sheet created by the Fax Wizard based on the answers you entered through the Fax Wizard.
- Click in the **Remarks area.** Type the text of the fax as shown in Figure 3.9c.
- Click the **Spelling button** to begin the spell check. Correct any misspellings or other errors. Enter the number of pages in the upper right corner. Click the check box "For your review".
- Save the document. Click the **Print button** on the Standard toolbar to print the completed document.
- Pull down the **File menu.** Click **Close** to close the Fax document but remain in Word.

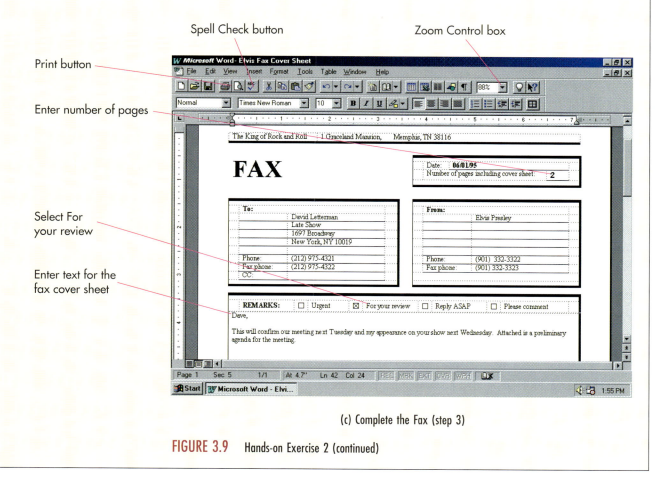

(c) Complete the Fax (step 3)

FIGURE 3.9 Hands-on Exercise 2 (continued)

ENHANCING A DOCUMENT 125

MICROSOFT FAX

The ***Microsoft Fax accessory*** enables you to send and receive fax messages provided you have a fax modem on your computer or local area network. The easiest way to fax an existing document is to right click the document from within My Computer or the Windows Explorer, click the Send To command, click Fax Recipient from the shortcut menu, then follow the on-screen instructions. If you are unable to load Microsoft Fax, it is most likely because it was not installed properly. Open My Computer, double click Control Panel, then double click the icon to Add/Remove programs. Click the Windows Setup tab, then check that Microsoft Exchange and Microsoft Fax are both installed.

STEP 4: The Other Documents Tab

➤ Pull down the **File menu.** Click **New** to produce the New dialog box. Click the **Other Documents tab** to display the documents shown in Figure 3.9d.

➤ Click the **Details button** to switch to the Details view to see the file name, type, size, and date of last modification.

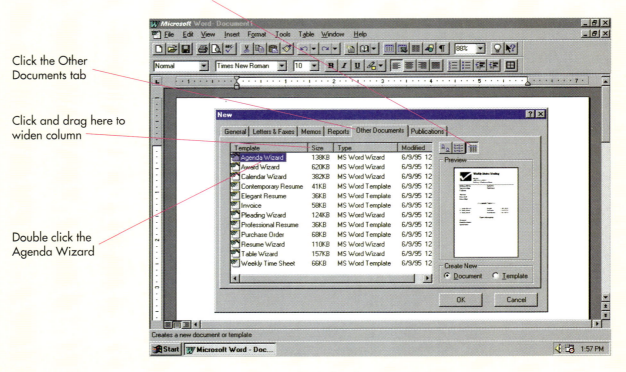

(d) The Other Documents (step 4)

FIGURE 3.9 Hands-on Exercise 2 (continued)

➤ Click and drag the vertical line between the Template and Size columns, to increase the size of the Template column, so that you can see the complete document name.

➤ Double click the **Agenda Wizard** to open the wizard and create an agenda.

STEP 5: The Agenda Wizard (continued)

➤ The Agenda Wizard asks a series of questions in order to build a template. Click the option button for the style you want—for example, **Boxes** in Figure 3.9e. Click **Next.**

➤ Enter the Date and Starting Time of the meeting. Click **Next.** Enter the main topic and location of the meeting. Click **Next.**

➤ Check (clear) the boxes corresponding to the items you want (don't want) placed on the agenda; for example, check the boxes for **Please read** and **Please bring.** Click **Next.**

➤ Check the boxes for the persons you want mentioned on the agenda; for example, check the boxes for note taker and the attendees. Click **Next.**

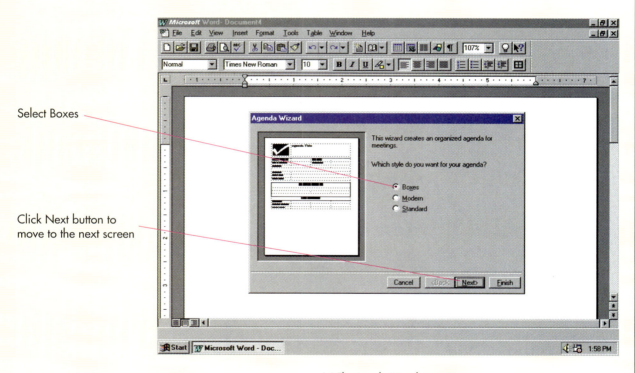

(e) The Agenda Wizard (step 5)

FIGURE 3.9 Hands-on Exercise 2 (continued)

STEP 6: The Agenda Wizard (continued)

➤ Enter the Agenda topics as shown in Figure 3.9f. Press the **Tab key** to move from one text box to the next. Click the **Next command button** when you have completed the topics.

➤ If necessary, reorder the topics by clicking the desired topic, then clicking the **Move Up** or **Move Down command button.** Click **Next** when you are satisfied with the agenda.

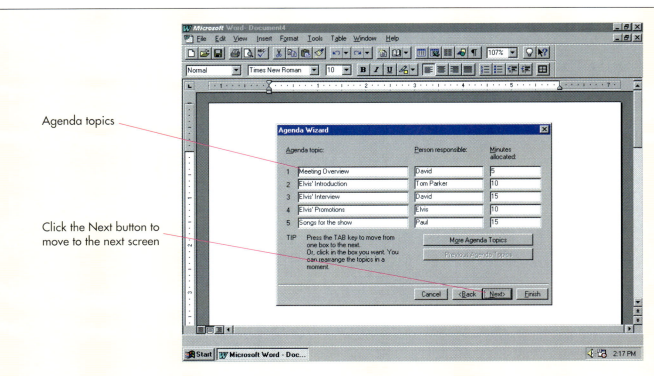

Agenda topics

Click the Next button to move to the next screen

(f) The Agenda Wizard, continued (step 6)

FIGURE 3.9 Hands-on Exercise 2 (continued)

➤ Click the **Yes** or **No button,** depending on whether or not you want a form to record the minutes of the meeting. Click **Next.**

➤ You will see a message indicating that the Agenda Wizard has all the information it needs. Click **Yes** or **No,** depending on whether or not you want to seek help as you complete the agenda.

➤ Click the **Finish command button.** Save the document as **Elvis Agenda.**

STEP 7: Complete the Agenda

➤ If necessary, change to the **Normal view** and zoom to **Page Width.** Figure 3.9g displays the agenda created by Agenda Wizard based on the answers you supplied.

➤ Complete the Agenda by entering the additional information, such as the names of the note taker and attendees as well as the specifics of what to read or bring, as shown in the figure.

➤ Save the document. Click the **Print button** on the Standard toolbar to print the completed document.

➤ Pull down the **File menu** and click the **Close command** to close the document and remain in Word.

STEP 8: Award Yourself

➤ Use the **Award Wizard** to create a certificate for yourself, citing the outstanding work you have done so far. The Award Wizard lets you choose one of four styles (formal, modern, decorative, or jazzy) in either portrait or landscape orientation. It's fun, it's easy, and you deserve it.

➤ Exit Word if you do not want to continue with the next exercise at this time.

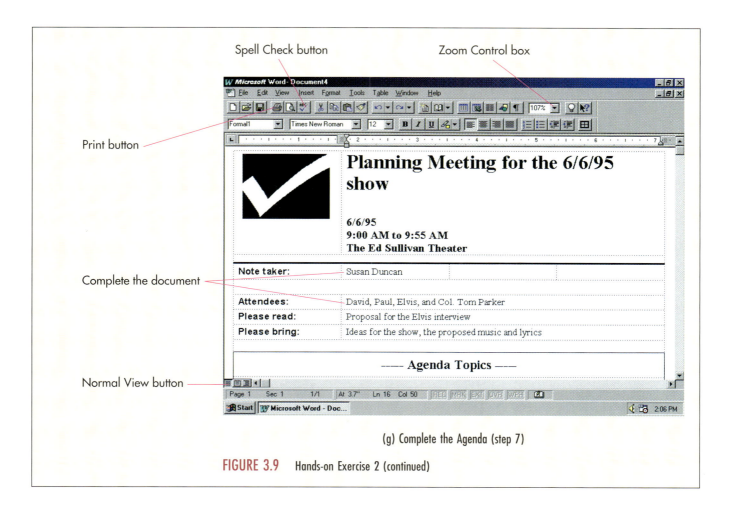

(g) Complete the Agenda (step 7)

FIGURE 3.9 Hands-on Exercise 2 (continued)

THE INSERT OBJECT COMMAND

One of the primary advantages of the Windows environment is the ability to create a *compound document* containing data from multiple applications. One way this can be accomplished is through the *Insert Object command* by which an *object* (any piece of data created by a Windows application) is embedded into a Word document.

The Microsoft Office includes not only Word, Excel, PowerPoint, and Access, but also several additional applications, including the ClipArt Gallery and Microsoft WordArt. The following discussion shows you how to insert objects created by these applications into a Word document, and in so doing, create some truly impressive documents.

Microsoft ClipArt Gallery

The right picture adds immeasurably to a document. *Clip art* (graphic images) is available from a variety of sources, including the Microsoft ClipArt Gallery, which is part of the Microsoft Office. The *ClipArt Gallery* contains more than 1,100 clip art images in 26 different categories as shown in Figure 3.10a. Select a category such as Cartoons, select an image such as the duck smashing the computer, then click the Insert command button to insert the clip art into a document.

After clip art has been inserted into a document, it should be placed into a frame to facilitate moving the image. A *frame* is a special type of (invisible) *container* that holds an object (e.g., a piece of clip art), and it provides the easiest

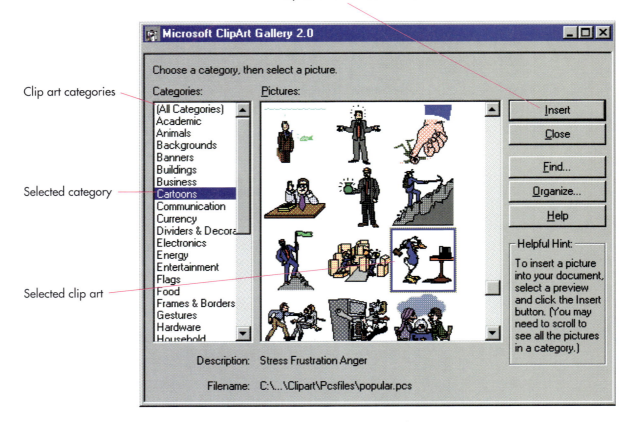

(a) The ClipArt Gallery

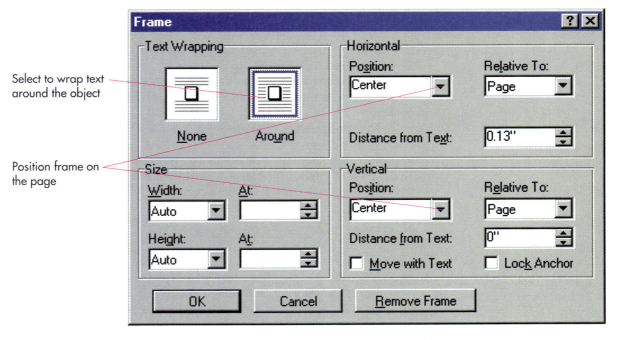

(b) Format Frame Command

FIGURE 3.10 Inserting Clip Art into a Document

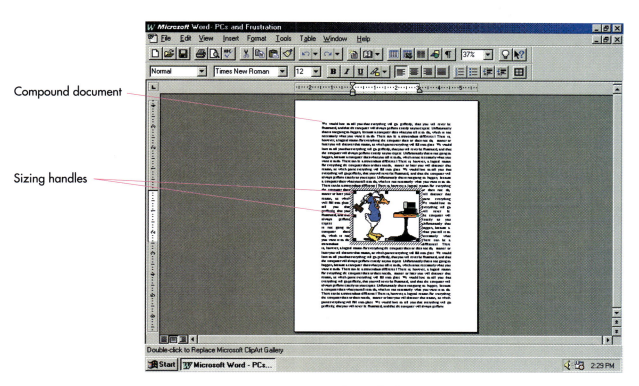

(c) The Completed Document

FIGURE 3.10   Inserting Clip Art into a Document (continued)

way to position the object within a document. Anything at all can be placed in a frame—a picture, a table, a dropped capital letter, or an object created by another application such as a spreadsheet created by Excel.

A frame (and its contents) can be dragged into position using the mouse or aligned more precisely using the ***Format Frame command*** shown in Figure 3.10b. Enclosing an object in a frame enables you to move the object freely on the page and/or wrap text around the object. Without a frame, the object is treated as an ordinary paragraph and movement is restricted to one of three positions (left, center, or right). Text cannot be wrapped around an unframed object.

Figure 3.10c displays the compound document containing text and the clip art cartoon. The text wraps around the graphic in accordance with the specifications in the Format Frame command of Figure 3.10b. The horizontal and vertical placement of the graphic is also consistent with the placement options within the command.

The graphic in Figure 3.10c is selected and surrounded by eight ***sizing handles*** that function identically in every Windows application. Click and drag any one of the four corner handles in the direction you want to go to change the length and width simultaneously and keep the graphic in proportion. Click and drag a border handle to change one dimension at a time.

Microsoft WordArt

Clip art is wonderful, but what if you cannot find an appropriate graphic? Microsoft Word anticipates this situation and includes a delightful application, ***Microsoft WordArt,*** that enables you to create special effects with text. It lets you rotate and/or flip text, display it vertically on the page, shade it, slant it, arch it, or even print it upside down.

WordArt is intuitively easy to use. In essence, you enter the text in the dialog box of Figure 3.11a, then choose a shape for the text from among the selections shown in Figure 3.11b. You can create special effects by choosing one of several different shadows as shown in Figure 3.11c. You can use any TrueType font on your system, and you can change the color of the WordArt object. Figure 3.11d shows the completed WordArt object. It's fun, it's easy, and you can create some truly dynamite documents.

(a) Enter Text

(b) Text Shapes

(c) Shadows

FIGURE 3.11 WordArt

(d) Completed Text

FIGURE 3.11   WordArt (continued)

OBJECT LINKING AND EMBEDDING

Object Linking and Embedding (OLE) enables you to create a compound document containing objects (data) from multiple Windows applications. In actuality, there are two distinct techniques, linking and embedding, and each can be implemented in different ways. OLE is one of the major benefits of working in the Windows environment, but it would be impossible to illustrate all of the techniques in a single exercise. Accordingly, we have created the icon at the left to help you identify the many examples of object linking and embedding that appear throughout the Exploring Windows series.

HANDS-ON EXERCISE 3

The ClipArt Gallery and WordArt

Objective: Enhance the appearance of a document through the Microsoft ClipArt Gallery and Microsoft WordArt. Insert an object into a frame, then move and size the frame within the document. Use Figure 3.12 as a guide in the exercise.

STEP 1: Insert Object Command
- Start Word. Open the **About the Internet** document in the Exploring Word folder. Save the document as **Modified Internet.** Check that the insertion point is at the beginning of the document.
- Pull down the **Insert menu.** Click **Object** to display the dialog box shown in Figure 3.12a. Click the **Create New tab** if necessary. (You may see a different set of object types from those in the figure, depending on the applications that are installed on your system.)
- Select the **Microsoft ClipArt Gallery.** Click **OK.**

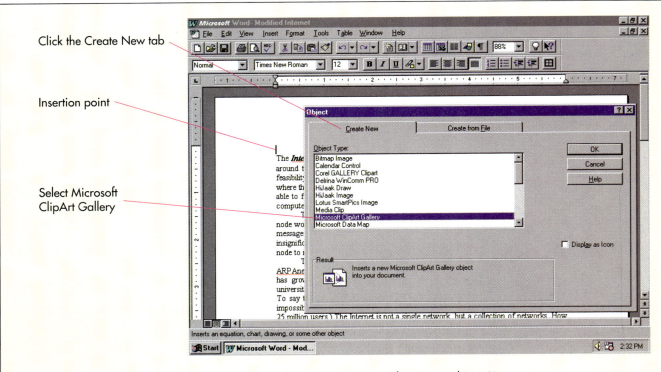

(a) Insert Object Command (step 1)

FIGURE 3.12 Hands-on Exercise 3

STEP 2: The ClipArt Gallery

➤ The dialog box for the Microsoft ClipArt Gallery should appear on your screen as shown in Figure 3.12b. Select (click) the **Maps - International** category as shown in the figure.

➤ Click the **World Map clip art image** to select the image. Click the **Insert command button** to place the clip art into your document.

➤ Click the **Save button** on the Standard toolbar to save the document.

MISSING CLIP ART

The ClipArt Gallery contains more than 1,100 clip art images in 26 different categories. If you do not see all of the clip art, it is because the clip art was not included in the original installation of Microsoft Office. Ask your instructor to reinstall the ClipArt Gallery (from the CD version of Microsoft Office) to obtain the full complement of clip art images. Be sure to include the clip art in the Value Pack folder.

STEP 3: Frame the Clip Art Object

➤ Click on the **clip art image** to select the image as indicated by the sizing handles shown in Figure 3.12c. (If you do not see the sizing handles, just point to the object and click the left mouse button.)

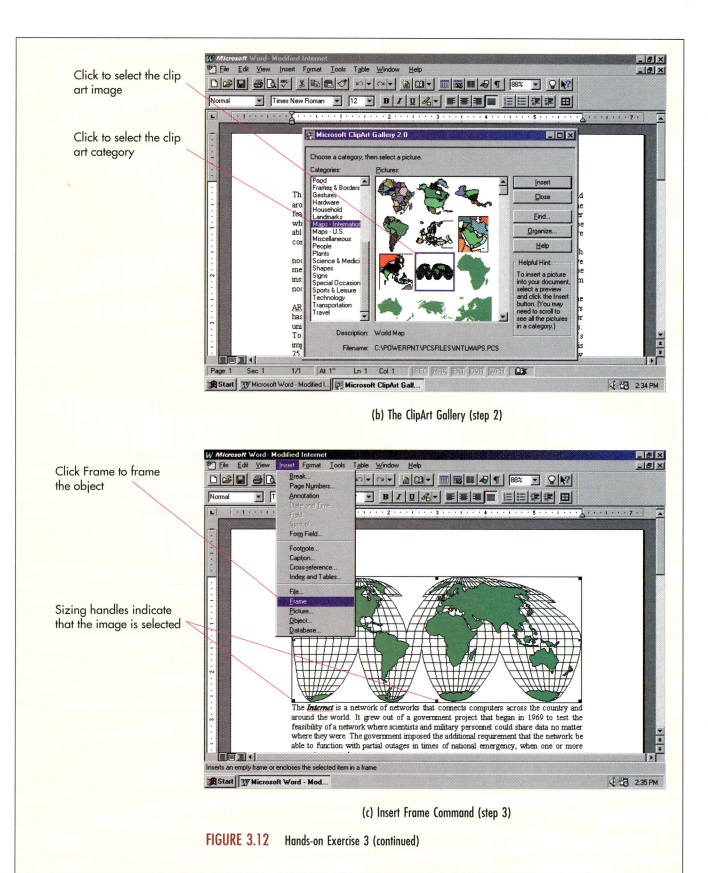

(b) The ClipArt Gallery (step 2)

(c) Insert Frame Command (step 3)

FIGURE 3.12 Hands-on Exercise 3 (continued)

➤ Pull down the **Insert menu.** Click **Frame** as shown in Figure 3.12c. The clip art will still be selected but will be surrounded by a shaded border to indicate that it is contained in a frame.

> ### USE THE RIGHT MOUSE BUTTON
>
> The easiest way to insert a frame is to use the right mouse button. Point to the clip art object, click the right mouse button to display a shortcut menu, then click the Frame Picture command. Point to the border of the newly inserted frame, click the right mouse button to display a different shortcut menu with commands appropriate to the frame, then click the Format Frame command to move and/or size the frame.

STEP 4: Move and Size the Object

➤ Pull down the **View menu** and check that you are in the Page Layout view (or click the **Page Layout button** above the status bar).

➤ Click the **drop-down arrow** in the **Zoom Control box** and change the magnification to **Whole Page.** You can see the entire document as shown in Figure 3.12d, which makes it easier to move and size the clip art.

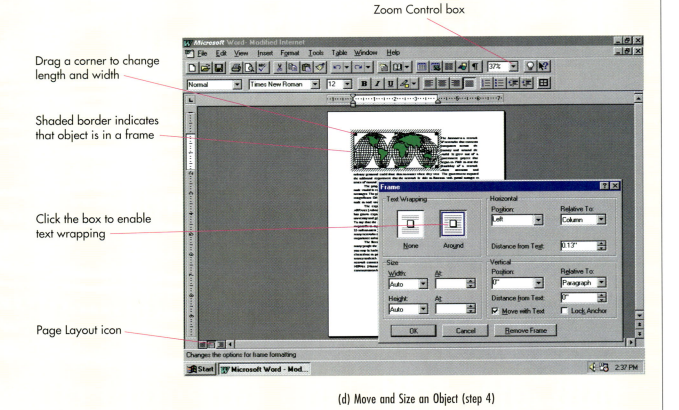

(d) Move and Size an Object (step 4)

FIGURE 3.12 Hands-on Exercise 3 (continued)

- Size the frame within the document:
  - Drag a corner handle (the mouse pointer changes to a double arrow) to change the length and width of the frame simultaneously and keep the graphic in proportion.
  - Drag a handle on the horizontal or vertical border to change one dimension only (which distorts the object in the frame).
- Point to a border of the clip art, click the **right mouse button** to display a shortcut menu, then click the **Format Frame** command from the resulting shortcut menu.
- Click the box to wrap text around the object as shown in Figure 3.12d. (You must allow at least one inch of text on each side of the object if you want to wrap text on both sides.) Click **OK.**
- Position the graphic along the right margin at the top of the second paragraph. (You can use the Format Frame command instead of the mouse for more precision.)
- Save the document.

TO CLICK OR DOUBLE CLICK

Clicking an object selects the object and produces the sizing handles to move and/or size the object. Double clicking an object loads the application that created the object and enables you to modify the object using that application.

STEP 5: Change the Clip Art
- Double click the **clip art image** to reload the ClipArt Gallery as shown in Figure 3.12e.
- Select (click) a different image such as the globe of the **Western hemisphere.** Click the **Insert command button** to insert the new image in place of the existing image.
- The frame in which the clip art image is contained retains its approximate position within the document. The size of the image has changed due to the different shape. Move and/or size the image as desired.
- Save the document.

FIND THE RIGHT CLIP ART

The Find command within the ClipArt Gallery enables you to search for clip art images containing specific text in their description. Some searches yield fruitful results such as a search on the word "computer," which returns multiple images in several categories. Other searches are less productive because there is less clip art. To initiate a search, click the Find button, click the down arrow on the description box, click and drag over the current contents in the Description box, then enter the desired text (e.g., "soccer"). Click the Find Now command button, then click the Insert button to insert the found image into a document.

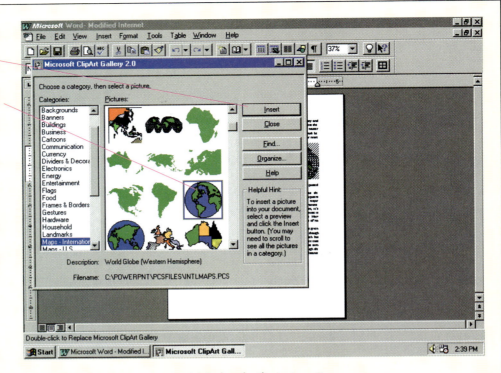

Click here to insert the new image, replacing the original one

Click to select a different clip art image

(e) Replace the Clip Art (step 5)

FIGURE 3.12 Hands-on Exercise 3 (continued)

STEP 6: WordArt

➤ Press **Ctrl+Home** to move to the beginning of the document. Pull down the **Insert menu** and click **Object** to produce the Insert Object dialog box.

➤ If necessary, click the **Create New tab,** then scroll until you can select **Microsoft WordArt 2.0** from the Object Type list box. Click **OK.**

➤ You should see a screen similar to Figure 3.12f. Type **About the Internet** as shown in the figure. Click **Update Display.**

➤ Click the **down arrow** on the **Shapes list box.** Click the **Deflate shape** as shown in Figure 3.12f. The shape of the text changes to match the shape you selected.

➤ Pull down the **Format menu** and click **Shadow** (or click the **Shadow button** on the WordArt toolbar) to display the available shadow effects. Choose (click) the effect that appeals to you. Click **OK.**

➤ Pull down the **Format menu** a second time. Click **Shading.** Choose a different foreground color (e.g., blue) and a different shading pattern. Click **OK.**

➤ Pull down the **Format menu** a third and final time and (if necessary) click the **Stretch to Frame** command. This ensures that the WordArt object will maintain its size and shape within its frame.

➤ Click outside the WordArt to deselect the object and return to Word.

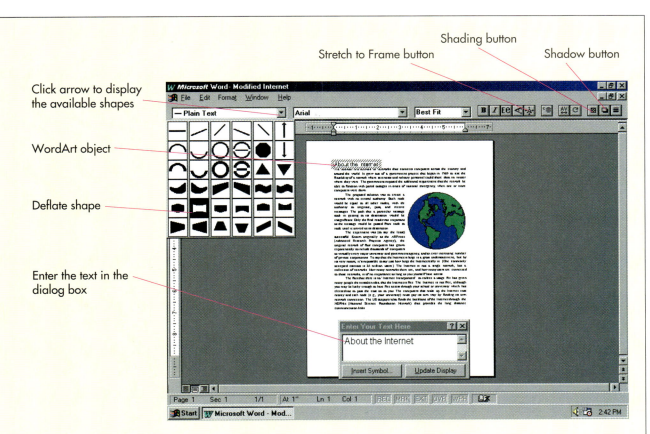

(f) WordArt (step 6)

FIGURE 3.12   Hands-on Exercise 3 (continued)

IN-PLACE EDITING

In-place editing enables you to double click a WordArt object within a Word document to edit the embedded object. You remain in Word (the client application), but the toolbar and pull-down menus are those of WordArt (the server application). The File menu is an exception and contains Word commands in order to save the compound document containing the embedded object.

STEP 7: Frame the WordArt Object

➤ The WordArt object should be selected with the sizing handles displayed. Pull down the **Insert menu** and click **Frame** (or right click the object to display the shortcut menu from where you can click the Frame Picture command).

➤ Move and/or size the WordArt frame to match the document in Figure 3.12g.

➤ Save the completed document. Print the completed document and submit it to your instructor as proof that you did the exercise. Exit Word.

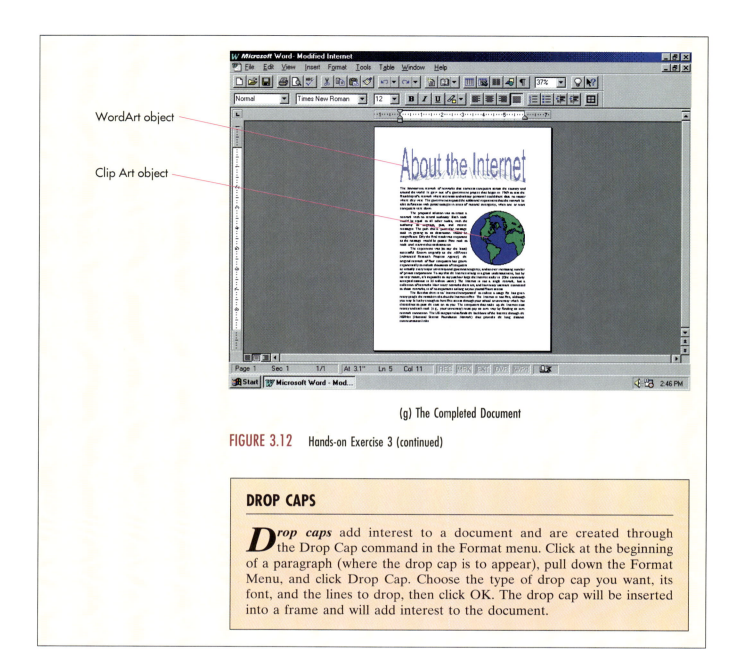

(g) The Completed Document

FIGURE 3.12 Hands-on Exercise 3 (continued)

DROP CAPS

Drop caps add interest to a document and are created through the Drop Cap command in the Format menu. Click at the beginning of a paragraph (where the drop cap is to appear), pull down the Format Menu, and click Drop Cap. Choose the type of drop cap you want, its font, and the lines to drop, then click OK. The drop cap will be inserted into a frame and will add interest to the document.

SUMMARY

The spell check compares the words in a document to those in a standard and/or custom dictionary. It will detect misspellings, duplicated phrases, and/or irregular capitalization, but will not flag properly spelled words that are used incorrectly.

The thesaurus suggests synonyms and/or antonyms. It can also recognize multiple forms of a word (noun, verb, and adjective) and offers suggestions for each. The grammar check searches for mistakes in punctuation, writing style, and word usage, by comparing strings of text within a document to a series of predefined rules.

An envelope is based on a different physical document from the letter it will contain. Microsoft Word saves you the trouble of having to change margins and orientation by providing the Envelopes and Labels command in the Tools menu.

The Insert Date and Time command places the date and/or time into a document either as a specific value or as a field. The latter is updated automatically whenever the document is opened in the Page Layout view or when it is printed.

The Insert Symbol command provides easy access to special characters, making it easy to place typographic characters into a document. Many special symbols are found in the Normal text, Wingdings, and Symbol fonts. All TrueType fonts are scaleable and may be displayed in any point size.

Wizards and templates help create professionally designed documents with a minimum of time and effort. A template is a partially completed document that contains formatting and other information. A wizard is an interactive program that creates a customized template based on the answers you supply.

One of the primary advantages of the Windows environment is the ability to create a compound document—that is, a document containing data from multiple applications. This can be accomplished through the Insert Object command where an object (any piece of data created by a Windows application) is inserted into a Word document.

The ClipArt Gallery contains more than 1,100 clip art images in 26 different categories. Microsoft WordArt enables you to add special effects to text. Each object (e.g., a clip art image or WordArt text) should be placed into a frame to facilitate moving it within a document. A frame (and its contents) can be dragged into position using the mouse or aligned more precisely using the dialog box within the Format Frame command. It can be sized by dragging the sizing handles.

KEY WORDS AND CONCEPTS

Agenda Wizard	Field code	Microsoft Fax accessory
Award Wizard	Field result	Microsoft WordArt
Calendar Wizard	Format Frame command	Object
Clip Art	Frame	Résumé Wizard
ClipArt Gallery	Grammar check	Sizing handle
Compound document	In-place editing	Spell check
Container	Insert Date and Time command	Template
Date field	Insert Frame command	Thesaurus
Drop Cap	Insert Object command	Wizard
Envelopes and Labels command	Insert Symbol command	WordArt
Fax Wizard		
Field		

MULTIPLE CHOICE

1. Which of the following will be detected by the spell check?
    (a) Duplicate words
    (b) Irregular capitalization
    (c) Both (a) and (b)
    (d) Neither (a) nor (b)

2. Which of the following is true about the thesaurus?
   (a) It recognizes different forms of a word such as a noun and a verb
   (b) It provides antonyms as well as synonyms
   (c) Both (a) and (b)
   (d) Neither (a) nor (b)

3. Which of the following is true about the Insert Symbol command?
   (a) It can insert a symbol in different type sizes
   (b) It can access any font installed on the system
   (c) Both (a) and (b)
   (d) Neither (a) nor (b)

4. Which of the following is true about the date field?
   (a) It is equivalent to typing the current date except that it is faster
   (b) It may be displayed during editing as either a field code or a field result
   (c) It may be displayed in only one format
   (d) All of the above are true

5. The grammar check:
   (a) Implements the identical rules for casual and business writing
   (b) Can be customized to include (omit) specific rules
   (c) Is run automatically in conjunction with a spell check
   (d) All of the above

6. The easiest way to create an envelope is to:
   (a) Use the Envelopes and Labels command in the Tools menu
   (b) Use the Envelopes command in the Insert menu
   (c) Change the margins and orientation using the Page Setup command in the File menu
   (d) All of the above are equally easy to implement

7. Which of the following is a true statement about wizards?
   (a) They are accessed through the New command in the File menu
   (b) They always produce a finished document
   (c) Both (a) and (b)
   (d) Neither (a) nor (b)

8. How do you access the wizards built into Microsoft Word?
   (a) Pull down the Wizards and Templates menu
   (b) Pull down the Insert menu and choose Wizards and Templates
   (c) Pull down the File menu and choose the New command
   (d) None of the above

9. Which of the following is true regarding wizards and templates?
   (a) A wizard may create a template
   (b) A template may create a wizard
   (c) Both (a) and (b)
   (d) Neither (a) nor (b)

10. Which of the following is controlled by the Format Frame command?
    (a) The horizontal and/or vertical placement of the frame
    (b) Wrapping (not wrapping) text around the framed object
    (c) Both (a) and (b)
    (d) Neither (a) nor (b)

11. What is the difference between clicking and double clicking an object?
    (a) Clicking selects the object; double clicking opens the application that created the object
    (b) Double clicking selects the object; clicking opens the application that created the object
    (c) Clicking changes to Normal view; double clicking changes to Page Layout view
    (d) Double clicking changes to Normal view; clicking changes to Page Layout view

12. The Microsoft ClipArt Gallery:
    (a) Is accessed through the Object command in the Insert menu
    (b) Is available to every application in the Microsoft Office
    (c) Enables you to search for a specific piece of ClipArt by specifying a key word in the description of the clip art
    (d) All of the above

13. Which view, and which magnification, offers the most convenient way to position a graphic within a document?
    (a) Page Width in the Page Layout view
    (b) Full Page in the Page Layout view
    (c) Page Width in the Normal view
    (d) Full Page in the Normal view

14. How do you frame a graphic object?
    (a) Click to select the object, pull down the Insert menu, and choose the Frame command
    (b) Right click the object, then select the Frame Picture command from the shortcut menu
    (c) Both (a) and (b)
    (d) Neither (a) nor (b)

15. How do you insert a date into a document so that the date is automatically updated when the document is retrieved?
    (a) Type the date manually
    (b) Use the Date and Time command in the Insert menu and clear the box to insert the date as a field
    (c) Use the Insert Date and Time command in the Insert menu and check the box to insert the date as a field
    (d) It cannot be done

ANSWERS

1. c	**6.** a	**11.** a
2. c	**7.** a	**12.** d
3. c	**8.** c	**13.** b
4. b	**9.** a	**14.** c
5. b	**10.** c	**15.** c

Exploring Microsoft Word

1. Use Figure 3.13 to match each action with its result; a given action may be used more than once or not at all.

   Action
   a. Click at 1
   b. Click at 2
   c. Click at 10, then click at 3
   d. Click at 4
   e. Click at 11, then click at 5
   f. Click at 7, then click at 6
   g. Click and drag at 8
   h. Click and drag at 9
   i. Double click at 9
   j. Click at 12

   Result
   ____ Insert the current date into the masthead
   ____ Spell check the document
   ____ Add a drop cap to the first paragraph
   ____ Save the document
   ____ Change the view to Whole Page
   ____ Move the clip art image
   ____ Size the clip art image
   ____ Change to a different clip art image
   ____ Find a synonym for "network"
   ____ Create a fax cover sheet

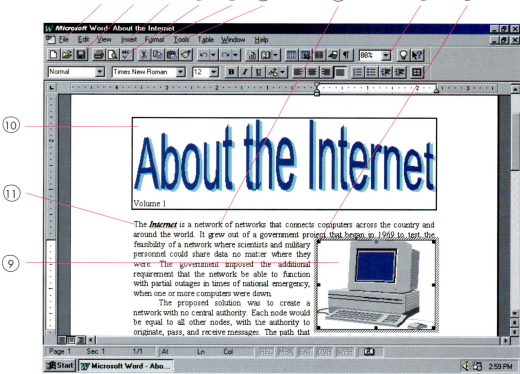

FIGURE 3.13 Screen for Problem 1

2. The need to check a document: The human eye is generally uncritical and sees what it wants or expects to see. For example, read the sentence in the box below, once, and only once, counting the number of times the letter "F" appears in the sentence.

Finished files are the result of years of scientific study combined with the experience of years

The average person spots only three or four, and you can feel reasonably proud if you found all six. Our point in this seemingly trivial exercise is that our eyes are less discriminating than we would like to believe, allowing misspellings and simple typos to go unnoticed. Use the spell check in every document!

3. The grammar check: Answer the following with respect to the screen in Figure 3.14:
   a. Which command displayed the dialog box in the figure?
   b. Which options are currently in effect? How do you change these settings?
   c. What is a cliché? How was the explanation displayed in the figure?
   d. What is a homonym? Will the grammar check look for homonyms?
   e. What is the effect of clicking the drop down arrow in the Use Grammar and Styles Rules list box?
   f. What is the effect of clicking the Grammar option button?
   g. What happens if you click the OK command button? the Cancel command button?

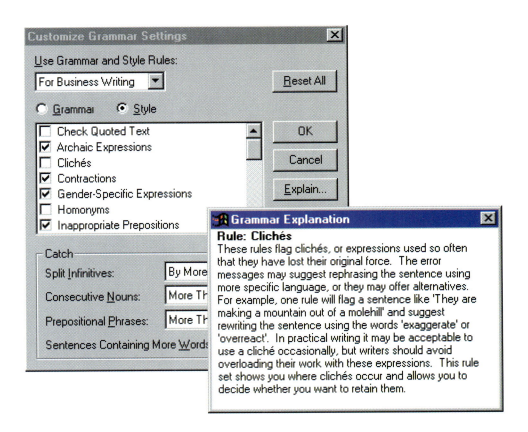

FIGURE 3.14   Screen for Problem 3

4. Answer the following with respect to the screen in Figure 3.15:
   a. Which command displayed the dialog box in the figure?
   b. Which font is selected? Which character is selected?
   c. How do you insert the selected character into the current document? What is the shortcut key to insert the character?
   d. How do you insert the copyright, registered, and trademark (©, ®, and ™) symbols into a document?
   e. What is a nonbreaking space? When would you want to insert this special character into a document?

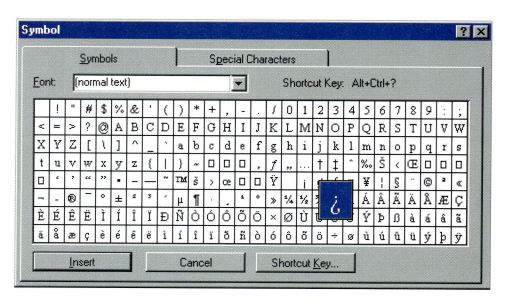

FIGURE 3.15 Screen for Problem 4

Practice with Microsoft Word

1. Figure 3.16 contains the draft version of the *Chapter 3 Practice 1* document contained on the data disk.
   a. Proofread the document and circle any mistakes in spelling, grammar, capitalization, or punctuation.

All documents should be thoroughly proofed before they be printed and distributed. This means that documents, at a minimum should be spell cheked,, grammar cheked, and proof read by the author. A documents that has spelling errors and/or grammatical errors makes the Author look unprofessional and illiterate and their is nothing worse than allowing a first impression too be won that makes you appear slopy and disinterested, and a document full or of misteakes will do exactly that. Alot of people do not not realize how damaging a bad first impression could be, and documents full of misteakes has cost people oppurtunities that they trained and prepared many years for.

FIGURE 3.16 Document for Practice with Word Exercise 1

b. Open the document in Word and run the spell check. Did Word catch any mistakes you missed? Did you find any errors that were missed by the program?

c. Use the thesaurus to come up with alternate words for *document*, which appears entirely too often within the paragraph.

d. Run the grammar check on the revised document. Did the program catch any grammatical errors you missed? Did you find any mistakes that were missed by the program?

e. Add your name to the revised document, save it, print it, and submit the completed document to your instructor.

f. Submit a title page with this assignment using WordArt, the ClipArt Gallery, or the Insert Symbol command to create a unique design.

2. Inserting Objects: Figure 3.17 illustrates a flyer that we created for a hypothetical computer sale. We embedded clip art and WordArt and created what we believe is an attractive flyer. Try to duplicate our advertisement, or better yet, create your own. Include your name somewhere in the document as a sales associate. Be sure to spell check your ad, then print the completed flyer and submit it to your instructor.

3. Exploring TrueType: Installing Windows 95 also installs several TrueType fonts, which in turn are accessible from any application. Two of the fonts, Symbol and Wingdings, contain a variety of special characters that can be used to create some unusual documents. Use the Insert Symbol command, your imagination, and the fact that TrueType fonts are scaleable to any point size, to recreate the documents in Figure 3.18. Better yet, use your imagination to create your own documents.

4. It's easier than it looks: The document in Figure 3.19 was created to illustrate the automatic formatting and correction facilities that are built into Microsoft Word. We want you to create the document, include your name at the bottom, then submit the completed document to your instructor as proof that you did the exercise. All you have to do is follow the instructions within the document and let Word do the formatting and correcting for you.

The only potential difficulty is that the options on your system may be set to negate some of the features to which we refer. Accordingly, you need to pull down the Tools menu, click the Options command, click the Auto-Format tab, then click the AutoFormat As You Type option button in order to verify that the options referenced in the document are in effect. You also need to review the table of predefined substitutions in the AutoCorrect command (pull down the Tools menu and click the AutoCorrect command) to learn the typewritten characters that will trigger the smiley faces, copyright, and registered trademark substitutions.

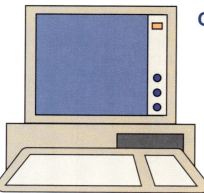

Computer World's Annual Pre-Inventory Sale

When: Saturday, October 21, 1995
8:00AM - 10:00 PM

Where: 13640 South Dixie Highway

Computer World

Computers
Printers
Fax/Modems
CD-ROM drives
Sound systems
Software
Etc.

Pre-Inventory Sale

Sales Associate: Bianca Costo

FIGURE 3.17   Document for Practice with Word Exercise 2

Valentine's Day
We'll serenade your sweetheart
Call 284-LOVE

STUDENT COMPUTER LAB
Fall Semester Hours

FIGURE 3.18 Documents for Practice with Word Exercise 3

It's Easier Than It Looks

This document was created to demonstrate the AutoCorrect and AutoFormat features that are built into Microsoft Word. In essence, you type as you always did and enter traditional characters, then let Word perform its "magic" by substituting symbols and other formatting for you. Among the many features included in these powerful commands are the:

1. Automatic creation of numbered lists by typing a number followed by a period, tab, or right parenthesis. Just remember to press the return key twice to turn off this feature.
2. Symbols for common fractions such as ½ or ¼.
3. Ordinal numbers with superscripts created automatically such as 1st, 2nd, or 3rd.
4. Copyright © and Registered trademark ® symbols.

AutoFormat will even add a border to a paragraph any time you type three or more hyphens, equal signs, or underscores on a line by itself.

===
_____

And finally, the AutoCorrect feature has built-in substitution for smiley faces that look best when set in a larger point size such as 72 points.

FIGURE 3.19   Document for Practice with Word Exercise 4

Case Studies

The Letterhead

A well-designed letterhead adds impact to your correspondence. Collect samples of professional stationery, then design your own letterhead, including your name, address, phone, and any other information you deem relevant. Include a fax number and/or e-mail address as appropriate. Use your imagination and design the letterhead for your planned career. Try different fonts and/or the Format Border command to add horizontal line(s) under the text. Consider a graphic logo, but keep it simple. You might also want to decrease the top margin so that the letterhead prints closer to the top of the page. Submit the completed letterhead for entry into a class contest.

An Ad for Travel

The ClipArt Gallery includes the maps and flags of many foreign countries. It also has maps of all 50 states as well as pictures of many landmarks. Design a one-page flyer for a place you want to visit, in the United States or abroad. Collect the assignments, then ask your instructor to hold a contest to decide the most appealing document. It's fun, it's easy, and it's educational. Bon voyage!

The Cover Page

Use WordArt and/or the ClipArt Gallery to create a truly original cover page that you can use with all of your assignments. The cover page should include the title of the assignment, your name, course information, and date. (Insert the date as a field so that it will be updated automatically every time you retrieve the document.) The formatting is up to you. Print the completed cover page and submit it to your instructor, then use the cover page for all future assignments.

A Junior Year Abroad

How lucky can you get? You are spending the second half of your junior year in Paris. The problem is you will have to submit your work in French, and the English version of Microsoft Word won't do. Is there a foreign language version available? What about the dictionary and thesaurus? How do you enter the accented characters that occur so frequently? You are leaving in two months, so you had better get busy. What are your options? Bon voyage.

THE PROFESSIONAL DOCUMENT: FOOTNOTES, TABLES, AND STYLES

OBJECTIVES

After reading this chapter you will be able to:

1. Create a bulleted or numbered list; change the default character in either type of list.
2. Enter and/or edit footnotes and endnotes in a document.
3. Explain conceptually the use of the tables feature; create a table and insert it into a document.
4. Explain conceptually how styles automate the formatting process and provide a consistent appearance to common elements in a document.
5. Use the AutoFormat command to apply styles to an existing document; create, modify, and apply a style to selected elements of a document.
6. Define a section; explain how section formatting differs from character and paragraph formatting.
7. Create a header and/or a footer; establish different headers or footers for the first, odd, or even pages in the same document.
8. Insert page numbers into a document; use the Edit menu's Go To command to move directly to a specific page in a document.
9. Create and update a table of contents.

OVERVIEW

This chapter presents a series of features that give a document a professional look. It contains a wealth of information that will be especially useful the next time you have to write a term paper with specific formatting requirements. We show you how to insert footnotes and endnotes and how to convert one type of note to the other. We show you how to create a bulleted or numbered list to emphasize important items within a paper. We also introduce the tables feature, which is one of the most powerful features in Microsoft Word. Tables provide an easy way to arrange text, numbers, and/or graphics.

The second half of the chapter develops the use of styles, or sets of formatting instructions that provide a consistent appearance to similar elements in a document. We describe the AutoFormat command that assigns styles to an existing document and greatly simplifies the formatting process. We show you how to create a new style, how to modify an existing style, and how to apply those styles to text within a document. We also discuss several items associated with longer documents, such as page numbers, headers and footers, and a table of contents.

The chapter contains four hands-on exercises to apply the material at the computer. This is one more exercise than our earlier chapters, but we think you will appreciate the practical application of these very important capabilities within Microsoft Word.

BULLETS AND LISTS

A list helps to organize information by emphasizing important topics. A ***bulleted list*** emphasizes (and separates) the items. A ***numbered list*** sequences (and prioritizes) the items and is automatically updated to accommodate additions or deletions to the list. Either type of list could be created through normal formatting operations, but Microsoft Word facilitates the process through implementation of the ***Bullets and Numbering command*** within the Format menu. Execution of the command displays the Bullets and Numbering dialog box shown in Figure 4.1.

The tabs within the Bullets and Numbering dialog box enable you to specify the precise appearance of either type of list. Different bullets may be chosen as shown in Figure 4.1a, or different numbering schemes as in Figure 4.1b. A hanging indent may be specified for either type of list. Additional flexibility is provided by clicking the Modify command button in either dialog box to change the distance between the numbers or bullets and the associated text, and/or to modify the bullet or number style or appearance.

Bullets and numbering is implemented at the paragraph level and is illustrated in a hands-on exercise which follows shortly.

> ### AUTOMATIC CREATION OF A NUMBERED LIST
>
> Word will automatically create a numbered list any time you begin a line with a number or letter, followed by a period, tab, or right parenthesis, then continue with additional text on that line. Pressing the enter key at the end of the line or paragraph automatically generates the next sequential number or letter in the list. (Press the enter key twice to terminate the list.) To turn the autonumbering feature on or off, pull down the Tools menu, click Options, click the AutoFormat tab, then click the AutoFormat As You Type option button. Check (clear) the box for Automatic Numbered lists.

FOOTNOTES AND ENDNOTES

Every academic discipline has specific rules for incorporating footnotes or endnotes within a document. A ***footnote*** provides additional information about an item, such as its source, and appears at the bottom of the page where the reference occurs. An ***endnote*** is similar in concept but appears at the end of a document. A horizontal line separates the notes from the rest of the document.

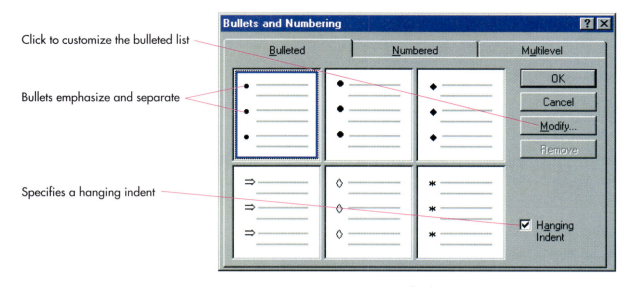

(a) Bulleted List

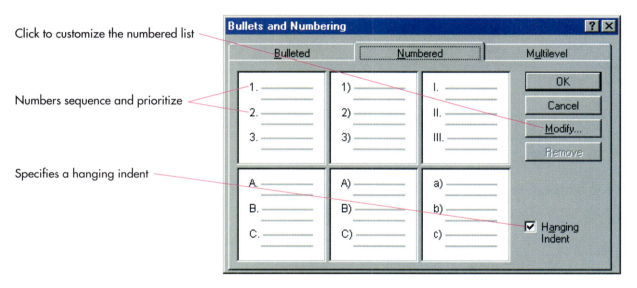

(b) Numbered List

FIGURE 4.1 Lists

The ***Insert Footnote command*** inserts a note into a document, and automatically assigns the next sequential number to that note. To create a note, position the insertion point where you want the reference, pull down the Insert menu, click Footnote to display the dialog box in Figure 4.2a, then choose either the Footnote or Endnote option button. A superscript reference is inserted into the document, and you will be positioned at the bottom of the page (a footnote) or at the end of the document (an endnote), where you enter the text of the note.

The Options command button in the Footnote and Endnote dialog box enables you to modify the formatting of either type of note as shown in Figure 4.2b. You can change the numbering format (e.g., to Roman numerals) and/or start numbering from a number other than one. You can also convert footnotes to endnotes or vice versa.

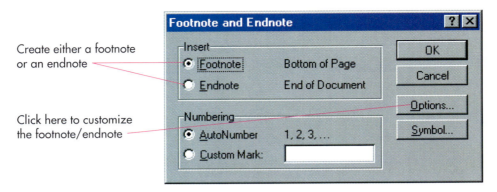

(a) Footnotes and Endnotes

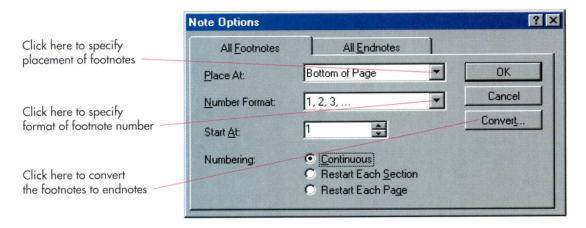

(b) Options

FIGURE 4.2 Footnotes and Endnotes

The Insert Footnote command is quite powerful and adjusts for last-minute changes, either in your writing or in your professor's requirements. It will, for example, renumber all existing notes to accommodate the addition or deletion of a footnote or endnote. [Existing notes are moved (or deleted) within a document by moving (deleting) the reference mark rather than the text of the footnote.]

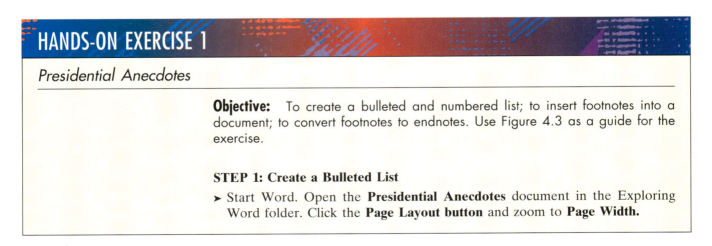

HANDS-ON EXERCISE 1

Presidential Anecdotes

Objective: To create a bulleted and numbered list; to insert footnotes into a document; to convert footnotes to endnotes. Use Figure 4.3 as a guide for the exercise.

STEP 1: Create a Bulleted List

➤ Start Word. Open the **Presidential Anecdotes** document in the Exploring Word folder. Click the **Page Layout button** and zoom to **Page Width.**

- Save the document as **Modified Presidential Anecdotes** so you can return to the original document if necessary.
- Click and drag to select the names of the presidents as shown in Figure 4.3a.
- Pull down the **Format menu.** Click **Bullets and Numbering.** If necessary, click the **Bulleted tab** to display the dialog box in the figure.
- Choose (click) a bullet style. Click **OK** to create the bulleted list and close the Bullets and Numbering dialog box.
- Check that the bulleted list is still selected. Click the **Bullets button** on the Standard toolbar to toggle the bullets off. Click the **Bullets button** a second time to restore the bullets.
- Click the **Increase Indent** button on the Formatting toolbar to indent the list to the next tab stop.

THE RIGHT MOUSE BUTTON

The right mouse button is the fastest way to access the Bullets and Numbering dialog box. Click and drag to select the items in a list, click the right mouse button to display a shortcut menu, then click the Bullets and Numbering command to display the dialog box. Click the appropriate tab (Bulleted or Numbered), click the style you want, then click the OK button to implement the list and close the dialog box.

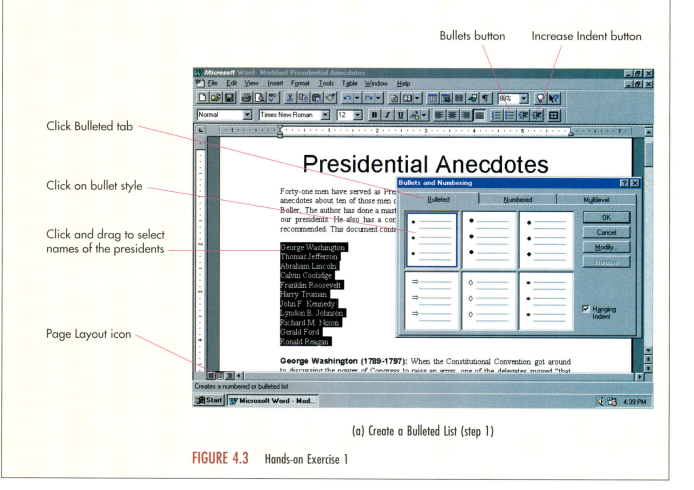

(a) Create a Bulleted List (step 1)

FIGURE 4.3 Hands-on Exercise 1

STEP 2: Create a Numbered List

➤ Check that the entire list is still selected. Click the **Numbering button** on the Formatting toolbar to convert the bulleted list to a numbered list.

➤ Click outside the list to deselect it. Click and drag to select **Franklin Roosevelt** as shown in Figure 4.3b. (You cannot select the number, only the text.)

➤ Press the **Del key** to erase the selected text, which automatically renumbers the rest of the list. (You may or may not have to press the **Del key** a second time to erase the number 5, depending on whether or not the paragraph mark was selected when you deleted Franklin Roosevelt.)

LISTS AND THE FORMATTING TOOLBAR

The Bullets and Numbering buttons on the Formatting toolbar facilitate the creation of either type of list. Click the Bullets button to create a bulleted list from selected items or to convert a numbered list to a bulleted list. Click the Numbering button to create a numbered list or to convert a bulleted list to numbers. The Bullets and Numbering buttons also function as toggle switches; for example, clicking the Bullets button when a bulleted list is already in effect will remove the bullets.

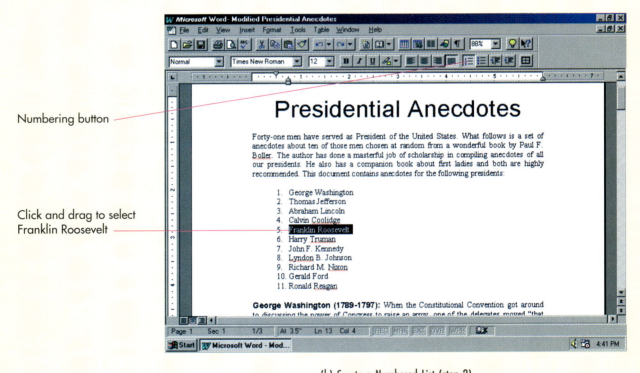

(b) Create a Numbered List (step 2)

FIGURE 4.3 Hands-on Exercise 1 (continued)

STEP 3: Create a Footnote

➤ Click the **drop-down arrow** on the **Zoom Control box** then click **Whole Page** to view the page before the footnotes are added. Click the **drop-down arrow** on the **Zoom Control box** a second time and click **Page Width** to facilitate the addition of the footnotes.

➤ Click immediately after the period following Paul Boller's name (the last word in the second sentence).

➤ Pull down the **Insert menu.** Click **Footnote** to display the Footnote and Endnote dialog box in Figure 4.3c.

➤ Click the **Footnote option button** as shown in the figure. Click **OK** to insert a footnote and close the dialog box.

➤ The insertion point moves automatically to the bottom of the page, where you will enter the text of the footnote. The existing footnotes are renumbered automatically to accommodate the new footnote.

➤ Type the text of the footnote, **Paul F. Boller, Jr.,** ***Presidential Anecdotes,*** **Penguin Books (New York, NY, 1981).** Be sure to italicize the title of the book in your footnote.

➤ Save the document.

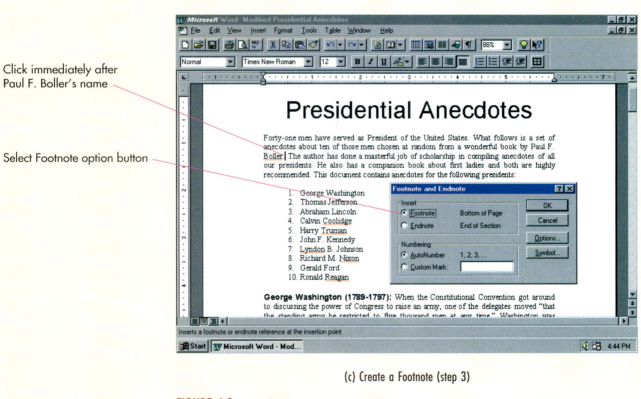

(c) Create a Footnote (step 3)

FIGURE 4.3   Hands-on Exercise 1 (continued)

FOOTNOTES AND STYLES

You can change the formatting (e.g., the font and point size) for individual footnotes just as you can change the formatting of any other element in a document. You can also change the formatting for all footnotes by changing the predefined style for the footnote text or reference. See the discussion on styles beginning on page 172 for additional information.

STEP 4: Renumber a Footnote

➤ The anecdotes in this document are out of chronological order in that Abraham Lincoln comes before Thomas Jefferson when it should be the other way around. The associated footnotes (Lincoln is currently number 3 and Jefferson is number 4) will be renumbered automatically when the associated text is moved. Thus:

- Select the paragraph containing the Lincoln anecdote (together with the blank line above the paragraph) as shown in Figure 4.3d.
- Drag the selected text below the anecdote for Thomas Jefferson. Release the mouse. The footnote for the Lincoln anecdote is renumbered to 4. The number of the Jefferson footnote changes to 3.

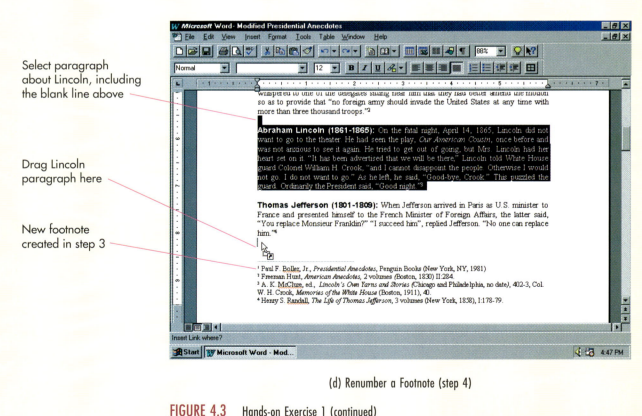

(d) Renumber a Footnote (step 4)

FIGURE 4.3 Hands-on Exercise 1 (continued)

➤ Click the **Undo button** to cancel the move. The Lincoln and Jefferson footnotes return to their original numbers, 3 and 4, respectively. Click the **Redo button** to restore the move and place the footnotes in their proper order.

➤ Save the document.

> ### THE WRONG VIEW
>
> Footnotes are visible only in the Page Layout view. Hence if you do not see a footnote, it is probably because you are in the wrong view, the Normal View, as opposed to the Page Layout view. Pull down the View menu and click the Page Layout command, or click the Page Layout button above the status bar. To edit (view) footnotes in the Normal view, double click the footnote reference mark, or pull down the View menu and click Footnote.

STEP 5: Delete a Footnote

➤ Click and drag to select the text of the second footnote as shown in Figure 4.3e. Press the **Del key** (in an attempt) to delete the footnote.

➤ The action is invalid and an error message appears. Click **OK** (or press **Esc**) to close the informational dialog box and continue working.

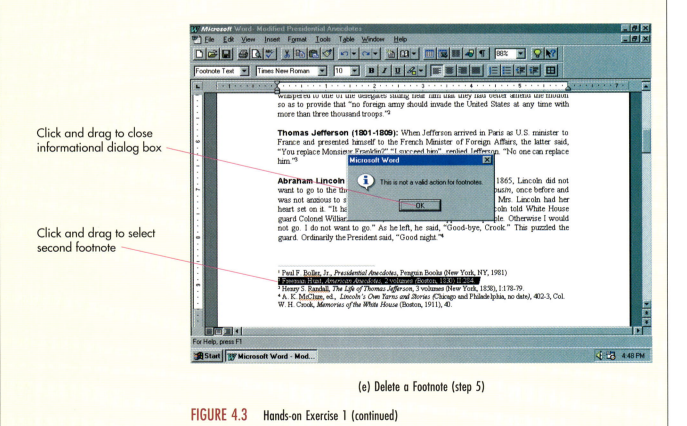

(e) Delete a Footnote (step 5)

FIGURE 4.3   Hands-on Exercise 1 (continued)

THE PROFESSIONAL DOCUMENT

➤ Click and drag to select the reference mark for the second footnote. Press the **Del key.** The text for the second footnote is deleted, and the existing footnotes are renumbered.

➤ Click the **Undo button** to cancel the deletion as we want the footnote to remain. You now know that a footnote is deleted (or moved) by deleting (or moving) the reference mark rather than the text of the footnote.

STEP 6: Convert Footnotes to Endnotes

➤ Pull down **Insert menu.** Click **Footnote** to display the Footnote and Endnote dialog box. Click the **Options command button** to display the Note Options dialog box in Figure 4.3f.

➤ Click the **Convert command button** to display the Convert Notes dialog box. (Your dialog boxes may be positioned differently from those in the figure.)

➤ Click the option button to **Convert All Footnotes to Endnotes.** Click **OK** to implement the conversion and close the Convert Notes dialog box. Click **OK** to close the Note Options dialog box.

➤ Click **Close** to exit the Footnotes and Endnotes dialog box.

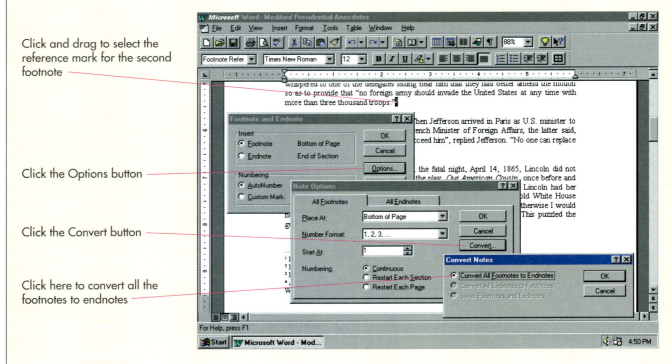

Click and drag to select the reference mark for the second footnote

Click the Options button

Click the Convert button

Click here to convert all the footnotes to endnotes

(f) Convert Footnotes to Endnotes (step 6)

FIGURE 4.3 Hands-on Exercise 1 (continued)

STEP 7: The Completed Document

➤ Press **Ctrl+end** to move to the end of the document, after the last anecdote but before the first endnote.

➤ Press **Ctrl+enter** to insert a page break. Type **References** in 24 point Arial. Click the **Center button** on the Formatting toolbar to center the heading. Add one or two blank lines as necessary.

➤ Pull down the **View menu.** Click **Zoom.** Click the **Many Pages option button,** then click the **monitor icon** to display a drop-down list, then click and drag to display three pages across. Release the mouse. Click **OK.**

➤ The completed document is shown in Figure 4.3g. Save the document a final time. Print the completed document and submit it to your instructor.

➤ Exit Word if you do not want to continue with the next exercise at this time.

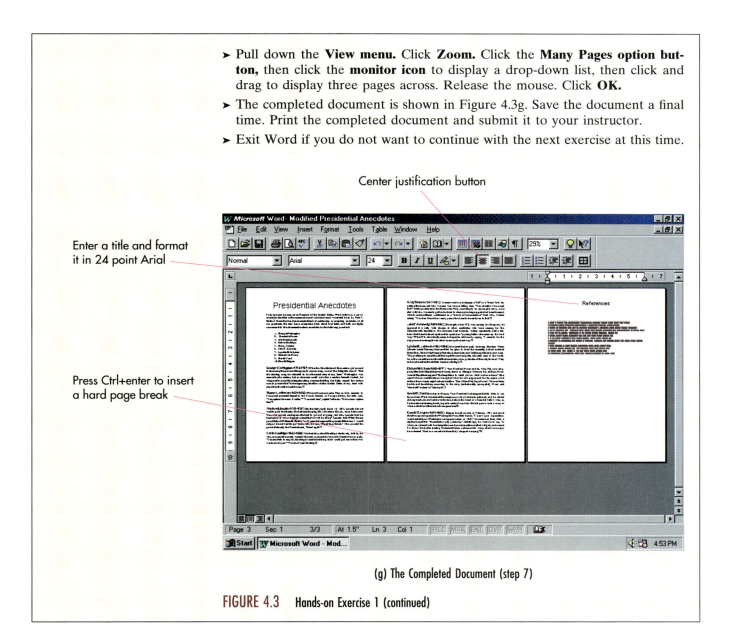

(g) The Completed Document (step 7)

FIGURE 4.3 Hands-on Exercise 1 (continued)

TABLES

The *tables feature* is one of the most powerful in Word and is the basis for an almost limitless variety of documents. The study schedule in Figure 4.4a, for example, is actually a 12 × 8 (12 rows and 8 columns) table as can be seen from the underlying structure in Figure 4.4b.

The rows and columns in a table intersect to form *cells,* which can contain text, numbers, and/or graphics. Commands operate on one or more cells. Individual cells can be joined together to form a larger cell as was done in the first and last rows of Figure 4.4. The rows within a table can be different heights, and each row may contain a different number of columns.

A table is created through the ***Insert Table command*** in the ***Table menu.*** The command produces a dialog box in which you enter the number of rows and columns. Once the table has been defined, you enter text in individual cells. Text wraps as it is entered within a cell, so that you can add or delete text in a cell

Weekly Class and Study Schedule

	Monday	Tuesday	Wednesday	Thursday	Friday	Saturday	Sunday
8:00 AM							
9:00 AM							
10:00 AM							
11:00 AM							
12:00 PM							
1:00 PM							
2:00 PM							
3:00 PM							
4:00 PM							
Notes							

(a) Completed Table

(b) Underlying Structure

FIGURE 4.4 The Tables Feature

without affecting the text in other cells. You can format the contents of an individual cell the same way you format an ordinary paragraph; that is, you can change the font, use boldface or italics, change the alignment, or apply any other formatting command. You can also select multiple cells and apply the formatting to all selected cells at once.

The Insert and Delete commands in the Table menu enable you to add new rows or columns, or delete existing rows or columns. You can invoke other commands to shade and/or border selected cells or the entire table. It's easy, and as you may have guessed, it's time for another hands-on exercise.

LEFT ALIGNED   **CENTERED**   **RIGHT ALIGNED**

Many documents call for left, centered, and/or right aligned text on the same line, an effect that is achieved through setting tabs, or more easily through a table. To achieve the effect shown in the first line of this tip, create a 1 × 3 table (one row and three columns), type the text in the three cells, then use the buttons on the Formatting toolbar to left align, center, and right align the respective cells.

HANDS-ON EXERCISE 2

Tables

Objective: To create a table; to change row heights and column widths; to join cells together; to apply borders and shading to selected cells. Use Figure 4.5 as a guide in the exercise.

STEP 1: Page Setup

➤ Start Word. If necessary, open a new document. Pull down the **File menu.** Click **Page Setup.** If necessary, click the **Paper Size tab** to display the dialog box in Figure 4.5a. Click the **Landscape option button.**

➤ Click the **Margins tab.** Change the top and bottom margins to **.75** inch. Change the left and right margins to **.5** inch each. Click **OK** to accept the settings and close the dialog box.

➤ Change to the **Page Layout** view. Zoom to **Page Width.**

➤ Save the document as **My Study Schedule** in the Exploring Word folder.

THE INSERT TABLE BUTTON

The fastest way to create a table is to use the Insert Table button on the Standard toolbar. Click the Insert Table button to display a grid, then drag the mouse across and down the grid until you have the desired number of rows and columns. Release the mouse to create the table.

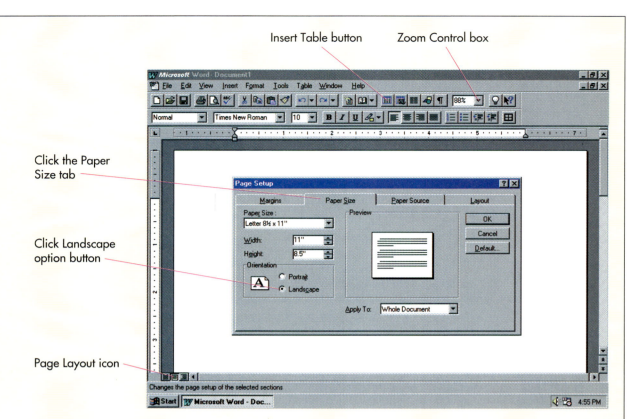

(a) Change the Orientation

FIGURE 4.5 Hands-on Exercise 2

STEP 2: Create the Table

➤ Pull down the **Table menu.** Click **Insert Table** to display the dialog box in Figure 4.5b. Enter **8** as the number of columns. Enter **12** as the number of rows.

➤ Click **OK** and the table will be inserted into the document. The cells in a table are separated by dotted lines known as gridlines, which appear on the monitor but not in the printed document.

➤ If you do not see the table, it is probably because the gridlines have been suppressed. Pull down the **Table menu** and click **Gridlines.**

TABLES AND THE SHOW/HIDE ¶ BUTTON

The Show/Hide ¶ button can be toggled on (off) to display (hide) the nonprinting characters associated with a table. The □ symbol indicates the end-of-cell (or end-of-row) marker and is analogous to the ¶ symbol at the end of a paragraph in a regular document.

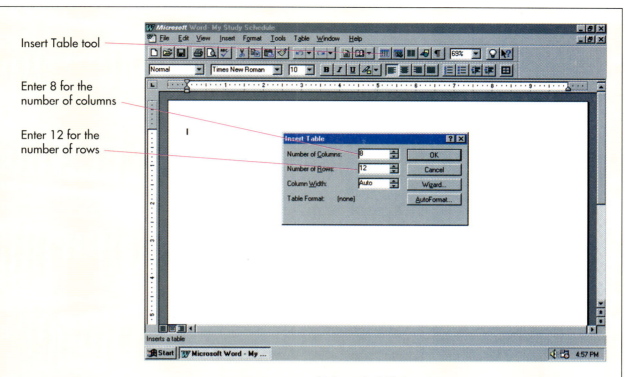

(b) Create the Table (step 2)

FIGURE 4.5 Hands-on Exercise 2 (continued)

STEP 3: Table Basics

➤ Practice moving within the table:
- If the cells in the table are empty (as they are now), press the **left** and **right arrow keys** to move from column to column. If the cells contain text (as they will later in the exercise), you must press **Tab** and **Shift+Tab** to move from column to column.
- Press the **up** and **down arrow keys** to move from row to row. This works for both empty cells and cells with text.

➤ Select a cell row, column, or block of contiguous cells:
- To select a single cell, click immediately to the right of the left gridline (the pointer changes to an arrow when you are in the proper position).

TABS AND TABLES

The Tab key functions differently in a table than in a regular document. Press the Tab key to move to the next cell in the current row (or to the first cell in the next row if you are at the end of a row). Press Tab when you are in the last cell of a table to add a new blank row to the bottom of the table. Press Shift+Tab to move to the previous cell in the current row (or to the last cell in the previous row). You must press Ctrl+Tab to insert a regular tab character within a cell.

- To select an entire row, click outside the table to the left of the first cell in that row.
- To select a column, click just above the top of the column (the pointer changes to a small black arrow).
- To select adjacent cells, drag the mouse over the cells.
- To select the entire table, drag the mouse over the table.

STEP 4: Merge the Cells

➤ Click outside the table to the left of the first cell in the first row to select the entire first row as shown in Figure 4.5c. Pull down the **Table menu.** Click **Merge Cells.**

➤ Type **Weekly Class and Study Schedule** and format the text in 24 point Arial bold. Center the text within the cell.

➤ Click outside the table to the left of the first cell in the last row to select the entire row. Pull down the **Table menu.** Click **Merge Cells** to join the cells into a single cell.

➤ Type **Notes:** and format the entry in 12 point Arial bold.

➤ Save the table.

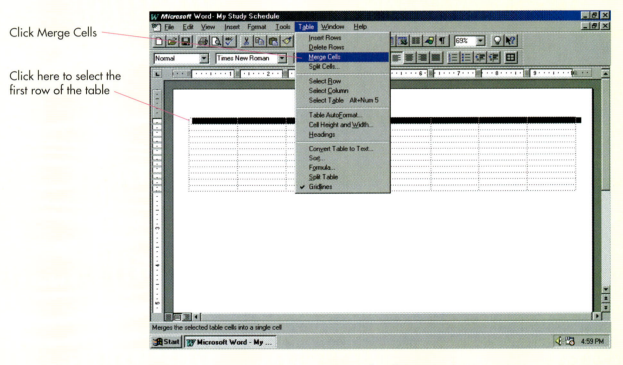

(c) Merge the Cells (step 4)

FIGURE 4.5 Hands-on Exercise 2 (continued)

STEP 5: Enter the Days and Hours

➤ Click the second cell in the second row. Type **Monday.**

➤ Press the **Tab** (or **right arrow) key** to move to the next cell. Type **Tuesday.** Continue until the days of the week have been entered.

➤ Use the Formatting Toolbar to change the font and alignment for the days of the week:
  - Select the entire row. Click the **Bold button.**
  - Click the **Font List box** to choose an appropriate font such as **Arial.**
  - Click the **Font Size List box** to choose an appropriate size such as **10** point.
  - Click the **Center button** on the Formatting toolbar.
➤ Click anywhere in the table to deselect the text and see the effect of the formatting change.
➤ Click the first cell in the third row. Type **8:00AM.** Press the **down arrow key** to move to the first cell in the fourth row. Type **9:00AM.**
➤ Continue in this fashion until you have entered the hourly periods up to **4:00PM.** Format as appropriate. (We right aligned the time periods and changed the font to Arial bold.) Your table should match Figure 4.5d. Save the table.

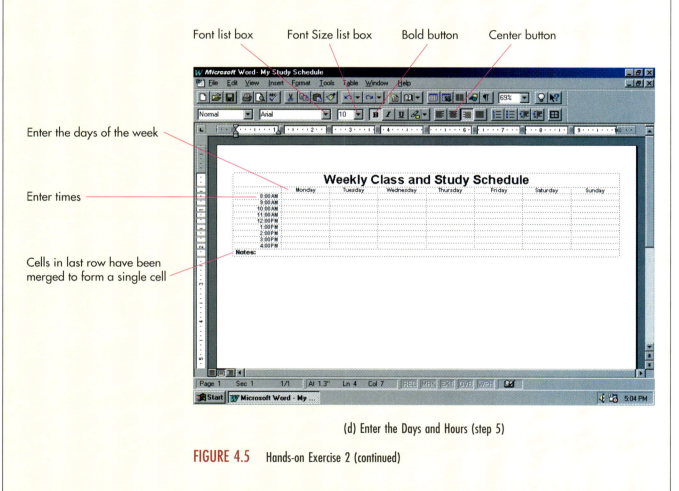

(d) Enter the Days and Hours (step 5)

FIGURE 4.5 Hands-on Exercise 2 (continued)

STEP 6: Change the Row Heights

➤ Click immediately after the word "notes." Press the **enter key** five times. The height of the cell increases automatically to accommodate the additional paragraphs.
➤ Select the cells containing the hours of the day. Pull down the **Table menu.** Click **Cell Height and Width** to display the dialog box in Figure 4.5e.

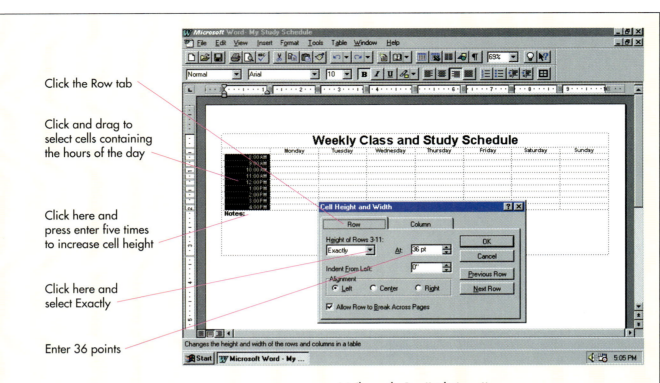

(e) Change the Row Height (step 6)

FIGURE 4.5   Hands-on Exercise 2 (continued)

➤ If necessary, click the **Row tab.** Click the arrow for the Height of Rows list box. Click **Exactly,** then enter **36** (36 points is equal to ½ inch) in the At text box.

➤ Click **OK.** Click anywhere to deselect the text and see the new row heights.

STEP 7: Borders and Shading

➤ Pull down the **Table menu** and click **Select Table** (or drag the mouse over the entire table).

➤ Pull down the **Format menu.** Click **Borders and Shading** to display the dialog box in Figure 4.5f.

➤ If necessary, click the **Borders Tab.** Click **Grid** in the **Presets** area. Click **OK** to close the dialog box. Click anywhere in the table to deselect the table and see the effect of the Borders command.

➤ Select the first row in the table. Pull down the **Format menu** a second time. Click **Borders and Shading.**

➤ Click the **Shading Tab.** Click **10%** in the Shading list box. Experiment with different colors for borders or shading (if you have a color printer).

➤ Click **OK** to close the dialog box. Click outside the selected text to see the shading. Save the table.

STEP 8: The Completed Table

➤ Zoom to **Whole Page** to see the completed schedule as shown in Figure 4.5g.

➤ Print the table. Exit Word if you do not want to continue with the next exercise at this time.

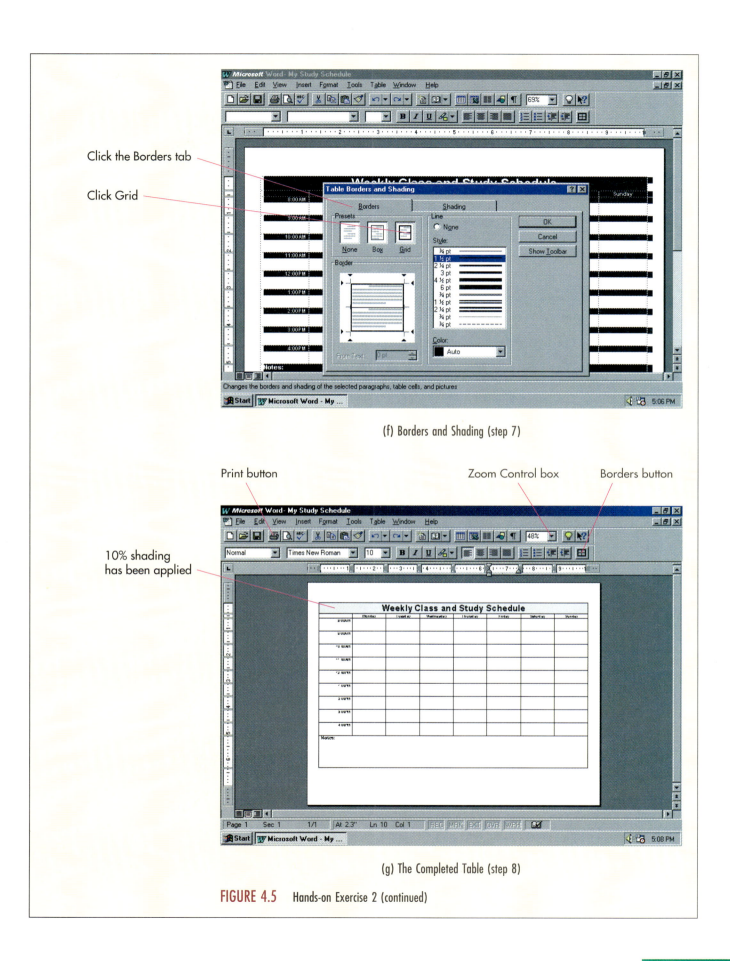

(f) Borders and Shading (step 7)

(g) The Completed Table (step 8)

FIGURE 4.5 Hands-on Exercise 2 (continued)

STYLES

A characteristic of professional documents is the use of uniform formatting for each element. Different elements can have different formatting; for example, headings may be set in one font and the text under those headings in a different font. You may want the headings centered and the text justified.

If you are like most people, you will change your mind several times before arriving at a satisfactory design, after which you will want consistent formatting for each element in the document. You can use the Format Painter (see page 73) to copy the formatting from one occurrence of an element to another, but it still requires you to select the individual elements and paint each one whenever formatting changes.

A much easier way to achieve uniformity is to store the formatting information as a *style,* then apply that style to multiple occurrences of the same element within the document. Change the style and you automatically change all text defined by that style.

Styles are created on the character or paragraph level. A **character style** stores character formatting (font, size, and style) and affects only the selected text. A **paragraph style** stores paragraph formatting (alignment, line spacing, indents, tabs, text flow, and borders and shading, as well as the font, size, and style of the text in the paragraph). A paragraph style affects the current paragraph or multiple paragraphs if several paragraphs are selected. The **Style command** in the Format menu is used to create and/or modify either type of style, then enables you to apply that style within a document.

Execution of the Style command displays the dialog box shown in Figure 4.6, which lists the styles in use within a document. The **Normal style** contains the default paragraph settings (left aligned, single spacing, and a default font) and is automatically assigned to every paragraph unless a different style is specified. The **Heading 1** and **Body Text** styles are used in conjunction with the AutoFormat command, which applies these styles throughout a document. (The AutoFormat command is illustrated in the next hands-on exercise.) The **Default Paragraph Font** is a character style that specifies the (default) font for new text.

The Description box displays the style definition; for example, Times New Roman, 10 point, flush left, single spacing, and widow/orphan control. The Paragraph Preview box shows how paragraphs formatted in that style will appear. The Modify command button provides access to the Format Paragraph and Format Font commands to change the characteristics of the selected style. The Apply command button applies the style to all selected paragraphs or to the current paragraph. The New command button enables you to define a new style.

Styles automate the formatting process and provide a consistent appearance to a document. Any type of character or paragraph formatting can be stored within a style, and once a style has been defined, it can be applied to multiple occurrences of the same element within a document to produce identical formatting.

STYLES AND PARAGRAPHS

A paragraph style affects the entire paragraph; that is, you cannot apply a paragraph style to only part of a paragraph. To apply a style to an existing paragraph, place the insertion point anywhere within the paragraph, pull down the Style list box on the Formatting toolbar, then click the name of the style you want

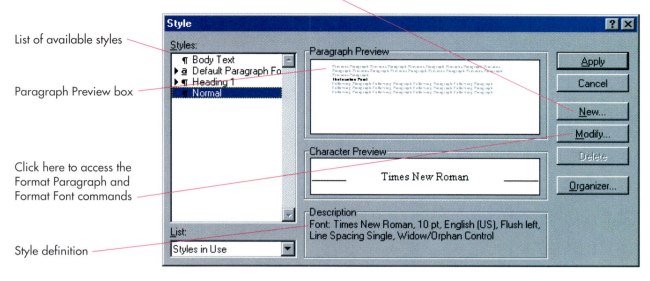

FIGURE 4.6 The Normal Style

The AutoFormat Command

The ***AutoFormat command*** enables you to format lengthy documents quickly, easily, and in a consistent fashion. In essence, the command analyzes a document and formats it for you. Its most important capability is the application of styles to individual paragraphs; that is, the command goes through an entire document, determines how each paragraph is used, then applies an appropriate style to each paragraph. The formatting process assumes that one-line paragraphs are headings and applies the predefined Heading 1 style to those paragraphs. It applies the Body Text style to ordinary paragraphs and can also detect lists and apply a numbered or bullet style to those lists.

The AutoFormat command will also add special touches to a document if you request those options. It can replace "ordinary quotation marks" with "smart quotation marks" that curl and face each other. It will also replace ordinal numbers (1st, 2nd, or 3rd) with the corresponding superscripts (1st, 2nd, or 3rd), or common fractions (1/2 or 1/4) with typographical symbols (½ or ¼).

AUTOMATIC BORDERS AND LISTS

The AutoFormat As You type option applies sophisticated formatting as text is entered. It creates a numbered list automatically any time a number is followed by a period, tab, or right parenthesis (press enter twice in a row to turn off the feature). It will also add a border to a paragraph any time you type three or more hyphens, equal signs, or underscores followed by the enter key. Pull down the Tools menu, click Options, click the AutoFormat tab, then click the AutoFormat As You Type option button to select the desired features. See practice exercise 4 on page 147 for additional examples.

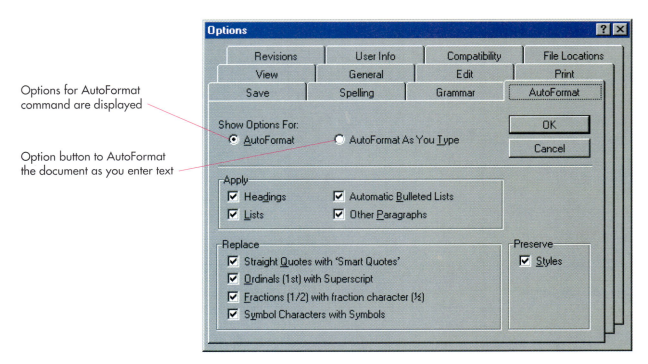

FIGURE 4.7 The AutoFormat Command

Options in the AutoFormat command are accessed from the dialog box shown in Figure 4.7. Once the options have been set, all formatting is done automatically by selecting the AutoFormat command from the Format menu. The changes are not final, however, as the command gives you the opportunity to review each formatting change individually, then accept the change or reject it as appropriate. (You can also format text automatically as it is entered according to the options specified under AutoFormat As You Type.)

HANDS-ON EXERCISE 3

Styles

Objective: To use the AutoFormat command on an existing document; to modify existing styles; to create a new style. Use Figure 4.8 as a guide for the exercise.

STEP 1: Load the Practice Document

➤ Start Word. Pull down the **File menu.** Open the document **Tips for Microsoft Word** from the Exploring Word folder. (This document contains 50 tips that appear throughout the text.)

➤ Pull down the **File menu** a second time. Save the document as **Styles** so that you can return to the original if necessary.

➤ If necessary, pull down the **View menu** and click **Normal** (or click the **Normal button** above the status bar). Pull down the **View menu** a second time, click **Zoom,** click **Page Width,** and click **OK** (or click the **arrow** on the **Zoom Control box** on the Standard toolbar and select **Page Width**).

STEP 2: The AutoFormat Command

➤ Press **Ctrl+Home** to move to the beginning of the document. Pull down the **Format menu.** Click **AutoFormat** to display the dialog box in Figure 4.8a.

➤ Click the **Options command button.** Be sure that every check box is selected to implement the maximum amount of automatic formatting. Click the **OK button** to close the dialog box.

➤ Click the **OK command button** in the AutoFormat dialog box in Figure 4.8a to format the document. You will see a message at the left side of the status bar as the formatting is taking place, then you will see a newly formatted document behind a dialog box.

➤ Click the **Accept command button** to accept the formatting changes. Save the document.

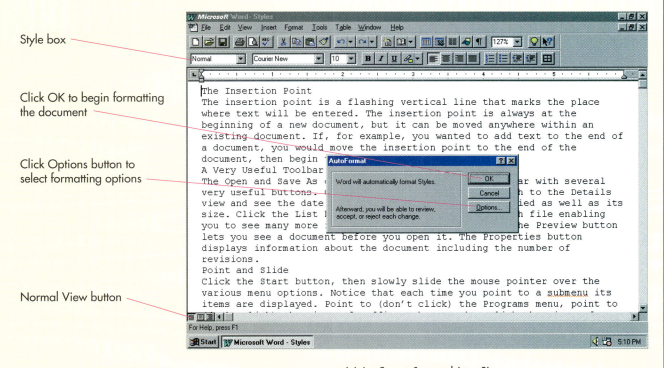

(a) AutoFormat Command (step 2)

FIGURE 4.8   Hands-on Exercise 3

STEP 3: Style Assignments

➤ Click anywhere in the heading of the first tip. The Style box on the Formatting toolbar displays Heading 1 to indicate that this style has been applied to the title of the tip.

➤ Click anywhere in the text of the first tip. The Style box on the Formatting toolbar displays Body Text to indicate that this style has been applied to the current paragraph.

➤ Click the title of any tip and you will see the Heading 1 style in the Style box. Click the text of any tip and you will see the Body Text style in the Style box.

STEP 4: Modify the Body Text Style

➤ Press **Ctrl+Home** to move to the beginning of the document. Click anywhere in the text of the first tip.

➤ Pull down the **Format menu.** Click **Style.** The Body Text style is automatically selected, and its characteristics are displayed within the description box.

➤ Click the **Modify command button** to produce the Modify Style dialog box in Figure 4.8b.

➤ Click the **Format command button.**
- Click **Paragraph** to produce the Paragraph dialog box.
- Click the **Indents and Spacing** tab.
- Click the **arrow** on the **Alignment list box.** Click **Justified.**
- Change the **Spacing After** to **12.**
- Click the **Text Flow tab** on the Paragraph dialog box.
- Click the **Keep Lines Together** check box so an individual tip will not be broken over two pages. Click **OK** to close the Paragraph dialog box.

➤ Click **OK** to close the Modify Style dialog box. Click the **Close command button** to return to the document. Save the document.

SPACE BEFORE AND AFTER

It's common practice to press the enter key twice at the end of a paragraph (once to end the paragraph, and a second time to insert a blank line before the next paragraph). The same effect can be achieved by setting the spacing before or after the paragraph using the Spacing Before or After list boxes in the Format Paragraph command. The latter technique gives you greater flexibility in that you can specify any amount of spacing (e.g., 6 points to leave only half a line) before or after a paragraph. It also enables you to change the spacing between paragraphs more easily because the spacing information can be stored within the paragraph style.

STEP 5: Review the Formatting

➤ All paragraphs in the document change automatically to reflect the new definition of the Body Text style.

➤ Click the **Help button** on the Standard toolbar; the mouse pointer changes to a large question mark. Click in any paragraph to display the formatting in effect for that paragraph as shown in Figure 4.8c.

➤ You will see formatting specifications for the Body Text style (Indent: Left 0″, Justified, Space After 12 pt, Keep Lines Together, Font Times New Roman, 10pt, and English (US)).

➤ Click in any other paragraph to see the formatting in effect for that paragraph.

➤ Click the **Help button** a second time (or press **Esc**) to return to normal editing.

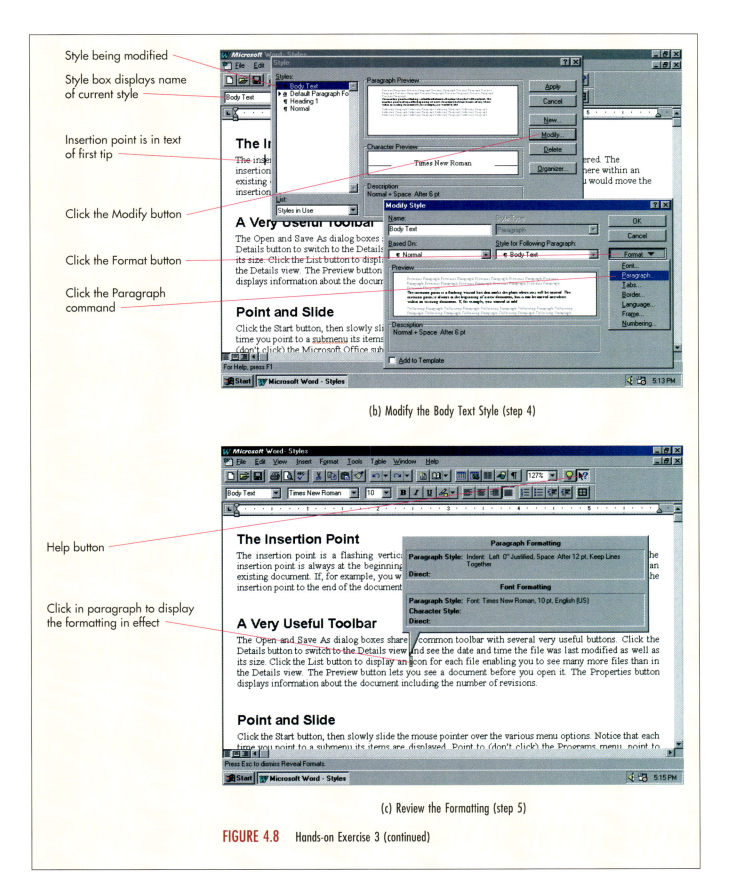

(b) Modify the Body Text Style (step 4)

(c) Review the Formatting (step 5)

FIGURE 4.8 Hands-on Exercise 3 (continued)

> **HELP WITH FORMATTING**
>
> It's all too easy to lose sight of the formatting in effect, so Word provides a Help button on the Standard toolbar. Click the button, and the mouse pointer assumes the shape of a large question mark. Click anywhere in a document to display the formatting in effect at that point. Click the Help button a second time to exit Help.

STEP 6: Modify the Heading 1 Style

➤ Click anywhere in the title of the first tip. The Style box on the Formatting toolbar contains Heading 1 to indicate that this style has been applied to the current paragraph.

➤ Pull down the **Format menu.** Click **Style.** The Heading 1 style is automatically selected, and its characteristics are displayed within the description box.

➤ Click the **Modify command button** to produce the Modify Style dialog box.

➤ Click the **Format command button.**

- Click **Paragraph** to produce the Paragraph dialog box. Click the **Indents and Spacing tab.**
- Change the **Spacing After** to **0** (there should be no space separating the heading and the paragraph).
- Change the **Spacing Before** to **0** (since there are already 12 points after the Body Text style as per the settings in step 6). Click **OK.**
- Click the **Format command button** a second time.
- Click **Font** to produce the Font dialog box.
- Click **10** in the Font size box. Click **OK.**

➤ Click **OK** to close the Modify Style dialog box. Click the **Close command button** to return to the document and view the changes.

➤ Save the document.

> **MODIFY STYLES BY EXAMPLE**
>
> The Modify command button in the Format Style command is one way to change a style, but it prevents the use of the toolbar buttons; thus it's easier to modify an existing style by example. Select any text that is defined by the style you want to modify, then reformat that text using the Formatting toolbar, shortcut keys, or pull-down menus. Click the Style box on the Formatting toolbar, make sure the selected style is the correct one, press enter, then click OK when asked if you want to redefine the style.

STEP 7: Create a New Style

➤ Press **Ctrl+Home** to move to the beginning of the document. Press **Ctrl+enter** to create a page break for a title page.

- Move the insertion point above the page break. Press the **enter key** five to ten times to move to an appropriate position for the title.
- Click the **Show/Hide ¶ button** on the Standard toolbar to display the nonprinting characters. Select the paragraph marks, pull down the **Style list** on the Formatting toolbar, and click **Normal.**
- Deselect the paragraph marks to continue editing.
- Place the insertion point to the left of the last hard return above the page break. Enter the title, **50 Tips in Microsoft Word,** and format it in 28 Point Arial Bold as shown in Figure 4.8d.
- Click the **Center button** on the Formatting toolbar.
- Check that the title is still selected, then click the **Styles List box** on the Formatting toolbar. The style name, Normal, is selected.
- Type **My Style** (the name of the new style). Press **enter.** You have just created a new style that we will use in the next exercise. Save the document.

> **MORE FONTS**
>
> We have restricted our design to the Arial and Times New Roman fonts because they are supplied with Windows and hence are always available. In all likelihood, you will have several additional fonts available, in which case you can modify the fonts in the Heading 1 and/or Body Text styles to create a completely different design.

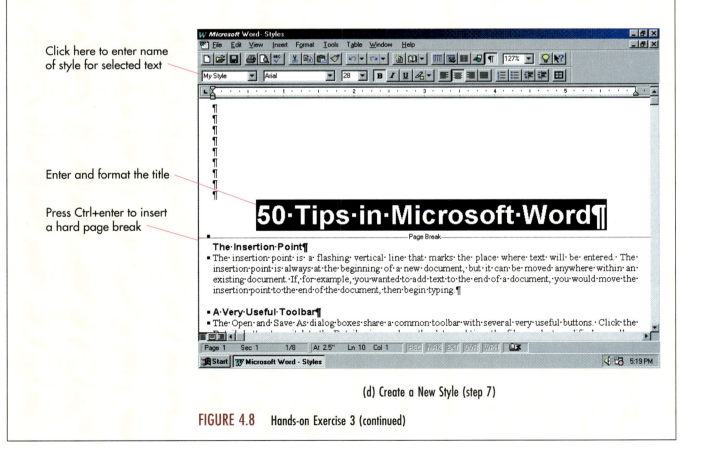

(d) Create a New Style (step 7)

FIGURE 4.8 Hands-on Exercise 3 (continued)

STEP 8: Complete the Title Page

➤ Click the **Page Layout button** on the status bar. Click the **arrow** on the **Zoom Control box** on the Standard toolbar. Click **Two Pages.**

➤ Scroll through the document to see the effects of your formatting.

➤ Press **Ctrl+Home** to return to the beginning of the document, then change to **Page Width** so that you can read what you are typing. Complete the title page as shown in Figure 4.8e.

➤ Click immediately to the left of the ¶ after the title to deselect the text. Press **enter** once or twice.

➤ Click the **arrow** on the **Font Size box** on the Formatting toolbar. Click **12.** Type **by Robert Grauer and Maryann Barber.** Press **enter.**

➤ Save the document. Print the document. Exit Word if you do not want to continue with the next exercise at this time.

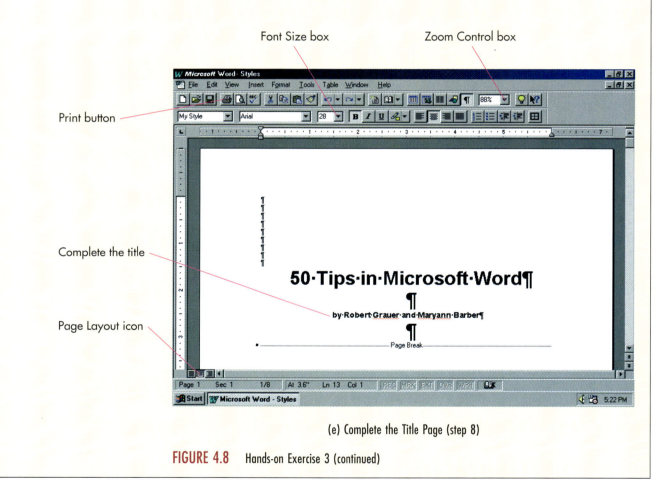

(e) Complete the Title Page (step 8)

FIGURE 4.8   Hands-on Exercise 3 (continued)

WORKING IN LONG DOCUMENTS

Long documents, such as term papers or reports, require additional formatting for better organization. These documents typically contain page numbers, headers and/or footers, and a table of contents. Each of these elements is discussed in turn and will be illustrated in a hands-on exercise.

Page Numbers

The ***Insert Page Numbers command*** is the easiest way to place ***page numbers*** into a document and is illustrated in Figure 4.9. The page numbers can appear at the top or bottom of a page, and can be left, centered, or right-aligned. Additional flexibility is provided as shown in Figure 4.9b; you can use Roman rather than Arabic numerals, and you need not start at page number one.

The Insert Page Number command is limited in two ways. It does not provide for additional text next to the page number, nor does it allow for different placements on the odd and even pages of a document as in a book or newsletter. Both restrictions are overcome by creating a header or footer which contains the page number.

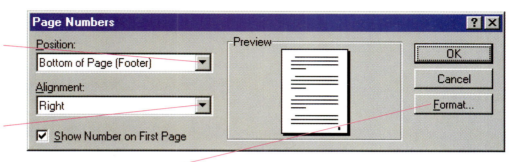

(a) Placement

(b) Format

FIGURE 4.9   Page Numbers

Headers and Footers

Headers and footers give a professional appearance to a document. A ***header*** consists of one or more lines that are printed at the top of every page. A ***footer*** is printed at the bottom of the page. A document may contain headers but not footers, footers but not headers, or both headers and footers.

Headers and footers are created from the View menu. (A simple header or footer is also created automatically by the Insert Page Number command, depending on whether the page number is at the top or bottom of a page.) Headers and footers are formatted like any other paragraph and can be centered, left- or right-aligned. They can be formatted in any typeface or point size and can include special codes to automatically insert the page number, date and/or time a document is printed.

The advantage of using a header or footer (over typing the text yourself at the top or bottom of every page) is that you type the text only once, after which it appears automatically according to your specifications. The placement of the headers and footers is adjusted for changes in page breaks caused by the insertion or deletion of text in the body of the document.

Headers and footers can change continually throughout a document. The Page Setup dialog box (in the File menu) enables you to specify a different header or footer for the first page, and/or different headers and footers for the odd and even pages. If, however, you wanted to change the header (or footer) midway through a document, you would need to insert a section break at the point where the new header (or footer) is to begin.

Sections

Formatting in Word occurs on three levels. You are already familiar with formatting at the character and paragraph levels that have been used throughout the text. Formatting at the section level controls headers and footers, page numbering, page size and orientation, margins, and columns. All of the documents in the text so far have consisted of a single ***section,*** and thus any section formatting applied to the entire document. You can, however, divide a document into sections and format each section independently.

Formatting at the section level may appear complicated initially, but it gives you the ability to create more sophisticated documents. You can use section formatting to:

- Change the margins within a multipage letter where the first page (the letterhead) requires a larger top margin than the other pages in the letter.
- Change the orientation from portrait to landscape to accommodate a wide table at the end of the document.
- Change the page numbering, for example to use Roman numerals at the beginning of the document for a table of contents and Arabic numerals thereafter.
- Change the number of columns in a newsletter, which may contain a single column at the top of a page for the masthead, then two or three columns in the body of the newsletter.

In all instances, you determine where one section ends and another begins by using the ***Insert menu*** to create a ***section break.*** You also have the option of deciding how the section break will be implemented on the printed page; that is, you can specify that the new section continue on the same page, that it begin on a new page, or that it begin on the next odd or even page even if a blank page has to be inserted.

Word stores the formatting characteristics of each section in the section break at the end of a section. Thus, deleting a section break also deletes the section formatting, causing the text above the break to assume the formatting characteristics of the next section.

Figure 4.10 displays a multipage view of a ten-page document. The document has been divided into two sections, and the insertion point is currently on the

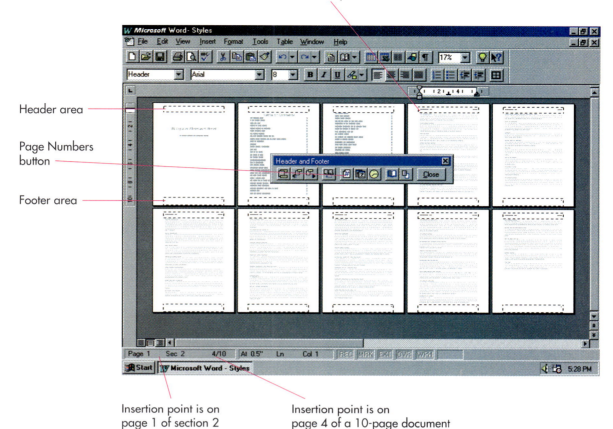

FIGURE 4.10 Headers and Footers

fourth page of the document (page four of ten), which is also the first page of the second section. Note the corresponding indications on the status bar and the position of the headers and footers throughout the document.

Figure 4.10 also displays the Headers and Footers toolbar, which contains various icons associated with these elements. As indicated, a header or footer may contain text and/or special codes—for example, the word "page" followed by a code for the page number. The latter is inserted into the header by clicking the appropriate button on the Headers and Footers toolbar.

THE SECTION VERSUS THE PARAGRAPH

Line spacing, alignment, tabs, and indents are implemented at the paragraph level. Change any of these parameters anywhere within the current (or selected) paragraph(s) and you change *only* those paragraph(s). Margins, headers and footers, page numbering, page size and orientation, and newspaper columns are implemented at the section level. Change these parameters anywhere within a section, and you change the characteristics of every page within that section.

Table of Contents

A *table of contents* lists headings in the order they appear in a document and the page numbers where the entries begin. Word will create the table of contents automatically, provided you have identified each heading in the document with a built-in heading style (Heading 1 through Heading 9). Word will also update the table automatically to accommodate the addition or deletion of headings and/or changes in page numbers brought about through changes in the document.

The table of contents is created through the **Index and Tables command** from the Insert menu as shown in Figure 4.11. You have your choice of several predefined formats and the number of levels within each format; the latter correspond to the heading styles used within the document. You can also choose the *leader character* and whether or not to right align the page numbers.

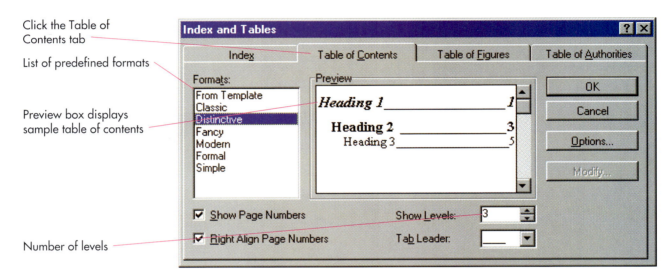

FIGURE 4.11 Index and Tables Command

The Go To Command

The *Go To command* moves the insertion point to the top of a designated page. The command is accessed from the Edit menu, or by pressing the F5 function key, or by double clicking the Page number on the status bar. After the command has been executed, you are presented with a dialog box in which you enter the desired page number. You can also specify a relative page number—for example, P+2 to move forward two pages, or P-1 to move back one page.

HANDS-ON EXERCISE 4

Working in Long Documents

Objective: To create a header (footer) that includes page numbers; to insert and update a table of contents; to insert a section break and demonstrate the Go To command; to view multiple pages of a document. Use Figure 4.12 as a guide for the exercise.

STEP 1: Applying a Style

➤ Open the **Styles document** from the first exercise. Scroll to the top of the second page. Click to the left of the first tip title. (If necessary, click the **Show/Hide ¶ button** on the Standard toolbar to hide the paragraph marks.)

➤ Type **Table of Contents.** Press the **enter key** two times.

➤ Click anywhere within the phrase "Table of Contents". Click the **arrow** on the **Styles list box** to pull down the styles for this document as shown in Figure 4.12a.

➤ Click **My Style** (the style you created at the end of the previous exercise). "Table of Contents" is centered in 28 point Arial bold according to the definition of My Style.

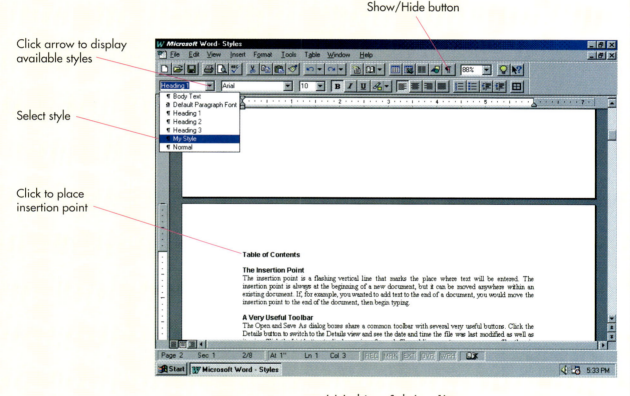

(a) Applying a Style (step 1)

FIGURE 4.12 Hands-on Exercise 4

STEP 2: View Many Pages

➤ Click the line immediately under the heading for the table of contents. Pull down the **View menu.** Click **Zoom** to display the dialog box in Figure 4.12b.

➤ Click the **monitor icon.** Click and drag the **page icon** within the monitor to display two pages down by five pages across as shown in the figure. Release the mouse.

➤ Click **OK.** The display changes to show all eight pages in the document.

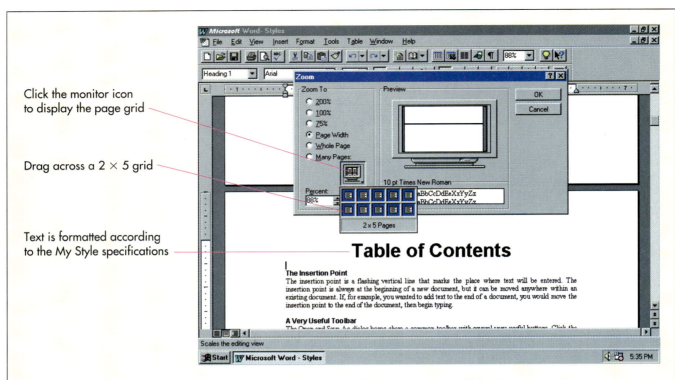

(b) View Zoom Command (step 2)

FIGURE 4.12 Hands-on Exercise 4 (continued)

STEP 3: Create the Table of Contents

➤ Pull down the **Insert menu.** Click **Index and Tables.** If necessary, click the **Table of Contents tab** to display the dialog box in Figure 4.12c.

➤ Check the boxes to **Show Page Numbers** and to **Right Align Page Numbers.**

➤ Click **Distinctive** in the **Formats list box.** Click the **arrow** in the **Tab Leader list box.** Choose a dot leader. Click **OK.** Word takes a moment to create the table of contents, which extends to two pages.

AUTOFORMAT AND THE TABLE OF CONTENTS

Word will create a table of contents automatically, provided you use the built-in heading styles to define the items for inclusion. If you have not applied the heading styles to the document, the AutoFormat command will do it for you. Once the heading styles are in the document, pull down the Insert command, click Index and Tables, then click the Table of Contents command.

STEP 4: Field Codes versus Field Text

➤ Click anywhere on the actual table of contents and it assumes a gray background. Click the **arrow** on the **Zoom Control box** on the Standard toolbar. Click **Page Width** in order to read the table of contents as in Figure 4.12d.

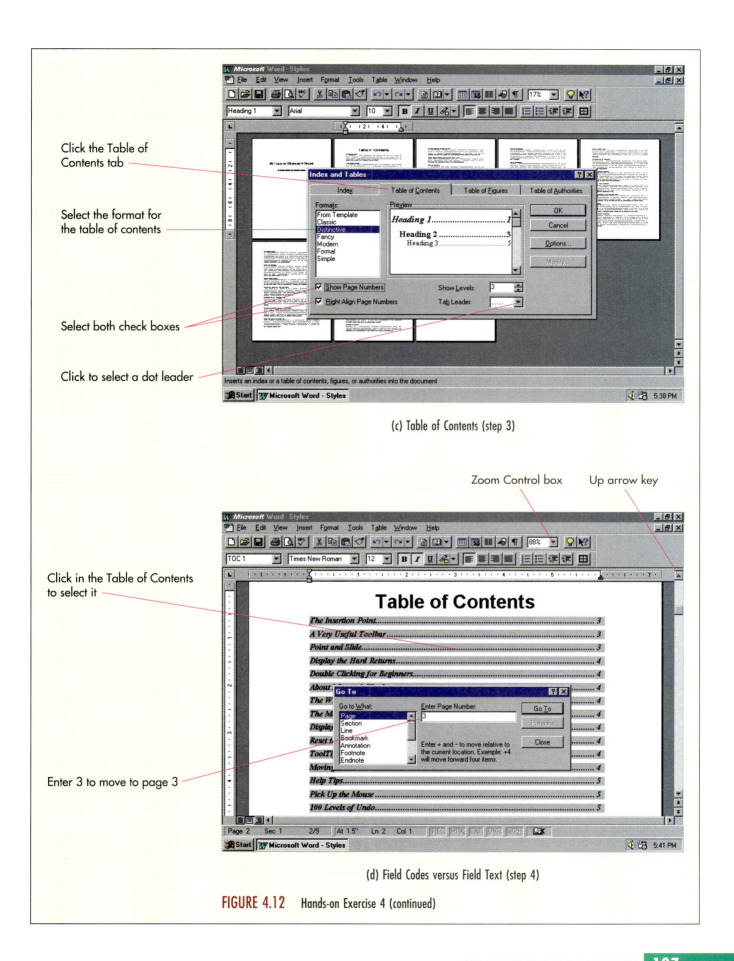

- Use the **up arrow key** to scroll to the beginning of the table of contents. Click in the first entry in the table of contents, then press **Shift+F9.** The entire table of contents is replaced by an entry similar to {TOC \o "1-3"} to indicate a field code; the exact code depends on your selections in step 4.
- Press **Shift+F9** a second time. The field code for the table of contents is replaced by text.
- Pull down the **Edit menu.** Click **Go To** to display the dialog box in Figure 4.12d.
- Type **3** and press the **enter key** to go to page 3. Click **Close.**

THE GO TO AND GO BACK COMMANDS

The F5 key is the shortcut equivalent of the Edit Go To command and produces a dialog box to move to a specific location (a page or section) within a document. The Shift+F5 combination executes the Go Back command and returns to a previous location of the insertion point; press Shift+F5 repeatedly to cycle through the last three locations of the insertion point.

STEP 5: Insert a Section Break
- Scroll down page three until you are at the end of the table of contents. Click to the left of the first tip heading as shown in Figure 4.12e.
- Pull down the **Insert menu.** Click **Break** to display the dialog box in Figure 4.12e.
- Click the **Next Page button** under Section Breaks. Click **OK** to create a section break, simultaneously forcing the first tip to begin on a new page.
- The status bar displays Page 1 Sec 2 to indicate you are on page one in the second section. (See the boxed tip on page numbering if the status bar indicates page 4.) The entry 4/10 indicates that you are physically on the fourth page of a ten-page document.

SECTIONS AND PAGE NUMBERING

Word gives you the option of numbering pages consecutively from one section to the next, or alternatively, of starting each section from page one. To view (change) the page numbering options in effect, pull down the Insert menu, click Page Numbers, click the Format command button, then click the option button for the page numbering you want. To start each section at page one, click the Start At option button, type 1 as the beginning page number, then click OK.

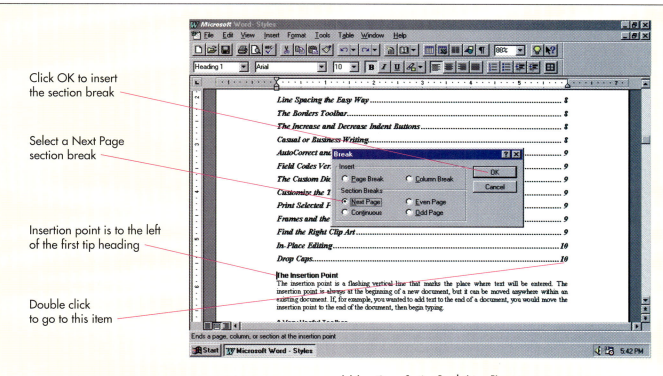

(e) Inserting a Section Break (step 5)

FIGURE 4.12   Hands-on Exercise 4 (continued)

> ### MOVING WITHIN LONG DOCUMENTS
>
> Double click the page indicator on the status bar to display the dialog box for the ***Edit Go To command.*** You can also double click a page number in the table of contents (created through the Index and Tables command in the Insert menu) to go directly to the associated entry.

STEP 6: Create the Header

➤ Pull down the **File menu.** Click **Page Setup.** If necessary, click the **Layout tab** to display the dialog box in Figure 4.12f.

➤ If necessary, clear the box for Different Odd and Even Pages and for Different First Page, as all pages in this section (section two) are to have the same header. Click **OK.**

STEP 7: Create the Header (continued)

➤ Pull down the **View menu.** Click **Header and Footer** to produce the screen in Figure 4.12g. The text in the document is faded to indicate that you are editing the header, as opposed to the document.

➤ The "Same as Previous" indicator is on since Word automatically uses the header from the previous section. Click the **Same as Previous button** on the Header and Footer toolbar to toggle the indicator off in order to create a different header for this section. The indicator disappears from the header.

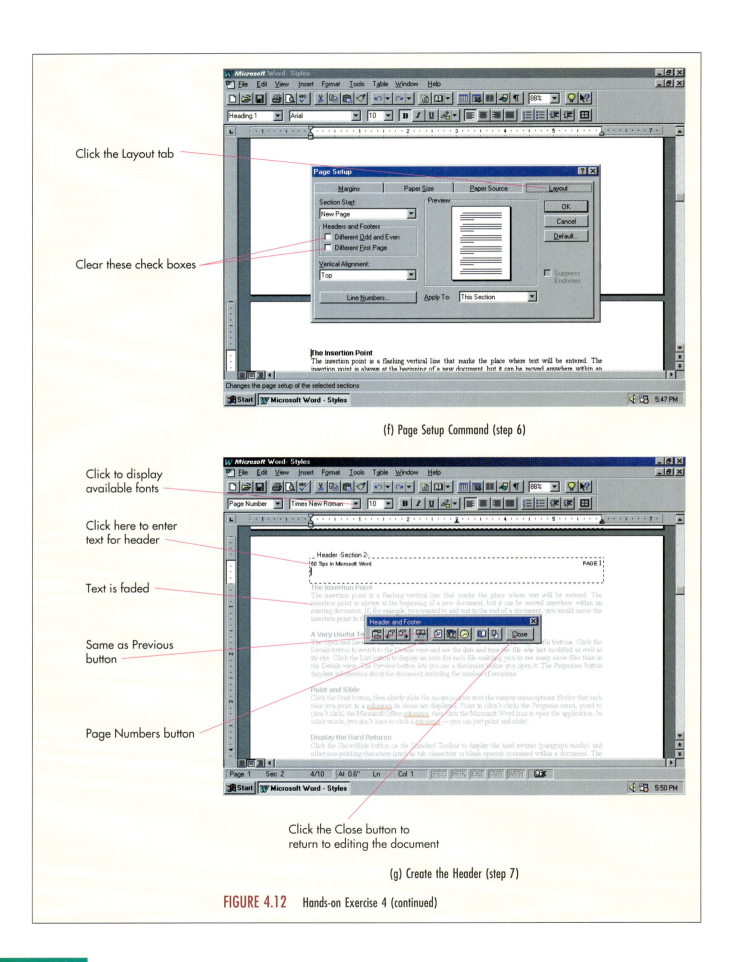

FIGURE 4.12 Hands-on Exercise 4 (continued)

➤ If necessary, click in the header. Click the **arrow** on the **Font list box** on the Formatting toolbar. Click **Arial**. Click the **arrow** on the Font size box. Click **8**. Type **50 Tips In Microsoft Word.**

➤ Press the **Tab key** twice. Type **PAGE**. Press the **space bar**. Click the **Page Numbers button** on the Header and Footer toolbar to insert a code for the page number. Press the **enter key** to insert a blank line in the header.

➤ Click the **Close button.** The header is faded, and the document text is available for editing.

➤ Save the document.

> ### HEADERS AND FOOTERS
>
> If you do not see a header or footer, it is most likely because you are in the wrong view. Headers and footers are displayed in the Page Layout view but not in the Normal view. (Click the Page Layout button on the status bar to change the view.) Even in the Page Layout view the header (footer) is faded, indicating that it cannot be edited unless it is selected (opened) by double clicking.

STEP 8: Update the Table of Contents

➤ Press **Ctrl+Home** to move to the beginning of the document. The status bar indicates Page 1, Sec 1.

➤ Click the **Next Page button** on the vertical scroll bar to move to the page containing the table of contents.

➤ Click anywhere in the table of contents and it assumes a gray background. The first tip, The Insertion Point, is shown to begin on page 3.

➤ Press the **F9 key** to update the table of contents. If necessary, click the **Update Entire Table** button as shown in Figure 4.12h, then click **OK.**

➤ The pages are renumbered to reflect the actual page numbers in the second section.

> ### UPDATING THE TABLE OF CONTENTS
>
> Use a shortcut menu to update the table of contents. Point anywhere in the table of contents, then press the right mouse button, to display a shortcut menu. Click Update Field, click the Update Entire Table command button, and click OK. The table of contents will be adjusted automatically to reflect page number changes as well as the addition or deletion of any items defined by any built-in heading style.

STEP 9: The Completed Document

➤ Pull down the **View menu.** Click **Zoom.** Click **Many Pages.** Click the **monitor icon.**

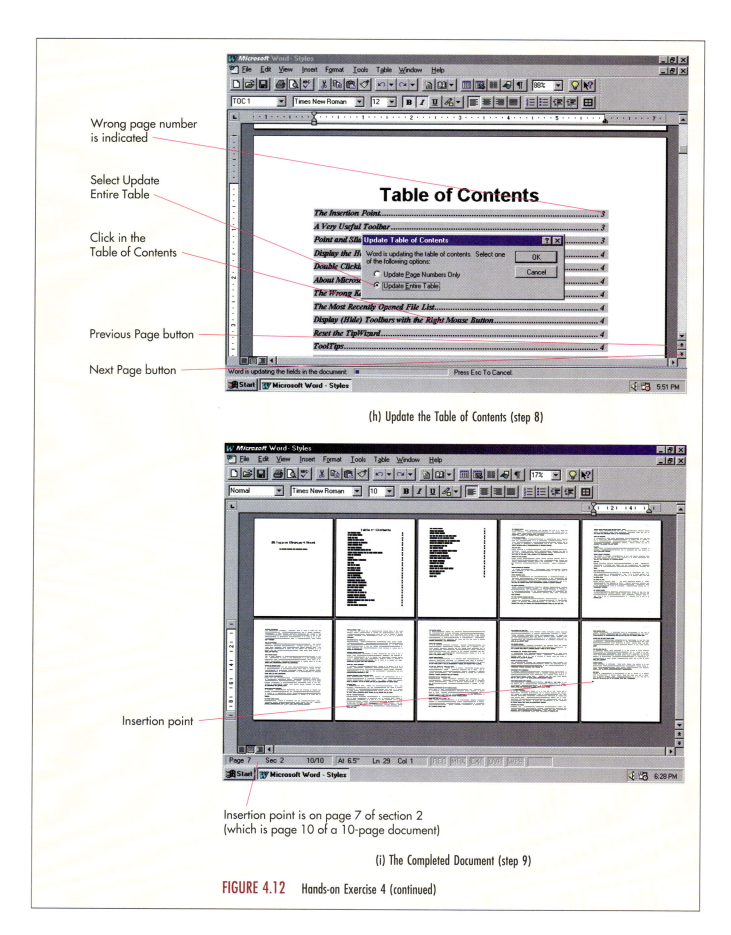

(h) Update the Table of Contents (step 8)

(i) The Completed Document (step 9)

FIGURE 4.12 Hands-on Exercise 4 (continued)

- Click and drag the **page icon** within the monitor to display two pages down by five pages. Release the mouse. Click **OK.**
- The completed document is shown in Figure 4.12i.
- Press **Ctrl+End** to move to the last page in the document.
- The status bar displays Page 7, Sec 2, 10/10 to indicate the seventh page in the second section, which is also the tenth page in the ten-page document.
- Save the document. Print the entire document. Exit Word.

> ### BOOKMARKS
>
> A *bookmark* is a predefined place in a document that is accessible through the Edit Go To command. Place the insertion point where you want the bookmark, pull down the Edit menu, click Bookmark, enter a name for the bookmark (40 or fewer characters consisting of letters, numbers, and/or the underscore), and click the Add command button. To return to the bookmark when subsequently editing the document, press the F5 key to display the dialog box for the Go To command, click Bookmark, choose the name of the bookmark from the displayed list, then click the Go To command button.

SUMMARY

A list helps to organize information by emphasizing important topics. A bulleted or numbered list can be created by clicking the appropriate button on the Formatting toolbar or by executing the Bullets and Numbering command in the Format menu.

Footnotes provide additional information about an item and appear at the bottom of the page where the reference occurs. Endnotes are similar in concept but appear collectively at the end of a document. The addition or deletion of a footnote or endnote automatically renumbers the notes that follow.

Tables represent a very powerful capability within Word and are created through the Insert Table command in the Table menu or by using the Insert Table button on the Standard toolbar. The cells in a table can contain text, numbers, and/or graphics. The cells in the table are separated by dotted lines known as gridlines, which appear on the monitor but not in the printed document.

A style is a set of formatting instructions that has been saved under a distinct name. Styles are created at the character or paragraph level and provide a consistent appearance to similar elements throughout a document. Existing styles can be modified to change the formatting of all text defined by that style.

The AutoFormat command analyzes a document and formats it for you. The command goes through an entire document, determines how each paragraph is used, then applies an appropriate style to each paragraph.

Formatting occurs at the character, paragraph, or section level. Section formatting controls margins, columns, page orientation and size, page numbering, and headers and footers. A header consists of one or more lines that are printed at the top of every (designated) page in a document. A footer is text that is printed at the bottom of designated pages. Page numbers may be added to either a header or footer.

A table of contents lists headings in the order they appear in a document with their respective page numbers. It can be created automatically, provided the built-in heading styles were previously applied to the items for inclusion. The Edit Go To command enables you to move directly to a specific page, section, or bookmark within a document.

KEY WORDS AND CONCEPTS

AutoFormat command	Format Style command	Normal style
Body Text style	Go To command	Numbered list
Bookmark	Header	Page numbers
Bulleted list	Heading 1 style	Paragraph style
Bullets and Numbering command	Index and Tables command	Section
Cell	Insert Footnote command	Section break
Character style		Style
Default Paragraph Font style	Insert menu	Style command
	Insert Page Numbers command	Table menu
Endnote		Table of contents
Footer	Insert Table command	Tables feature
Footnote	Leader character	

Multiple Choice

1. Which of the following can be stored within a paragraph style?
   (a) Tabs and indents
   (b) Line spacing and alignment
   (c) Shading and borders
   (d) All of the above

2. What is the easiest way to change the alignment of five paragraphs scattered throughout a document, each of which has been formatted with the same style?
   (a) Select the paragraphs individually, then click the appropriate alignment button on the Formatting toolbar
   (b) Select the paragraphs at the same time, then click the appropriate alignment button on the Formatting toolbar
   (c) Change the format of the existing style, which changes the paragraphs
   (d) Retype the paragraphs according to the new specifications

3. The AutoFormat command will do all of the following except:
   (a) Apply styles to individual paragraphs
   (b) Apply boldface italics to terms that require additional emphasis
   (c) Replace ordinary quotes with smart quotes
   (d) Substitute typographic symbols for ordinary letters—such as © for (C)

4. Which of the following is true?
   (a) The addition or deletion of a footnote automatically renumbers the notes that follow
   (b) The addition or deletion of an endnote automatically renumbers the notes that follow
   (c) Both (a) and (b)
   (d) Neither (a) nor (b)

5. In which view do you see headers and/or footers?
   (a) Page Layout view
   (b) Normal view
   (c) Both (a) and (b)
   (d) Neither (a) nor (b)

6. Which of the following numbering schemes can be used with page numbers?
   (a) Roman numerals (I, II, III . . . or i, ii, iii)
   (b) Regular numbers (1, 2, 3, . . .)
   (c) Letters (A, B, C . . . or a, b, c)
   (d) All of the above

7. Which of the following is true regarding headers and footers?
   (a) Every document must have at least one header
   (b) Every document must have at least one footer
   (c) Both (a) and (b)
   (d) Neither (a) nor (b)

8. Which of the following is a *false* statement regarding lists?
   (a) A bulleted list can be changed to a numbered list and vice versa
   (b) The symbol for the bulleted list can be changed to a different character
   (c) The numbers in a numbered list can be changed to letters or roman numerals
   (d) The bullets or numbers cannot be removed

9. Page numbers can be specified in:
   (a) A header but not a footer
   (b) A footer but not a header
   (c) A header or a footer
   (d) Neither a header nor a footer

10. Which of the following is true regarding the formatting within a document?
   (a) Line spacing and alignment are implemented at the section level
   (b) Margins, headers, and footers are implemented at the paragraph level
   (c) Both (a) and (b)
   (d) Neither (a) nor (b)

11. What happens when you press the Tab key from within a table?
   (a) A Tab character is inserted just as it would be for ordinary text
   (b) The insertion point moves to the next column in the same row or the first column in the next row if you are at the end of the row
   (c) Both (a) and (b)
   (d) Neither (a) nor (b)

12. Which of the following is true, given that the status bar displays Page 1, Section 3, followed by 7/9?
    (a) The document has a maximum of three sections
    (b) The third section begins on page 7
    (c) The insertion point is on the very first page of the document
    (d) All of the above

13. The Edit Go To command enables you to move the insertion point to:
    (a) A specific page
    (b) A relative page forward or backward from the current page
    (c) A specific section
    (d) Any of the above

14. Once a table of contents has been created and inserted into a document:
    (a) Any subsequent page changes arising from the insertion or deletion of text to existing paragraphs must be entered manually
    (b) Any additions to the entries in the table arising due to the insertion of new paragraphs defined by a heading style must be entered manually
    (c) Both (a) and (b)
    (d) Neither (a) nor (b)

15. How do you print the lines separating the cells within a table in the printed document?
    (a) Select the gridlines option from the Table menu
    (b) Use the Format Border command
    (c) Either (a) or (b) but not both
    (d) Both (a) and (b) must be in effect at the same time

ANSWERS

1. d	**6.** d	**11.** b
2. c	**7.** d	**12.** b
3. b	**8.** d	**13.** d
4. c	**9.** c	**14.** d
5. a	**10.** d	**15.** b

EXPLORING MICROSOFT WORD

1. Use Figure 4.13 to match each action with its result; a given action may be used more than once or not at all.

   Action
   a. Click at 1, click at 7
   b. Click at 2

   Result
   ____ Change to landscape orientation
   ____ Insert page numbers into the document

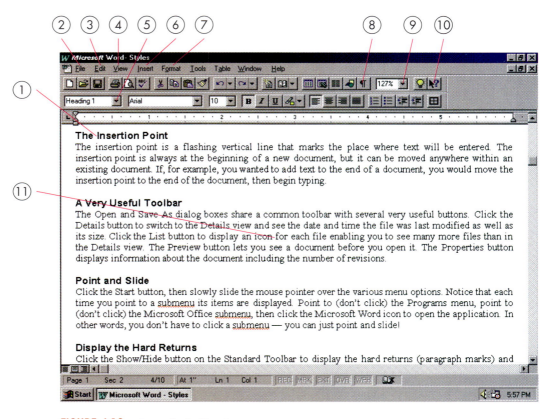

FIGURE 4.13 Screen for Problem 1

    c. Click at 3   ____ View the list of existing styles
    d. Click at 4   ____ Show the paragraph marks
    e. Click at 5   ____ Create a table of contents
    f. Click at 6   ____ Zoom to two pages
    g. Click at 7   ____ Go to page six
    h. Click at 8   ____ Edit the existing style
    i. Click at 9   ____ View the paragraph's formatting specifications
    j. Click at 10, click at 11   ____ Create a header

2. Adding emphasis: Figure 4.14 illustrates the use of a pull quote to add emphasis to a paragraph within a document. Figure 4.14a displays a paragraph set to the specifications of the style in Figure 4.14b.
   a. What is the name of the style?
   b. Which typeface, point size, and other font attributes are specified?
   c. Which paragraph attributes are specified?
   d. Which border attributes are specified?
   e. What is the easiest way to create the style; that is, should the style be created before or after the commands in parts b through d are executed?
   f. How would you modify the style to use a drop shadow rather than the parallel lines at the top and bottom?
   g. How would you modify the style so that the text is shaded?

Horizontal rules are effective to separate one topic from another, emphasize a subhead, or call attention to a pull quote, a phrase or sentence taken from an article to emphasize a point.

(a) Printed Paragraph

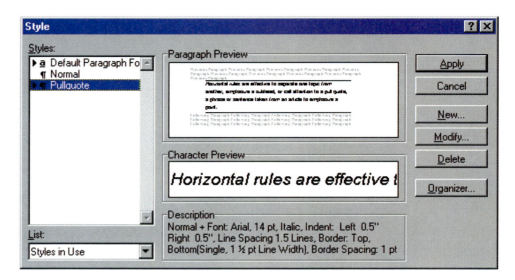

(b) Style Specifications

FIGURE 4.14   Pull Quotes

3. Answer the following with respect to the screen in Figure 4.15:
   a. How many sections are in the document? How many pages?
   b. What is the location of the insertion point? What does the indication "2/2" on the status bar mean?
   c. Which command was used to create the section break(s)?
   d. What is the orientation in the first section? In the second section?
   e. What are the margins in the first section? (Assume the default margins are in effect.) Are the margins the same in the second section?

4. Answer the following with respect to the screen displayed in Figure 4.16:
   a. What are the dimensions of the table? Which cells (if any) have been merged?
   b. What happens if you press the Tab key from within any cell in the table? If you press Ctrl+Tab?
   c. How does the appearance of the ruler change to reflect the fact that the insertion point is positioned within the table?
   d. Will the gridlines appear with the printed table? How do you place a border around the entire table so that the border prints with the table?
   e. Which command produced the dialog box in the figure?
   f. What is meant by automatic row height? What other way(s) will specify the height of a row?

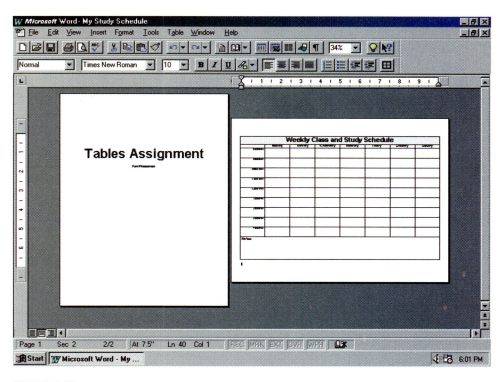

FIGURE 4.15 Screen for Problem 3

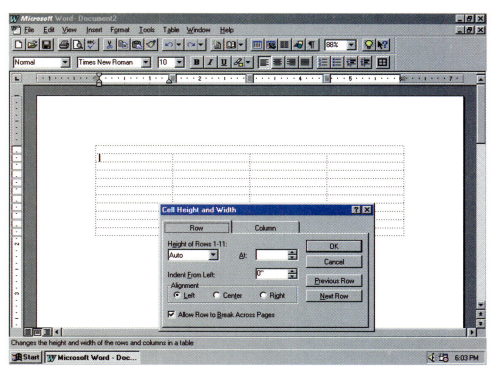

FIGURE 4.16 Screen for Problem 4

Practice with Microsoft Word

1. For the health conscious: Figure 4.17 displays the first five tips in a document describing tips for healthier living. Retrieve the document *Chapter 4 Practice 1* from the data disk, then modify it as follows:
   a. Use the AutoFormat command to apply the Heading 1 and Body Text styles throughout the document.
   b. Change the specifications for the Body Text and Heading 1 styles so that your document matches the document in the figure. The Heading 1 style calls for 12 point Arial bold with a blue top border (which requires a color printer). The Body Text style is 12 point Times New Roman, justified, with a ¼ inch left indent.
   c. Create a title page for the document consisting of the title, *Tips for Healthy Living,* the author, *Marion B. Grauer,* and an additional line, indicating that the document was prepared for you.
   d. Create a header for the document consisting of the title, *Tips for Healthy Living,* and a page number. The header is not to appear on the title page.

Start a Diet Journal
Keep a daily record of your weight and the foods you've eaten. Study your journal to become aware of your eating behavior. It will tell you when you're eating too much or if you're eating the wrong foods.

Why Do You Want to Lose Weight?
Write a list of reasons in your diet journal and refer to it often to sustain your motivation. Good health, good looks, more self-confidence, and new romantic possibilities are only the beginning.

Fighting Fatigue
Paradoxically, the more you do, the less tired you'll feel. Regular balanced exercise will speed up your metabolism, burn calories more efficiently, raise your energy level, and lift your spirits.

You Are What You Eat
Foods laden with fat, salt, and sugar leave you feeling lethargic and depressed. They set you up for more overeating. A nutritious low-fat diet has the opposite effect. You feel energized, revitalized, and happier.

"Water is the only drink for a wise man." Thoreau
Water is the perfect weight-loss beverage. It fills your stomach, curbs your appetite, and cleanses your entire system. Add a twist of lemon or lime to improve the taste, and drink eight glasses every day.

FIGURE 4.17 Document for Practice with Word Exercise 1

2. **Sports fans:** The tables feature is perfect to display the standings of any league, be it amateur or professional. Figure 4.18, for example, shows hypothetical standings in baseball and was a breeze. Pick any sport or league that you like and create a table with the standings as of today.

American League
Standings as of June 4, 1995

East	Wins	Losses	Percent
Boston Red Sox	22	11	.667
Baltimore Orioles	15	18	.455
Toronto Blue Jays	15	19	.441
Detroit Tigers	15	20	.429
New York Yankees	13	19	.406
Central	**Wins**	**Losses**	**Percent**
Cleveland Indians	23	10	.697
Kansas City Royals	18	15	.545
Milwaukee Brewers	15	19	.441
Chicago White Sox	13	20	.394
Minnesota Twins	11	25	.306
West	**Wins**	**Losses**	**Percent**
California Angels	22	13	.629
Seattle Mariners	19	15	.559
Texas Rangers	20	16	.556
Oakland A's	17	18	.486

FIGURE 4.18 Document for Practice with Word Exercise 2

3. **Form design:** The tables feature is ideal to create forms as shown by the document in Figure 4.19, which displays an employment application. Reproduce the document shown in the figure or design your own application. Submit the completed document to your instructor.

4. **Graphics:** A table may contain anything; text, graphics, or numbers as shown by the document in Figure 4.20, which displays a hypothetical computer advertisement. It's not complicated; in fact, it was really very easy; just follow the steps below:

   a. Create a 7 × 4 table.

   b. Merge all of the cells in row one and enter the heading. Merge all of the cells in row two and type the text describing the sale.

   c. Use the ClipArt Gallery to insert a picture into the table. (Various computer graphics are available in the Business and Technology categories.)

   d. Enter the sales data in rows three through seven of the table; all entries are centered within the respective cells.

   e. Use the Format Borders command to implement lines and shading, then print the completed document.

   Of course, it isn't quite as simple as it sounds, but we think you get the idea. Good luck and feel free to improve on our design.

Computer Consultants, Inc.
Employee Application Form

Last Name:	First Name:	Middle Name:

Address:

City:	State:	Zip Code:	Telephone:

Date of Birth:	Place of Birth:	Citizenship:

Highest Degree Attained:	List Schools Attended (include years attended):
High School Diploma Bachelor's Degree Master's Degree Ph.D.	

List Specific Computer Skills:

List Relevant Computer Experience:

References (list name, title, and current mailing address):

1.

2.

3.

FIGURE 4.19 Document for Practice with Word Exercise 3

Computers to Go

Our tremendous sales volume enables us to offer the fastest, most powerful series of Pentium computers at prices almost too good to be true. Each microprocessor is offered in a variety of configurations so that you get exactly what you need. All configurations include a local bus video, a 15-inch monitor, a mouse, and Windows 95.

Capacity	Configuration 1 8 Mb RAM 540 Mb Hard Drive	Configuration 2 16 Mb RAM 1 Gb Hard Drive	Configuration 3 24 Mb RAM 2 Gb Hard Drive
Pentium - 60 Mz	$1,999	$2,099	$2,599
Pentium - 75 Mz	$2,199	$2,399	$2,899
Pentium - 100 Mz	$2,399	$2,699	$3,199
Pentium - 120 Mz	$2,599	$2,999	$3,499

FIGURE 4.20   Document for Practice with Word Exercise 4

CASE STUDIES

Milestones in Communications

We take for granted immediate news of everything that is going on in the world, but it was not always that way. Did you know, for example, that it took five months for Queen Isabella to hear of Columbus' discovery, or that it took two weeks for Europe to learn of Lincoln's assassination? We've done some research on milestones in communications and left the file for you (Milestones in Communications). It runs for two, three, or four pages, depending on the formatting, which we leave to you. We would like you to include a header, and we think you should box the quotations that appear at the end of the document (it's your call as to whether to separate the quotations or group them together). Please be sure to number the completed document and don't forget a title page.

The Term Paper

Go to your most demanding professor and obtain the formatting requirements for the submission of a term paper. Be as precise as possible; for example, ask about margins, type size, and so on. What are the requirements for a title page? Is there a table of contents? Are there footnotes or endnotes, headers or footers? What is the format for the bibliography? Summarize the requirements, then indicate the precise means of implementation within Microsoft Word.

Forms, Forms, and More Forms

Every business uses a multitude of forms. Job applicants submit an employment application, sales personnel process order forms, and customers receive invoices. Even telephone messages have a form of their own. The office manager needs forms for everything, and she has come to you for help. You remember reading something about a tables feature and suggest that as a starting point. She needs more guidance so you sit down with her and quickly design two forms that meet with her approval. Bring the two forms to class and compare your work with that of your classmates.

Tips for Windows 95

The appendix on Windows 95 that appears at the end of this text contains introductory information about the new operating system. We captured many of the tips in that appendix, together with additional tips on other topics, and placed them into a *Tips for Windows 95* document that can be found on the data disk. The tips are not formatted, however, and we would like you to use the AutoFormat command to create an attractive document. There are lots of tips so a table of contents is also appropriate. Add a cover page with your name and date, then submit the completed document to your instructor.

DESKTOP PUBLISHING: CREATING A NEWSLETTER

OBJECTIVES

After reading this chapter you will be able to:

1. Describe one advantage and one disadvantage of using the Newsletter Wizard, as opposed to creating a document from scratch.
2. Create a multicolumn newsletter; explain how sections are used to vary the number of columns in a document.
3. Use the Format Borders command to create boxes, shading, and reverses within a newsletter.
4. Use the Insert Picture command to insert clip art into a document; explain how frames are used to move and/or size the graphic.
5. Differentiate between clicking and double-clicking an object; modify a picture using the drawing tools within Microsoft Word.
6. Discuss the importance of a grid in the design of a document; describe the use of white space as a design element.

OVERVIEW

Desktop publishing evolved through a combination of technologies including faster computers, laser printers, and sophisticated page composition software to manipulate text and graphics. Today's generation of word processors has matured to such a degree that it is difficult to tell where word processing ends and desktop publishing begins. Microsoft Word is, for all practical purposes, a desktop publishing program that can be used to produce all types of documents.

The essence of desktop publishing is the merger of text with graphics to produce a professional-looking document without reliance on external services. Desktop publishing will save you time and money because you are doing work that used to be done by others. In practice it is not as easy as it sounds, because you are doing work that was previously done by others who were skilled in their respective areas. Thus, in addition to learning the commands within Microsoft Word to implement desktop publishing, you need to learn the basics of graphic design.

The chapter focuses on desktop publishing as it is implemented in Microsoft Word, followed by a brief introduction to graphic design. We show you how to create a multicolumn document, how to import graphic images, and how to edit those images as embedded objects. We also review material from earlier chapters on bullets and lists, borders and shading, and section formatting, all of which will be used to create a newsletter in this chapter. We also discuss several guidelines of graphic design to help you create a more polished document.

THE NEWSLETTER

The chapter is organized around the newsletter in Figure 5.1, which illustrates basic capabilities in ***desktop publishing.*** The hands-on exercises help you create the newsletter(s) in the figure. We think you will be pleased at how easy the process is and hope that you go on to create more sophisticated designs.

Figure 5.1a shows the newsletter as it exists on the data disk. We supply the text, but the formatting will be up to you. Figure 5.1b shows the newsletter at the end of the first hands-on exercise. It contains balanced newspaper columns, a ***masthead*** (a heading for the newsletter) that is set between thick parallel lines, and a bulleted list.

Figure 5.1c displays a more interesting design that contains a graphic, columns of different widths, a vertical line to separate the columns, and a dropped capital letter to emphasize the lead article. The figure uses shading to emphasize a specific paragraph and a ***reverse*** (white text on a black background) to accentuate the masthead.

Figure 5.1d illustrates an alternate design using three columns rather than two. The figure incorporates a ***pull quote*** (a phrase or sentence taken from an article) to emphasize a point. It also uses a more dynamic masthead that was developed with Microsoft WordArt (see pages 131–133).

The choice between the various newsletters in the figure is one of personal taste. All of the newsletters contain the identical text, but vary in their presentation of the written material. The easy part of desktop publishing is to implement a specific design using commands within Microsoft Word. The more difficult aspect is to create the design in the first place. We urge you therefore to experiment freely and to realize that good design is often the result of trial and error.

> **ADDING INTEREST**
>
> Boxes, shading, and reverses (light text on a dark background) add interest to a document. Horizontal (vertical) lines are also effective in separating one topic from another, emphasizing a subhead, or calling attention to a pull quote (a phrase or sentence taken from the article to emphasize a key point).

Typography

Typography—the selection of typefaces, styles, and sizes—is a critical element in the design of any document. The basics were presented in Chapter 2, where we distinguished between a serif and a sans serif typeface. We noted that serif type-

Contest Winner
Congratulations to Carol Vazquez Villar who submitted the winning entry for our logo. Carol wins a pair of running shoes, which she promises to show off at the upcoming Jungle Jog.

Warming Up
Ever pull a muscle running your first mile or playing your first game of tennis? You should have stretched before you started -- right? Not according to a panel of sports medicine experts put together by the National Strength and Conditioning Association.

Warming up, not stretching, is the most important thing you can do to prevent injuries. Muscles that are cold are not very pliable and thus are susceptible to injury. Even stretching should be put off until you warm up with a few minutes of light jogging to increase your metabolic rate and raise your body's core temperature. When should you stretch? After your exercise -- when your muscles are warm.

Cold muscles injure easily
Begin with light jogging
Stretch after exercising
Be kind to your muscles

Better Fit Than Fat
There is nothing like finishing a meal with a delicate French pastry or a luscious chocolate mousse, but how much will that indulgence cost in calories? And what will you look like on the beach if you keep treating yourself to such delights?

Exercise is important to weight control, giving you more caloric leeway in your diet and suppressing your appetite. The number of calories burned during physical exercise depends on many factors -- how big you are (thinner, smaller people burn fewer calories at the same activity level than heavier, larger people), how hard or fast you work out (the harder the labor or faster the speed, the more calories you burn per minute), the air temperature (the colder the weather, the more calories you burn), the clothes you wear, the type of activity you choose, and the amount of time you spend doing it.

Some sports burn more fat than others. Start-stop activities, such as tennis or sprinting, are primarily carbohydrate-burning activities and use 60-70% carbohydrates and only 40-30% fat. Continuous sports on the other hand, such as walking or jogging, consume 50 - 60% fat and 50-40% carbohydrates.

Any strenuous workout, be it jogging, energetic walking, biking, or swimming, is fine. The important thing is to make a commitment to exercise regularly, at least three to five times a week, every week. If you haven't exercised in a while, start off slowly and gradually build up to the level that you desire.

Exercise and Income
According to a recent Gallup poll, the higher a person's income, the more likely he or she is to exercise; for example, in households with an income over $30,000, 68% of the men and 60% of the women exercise regularly. In addition, people with college degrees are more likely to exercise than those with only high school diplomas.

The Sun and Your Skin
If you have blond or red hair and your eyes are blue, green, or gray, you are more prone to skin cancer. The harmful rays of the sun are the ultraviolet (UV) ones. Unlike the infrared rays that are screened by the clouds, the UV rays go right through. So even on overcast days you need to protect your skin with a sunscreen with a high SPF factor. The best sunscreens are those that contain PABA esters and benzophenones that protect against both UVA and UVB rays.

As a precaution against skin cancer, examine brown spots, birth marks, moles, and sores that don't heal within two weeks. See your doctor immediately if you notice any change in shape or color.

Jungle Jog
Run the trails at the City Zoo on Saturday, March 15th at 7:00 AM, then meet at the Pavilion for breakfast among the beasts. Robert Plant will defend his title from last year. 35:55 is the time to beat.

(a) Text for the Newsletter

The Athlete's Hi

Contest Winner
Congratulations to Carol Vazquez Villar who submitted the winning entry for our logo. Carol wins a pair of running shoes, which she promises to show off at the upcoming Jungle Jog.

Warming Up
Ever pull a muscle running your first mile or playing your first game of tennis? You should have stretched before you started -- right? Not according to a panel of sports medicine experts put together by the National Strength and Conditioning Association.

Warming up, not stretching, is the most important thing you can do to prevent injuries. Muscles that are cold are not very pliable and thus are susceptible to injury. Even stretching should be put off until you warm up with a few minutes of light jogging to increase your metabolic rate and raise your body's core temperature. When should you stretch? After your exercise -- when your muscles are warm.

- Cold muscles injure easily
- Begin with light jogging
- Stretch after exercising
- Be kind to your muscles

Better Fit Than Fat
There is nothing like finishing a meal with a delicate French pastry or a luscious chocolate mousse, but how much will that indulgence cost in calories? And what will you look like on the beach if you keep treating yourself to such delights?

Exercise is important to weight control, giving you more caloric leeway in your diet and suppressing your appetite. The number of calories burned during physical exercise depends on many factors -- how big you are (thinner, smaller people burn fewer calories at the same activity level than heavier, larger people), how hard or fast you work out (the harder the labor or faster the speed, the more calories you burn per minute), the air temperature (the colder the weather, the more calories you burn), the clothes you wear, the type of activity you choose, and the amount of time you spend doing it.

Some sports burn more fat than others. Start-stop activities, such as tennis or sprinting, are primarily carbohydrate-burning activities and use 60–70% carbohydrates and only 40–30% fat. Continuous sports on the other hand, such as walking or jogging, consume 50–60% fat and 50–40% carbohydrates.

Any strenuous workout, be it jogging, energetic walking, biking, or swimming, is fine. The important thing is to make a commitment to exercise regularly, at least three to five times a week, every week. If you haven't exercised in a while, start off slowly and gradually build up to the level that you desire.

Exercise and Income
According to a recent Gallup poll, the higher a person's income, the more likely he or she is to exercise; for example, in households with an income over $30,000, 68% of the men and 60% of the women exercise regularly. In addition, people with college degrees are more likely to exercise than those with only high school diplomas.

The Sun and Your Skin
If you have blond or red hair and your eyes are blue, green, or gray, you are more prone to skin cancer. The harmful rays of the sun are the ultraviolet (UV) ones. Unlike the infrared rays that are screened by the clouds, the UV rays go right through. So even on overcast days you need to protect your skin with a sunscreen with a high SPF factor. The best sunscreens are those that contain PABA esters and benzophenones that protect against both UVA and UVB rays.

As a precaution against skin cancer, examine brown spots, birth marks, moles, and sores that don't heal within two weeks. See your doctor immediately if you notice any change in shape or color.

Jungle Jog
Run the trails at the City Zoo on Saturday, March 15th at 7:00 AM, then meet at the Pavilion for breakfast among the beasts. Robert Plant will defend his title from last year. 35:55 is the time to beat.

(b) At End of Exercise 1

The Athlete's Hi

Contest Winner
Congratulations to Carol Vazquez Villar who submitted the winning entry for our logo. Carol wins a pair of running shoes, which she promises to show off at the upcoming Jungle Jog.

Warming Up
Ever pull a muscle running your first mile or playing your first game of tennis? You should have stretched before you started -- right? Not according to a panel of sports medicine experts put together by the National Strength and Conditioning Association.

Warming up, not stretching, is the most important thing you can do to prevent injuries. Muscles that are cold are not very pliable and thus are susceptible to injury. Even stretching should be put off until you warm up with a few minutes of light jogging to increase your metabolic rate and raise your body's core temperature. When should you stretch? After your exercise -- when your muscles are warm.

- Cold muscles injure easily
- Begin with light jogging
- Stretch after exercising
- Be kind to your muscles

Better Fit Than Fat
There is nothing like finishing a meal with a delicate French pastry or a luscious chocolate mousse, but how much will that indulgence cost in calories? And what will you look like on the beach if you keep treating yourself to such delights?

Exercise is important to weight control, giving you more caloric leeway in your diet and suppressing your appetite. The number of calories burned during physical exercise depends on many factors -- how big you are (thinner, smaller people burn fewer calories at the same activity level than heavier, larger people), how hard or fast you work out (the harder the labor or faster the speed, the more calories you burn per minute), the air temperature (the colder the weather, the more calories you burn), the clothes you wear, the type of activity you choose, and the amount of time you spend doing it.

Some sports burn more fat than others. Start-stop activities, such as tennis or sprinting, are primarily carbohydrate-burning activities and use 60–70% carbohydrates and only 40–30% fat. Continuous sports on the other hand, such as walking or jogging, consume 50–60% fat and 50–40% carbohydrates.

Any strenuous workout, be it jogging, energetic walking, biking, or swimming, is fine. The important thing is to make a commitment to exercise regularly, at least three to five times a week, every week. If you haven't exercised in a while, start off slowly and gradually build up to the level that you desire.

Exercise and Income
According to a recent Gallup poll, the higher a person's income, the more likely he or she is to exercise; for example, in households with an income over $30,000, 68% of the men and 60% of the women exercise regularly. In addition, people with college degrees are more likely to exercise than those with only high school diplomas.

The Sun and Your Skin
If you have blond or red hair and your eyes are blue, green, or gray, you are more prone to skin cancer. The harmful rays of the sun are the ultraviolet (UV) ones. Unlike the infrared rays that are screened by the clouds, the UV rays go right through. So even on overcast days you need to protect your skin with a sunscreen with a high SPF factor. The best sunscreens are those that contain PABA esters and benzophenones that protect against both UVA and UVB rays.

As a precaution against skin cancer, examine brown spots, birth marks, moles, and sores that don't heal within two weeks. See your doctor immediately if you notice any change in shape or color.

Jungle Jog
Run the trails at the City Zoo on Saturday, March 15th at 7:00 AM, then meet at the Pavilion for breakfast among the beasts. Robert Plant will defend his title from last year. 35:55 is the time to beat.

(c) At End of Exercise 3

The Athlete's Hi

Volume 1, Number 1 **Winter 1996**

Contest Winner
Congratulations to Carol Vazquez Villar who submitted the winning entry for our logo. Carol wins a pair of running shoes, which she promises to show off at the upcoming Jungle Jog.

Warming Up
Ever pull a muscle running your first mile or playing your first game of tennis? You should have stretched before you started -- right? Not according to a panel of sports medicine experts put together by the National Strength and Conditioning Association.

Warming up, not stretching, is the most important thing you can do to prevent injuries. Muscles that are cold are not very pliable and thus are susceptible to injury. Even stretching should be put off until you warm up with a few minutes of light jogging to increase your metabolic rate and raise your body's core temperature. When should you stretch? After your exercise -- when your muscles are warm.

- Cold muscles injure easily
- Begin with light jogging
- Stretch after exercising
- Be kind to your muscles

Better Fit Than Fat
There is nothing like finishing a meal with a delicate French pastry or a luscious chocolate mousse, but how much will that indulgence cost in calories? And what will you look like on the beach if you keep treating yourself to such delights?

Exercise is important to weight control, giving you more caloric leeway in your diet and suppressing your appetite. The number of calories burned during physical exercise depends on many factors -- how big you are (thinner, smaller people burn fewer calories at the same activity level than heavier, larger people), how hard or fast you work out (the harder the labor or faster the speed, the more calories you burn per minute), the air temperature (the colder the weather, the more calories you burn), the clothes you wear, the type of activity you choose, and the amount of time you spend doing it.

Some sports burn more fat than others. Start-stop activities, such as tennis or sprinting, are primarily carbohydrate-burning activities and use 60–70% carbohydrates and only 40–30% fat. Continuous sports on the other hand, such as walking or jogging, consume 50–60% fat and 50–40% carbohydrates.

Any strenuous workout, be it jogging, energetic walking, biking, or swimming, is fine. The important thing is to make a commitment to exercise regularly, at least three to five times a week, every week. If you haven't exercised in a while, start off slowly and gradually build up to the level that you desire.

Exercise and Income
According to a recent Gallup poll, the higher a person's income, the more likely he or she is to exercise; for example, in households with an income over $30,000, 68% of the men and 60% of the women exercise regularly. In addition, people with college degrees are more likely to exercise than those with only high school diplomas.

"The important thing is to make a commitment to exercise regularly, at least three to five times a week, every week"

The Sun and Your Skin
If you have blond or red hair and your eyes are blue, green, or gray, you are more prone to skin cancer. The harmful rays of the sun are the ultraviolet (UV) ones. Unlike the infrared rays that are screened by the clouds, the UV rays go right through. So even on overcast days you need to protect your skin with a sunscreen with a high SPF factor. The best sunscreens are those that contain PABA esters and benzophenones that protect against both UVA and UVB rays.

As a precaution against skin cancer, examine brown spots, birth marks, moles, and sores that don't heal within two weeks. See your doctor immediately if you notice any change in shape or color.

Jungle Jog
Run the trails at the City Zoo on Saturday, March 15th at 7:00 AM, then meet at the Pavilion for breakfast among the beasts. Robert Plant will defend his title from last year. 35:55 is the time to beat.

(d) An Alternate Design

FIGURE 5.1 The Newsletter

faces were preferable for large amounts of text, and that sans serif was preferable for headings and titles. We also said that type size was measured in points and that there were 72 points to the inch. Large amounts of text are typically set in 10 or 12 point type. This book, for example, is set in 10 point type.

Typography influences the appearance of a document more than any other element. Good typography goes almost unnoticed, whereas poor typography calls attention to itself and distracts from the document. There are no hard and fast rules, only guidelines and common sense, and what works in one instance may not work in another.

One generally accepted guideline is to limit the number of typefaces in a document to two, but to use multiple styles and sizes of those typefaces. Boldface and/or italics are recommended for emphasis, as opposed to underlining or all uppercase letters. Different point sizes can also be used to differentiate between headings, subheadings, and text, but a variation of at least two points is necessary to be noticeable.

The point size should also be consistent with the length of a line or the width of a column. Larger point sizes require longer lines or wider columns. Conversely, the shorter the line or narrower the column, the smaller the point size. Very narrow columns or very short lines should be avoided because they are choppy and difficult to read. Overly wide columns or very long lines are just as bad because the reader can easily get lost.

Columns

The ***Columns command*** in the Format menu enables you to define ***newspaper-style columns*** in which text flows continuously from the bottom of one column to the top of the next. You specify the number of columns and, optionally, the space between columns. Microsoft Word does the rest, calculating the width of each col-

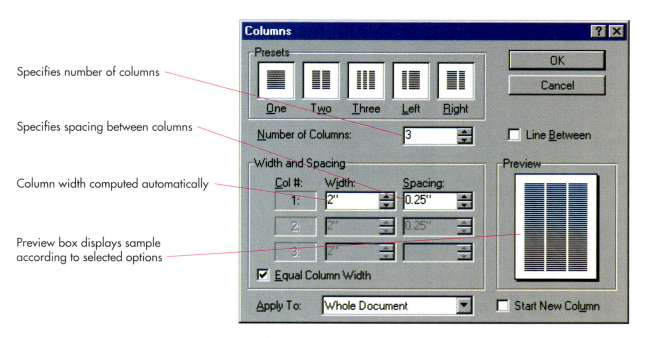

FIGURE 5.2 The Columns Command

umn according to the left and right margins on the page and the specified (default) space between columns.

The dialog box in Figure 5.2 specifies three equal columns with .25 inch between each column. The two-inch width of each column is computed automatically based on left and right page margins of one inch each and the ¼ inch spacing between columns. The space in the margins and between the columns, a total of 2½ inches in this example, is subtracted from the page width of 8½ inches. The remaining 6 inches is divided by three, resulting in a column width of two inches.

The number of columns can vary within a document. Each of the newsletters in Figure 5.1, for example, uses a single column at the top of the page for the masthead and multiple columns on the rest of the page. Columns are implemented at the section level, and thus a **section break** must be inserted whenever the column specification changes. (Section formatting was described in Chapter 4 in conjunction with changing margins, headers and footers, page numbering, size, and orientation.)

UNEQUAL COLUMNS

Add interest to a document by creating columns of different widths. Pull down the Format menu, click Columns, then click the Left or Right icon in the Presets area. Change the number, width, and/or spacing between columns, and Microsoft Word automatically changes the other parameters to match your specifications. Add a line between columns by checking the Line Between box in the Columns dialog box.

THE NEWSLETTER WIZARD

At first glance the **Newsletter Wizard** appears to answer the prayers of the would-be desktop publisher. Like any wizard (wizards were introduced in Chapter 3), the Newsletter Wizard asks you a series of questions, then creates a template for you on which to base a document.

The Newsletter Wizard provides a considerable amount of flexibility as can be inferred from the screens in Figure 5.3a, b, c, and d, which let you specify the style, number of columns, title, and elements to include. The resulting template in Figure 5.3e is based on your answers, and further, incorporates good typography and other elements of graphic design.

What, then, is the drawback, and why would you not use the Newsletter Wizard for every newsletter you create? The problem is one of adaptability in that the wizard may not be suitable for the newsletter you wish to create. What if you wanted to include two graphics, rather than one, or you wanted the graphic(s) in a different position? What if you needed a newsletter with columns of varying width, or you wanted to include a pull quote or a reverse?

You could, of course, use the template created by the wizard as the starting point for the newsletter, then execute the necessary commands in Word to modify the document according to your specifications. You will find, however, that it is just as easy to create the newsletter from the beginning and bypass the wizard entirely. You will wind up with a superior document that is exactly what you need and not what the wizard thinks you need. Creating a newsletter is a lot easier than you might imagine as you will see in the exercise that begins on page 211.

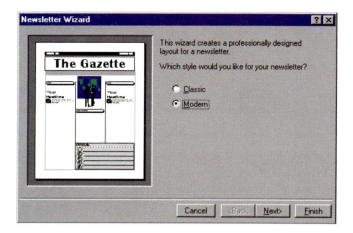

(a) The Newsletter Wizard

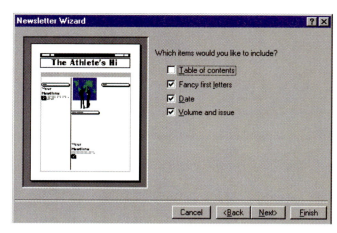

(d) Select the Items to Include

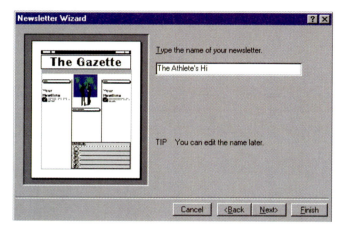

(b) Enter the Title

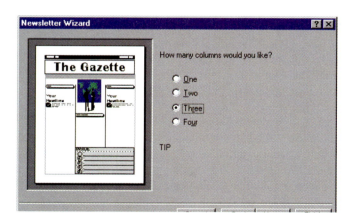

(c) Specify the Number of Columns

(e) The Completed Template

FIGURE 5.3   The Newsletter Wizard

HANDS-ON EXERCISE 1

Newspaper Columns

Objective: To create a multicolumn document with equal text in each column, to create a masthead, and to implement a bulleted or numbered list. Use Figure 5.4 as a guide for the exercise.

STEP 1: Load the Text of the Newsletter
- Start Word. Open the **Text for Newsletter** document in the Exploring Word folder.
- If necessary, click the **Page Layout button** on the status bar. Set the magnification (zoom) to **Page Width** to match the document in the figure.
- Save the document as **Modified Newsletter** so that you can return to the original document if necessary.

> ### VIEWS AND COLUMNS
>
> You must be in the Page Layout view, not the Normal view, in order to see columns displayed side-by-side within a document. Thus, if you do not see columns, it is probably because you are in the wrong view. Click the Page Layout button on the status bar to change the view, then click the arrow on the Zoom control box on the Standard toolbar to see as more or less of the page as necessary.

STEP 2: Newspaper Columns
- Pull down the **Format menu.** Click **Columns** to produce the dialog box in Figure 5.4a.
- Click the **Presets icon** for **Two.** The column width for each column and the spacing between columns will be determined automatically from the existing margins.
- If necessary, clear the **Line Between box.** Click **OK** to accept the settings and exit the dialog box. The text of the newsletter should be displayed in two columns.

> ### THE COLUMNS BUTTON
>
> The Columns button on the Standard toolbar is the fastest way to create columns in a document. Click the button, drag the mouse to choose the number of columns, then release the mouse to create the columns. The toolbar lets you change the number of columns, but not the spacing between columns. The toolbar is also limited in that you cannot create columns of different widths or select (deselect) a line between columns.

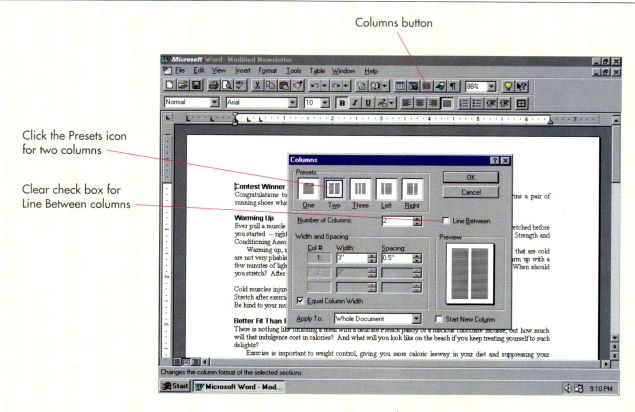

(a) Newspaper Columns (step 1)

FIGURE 5.4 Hands-on Exercise 1

STEP 3: Balance the Columns

➤ Use the **Zoom Control box** on the Standard toolbar to zoom to **Whole Page** to see the entire newsletter as in Figure 5.4b. Do not be concerned if the columns are of different lengths.

➤ Press **Ctrl+End** to move to the end of the document. Pull down the **Insert Menu.** Click **Break** to produce the dialog box of Figure 5.4b.

➤ Click the **Continuous button** under Section Breaks. Click **OK.** The columns should be balanced although one column may be one line longer (shorter) than the other.

USE THE RULER TO CHANGE COLUMN WIDTH

You can use the ruler to change column widths simply by dragging a column marker. Changing the width of one column in a document with equal-sized columns changes the width of all other columns so that they remain equal. Changing the width in a document with unequal columns changes only that column. You can also double click the top of the ruler to display the Page Setup dialog box, then click the Margins tab to change the left and right margins, which in turn will change the column width.

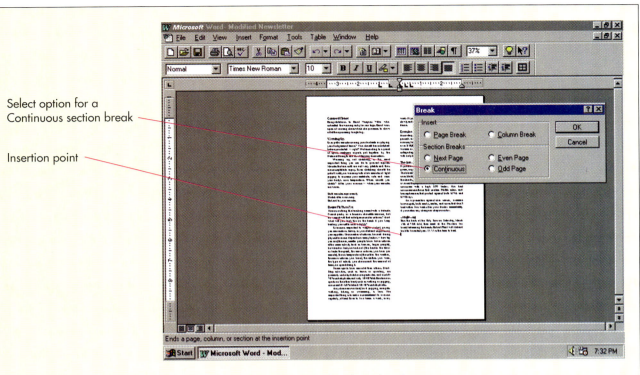

(b) Balance the Columns (step 3)

FIGURE 5.4 Hands-on Exercise 1 (continued)

STEP 4: Create the Masthead

➤ Use the **Zoom Control box** on the Standard toolbar to change to **Page Width.** Click the **Show/Hide ¶ button** to display the paragraph (and section) marks.

➤ Press **Ctrl+Home** to move to the beginning of the document.

➤ Pull down the **Insert menu.** Click **Break.** Click the **Continuous button.** Click **OK** to produce a double dotted line, indicating a section break as shown in Figure 5.4c.

➤ Click above the dotted line, which will place the insertion point to the left of the line. Check the status bar to be sure you are in section one, then format this section as a single column as follows:

- Pull down the **Format menu,** click **Columns,** choose **One** from the Presets column formats, and click **OK,** or
- Click the **Columns button** on the Standard toolbar and select one column.

COLUMNS AND SECTIONS

Columns are implemented at the section level, and thus a new section is required whenever the number of columns changes within a document. Select the text that is to be formatted in columns, click the Columns button on the Standard toolbar, then drag the mouse to set the desired number of columns. Microsoft Word will automatically insert the section breaks before and after the selected text.

➤ Type **The Athlete's Hi** and press **enter** twice. Select the newly entered text as shown in Figure 5.4c. Click the **Center button** on the Formatting toolbar. Change the font to **60 pt Arial Bold.**

➤ Save the newsletter.

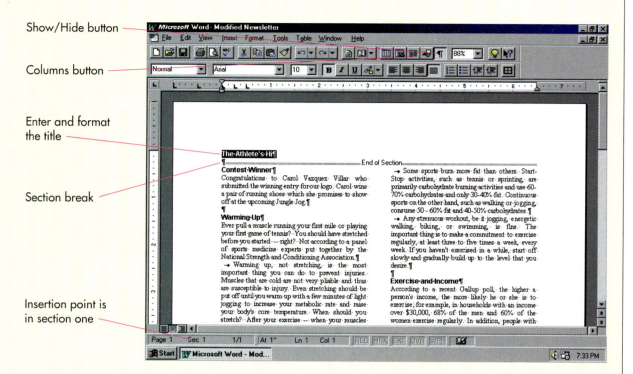

(c) Create the Masthead (step 4)

FIGURE 5.4 Hands-on Exercise 1 (continued)

STEP 5: Add Lines to the Masthead

➤ Press **Ctrl+Home** to move to the beginning of the newsletter. Click anywhere within the paragraph containing **The Athlete's Hi.**

➤ Pull down the **Format menu.** Click **Borders and Shading.** If necessary, click the **Borders tab** to produce the dialog box in Figure 5.4d.

BORDERS AND SHADING

The ***Borders and Shading command*** takes practice, but once you get used to it, you will love it. To place a border around multiple paragraphs (the paragraphs should have the same indents or else a different border will be placed around each paragraph), select the paragraphs prior to execution of the Borders and Shading command. Select (click) the line style you like, then click the Box or Shadow Preset button to place the border around the selected paragraphs. To change the border on one side, select (click) the side within the border model, then click the desired style. Click OK to exit the dialog box.

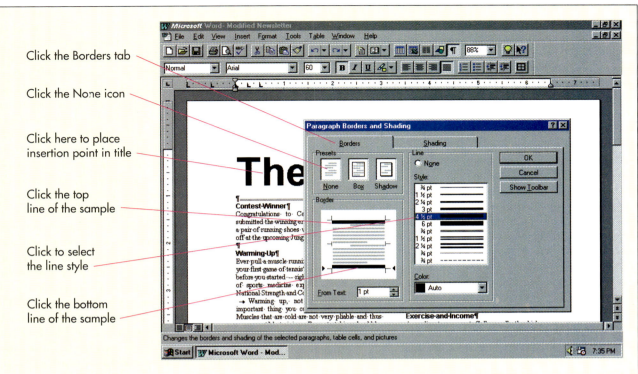

(d) Format the Masthead (step 5)

FIGURE 5.4 Hands-on Exercise 1 (continued)

➤ Click the **None icon** in the Presets area. Click the **top line** of the border model to apply a top border. Click the **4½ point** line style. Click the **bottom line** of the model to apply the same line to the bottom border.

➤ Click **OK** to return to the document. The masthead should be enclosed in parallel horizontal lines.

➤ Save the newsletter.

STEP 6: Bulleted and Numbered Lists

➤ Scroll in the document until you come to the list at the end of the Warming Up paragraph. Select the entire list as shown in Figure 5.4e.

➤ Pull down the **Format menu.** Click **Bullets and Numbers.** If necessary, click the **Numbered tab** to produce the dialog box in the figure.

➤ Choose a number style. Click **OK** to return to the document, which now contains a numbered list.

➤ Click at the end of the first item on the list. Press the **enter key** to begin a new line and enter a new item, **Begin with light jogging.** Microsoft Word automatically renumbers the list to include the item you just typed.

➤ Drag the mouse to select all four items on the list (the numbers will not be highlighted). Click the **Bullets button** on the Formatting toolbar to change to a bulleted list.

➤ Click the **Increase Indent button** on the Formatting toolbar to indent the entire list to the next tab stop. Click the **Decrease Indent button** to move the list to the previous tab stop. Click the **Increase Indent button** a second time to end with the bulleted items indented one tab stop.

➤ Click anywhere in the document to deselect the text. Save the newsletter.

DESKTOP PUBLISHING 215

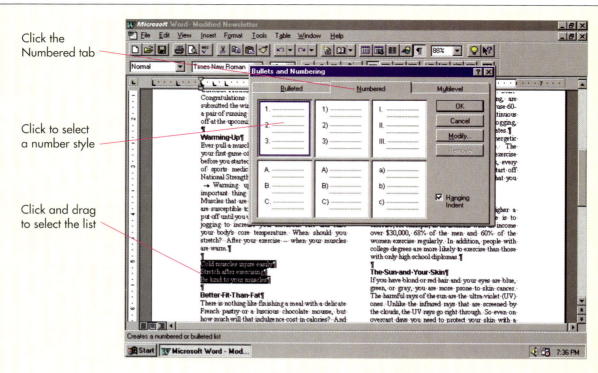

(e) Bullets and Numbering (step 6)

FIGURE 5.4 Hands-on Exercise 1 (continued)

LISTS AND THE FORMATTING TOOLBAR

The Formatting toolbar contains four buttons for use with bulleted and numbered lists. The Increase Indent and Decrease Indent buttons move the selected items one tab stop to the right and left, respectively. The Bullets button creates a bulleted list from unnumbered items or converts a numbered list to a bulleted list. The Numbering button creates a numbered list or converts a bulleted list to numbers. The Bullets and Numbering buttons also function as toggle switches; for example, clicking the Bullets button when a bulleted list is in effect will remove the bullets.

STEP 7: The Completed Newsletter

➤ Use the **Zoom Control box** on the Standard toolbar to zoom to **Whole Page** to see the entire newsletter as in Figure 5.4f.

➤ Click the **Show/Hide ¶ button** to suppress the paragraph markers.

➤ Pull down the **File menu.** Click **Exit** if you do not want to continue with the next exercise at this time. Click **Close** to close the document and remain in Word.

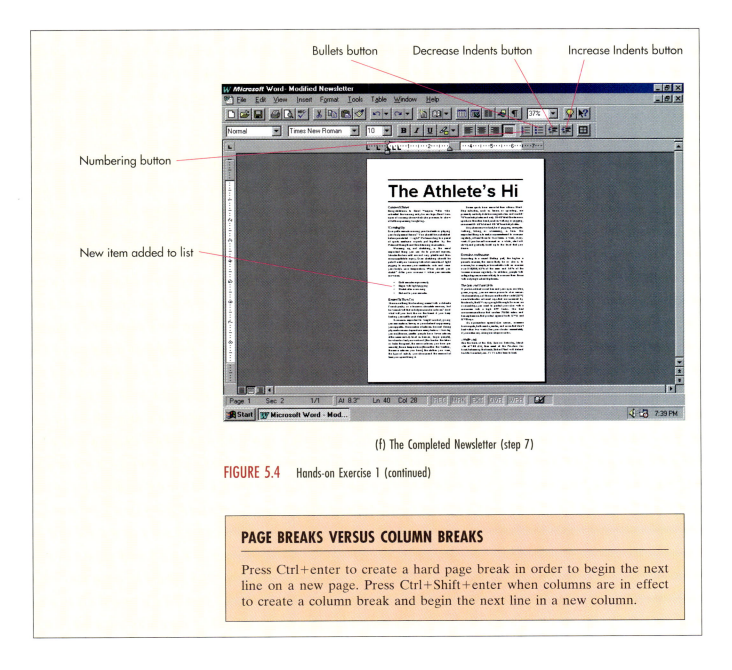

(f) The Completed Newsletter (step 7)

FIGURE 5.4 Hands-on Exercise 1 (continued)

PAGE BREAKS VERSUS COLUMN BREAKS

Press Ctrl+enter to create a hard page break in order to begin the next line on a new page. Press Ctrl+Shift+enter when columns are in effect to create a column break and begin the next line in a new column.

GRAPHICS

The right picture adds immeasurably to a document. ***Clip art*** (graphic images) is available from a variety of sources. You can use the Insert Object command to insert an image from the Microsoft ClipArt Gallery, as we discussed in Chapter 3. You can also use the Insert Picture command to select from an entirely different set of clip art images.

The ***Insert Picture command*** enables you to select a clip art image from anywhere on your system. A set of sample images is installed automatically in a Clipart folder when you install Microsoft Word or Microsoft Office. Execution of the Insert Picture command displays the dialog box of Figure 5.5a, which lets you preview a picture prior to inserting it. The available pictures (e.g., the graphics in the Clipart folder) are shown in the Name list box. All you do is select (click) a graphic, then click the OK command button to insert the graphic into the document.

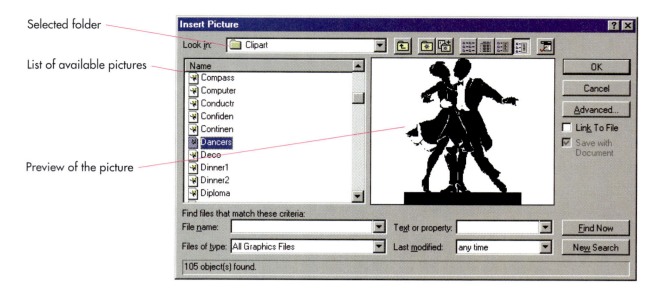

(a) Insert Picture Command

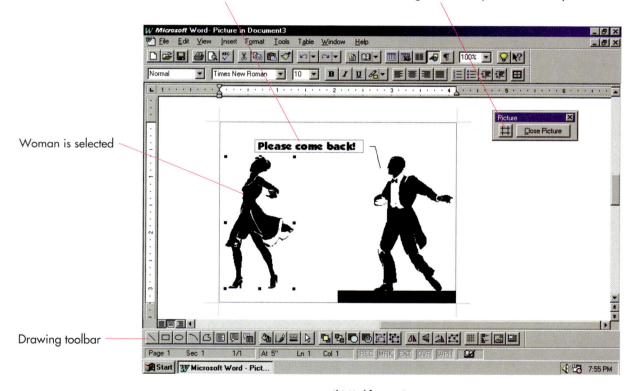

(b) Modifying a Picture

FIGURE 5.5 Graphics

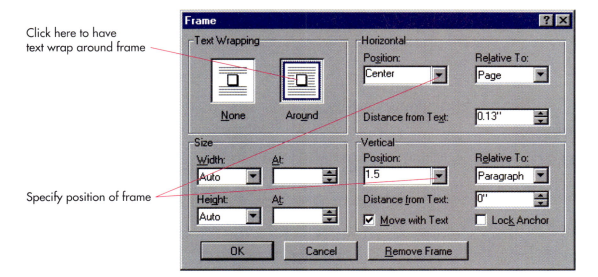

Click here to have text wrap around frame

Specify position of frame

(c) Format Frame Command

Once a graphic has been inserted into a document, you can change its size, change its position, or even modify its content. Clicking the object selects it and lets you move or size the object within the document. Double clicking the object loads the drawing portion of Word in order to modify the picture. Once a graphic has been inserted into a document, you can change its size, change its position, or even modify its content. Clicking the object selects it and lets you move or size the object within the document. Double clicking the object loads the drawing portion of Word in order to modify the picture.

Once a graphic has been inserted into a document, you can change its size, change its position, or even modify its content. Clicking the object selects it and lets you move or size the object within the document. Double clicking the object loads the drawing portion of Word in order to modify the picture. Once a graphic has been inserted into a document, you can change its size, change its position, or even modify its content. Clicking the object selects it and lets you move or size the object within the document. Double clicking the object loads the drawing portion of Word in order to modify the picture. Once a graphic has been inserted into a document, you can change its size, change its position, or even modify its content. Clicking the object selects it and lets you move or size the object within the document. Double clicking the object loads the drawing portion of Word in order to modify the picture. Once a graphic has been inserted into a document, you can change its size, change its position, or even modify its content. Clicking the object selects it and lets you move or size the object within the document. Double clicking the object loads the drawing portion of Word in order to modify the picture.

(d) The Completed Document

FIGURE 5.5 Graphics (continued)

Once a graphic has been inserted into a document, you can change its size or position or even modify its content. Clicking the object selects it and lets you align or size the object within the document. Double clicking the object loads the program that created the graphic in order to modify the picture, as shown in Figure 5.5b.

Microsoft Word includes a complete set of drawing tools to create and/or modify the graphics supplied with Word. The picture is displayed in the window with the ***drawing toolbar*** displayed at the bottom of the window. You can add shapes, change colors, flip or rotate the image, or add callouts. (ToolTips are displayed when you point to a tool to indicate its function.) Online help is available just as it is for every other Windows application. So too is the Undo command, which we find invaluable.

The complete capabilities of the drawing program are beyond the present discussion, but you will be surprised at what you can do with a little bit of experimentation. We modified the Dancers graphic by selecting the woman, clicking the tool to rotate her about the vertical axis, then dragging her away from her partner. We also added a call out in which the man asks her to come back.

DROP CAPS

*D**rop caps* add interest to a document and are created through the Drop Cap command in the Format menu. Click at the beginning of a paragraph (where the drop cap is to appear), pull down the Format Menu, and click Drop Cap. Choose the type of drop cap you want, its font, and the number of lines to drop, then click OK. The drop cap will be inserted into a frame in the document.

Frames

Frames were introduced in Chapter 3 in conjunction with inserting an object from the Microsoft ClipArt Gallery into a document. A frame should also be inserted around a picture to facilitate positioning the picture within a document and/or wrapping text around the picture. Anything at all can be placed into a frame—a picture, a table, a dropped capital letter, or an object created by another application, such as a spreadsheet created by Microsoft Excel.

Once an object has been placed in a frame, it can be dragged into position using the mouse or aligned more precisely using the dialog box within the ***Format Frame command*** shown in Figure 5.5c. The command enables you to specify the precise horizontal and vertical location of the frame. It also determines whether or not text is to wrap around the frame.

Figure 5.5d displays a document containing text and the Dancers graphic. (We decided to reunite our dancers and use the original picture). The text wraps around the graphic in accordance with the specifications in the Format Frame command of Figure 5.5c. The horizontal and vertical placement of the graphic are also consistent with the placement options within the Format Frame command. (Placing an object in a frame does not create a border for the object, which is done through the Borders and Shading command.)

TO FRAME OR NOT TO FRAME

Enclosing an object in a frame lets you position it freely on the page and/or wrap text around the object. Without a frame, the object is treated as an ordinary paragraph, and movement is restricted to one of three positions (left, center, or right). Text cannot be wrapped around an unframed object.

HANDS-ON EXERCISE 2

Graphics

Objective: Insert a picture into a document, then modify the picture to include your initials; frame the picture, then size and move the graphic within the document. Create a drop cap, boxed text, and reverse for emphasis. Use Figure 5.6 as a guide.

STEP 1: Load the Newsletter

➤ Open the **Modified Newsletter document** from the previous exercise. If necessary, change to the **Page Layout** view and zoom to **Page Width.**

➤ Pull down the **File menu,** click **Page Setup,** and if necessary, click the **Margins tab** to produce the dialog box in Figure 5.6a.

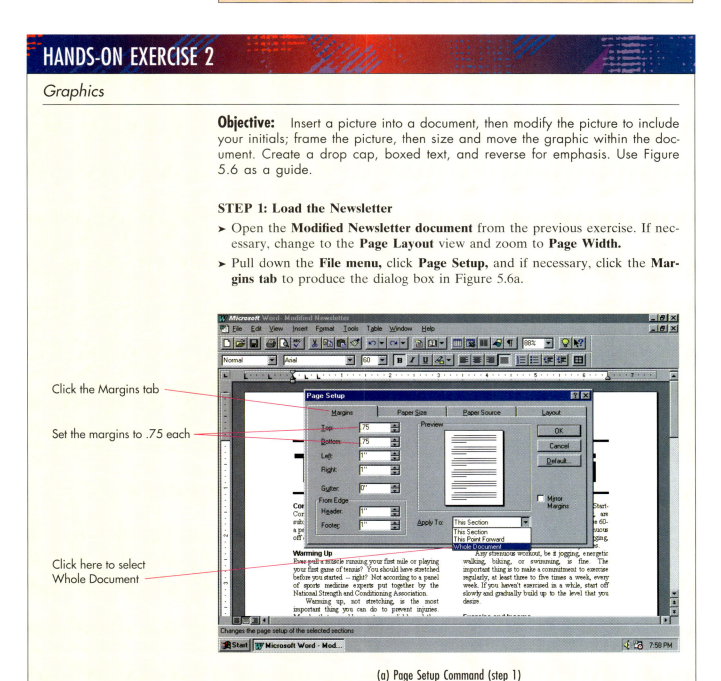

(a) Page Setup Command (step 1)

FIGURE 5.6   Hands-on Exercise 2

➤ Change the top and bottom margins to **.75** and **.75** as shown in the figure. Click the **arrow** in the **Apply To list box** and select **Whole Document.** Click **OK.**

STEP 2: Add the Graphic

➤ Click in the blank line at the end of the paragraph announcing the contest winner. Pull down the **Insert menu.** Click **Picture** to produce the dialog box of Figure 5.6b.

➤ The Clipart folder should already be selected, but if not, you must indicate where the clip art can be found.

- Click the **down arrow** in the **Look in box.** Click drive C, the drive where Microsoft Word or Microsoft Office is typically installed.
- Scroll until you can double click the **Winword** or **MSOffice folder** (depending on whether Word or Microsoft Office has been installed) to display its contents, which should include the Clipart folder. Double click the **Clipart folder.**

➤ The list of available figures should be visible as shown in Figure 5.6b. Click the **Preview button** if necessary, then scroll until you can select (click) the **Sports graphic.** Click **OK** to insert the figure into the document.

➤ Save the document.

(b) Insert the Picture (step 2)

FIGURE 5.6 Hands-on Exercise 2 (continued)

THE FIND NOW COMMAND

The Find Now button, as its name implies, enables you to search for a specific graphic. Pull down the Insert menu, click Picture, then enter the (expected) title of the graphic you are searching for in the File name text box. Type "Sport", for example, if you are looking for a sports picture, then click the Find Now command button. Word will search for all graphic files that include "sport" in their title, then display only those files, making the selection of an appropriate picture much easier.

STEP 3: Insert a Frame

➤ Point to the graphic, then click the **left mouse button** to select the graphic and display the sizing handles. Pull down the **Insert menu.** Click **Frame.** The picture is now enclosed within a shaded border to indicate a frame.

➤ Check that the frame is still selected. Pull down the **Format menu.** Click **Frame** to produce the dialog box in Figure 5.6c.
- Click the **arrow** on the **Horizontal Position box.** Click **Center.**
- Click the **arrow** on the **Horizontal Relative To box.** Click **Column.**

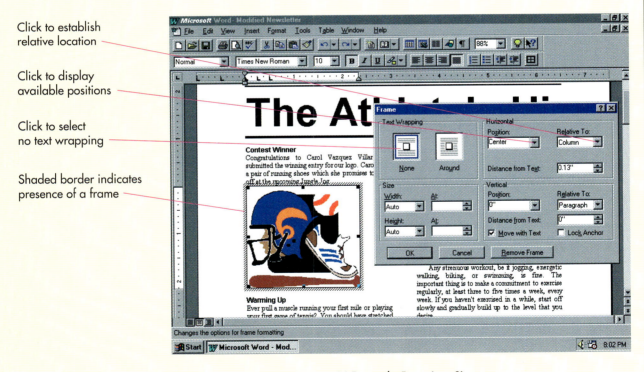

(c) Format the Frame (step 3)

FIGURE 5.6   Hands-on Exercise 2 (continued)

DESKTOP PUBLISHING   **223**

- The text may or may not wrap around the picture, depending on the size of the picture and the options in effect. (A minimum of one inch of text is required in order for the text to wrap.)
- If necessary, click the button to indicate **None** for Text Wrapping. Click **OK.** The sports picture should be centered within the left column.

➤ Save the newsletter.

> ### PICTURES, FRAMES, AND SHORTCUT MENUS
>
> Point to the border of a picture, then click the right mouse button to produce a shortcut menu. The commands in the menu will be appropriate for the selected object; that is, the menu will contain either the Frame Picture or the Format Frame command, depending on whether or not the graphic has already been framed.

STEP 4: Move and Size the Frame

➤ Use the **Zoom Control box** on the Standard toolbar to change to **Two Pages** as shown in Figure 5.6d; the newsletter may or may not spill to the second page, depending on the precise content of your document.

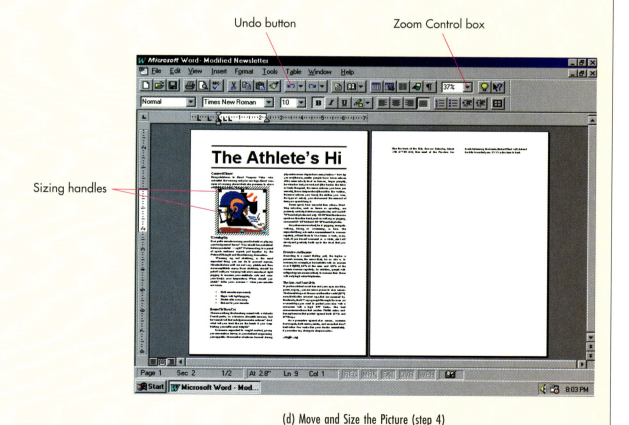

(d) Move and Size the Picture (step 4)

FIGURE 5.6   Hands-on Exercise 2 (continued)

➤ Point to the **graphic** (frame), then click the **left mouse button** to select the graphic and enclose it within the sizing handles. Experiment with moving and sizing the frame as follows:
- Drag a corner handle (the mouse pointer changes to a double arrow) to change the length and width simultaneously and keep the graphic in proportion.
- Drag a handle on the horizontal or vertical border to change one dimension only, which distorts the graphic.
- Drag any handle outward to increase the size of the picture or inward to shrink it.
- To move the frame, click the frame to select it, then drag the frame to its new position.
- To undo a move or sizing operation, click outside the frame to deselect it, then click the **Undo button** on the Standard toolbar.

➤ Move and/or size the frame so that the newsletter fits on a single page. Save the document.

STEP 5: Modify the Graphic

➤ Double click the **Sports graphic** in order to edit the picture in its own window as shown in Figure 5.6e. Click the **arrow** on the **Zoom Control box** on the toolbar and zoom to **200%.**

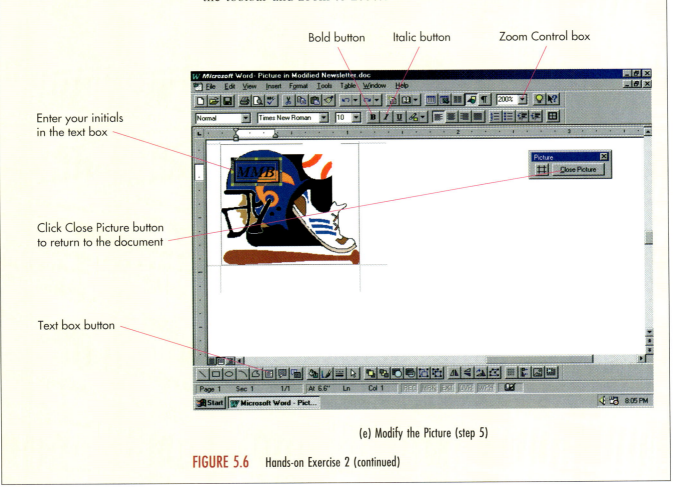

(e) Modify the Picture (step 5)

FIGURE 5.6 Hands-on Exercise 2 (continued)

- Click the **Text Box button** on the Drawing toolbar at the bottom of the window. Click the helmet in the drawing (the mouse pointer changes to a tiny cross) and drag the mouse to create a text box as shown in Figure 5.6e.
- Click the **Bold** and **Italics buttons** on the Formatting toolbar, then type your initials. (If you can't see all of your initials, click the border around the text box, then drag the sizing handles until you can see your initials.)
- Click the **Close Picture command button** to exit the drawing and return to the newsletter.

➤ Use the **Zoom Control box** to change to **Page Width.**
➤ Save the newsletter.

> ### TO CLICK OR DOUBLE CLICK
>
> Clicking an object selects the object and produces the sizing handles to move and/or size the object. Double clicking an object loads the application that created it and enables you to modify the object using the tools of that application.

STEP 6: The Masthead
➤ Press **Ctrl+Home** to move to the beginning of the document.
➤ Click the **Borders button** on the Formatting toolbar to display the Borders toolbar shown in Figure 5.6f.
➤ Click the **arrow** on the **Shading box** on the Borders toolbar. Choose **Solid (100%)** shading.
➤ Click outside the masthead to see the results. You should see white letters on a solid background (which is called a reverse).
➤ Save the newsletter.

STEP 7: Boxed and Shaded text
➤ Press **Ctrl+End** to move to the end of the newsletter. Select the paragraphs containing the Jungle Jog announcement along with its title.
➤ Click the **arrow** in the **Shading box** on the Borders toolbar. Choose **10%** shading.
➤ Click the **arrow** on the **Line style list box** to increase (decrease) the thickness of the line as you see fit. Click the **Outside border button** on the Borders toolbar to apply a border around the selected paragraphs.
➤ Click outside the selected text to see the results. Save the newsletter.

STEP 8: Add a Drop Cap
➤ Scroll to the beginning of the newsletter. Click immediately before the C in "Congratulations".
➤ Pull down the **Format menu.** Click **Drop Cap** to produce the dialog box in Figure 5.6g.

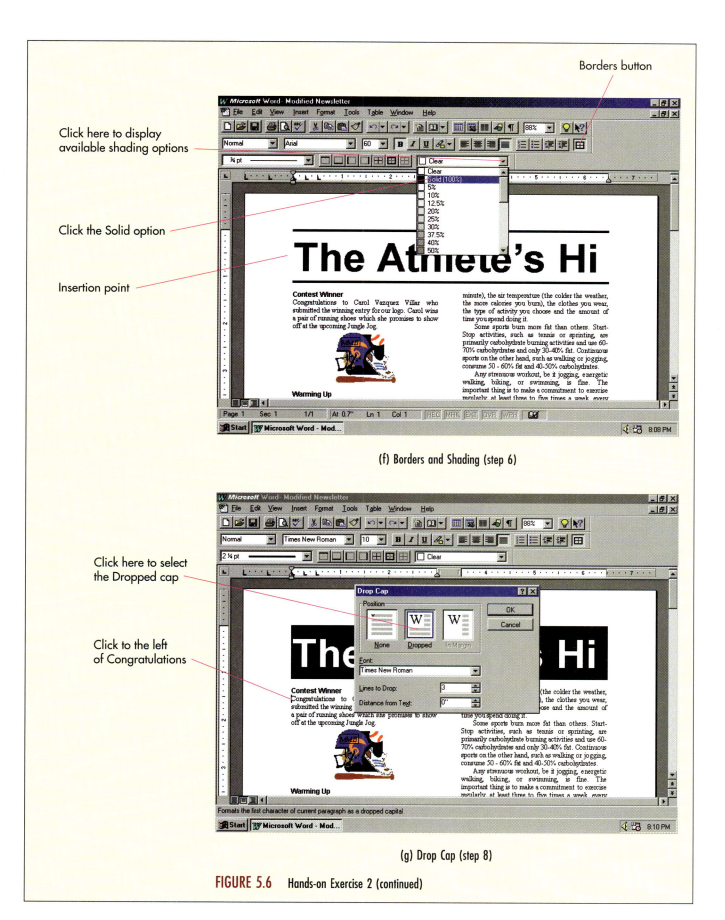

(f) Borders and Shading (step 6)

(g) Drop Cap (step 8)

FIGURE 5.6   Hands-on Exercise 2 (continued)

➤ Click the **Position icon** for **Dropped** as shown in the figure. You can also change the font, size (lines to drop), or distance from the text by clicking the arrow on the appropriate list box.

➤ Click **OK** to create the drop cap, exit the dialog box, and return to the document. Click outside the frame around the drop cap.

➤ Save the newsletter.

STEP 9: Change Column Formatting

➤ Click anywhere in the body of the newsletter, making sure you are in the second section.

➤ Pull down the **Format menu.** Click **Columns** to produce the dialog box in Figure 5.6h.

➤ Click the **Left Presets icon.** Change the width of the first column to **2″**, which automatically changes the width of the second column to 4″.

➤ Click the **Lines Between box.** Click **OK.**

➤ Use the **Zoom Control box** to zoom to **Whole Page** to display the completed newsletter as shown in Figure 5.6i. If necessary, size the graphic so that the newsletter fits on one page.

➤ Save the document a final time, then print the newsletter. Close the document. Exit Word.

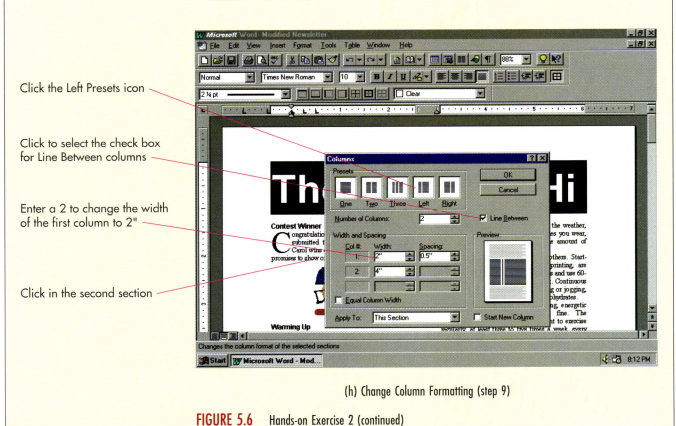

(h) Change Column Formatting (step 9)

FIGURE 5.6 Hands-on Exercise 2 (continued)

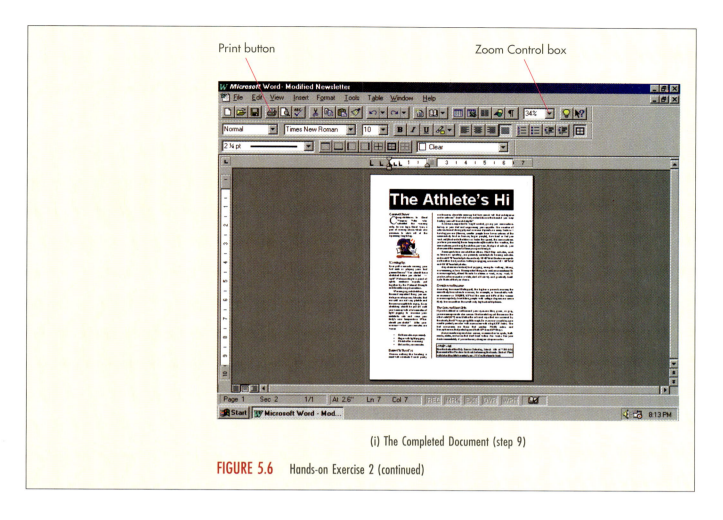

(i) The Completed Document (step 9)

FIGURE 5.6   Hands-on Exercise 2 (continued)

ELEMENTS OF GRAPHIC DESIGN

We trust you have completed the hands-on exercises without difficulty and that you were able to reproduce the newsletter. Realize, however, that the mere availability of Microsoft Word and a laser printer does not guarantee success in desktop publishing, any more than a word processor turns its author into a Shakespeare or a Hemingway. Other skills are necessary, and so we conclude with an introduction to basic principles of graphic design.

Much of what we say is subjective, and what works in one situation will not necessarily work in another. Your eye is the best judge of all, and you should stick to your own instincts. Experiment freely and realize that successful design is the result of trial and error. Seek inspiration from others by maintaining a file of publications, with examples of both good and bad design, and use the file as the basis for your own publications.

The Grid

The design of a document should be developed on a *grid,* an underlying, but *invisible,* set of horizontal and vertical lines that determine the placement of the major elements. A grid establishes the overall structure of a document by indicating the number of columns, the space between columns, the size of the margins, the placement of headlines, art, and so on. The grid does *not* appear in the printed document nor on the screen.

A grid may be simple or complex, but is always distinguished by the number of columns it contains. The three-column grid of Figures 5.7a and 5.7b is one of the most common and utilitarian designs. Figure 5.7c shows a four-column design for the same document, with unequal column widths to provide interest. Figure 5.7d illustrates a five-column grid that is often used with large amounts of text. Many other designs are possible as well. A one-column grid is used for term papers and letters. A two-column, wide and narrow format is appropriate for textbooks and manuals. Two- and three-column formats are used for newsletters and magazines.

The simple concept of a grid should make the underlying design of any document obvious, which in turn gives you an immediate understanding of page composition. Moreover, the conscious use of a grid will help you organize your material and result in a more polished and professional-looking publication. It will also help you to achieve consistency from page to page within a document (or from issue to issue of a newsletter). Indeed, much of what goes wrong in desktop publishing stems from failing to follow or use the underlying grid.

White Space

White space, or space that is free of text and art, is underutilized by most newcomers to graphic design. White space is essential, however, to provide contrast, and to give the eye a place to rest; conversely, the lack of white space makes a document crowded and difficult to read, as seen in Figure 5.8a.

White space is introduced into a document in several ways, but not every document will use every technique. White space will appear:

- Around a headline; surrounding a headline with white space gives it additional emphasis.
- In the page margins (left, right, top, and bottom); a minimum of one inch all around is a generally accepted guideline.
- Between columns in a multicolumn layout; the wider the columns, the more space is required between the columns.
- Between lines of text through adequate space between the lines.
- In paragraph indents and/or the ragged line endings of left-aligned type.
- Around a figure to emphasize the art.
- Between paragraphs through use of a paragraph spacing command; this subtlety increases the space after a hard carriage return and gives a more professional appearance than double spacing between paragraphs, which adds too much space.

White space can be used as a design element by leaving a column empty (or almost empty) as was done in Figures 5.8b and 5.8c. The use of vertical white space in this fashion is a very effective tool. White space is *not* attractive, however, when it is trapped in the middle of a page as in Figure 5.8d.

Emphasis

Good design makes it easy for the reader to determine what is important. ***Emphasis*** is achieved in several ways, the easiest being variations in type size and/or type style. Headings should be set in type sizes (at least two points) larger than the subheadings, which in turn should be larger than body copy. The use of **boldface** is effective as are *italics*, but both should be done in moderation. Shading, reverses (white letters on a black background), or boxes are also effective.

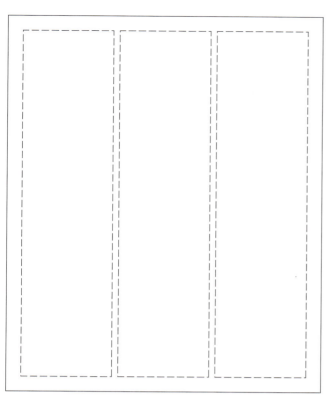

(a) Empty Three-column Grid

(b) Three-column Grid

(c) Four-column Grid

(d) Five-column Grid

FIGURE 5.7 The Grid System of Design

An Uninviting Morass of Text

I came to his garden alone, while the dew was still on the roses. Sweet fragrances and the song of birds filled the air. His voice I heard, soft and clear, saying that this is an organic garden. All the flowers, shrubs and trees were so beautiful not because of chemicals, but because of supplying the correct natural nutrients needed by each of them. There were no harmful insects because these plantings were strong and full of vitality. The birds, which also doubled as bug snatchers, were attracted by the various flowers and berries. Indeed Mrs. Crabtree was a lucky woman to have such a delightful garden and such an inspired man as Adam to tend it.

I came to his garden alone, while the dew was still on the roses. Sweet fragrances and the song of birds filled the air. His voice I heard, soft and clear, saying that this is an organic garden. All the flowers, shrubs and trees were so beautiful not because of chemicals, but because of supplying the correct natural nutrients needed by each of them. There were no harmful insects because these plantings were strong and full of vitality. The birds, which also doubled as bug snatchers, were attracted by the various flowers and berries. Indeed Mrs. Crabtree was a lucky woman to have such a delightful garden and such an inspired man as Adam to tend it.

I came to his garden alone, while the dew was still on the roses. Sweet fragrances and the song of birds filled the air. His voice I heard, soft and clear, saying that this is an organic garden. All the flowers, shrubs and trees were so beautiful not because of chemicals, but because of supplying the correct natural nutrients needed by each of them. There were no harmful insects because these plantings were strong and full of vitality. The birds, which also doubled as bug snatchers, were attracted by the various flowers and berries. Indeed Mrs. Crabtree was a lucky woman to have such a delightful garden and such an inspired man as Adam to tend it.

I came to his garden alone, while the dew was still on the roses. Sweet fragrances and the song of birds filled the air. His voice I heard, soft and clear, saying that this is an organic garden. All the flowers, shrubs and trees were so beautiful not because of chemicals, but because of the correct ▼

(a) Crowded Page

A Page Should Leave a Place for the Bird to Fly

I came to his garden alone, while the dew was still on the roses. Sweet fragrances and the song of birds filled the air. His voice I heard, soft and clear, saying that this is an organic garden. All the flowers, shrubs and trees were so beautiful not because of chemicals, but because of supplying the correct natural nutrients needed by each of them. There were no harmful insects because these plantings were strong and full of vitality. The birds, which also doubled as bug snatchers, were attracted by the various flowers and berries. Indeed Mrs. Crabtree was a lucky woman and to have such a delightful garden and such an inspired man as Adam to tend it.

I came to his garden alone, while the dew was still on the roses. Sweet fragrances and the song of birds filled the air. His voice I heard, soft and clear, saying that this is an organic garden. All the flowers, shrubs and trees were so beautiful not because of chemicals, but because of supplying the correct natural nutrients needed by each of them. There were no harmful insects because these plantings were strong and full of vitality. The birds, which also doubled as bug snatchers, were attracted by the various flowers and berries. Indeed Mrs. Crabtree was a lucky woman and to have such a delightful garden and such an inspired man as Adam to tend it.

I came to his garden alone, while the dew was still on the roses. Sweet fragrances and the song of birds filled the air. His voice I heard, soft and clear, saying that this is an organic garden. All the flowers, shrubs and trees were so beautiful not because of chemicals, but because of supplying the correct natural nutrients needed by each of them. There were no harmful insects because these plantings were strong and full of vitality. The birds, which also doubled as bug snatchers, were attracted by the various flowers and berries. Indeed Mrs. Crabtree was a lucky woman and to have such a delightful garden and such an inspired man as Adam to tend it. ▼

(b) White Space

(c) Emphasis

(d) Trapped White Space

FIGURE 5.8 White Space as a Design Element

Facing Pages

A multipage document such as a manual, newsletter, or brochure is typically viewed two pages at a time by the reader. If this is true for your publication, it makes sense to develop *facing pages* as a unit, as opposed to creating the pages individually. This is illustrated by Figure 5.9a, which shows individually balanced pages that do not look very good together. Figure 5.9b rearranges the same material in a more appealing fashion. Use the Page Layout view in Microsoft Word and zoom to two pages to work on your document.

(a) Pages Balanced Individually

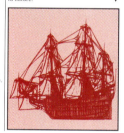

(b) Pages Balanced as a Unit

FIGURE 5.9 Balancing Facing Pages

SUMMARY

The essence of desktop publishing is the merger of text with graphics to produce a professional-looking document. Proficiency in desktop publishing requires not only knowledge of Microsoft Word, but familiarity with the basics of graphic design.

The Newsletter Wizard can be used to create a template for a newsletter. It is preferable, however, to create the newsletter entirely in Microsoft Word so that it better suits your needs.

A document can be divided into any number of newspaper-style columns in which text flows from the bottom of one column to the top of the next. Columns are implemented by clicking the Columns button on the Standard toolbar or by selecting the Columns command from the Format menu. Sections are required if different column arrangements are present in the same document. The Page Layout view is required to see the columns displayed side-by-side.

The Insert Picture command places a picture into a document, which can subsequently be modified using the drawing tools within Microsoft Word. A frame facilitates moving and/or wrapping text around the graphic.

The successful use of desktop publishing requires knowledge of graphic design in addition to proficiency in Word. The use of a grid, white space, and appropriate emphasis are basic design techniques.

KEY WORDS AND CONCEPTS

Borders and Shading command	Emphasis	Newsletter Wizard
Clip art	Facing pages	Newspaper-style columns
Column break	Format Frame command	Pull quote
Columns command	Frame	Reverse
Desktop publishing	Grid	Section break
Drawing toolbar	Insert Picture command	Typography
Drop cap	Masthead	White space

MULTIPLE CHOICE

1. Which of the following *must* be specified by the user?
   (a) The number of columns
   (b) The width of each column
   (c) Both (a) and (b)
   (d) Neither (a) nor (b)

2. Which view enables you to see a multicolumn document as it will appear on the printed page?
   (a) Normal view at any magnification
   (b) Page Layout view at any magnification
   (c) Normal or Page Layout view at 100% magnification
   (d) Normal or Page Layout view at Full Page magnification

3. How is clip art inserted into a document?
   (a) Through the Insert Picture Command
   (b) Through the Microsoft ClipArt Gallery
   (c) Both (a) and (b)
   (d) Neither (a) nor (b)

4. What is the minimum number of sections in a three-column newsletter whose masthead extends across all three columns?
   (a) One
   (b) Two
   (c) Three
   (d) Four

5. What is the difference between clicking and double clicking an object such as the sports graphic in the newsletter?
   (a) Clicking selects the object; double clicking enables you to edit the object
   (b) Double clicking selects the object; clicking enables you to edit the object
   (c) Clicking changes to Normal view; double clicking changes to Page Layout view
   (d) Double clicking changes to Normal view; clicking changes to Page Layout view

6. Which of the following is correct with respect to page and column breaks?
   (a) Press Ctrl+enter to create a page break
   (b) Press Ctrl+Shift+enter to create a column break
   (c) Both (a) and (b)
   (d) Neither (a) nor (b)

7. Which of the following can be placed into a frame?
   (a) A picture or dropped capital letter
   (b) A table or object created by another application
   (c) Both (a) and (b)
   (d) Neither (a) nor (b)

8. Which of the following is controlled by the Format Frame command?
   (a) The horizontal and/or vertical placement of the frame
   (b) Wrapping (not wrapping) text around the framed object
   (c) Both (a) and (b)
   (d) Neither (a) nor (b)

9. What is the effect of dragging one of the four corner handles on a selected object?
   (a) The length of the object is changed but the width remains constant
   (b) The width of the object is changed but the length remains constant
   (c) The length and width of the object are changed in proportion to one another
   (d) Neither the length nor width of the object is changed

10. Which type size is the most reasonable for columns of text, such as those appearing in the newsletter created in the chapter?
    (a) 6 point
    (b) 10 point
    (c) 14 point
    (d) 18 point

11. A grid is applicable to the design of
    (a) Documents with one, two, or three columns and moderate clip art
    (b) Documents with four or more columns and no clip art
    (c) Both (a) and (b)
    (d) Neither (a) nor (b)

12. Which of the following is *not* an appropriate place to introduce white space in a document?
    (a) Between columns of a multicolumn document
    (b) Trapped in the middle of a page
    (c) In the page margins
    (d) Between paragraphs

13. Which of the following can be used to add emphasis to a document in the absence of clip art?
    (a) Boxes and shading
    (b) Pull quotes and reverses
    (c) Both (a) and (b)
    (d) Neither (a) nor (b)

14. Which of the following is a universally accepted guideline in the design of a document?
    (a) Use wider columns for larger type sizes
    (b) Use the same type size for the heading and text of an article
    (c) Both (a) and (b)
    (d) Neither (a) nor (b)

15. Which of the following are implemented at the section rather than the paragraph level?
    (a) Columns
    (b) Margins
    (c) Both (a) and (b)
    (d) Neither (a) nor (b)

ANSWERS

1. a	6. c	11. c
2. b	7. c	12. b
3. c	8. c	13. c
4. b	9. c	14. a
5. a	10. b	15. c

EXPLORING MICROSOFT WORD

1. Use Figure 5.10 to match each action with its result; a given action may be used more than once or not at all.

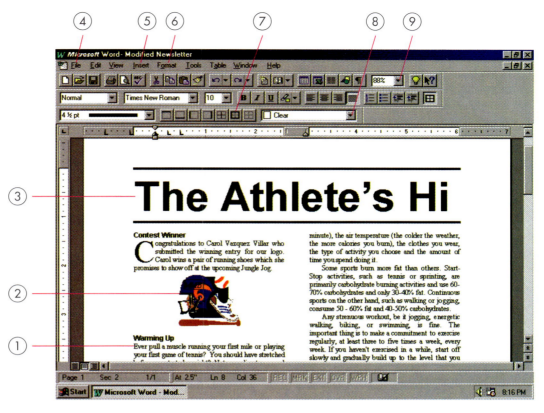

FIGURE 5.10 Screen for Problem 1

Action	Result
a. Click at 1, click at 6	____ Size the graphic
b. Double click at 2	____ Allow text to wrap around the graphic
c. Click at 2, drag a handle	____ Change the newsletter to three columns
d. Click at 2, click at 5	
e. Click at 2, click at 6	____ Modify the picture
f. Click at 2, click at 7	____ Insert the picture in a frame
g. Click at 3, click at 8	____ Put a border around the picture
h. Click at 4	____ Shade the masthead
i. Click at 6	____ Add a drop cap for the second article
j. Click at 9	
	____ Change the zoom to Whole Page
	____ Change the top and bottom margins

2. Answer the following with respect to the screen in Figure 5.11:
   a. What is the name of the style that is in effect at the insertion point? What are the specifications for that style?
   b. How would you change the typeface or point size for the style in part a?

DESKTOP PUBLISHING **237**

FIGURE 5.11 Screen for Problem 2

   c. Which command displayed the dialog box in Figure 5.11? How can you use the dialog box to display the specifications for the Body Text style? How would you change the specifications for that style?
   d. How was the newsletter in the figure created?

3. Answer the following with respect to the screen in Figure 5.12:
   a. Which command produced the dialog box in the figure?
   b. What are the left and right margins in effect? How wide is each column with the current margins?
   c. How wide would each column be if you changed the left and right margins to .5 inch each and retained the current spacing between columns?
   d. What would the width of each column be if you changed the margins and reduced the space between columns to .25 inch?
   e. Which point size, 10 point or 12 point, would be preferable for the design in part d?
   f. Explain why it is not possible to create a design of four unequal columns (2.5 inches for the first column and 1.5 inches for the other three columns) with left and right margins of .5 inch each?
   g. Regardless of the parameters chosen, the document will not be displayed in columns after clicking the OK button and closing the dialog box. Why?

4. The examples in Figure 5.13 contain two versions of the same page, one that violates basic rules of design and one that follows them. Describe the problems in the poorly designed page, then indicate how they were corrected in the revised version.

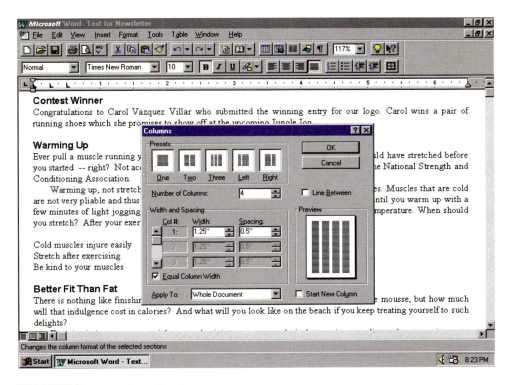

FIGURE 5.12 Screen for Problem 3

Poor Design

Improved Design

(a) Example 1

FIGURE 5.13 Pages for Problem 4

Poor Design   Improved Design

(b) Example 2

FIGURE 5.13 Pages for Problem 4 (continued)

PRACTICE WITH MICROSOFT WORD

1. The flyers in Figure 5.14 were created using the Insert Picture command to import the Jazz and Books graphics, respectively. Once the clip art was brought into the document, it was moved and sized as necessary to create the documents in the figure. It's easy, provided you remember to frame the picture as soon as you bring it into the document. Reproduce either or both of our flyers, or better yet, create your own.

2. Figure 5.15 displays three additional mastheads suitable for the newsletter that was developed in the chapter. Each masthead was created as follows:
   a. A two-by-two table was used in Figure 5.15a in order to right justify the date of the newsletter. The use of a table to right align text was suggested in the tip on page 165.
   b. A different font was used for the masthead in Figure 5.15b. The border around the masthead is a drop shadow.
   c. Microsoft WordArt was used to create the masthead in Figure 5.15c.

   Choose the masthead you like best, then modify the newsletter as it existed at the end of the second hands-on exercise to include the new masthead. Submit the modified newsletter to your instructor as proof that you did the hands-on exercises in this chapter as well as this problem.

UM Jazz Band
Plays Dixieland

Where: Gusman Hall

When: Friday,
      November 10

Time: 8:00 PM

(a) UM Jazz Band

CIS 120 Study Sessions

For those who don't know a bit from a byte
Come to Stanford College this Tuesday night
We'll study the concepts that aren't always clear
And memorize terms that hackers hold dear

We'll hit the books from 7 to 10
And then on Thursday we'll do it again
It can't hurt to try us — so come on by
And give the CIS tutors that old college try!

(b) CIS 120 Study Sessions

FIGURE 5.14 Flyers for Practice with Word Exercise 1

The Athlete's Hi
Volume 1   November 1995

(a) With Volume Number and Date

The Athlete's Hi

(b) Alternate Font and Drop Shadow

The Athlete's Hi

(c) Microsoft WordArt

FIGURE 5.15   Mastheads for Practice with Word Exercise 2

3. Create a newsletter containing at least one graphic from the Clipart folder. The intent of this problem is simply to provide practice in graphic design. There is no requirement to write meaningful text, but the headings in the newsletter should follow the theme of the graphic.

   a. Select a graphic, then write one or two sentences in support of that graphic. If, for example, you choose the Books graphic, you could write a sentence describing how you intend to hit the books in an effort to boost your GPA and make the Dean's List.

   b. As indicated, there is no requirement to write meaningful text for the newsletter; just copy the sentences from part (a) once or twice to create a paragraph, then copy the paragraph several times to create the newsletter. You should, however, create meaningful headings to add interest to the document.

   c. Develop an overall design away from the computer—that is, with pencil and paper. Use a grid to indicate the placement of the articles, headings, clip art, and masthead. You may be surprised to find that it is easier to master commands in Word than it is to design the newsletter; do not, however, underestimate the importance of graphic design in the ultimate success of your document.

d. More is not better; that is, do not use too many fonts, styles, sizes, and clip art just because they are available. Don't crowd the page, and remember that white space is a very effective design element. There are no substitutes for simplicity and good taste.

4. A guide to smart shopping: This problem is more challenging than the previous exercises in that you are asked to consider content as well as design. The objective is to develop a one- (or two-) page document with helpful tips to the novice on buying a computer. We have, however, written the copy for you and put the file on the data disk.

   a. Open and print the *Chapter 5 Practice 4* document on the data disk, which takes approximately a page and a half as presently formatted. Read our text and determine the tips you want to retain and those you want to delete. Add other tips as you see fit.

   b. Examine the available clip art through the Insert Picture command or through the Microsoft ClipArt Gallery. There is no requirement, however, to include a graphic; that is, use clip art only if you think it will enhance the document.

   c. Consult a current computer magazine (or another source) to determine actual prices for one or more configurations, then include this information prominently in your document.

   d. Create the masthead for the document, then develop with pencil and paper a rough sketch of the completed document showing the masthead, the placement of the text, clip art, and special of the month (the configuration in part c).

   e. Return to the computer and implement the design of part d. Try to create a balanced publication that completely fills the space allotted; that is, your document should take exactly one or two pages (rather than the page and a half in the original document on the data disk).

CASE STUDIES

Before and After

The best way to learn about the do's and don'ts of desktop publishing is to study the work of others. Choose a particular type of document—such as a newsletter, résumé, or advertising flyer—then collect samples of that document. Choose one sample that is particularly bad and redesign the document. You need not enter the actual text, but you should keep all of the major headings so that the document retains its identity. Add or delete clip art as appropriate. Bring the before and after samples to class and hold a contest to determine the most radical improvement.

Clip Art

Clip art—you see it all the time, but where do you get it, and how much does it cost? Some images are supplied with a word processor, but you grow tired of these and yearn for more. Scan the computer magazines and find at least two sources for additional clip art. Return to class with specific information on price and the nature of the clip art. Be sure to determine in advance how much disk space the clip art will require; the answer may surprise you.

The Flyer

It's rush week and you're the publicity chairperson for your fraternity or sorority. Needless to say, it's highly competitive and you need effective flyers to attract new members. This is an absolutely critical assignment, and people are counting on you. Don't blow it!

Intramurals

The ClipArt Gallery includes a Sports and Leisure category with graphics on many different sports. You have been appointed acting head of Campus Intramurals and need to create a flyer seeking participation in an upcoming league. Choose your sport, choose the graphic, and see how creative you can be.

APPENDIX A: OBJECT LINKING AND EMBEDDING

OVERVIEW

The ability to create a **compound document** is one of the primary advantages of the Windows environment. A compound document, such as the memo in Figure A.1, is a document that contains data (objects) from multiple applications. The memo was created in Microsoft Word, and it contains an object (a worksheet) that was created in Microsoft Excel. The **container** (the Word document) is created in the **client application** (Microsoft Word in this example). The object it contains (a worksheet) is created in the **server application** (Microsoft Excel in this example). **Object Linking and Embedding** (OLE—pronounced "OH-lay") is the means by which you develop compound documents.

The essential difference between linking and embedding is whether the object is stored within the compound document (embedding) or in its own file (linking). An **embedded object** is stored in the compound document, which in turn becomes the only user (client) of that object. A **linked object** is stored in its own file, and the compound document is one of many potential containers of that object. The compound document does not contain the linked object per se, but only a representation of the object as well as a pointer (link) to the file containing the object. The advantage of linking is that the object in the compound document is updated automatically if the object is changed in the source file in which it was created.

The choice between linking and embedding depends on how the object will be used. Linking is preferable if the object is likely to change, and the compound document requires the latest version. Linking should also be used when the same object is placed in many documents so that any change to the object has to be made in only one place. Embedding is preferable if you intend to edit the compound document on a computer other than the one on which it was created.

The exercise that follows shows you how to create the compound document in Figure A.1. The exercise uses the **Insert Object command** to embed a copy of the Excel worksheet into a Word document. (The

Lionel Douglas
402 Mahoney Hall • Coral Gables, Florida 33124

June 25, 1995

Dear Folks,

I heard from Mr. Black, the manager at University Commons, and the apartment is a definite for the Fall. Ken and I are very excited, and can't wait to get out of the dorm. The food is poison, not that either of us are cooks, but anything will be better than this! I have been checking into car prices (we are definitely too far away from campus to walk!), and have done some estimating on what it will cost. The figures below are for a Jeep Wrangler, the car of my dreams:

Price of car	$11,995			
Manufacturer's rebate	$1,000			
Down payment	$3,000		**My assumptions**	
Amount to be financed	$7,995		Interest rate	7.90%
Monthly payment	$195		Term (years)	4
Gas	$40			
Maintenance	$50			
Insurance	$100			
Total per month	$385			

My initial estimate was $471 based on a $2,000 down payment and a three year loan at 7.9%. I know this is too much so I plan on earning an additional $1,000 and extending the loan to four years. That will bring the total cost down to a more manageable level (see the above calculations). If that won't do it, I'll look at other cars.

Lionel

FIGURE A.1   A Compound Document

Insert Object command was introduced in Chapter 3 to embed objects from the Microsoft ClipArt Gallery and from Microsoft WordArt into a Word document.)

Once an object has been embedded into a document, it can be modified through *in-place editing.* In-place editing enables you to double click an embedded object (the worksheet) and change it, using the tools of the server application (Excel). In other words, you remain in the client application (Microsoft Word in this example), but you have access to the Excel toolbar and pull-down menus. In-place editing modifies the copy of the embedded object in the compound document. It does *not* change the original object because there is no connection (or link) between the object and the compound document.

HANDS-ON EXERCISE 1

Embedding

Objective: To embed an Excel worksheet into a Word document; to use in-place editing to modify the worksheet within Word. Use Figure A.2 as a guide in the exercise.

STEP 1: Open the Word Document

➤ Start Word. Open the **Car Request document** in the **Exploring Word folder.** Zoom to **Page Width** so that the display on your monitor matches ours.

➤ Save the document as **Modified Car Request** so that you can return to the original document if you edit the duplicated file beyond redemption.

➤ The date displayed on your monitor will be May 31, 1995, and needs to be updated. Point to the date field, click the **right mouse button** to display the shortcut menu in Figure A.2a, then click the **Update Field command.**

> ### THE DATE FIELD
>
> The Insert Date and Time command enables you to insert the date as a specific value (the date on which a document is created) or as a field. The latter will be updated automatically whenever the document is printed or when the document is opened in Page Layout view. Opening the document in the Normal view requires the date field to be updated manually.

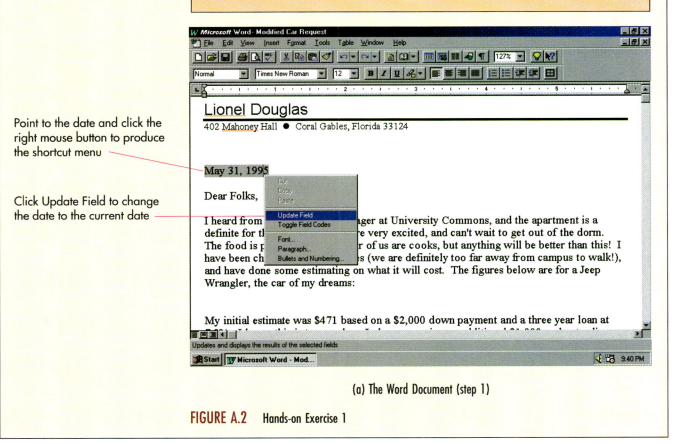

Point to the date and click the right mouse button to produce the shortcut menu

Click Update Field to change the date to the current date

(a) The Word Document (step 1)

FIGURE A.2 Hands-on Exercise 1

APPENDIX A 247

STEP 2: Insert an Object

➤ Click the blank line above paragraph two as shown in Figure A.2b. This is the place in the document where the worksheet is to go.

➤ Pull down the **Insert menu**, and click the **Object command** to display the Object dialog box in Figure A.2b.

➤ Click the **Create from File tab,** then click the **Browse command button** in order to open the Browse dialog box and select the object.

➤ Click (select) the **Car Budget workbook** (note the Excel icon), which is in the Exploring Word folder.

➤ Click **OK** to select the workbook and close the Browse dialog box.

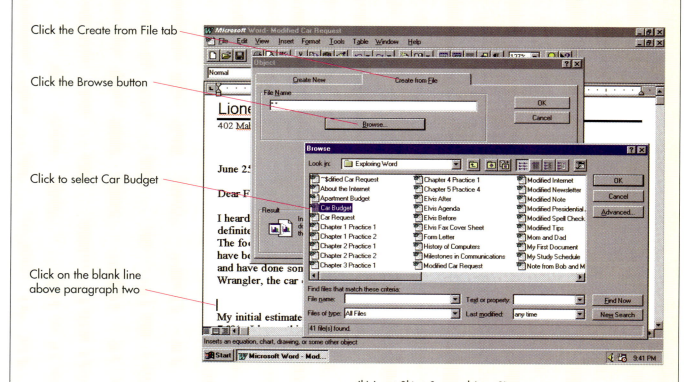

(b) Insert Object Command (step 2)

FIGURE A.2 Hands-on Exercise 1 (continued)

STEP 3: Insert an Object (continued)

➤ The file name of the object (Car Budget.xls) has been placed into the File Name text box, as shown in Figure A.2c.

➤ Verify that the Link to File and Display as Icon check boxes are clear, as shown in Figure A.2c. Note, too, the description at the bottom of the Object dialog box, which indicates that you will be able to edit the object using the application that created the file.

➤ Click **OK** to insert the Excel worksheet into the Word document. Save the document.

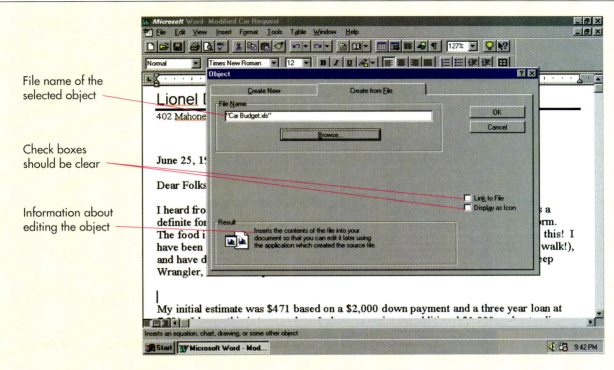

(c) Insert Object Command, continued (step 3)

FIGURE A.2   Hands-on Exercise 1 (continued)

STEP 4: Frame the Worksheet

➤ Point to the worksheet, then click the **right mouse button** to select the worksheet and display a shortcut menu. Click the **Frame Picture** command to frame the worksheet in order to position it more easily within the document.

➤ You will see the informational box in Figure A.2d, asking whether you want to switch to the Page Layout view. Click **Yes.** The worksheet is surrounded by a shaded (thatched) border to indicate a frame.

THE FORMAT FRAME COMMAND

All objects should be placed into a frame, a special type of (invisible) container in Microsoft Word that facilitates positioning an object within a Word document. An unframed object is treated as an ordinary paragraph, and movement is restricted to one of three alignments (left, center, or right). Additionally, text cannot be wrapped around an unframed object. A framed object, however, can be precisely positioned by right clicking the object, selecting the Format Frame command, then entering the information about the object's desired position.

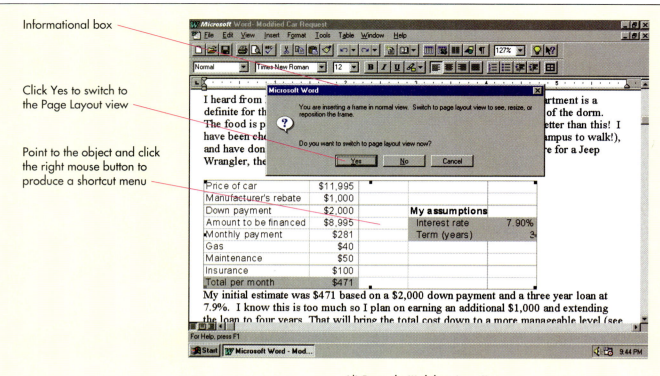

(d) Frame the Worksheet (step 4)

FIGURE A.2   Hands-on Exercise 1 (continued)

STEP 5: The Format Frame Command

➤ Pull down the **Format menu** and click **Frame** to display the Frame dialog box shown in Figure A.2e.

➤ Click the box for no text wrapping.

➤ Click the **drop-down arrow** on the list box for the Horizontal position and click **Center.** Click **OK** to accept the settings and close the Frame dialog box.

➤ The worksheet is centered within the memo, but you may want to insert a blank line(s) between the paragraphs to give the worksheet additional room.

➤ Save the document.

STEP 6: In-place Editing

➤ The worksheet should still be selected as indicated by the sizing handles. The monthly total of $471 needs to be changed to reflect Lionel's additional $1,000 for the down payment. Double click the worksheet object to edit the worksheet in place.

➤ Be patient as this step takes a while, even on a fast machine. The Excel grid, consisting of the row and column labels, will appear around the worksheet, as shown in Figure A.2f.

➤ You are still in Word, as indicated by the title bar (Microsoft Word - Modified Car Request), but the Excel toolbars are displayed.

➤ Click in cell **B3,** type the new down payment of **$3,000,** and press **enter.**

➤ Click in cell **E5,** type **4,** and press **enter.** The Monthly payment (cell B5) and Total per month (cell B9) drop to $195 and $385, respectively.

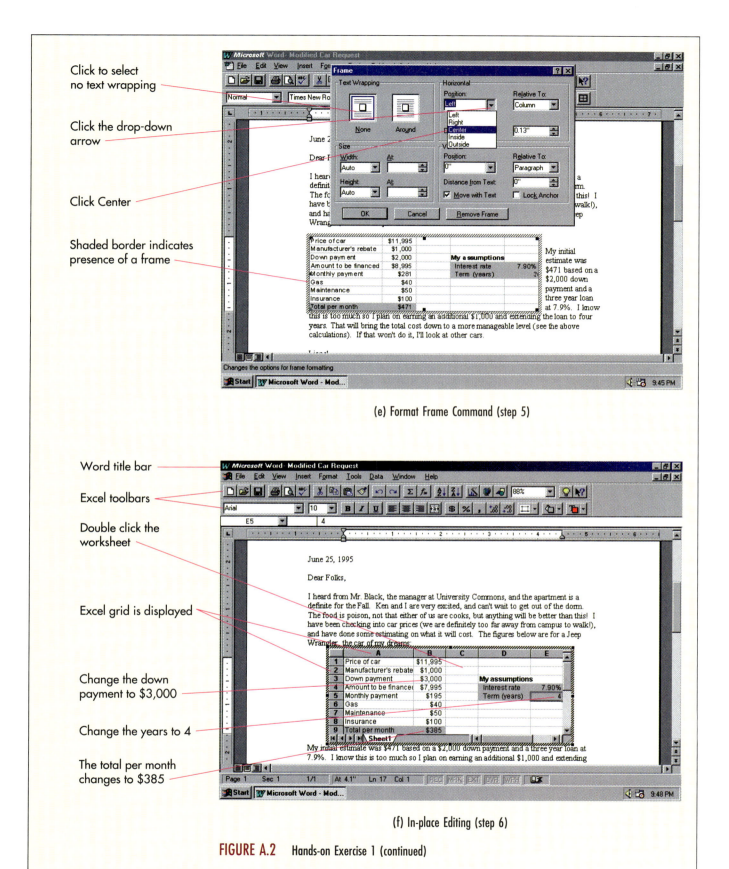

(e) Format Frame Command (step 5)

(f) In-place Editing (step 6)

FIGURE A.2 Hands-on Exercise 1 (continued)

IN-PLACE EDITING

In-place editing enables you to edit an embedded object using the toolbar and pull-down menus of the server application. Thus, when editing an Excel worksheet embedded into a Word document, the title bar is that of the client application (Microsoft Word), but the toolbars and pull-down menus reflect the server application (Excel). There are, however, two exceptions; the File and Window menus are those of the client application (Word) so that you can save the compound document and/or arrange multiple documents within the client application.

STEP 7: Save the Word Document

➤ Click anywhere outside the worksheet to deselect it and view the completed word document as shown in Figure A.2g.

➤ Pull down the **File menu** and click **Save** (or click the **Save button** on the Standard toolbar).

➤ Pull down the **File menu** a second time. Click **Exit** if you do not want to continue with the next hands-on exercise once this exercise is completed; otherwise click **Close** to remove the document from memory but leave Word open.

STEP 8: View the Original Object

➤ Click the **Start Button,** click (or point to) the **Programs menu,** then click **Microsoft Excel** to open the program.

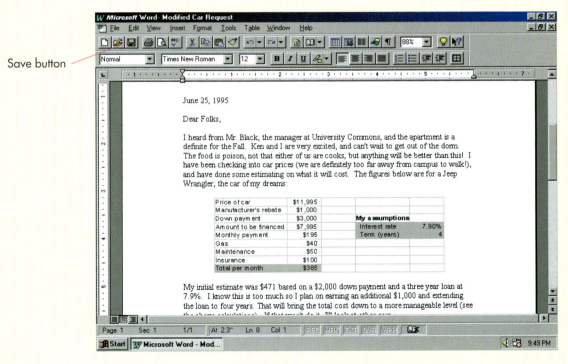

Save button

(g) The Completed Word Document (step 7)

FIGURE A.2   Hands-on Exercise 1 (continued)

➤ If necessary, click the **Maximize button** in the application window so that Excel takes the entire desktop, as shown in Figure A.2h.

➤ Pull down the **File menu** and click **Open** (or click the **Open button** on the Standard toolbar) to display the Open dialog box.

- Click the **drop-down arrow** on the Look In list box. Click the appropriate drive, drive C or drive A, depending on the location of your data.
- Double click the **Exploring Word folder** to make it the active folder.
- Click (select) **Car Budget** to select the workbook that we have used throughout the exercise.
- Click the **Open command button** to open the workbook, as shown in Figure A.2h.
- Click the **Maximize button** in the document window (if necessary) so that the document window is as large as possible.

➤ You should see the original (unmodified) worksheet, with a down payment of $2,000, a three-year loan, a monthly car payment of $281, and total expenses per month of $471. The changes that were made in step 6 were made to the compound document and are *not* reflected in the source file.

➤ Pull down the **File menu.** Click **Exit** to exit Microsoft Excel.

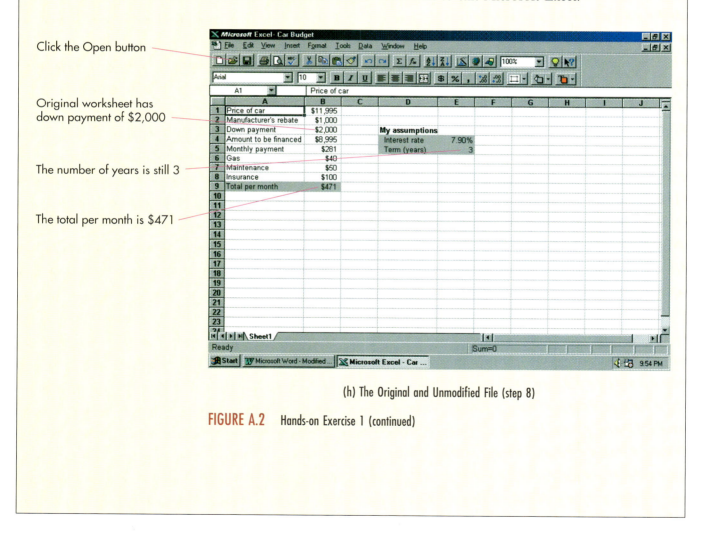

(h) The Original and Unmodified File (step 8)

FIGURE A.2   Hands-on Exercise 1 (continued)

LINKING

The exercise just completed used embedding rather than linking to place a copy of the Excel worksheet into the Word document. The last step in the exercise demonstrated that the original worksheet was unaffected by changes made to the embedded copy within the compound document.

Linking is very different from embedding as you shall see in the next exercise. Linking maintains a dynamic connection between the server and client. Embedding does not. With linking, the object created by the server application

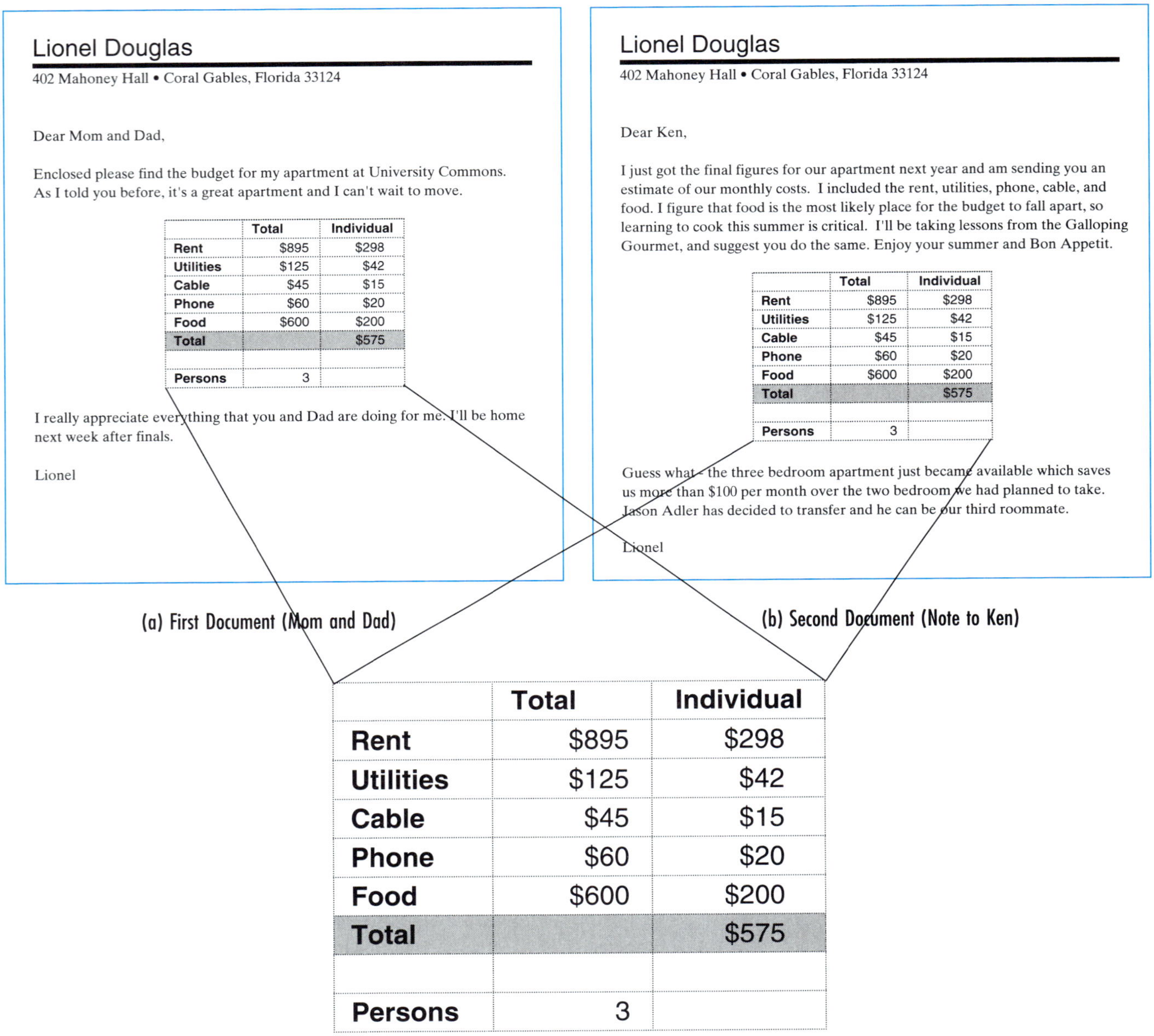

(a) First Document (Mom and Dad)

(b) Second Document (Note to Ken)

	Total	Individual
Rent	$895	$298
Utilities	$125	$42
Cable	$45	$15
Phone	$60	$20
Food	$600	$200
Total		$575
Persons	3	

(c) Worksheet (Apartment Budget)

FIGURE A.3 Linking

(e.g., an Excel worksheet) is tied to the compound document (e.g., a Word document) in such a way that any changes in the Excel worksheet are automatically reflected in the Word document. The Word document does not contain the worksheet per se, but only a representation of the worksheet, as well as a pointer (or link) to the Excel workbook.

Linking requires that an object be saved in its own file because the object does not actually exist within the compound document. Embedding, on the other hand, lets you place the object directly in a compound document without having to save it as a separate file. (The embedded object simply becomes part of the compound document.)

Consider now Figure A.3, in which the same worksheet is linked to two different documents. Both documents contain a pointer to the worksheet, which may be edited by double clicking the object in either compound document. Alternatively, you may open the server application and edit the object directly. In either case, changes to the Excel workbook are reflected in every compound document that is linked to the workbook.

The next exercise links a single Excel worksheet to two different Word documents. During the course of the exercise both applications (client and server) will be explicitly open, and it will be necessary to switch back and forth between the two. Thus, the exercise also demonstrates the multitasking capability within Windows 95 and the use of the taskbar to switch between the open applications.

HANDS-ON EXERCISE 2

Linking

Objective: To demonstrate multitasking and the ability to switch between applications; to link an Excel worksheet to multiple Word documents. Use Figure A.4 as a guide in the exercise.

STEP 1: Open the Word Document

➤ Check the taskbar to see whether there is a button for Microsoft Word indicating that the application is already active in memory. Start Word if you do not see its button on the taskbar.

➤ Open the **Mom and Dad document** in the **Exploring Word folder** as shown in Figure A.4a. The document opens in the Normal view (the view in which it was last saved). If necessary, zoom to **Page Width** so that the display on your monitor matches ours.

➤ Save the document as **Modified Mom and Dad.**

STEP 2: Open the Excel Worksheet

➤ Click the **Start button,** click (or point to) the **Programs menu,** then click **Microsoft Excel** to open the program.

➤ If necessary, click the **Maximize button** in the application window so that Excel takes the entire desktop. Click the **Maximize button** in the document window (if necessary) so that the document window is as large as possible.

➤ The taskbar should now contain buttons for both Microsoft Word and Microsoft Excel. Click either button to move back and forth between the open applications. End by clicking the Microsoft Excel button, since you want to work in that application.

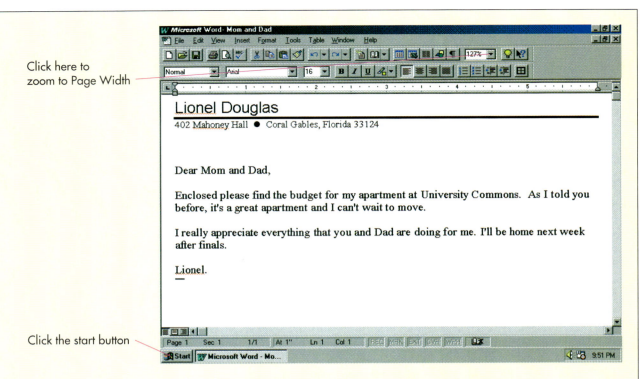

(a) Open the First Word Document (step 1)

FIGURE A.4 Hands-on Exercise 2

➤ Pull down the **File menu** and click **Open** (or click the **Open button** on the Standard toolbar) to display the Open dialog box in Figure A.4b.
➤ Click the **drop-down arrow** on the Look In list box. Click the appropriate drive, drive C or drive A, depending on the location of your data. Double click the **Exploring Word folder** to make it the active folder. Double click **Apartment Budget** to open the workbook.

THE COMMON USER INTERFACE

The *common user interface* provides a sense of familiarity from one Windows application to the next. Even if you have never used Excel, you will recognize many of the elements present in Word. Both applications share a common menu structure with consistent ways to execute commands from those menus. The Standard and Formatting toolbars are present in both applications. Many keyboard shortcuts are also common—for example Ctrl+Home and Ctrl+End to move to the beginning and end of a document.

STEP 3: Copy the Worksheet to the Clipboard
➤ Click in cell **A1.** Drag the mouse over cells **A1 through C9** so that the entire worksheet is selected as shown in Figure A.4c.

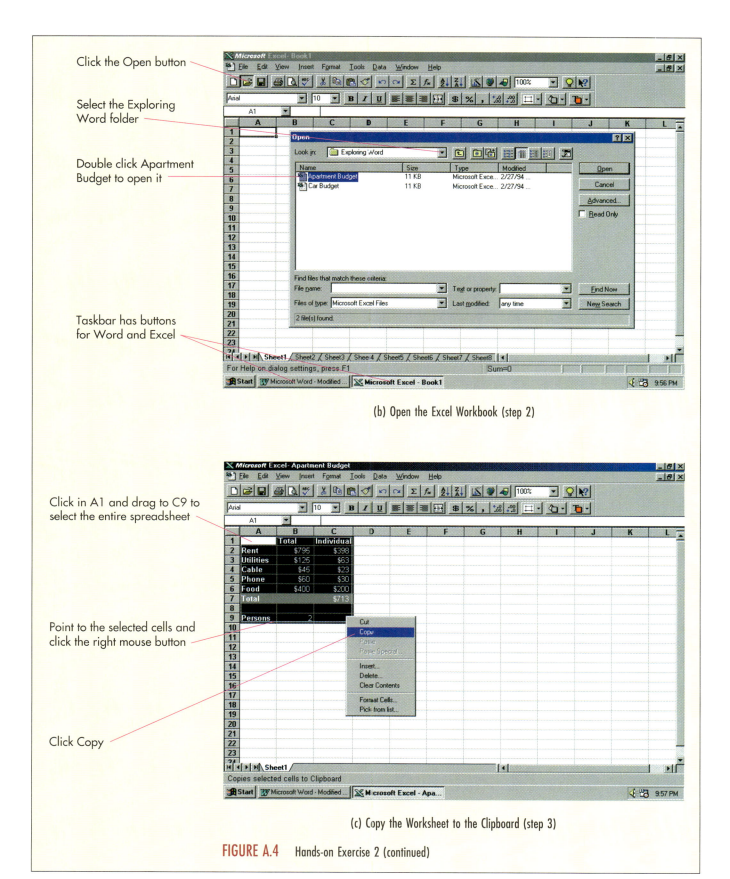

(b) Open the Excel Workbook (step 2)

(c) Copy the Worksheet to the Clipboard (step 3)

FIGURE A.4 Hands-on Exercise 2 (continued)

APPENDIX A

- Point to the selected cells, then click the **right mouse button** to display the shortcut menu shown in the figure. Click **Copy.** A moving border appears around the selected area in the worksheet, indicating that it has been copied to the clipboard.
- Click the **Microsoft Word button** on the taskbar to return to the Word document.

> ### THE WINDOWS 95 TASKBAR
>
> *Multitasking,* the ability to run multiple applications at the same time, is one of the primary advantages of the Windows environment. Each button on the taskbar appears automatically when its application or folder is opened and disappears upon closing. (The buttons on are resized automatically according to the number of open windows.) You can customize the taskbar by right clicking an empty area to display a shortcut menu, then clicking the Properties command. You can resize the taskbar by pointing to its inside edge, then dragging when you see a double-headed arrow. You can also move the taskbar to the left or right edge of the desktop, or to the top of the desktop, by dragging a blank area of the taskbar to the desired position.

STEP 4: Create the Link
- Click in the document between the two paragraphs. Press **enter** to enter an additional blank line.
- Pull down the **Edit menu.** Click **Paste Special** to produce the dialog box in Figure A.4d.
- Click the **Paste Link option button.** Click **Microsoft Excel Worksheet Object.** Click **OK** to insert the worksheet into the document. You may want to insert a blank line before and/or after the worksheet to make it easier to read.
- Save the document containing the letter to Mom and Dad.

> ### LINKING VERSUS EMBEDDING
>
> The *Paste Special command* will link or embed an object, depending on whether the Paste Link or Paste Option button is checked. Linking stores a pointer to the file containing the object together with a reference to the server application, and changes to the object are automatically reflected in all compound documents that are linked to the object. Embedding stores a copy of the object with a reference to the server application, but any changes to the copy of the object within the compound document are not reflected in the original object. With both linking and embedding, however, you can double click the object in the compound document to edit the object by using the tools of the server application.

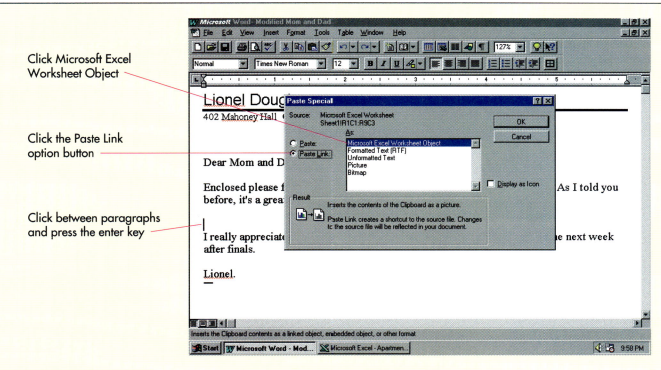

(d) Create the Link (step 4)

FIGURE A.4 Hands-on Exercise 2 (continued)

STEP 5: Open the Second Word Document

➤ Open the **Note to Ken document** in the **Exploring Word folder.** Save the document as **Modified Note to Ken** so that you can always return to the original document.

➤ The Apartment Budget worksheet is still in the clipboard since the contents of the clipboard have not been changed. Click at the end of the first paragraph (after the words Bon Appetit). Press the **enter key** to insert a blank line after the paragraph.

➤ Pull down the **Edit menu.** Click **Paste Special.** Click the **Paste Link option button.** Click **Microsoft Excel Worksheet Object.** Click **OK** to insert the worksheet into the document, as shown in Figure A.4e.

➤ If necessary, enter a blank line before or after the object to improve the appearance of the document. Save the document.

➤ Click anywhere on the worksheet to select the worksheet, as shown in Figure A.4e. The message on the status bar indicates you can double click the worksheet to edit the object.

STEP 6: Modify the Worksheet

➤ The existing spreadsheet indicates the cost of a two-bedroom apartment, but you want to show the cost of a three-bedroom apartment. Double click the worksheet in order to change it.

➤ The system pauses (the faster your computer, the better) as it switches back to Excel. Maximize the document window.

➤ Cells **A1 through C9** are still selected from step 3. Click outside the selected range to deselect the worksheet.

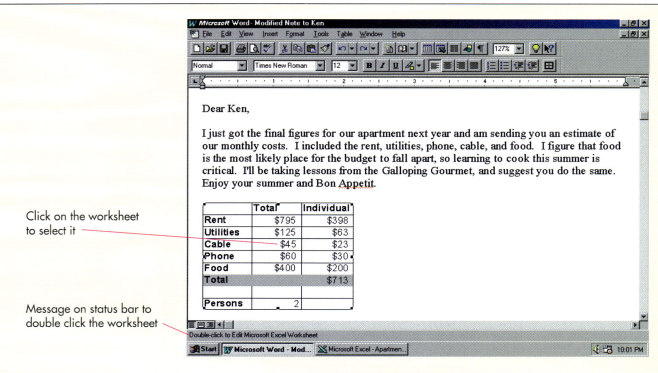

(e) Open the Second Document (step 5)

FIGURE A.4 Hands-on Exercise 2 (continued)

- Click in cell **B2.** Type **$895** (the rent for a three-bedroom apartment).
- Click in cell **B6.** Type **$600** (the increased amount for food).
- Click in cell **B9.** Type **3** to change the number of people sharing the apartment. Press **enter.** The total expenses (in cell C9) change to $575, as shown in Figure A.4f.
- Save the worksheet.

STEP 7: View the Modified Document

- Click the **Microsoft Word button** on the taskbar to return to Microsoft Word and the note to Ken, as shown in Figure A.4g.
- The note to Ken displays the modified worksheet because of the link established earlier.
- Click at the end of the worksheet and to add the additional text shown in Figure A.4g to let Ken know about the new apartment.
- Save the document.

STEP 8: View the Completed Note to Mom and Dad

- Pull down the **Window menu.** Click **Modified Note to Mom and Dad** to switch to this document.
- The note to your parents also contains the updated worksheet (with three roommates) because of the link established earlier.
- Save the completed document.

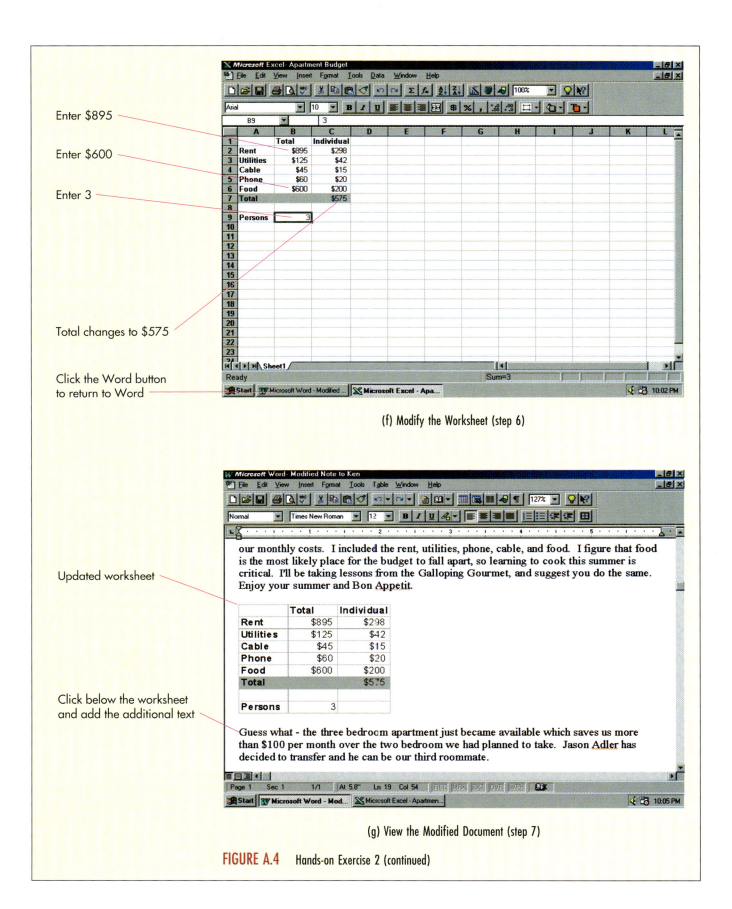

(f) Modify the Worksheet (step 6)

(g) View the Modified Document (step 7)

FIGURE A.4 Hands-on Exercise 2 (continued)

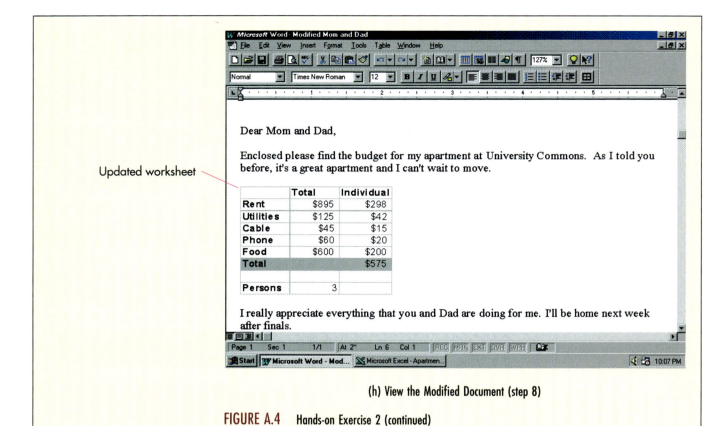

(h) View the Modified Document (step 8)

FIGURE A.4 Hands-on Exercise 2 (continued)

ALT+TAB STILL WORKS

Alt+Tab was a treasured shortcut in Windows 3.1 that enabled users to switch back and forth between open applications. The shortcut also works in Windows 95. Press and hold the Alt key while you press and release the Tab key repeatedly to cycle through the open applications. Note that each time you release the Tab key the icon of a different application is selected in the small rectangular window that is displayed in the middle of the screen. Release the Alt key when you have selected the icon for the application you want.

STEP 9: Exit

➤ Exit Word. Save the files if you are requested to do so. The button for Microsoft Word disappears from the taskbar.

➤ Exit Excel. Save the files if you are requested to do so. The button for Microsoft Excel disappears from the taskbar.

SUMMARY

The essential difference between linking and embedding is that linking does not place the object into the compound document, but only a pointer (link) to the object. Embedding places (a copy of) the actual object into the compound document. Linking is dynamic in nature, whereas embedding is not.

Linking requires that the object be saved in its own file, and further that the link between the object and the compound (container) document be maintained. Linking is especially useful when the same object is present in multiple documents because any subsequent change to the object is made in only one place, but is automatically reflected in the multiple compound documents.

Embedding does not require the object to be saved in a separate file because the object is contained within the compound document. Embedding lets you give your colleague a copy of the compound document, without a copy of the object, and indeed, there need not be a separate file for the object. You would not, however, want to embed the same object into multiple documents because any subsequent change to the object would have to be made in every document.

KEY WORDS AND CONCEPTS

Client application
Clipboard
Common user interface
Compound document
Container
Dynamic connection
Embedded object
In-place editing
Insert Object command
Linked object
Multitasking
Object Linking and
  Embedding (OLE)
Paste Special command
Server application

APPENDIX B: MAIL MERGE

OVERVIEW

A ***mail merge*** takes the tedium out of sending ***form letters,*** as it creates the same letter many times, changing the name, address, and other information as appropriate from letter to letter. You might use a mail merge to look for a job upon graduation, when you send essentially the same letter to many different companies. The concept is illustrated in Figure B.1, in which John Smith drafts a letter describing his qualifications, then merges that letter with a set of names and addresses, to produce the individual letters.

The mail merge process uses two files as input, a main document and a data source. A set of form letters is created as output. The ***main document*** (e.g., the cover letter in Figure B.1a) contains standardized text together with one or more ***merge fields*** that indicate where variable information is to be inserted into the individual letters. The ***data source*** (the set of names and addresses in Figure B.1b) contains the information that varies from letter to letter.

The first row in the data source is called the header row and identifies the fields in the remaining rows. Each additional row contains the data to create one letter and is called a ***data record.*** Every data record contains the same fields in the same order—for example, Title, FirstName, LastName, and so on.

The main document and the data source work in conjunction with one another, with the merge fields in the main document referencing the corresponding fields in the data source. The first line in the address of Figure B.1a, for example, contains the entries in angled brackets, <<*Title*>> <<*FirstName*>> <<*LastName*>>. (These entries are not typed explicitly but are entered through special commands as described in the hands-on exercise that follows shortly.) The merge process examines each record in the data source and substitutes the appropriate field values for the corresponding merge fields as it creates the individual form letters. For example, the first three fields in the first record will

John H. Smith
426 Jenny Lake Drive • Coral Gables, FL 33146 • (305) 666-4801

June 25, 1995

« Title » «FirstName» «LastName»
«JobTitle»
«Company»
«Address1»
«City», «State» «PostalCode»

Dear «Title» «LastName»:

I am writing to inquire about a position with «Company» as an entry level computer programmer. I have just graduated from the University of Miami with a Bachelor's Degree in Computer Information Systems (May, 1995) and I am very interested in working for you. I have a background in both microcomputer applications (Windows 95, Word, Excel, PowerPoint, and Access) as well as extensive experience with programming languages (Visual Basic, C++ and COBOL). I feel that I am well qualified to join your staff as over the past two years I have had a great deal of experience designing and implementing computer programs, both as a part of my educational program and during my internship with Personalized Computer Designs, Inc.

I am eager to put my skills to work and would like to talk with you at your earliest convenience. I have enclosed a copy of my résumé and will be happy to furnish the names and addresses of my references, if you so desire. You may reach me at the above address and phone number. I look forward to hearing from you.

Sincerely,

John Smith

(a) The Main Document

FIGURE B.1 The Mail Merge

produce *Mr. Jason Frasher.* The same fields in the second record will produce *Ms. Elizabeth Schery,* and so on.

In similar fashion, the second line in the address of the main document contains the <<*JobTitle*>> field. The third line contains the <<*Company*>> field. The fourth line references the <<*Address1*>> field, and the last line contains the <<*City*>>, <<*State*>, and <<*PostalCode*>> fields. The salutation repeats the <<*Title*>> and <<*LastName*>> fields. The first sentence uses the <<*Company*>> field a second time. The mail merge prepares the letters one at a time, with one letter created for every record in the data source until the file of names and addresses is exhausted. The individual form letters are shown in Figure B.1c. Each letter begins automatically on a new page.

Title	FirstName	LastName	JobTitle	Company	Address1	City	State	PostalCode
Mr.	Jason	Frasher	President	Frasher Systems	100 S. Miami Avenue	Miami	FL	33103
Ms.	Elizabeth	Schery	Director of Personnel	Custom Computing	8180 Kendall Drive	Miami	FL	33156
Ms.	Lauren	Howard	President	Unique Systems	475 LeJeune Road	Coral Gables	FL	33146

(b) The Data Source

John H. Smith

426 Jenny Lake Drive • Coral Gables, FL 33146 • (305) 666-4801

June 25, 1995

Mr. Jason Frasher
President
Frasher Systems
100 S. Miami Avenue
Miami, FL 33103

Dear Mr. Frasher:

I am writing to inquire about a position with Frasher Systems as an entry level computer programmer. I have just graduated from the University of Systems (May, 1995) and I am very interested microcomputer applications (Windows 95, experience with programming languages (V to join your staff as over the past two years I implementing computer programs, both as with Personalized Computer Designs, Inc.

I am eager to put my skills to work and wo enclosed a copy of my résumé and will be h you so desire. You may reach me at the ab from you.

Sincerely,

John Smith

John H. Smith

426 Jenny Lake Drive • Coral Gables, FL 33146 • (305) 666-4801

June 25, 1995

Ms. Elizabeth Schery
Director of Personnel
Custom Computing
8180 Kendall Drive
Miami, FL 33156

Dear Ms. Schery:

I am writing to inquire about a position with Custom Computing as an entry level computer programmer. I have just graduated from the University of Systems (May, 1995) and I am very interested microcomputer applications (Windows 95, W experience with programming languages (Vis to join your staff as over the past two years I implementing computer programs, both as a p with Personalized Computer Designs, Inc.

I am eager to put my skills to work and would enclosed a copy of my résumé and will be hap you so desire. You may reach me at the abov from you.

Sincerely,

John Smith

John H. Smith

426 Jenny Lake Drive • Coral Gables, FL 33146 • (305) 666-4801

June 25, 1995

Ms. Lauren Howard
President
Unique Systems
475 LeJeune Road
Coral Gables, FL 33146

Dear Ms. Howard:

I am writing to inquire about a position with Unique Systems as an entry level computer programmer. I have just graduated from the University of Miami with a Bachelor's Degree in Computer Information Systems (May, 1995) and I am very interested in working for you. I have a background in both microcomputer applications (Windows 95, Word, Excel, PowerPoint, and Access) as well as extensive experience with programming languages (Visual Basic, C++ and COBOL). I feel that I am well qualified to join your staff as over the past two years I have had a great deal of experience designing and implementing computer programs, both as a part of my educational program and during my internship with Personalized Computer Designs, Inc.

I am eager to put my skills to work and would like to talk with you at your earliest convenience. I have enclosed a copy of my résumé and will be happy to furnish the names and addresses of my references, if you so desire. You may reach me at the above address and phone number. I look forward to hearing from you.

Sincerely,

John Smith

(c) The Printed Letters

FIGURE B.1 The Mail Merge (continued)

FILE DESIGN

The zip code should be defined as a separate field in the data source in order to sort on zip code and take advantage of bulk mail. A person's first and last name should also be defined separately, so that you have access to either field, perhaps to create a friendly salutation such as Dear Joe or to sort on last name.

MAIL MERGE HELPER

The implementation of a mail merge in Microsoft Word is easy, provided you understand the basic concept. In essence, there are three things you must do:

1. Create and save the main document
2. Create and save the data source
3. Merge the main document and data source to create the individual letters

The Mail Merge command is located in the Tools menu. Execution of the command displays the **Mail Merge Helper,** which lists the steps in the mail merge process and guides you every step of the way.

The screen in Figure B.2 shows the Mail Merge Helper as it appears after steps 1 and 2 have been completed. The main document is the file *Finished Form Letter.doc*. The data source is the file *Names and Addresses.doc*. All that remains is to merge the files and create the individual form letters. The options in effect

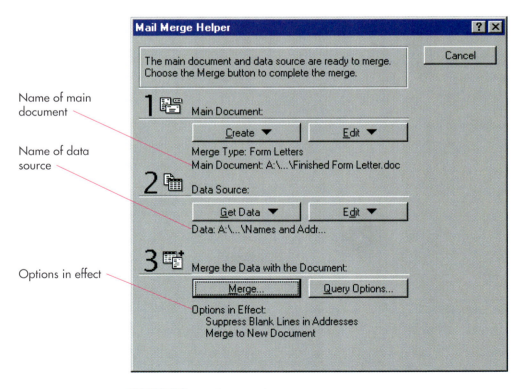

FIGURE B.2   Mail Merge Helper

indicate that the letters will be created in a new document and that blank lines, if any, in addresses (e.g., a missing company or title) will be suppressed. The Query Options command button lets you select and/or *sort* the records in the data source prior to the merge. These options are discussed after the hands-on exercise.

> ### PAPER MAKES A DIFFERENCE
>
> Most of us take paper for granted, but the right paper can make a significant difference in the effectiveness of the document. Reports and formal correspondence are usually printed on white paper, but you would be surprised how many different shades of white there are. Other types of documents lend themselves to colored paper for additional impact. In short, the choice of paper you use is far from an automatic decision. Our favorite source for paper is a company called PAPER DIRECT (1-800-APAPERS). Ask for a catalog, then consider the use of a specialty paper the next time you have an important project, such as the cover letter for your résumé.

HANDS-ON EXERCISE 1

Mail Merge

Objective: To create a main document and associated data source; to implement a mail merge and produce a set of form letters. Use Figure B.3 as a guide in the exercise.

STEP 1: Open the Cover Letter
- Open the **Form Letter document** in the **Exploring Word Folder** as shown in Figure B.3a. (The dialog box will not yet be displayed.)
  - If necessary, pull down the **View menu** and click **Page Layout** (or click the **Page Layout button** above the status bar).
  - If necessary, click the **Zoom Control arrow** to change to **Page Width.**
- Save the document as **Modified Form Letter** so that you can return to the original document if necessary.

> ### THE LETTER WIZARD
>
> It is the rare individual who has never been confronted by writer's block and the frustration of a blank screen and a flashing cursor. The Letter Wizard is Microsoft's attempt to get you started. Pull down the File menu, click New, click the Letters & Faxes tab in the New dialog box, then double click the Letter Wizard. The Wizard asks you a series of questions about the type of letter you want to write, then supplies a template for you to complete. It will even let you choose one of several prewritten letters, including a résumé cover letter. It's not perfect, but it is a starting point, and that may be all you need.

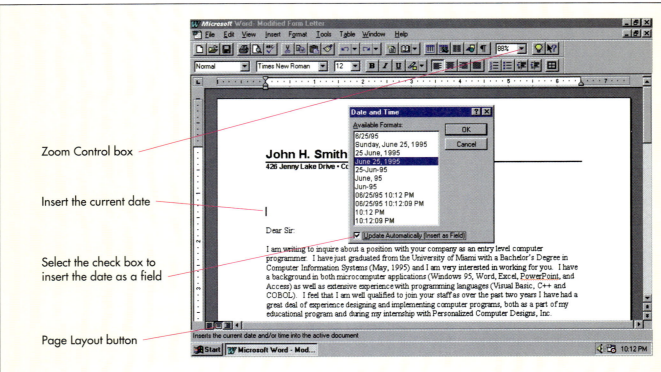

(a) Insert the Date (step 2)

FIGURE B.3 Hands-on Exercise 1

STEP 2: Insert Today's Date

➤ Click to the left of the "D" in Dear Sir, then press **enter** twice to insert two lines. Press the **up arrow** two times to return to the first line you inserted.

➤ Pull down the **Insert menu** and click the **Date and Time command** to display the dialog box in Figure B.3a.

➤ Select (click) the date format you prefer and, if necessary, check the box to insert the date as a field. Click **OK** to close the dialog box.

FIELD CODES VERSUS FIELD RESULTS

All fields are displayed in a document in one of two formats, as a ***field code*** or as a ***field result.*** A field code appears in braces and indicates instructions to insert variable data when the document is printed; a field result displays the information as it will appear in the printed document. You can toggle the display between the field code and field result by pressing Shift+F9 during editing.

STEP 3: Create the Main Document

➤ Pull down the **Tools menu.** Click **Mail Merge.** Click the **Create command button** under step 1 to create the main document as shown in Figure B.3b.

➤ Click **Form Letters,** then click **Active Window** to indicate that you will use the Form Letter document (in the active window) as the main document.

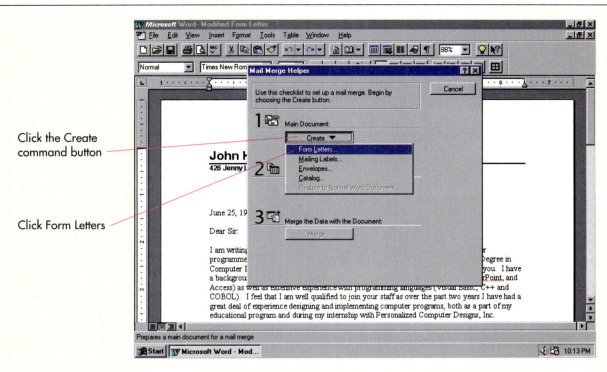

(b) Create the Main Document (step 3)

FIGURE B.3 Hands-on Exercise 1 (continued)

STEP 4: Create the Data Source

➤ Click **Get Data** under step 2, then click **Create Data Source** to display the dialog box in Figure B.3c.

➤ Word provides commonly used field names for the data source, but not all of the data fields are necessary. Click **Address2,** then click the **Remove Field Name command button.** Delete the Country, HomePhone, and WorkPhone fields in similar fashion.

➤ Click **OK** to complete the definition of the data source. You will then be presented with the Save As dialog box as you need to save the data source.

➤ Type **Names and Addresses** in the File Name text box as the name of the data source. Click **Save** to save the file.

➤ You will see a message indicating that the data source does not contain any data records. Click **Edit Data Source** in order to add records at this time.

STEP 5: Add the Data

➤ Enter data for the first record. Type **Mr.** in the Title field. Press **Tab** to move to the next (FirstName) field, and type **Jason.** Continue in this fashion until you have completed the first record as shown in Figure B.3d.

➤ Click **Add New** to enter the data for the next person to receive the letter:
- Ms. Elizabeth Schery
- Director of Personnel
- Custom Computing
- 8180 Kendall Drive
- Miami, FL 33156

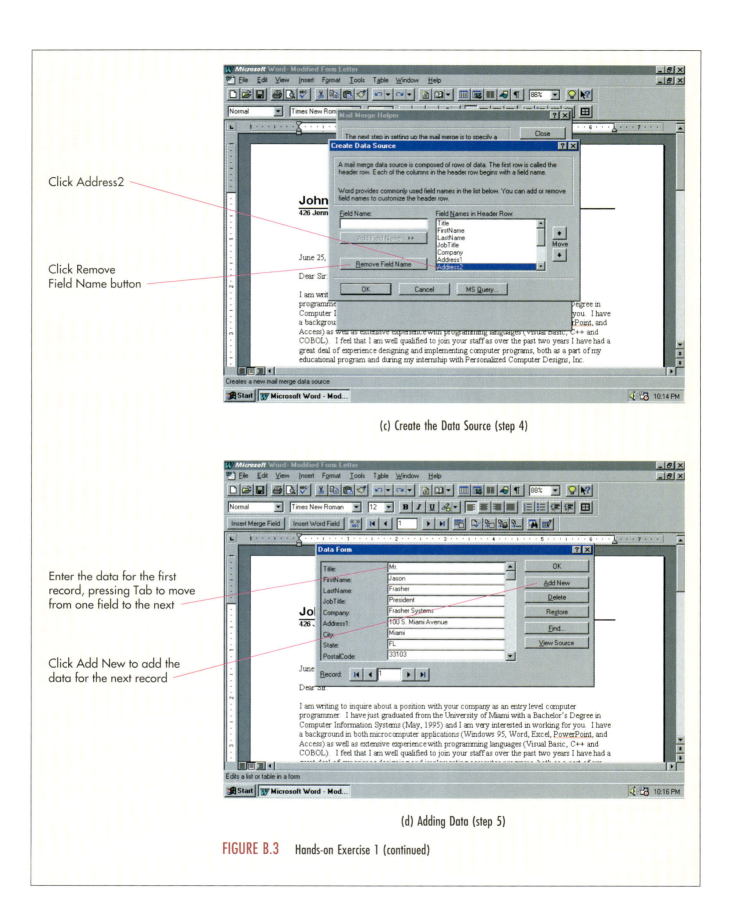

FIGURE B.3 Hands-on Exercise 1 (continued)

➤ Click **Add New** to enter the data for the third and last recipient:
  - Ms. Lauren Howard
  - President
  - Unique Systems
  - 475 LeJeune Road
  - Coral Gables, FL 33146
➤ Click **OK** to end the data entry and return to the main document. The Mail Merge toolbar is displayed immediately below the Formatting toolbar.

STEP 6: Add the Data Fields
➤ Click in the main document immediately below the date. Press **enter** to leave a blank line between the date and the first line of the address.
➤ Click the **Insert Merge Field button** on the Merge toolbar. Click **Title** from the list of fields within the data source. The title field is inserted into the main document and enclosed in angled brackets as shown in Figure B.3e.
➤ Press the **space bar** to add a space between the words. Click the **Insert Merge Field button** a second time. Click **FirstName.** Press the **space bar.**
➤ Click the **Insert Merge Field button** again. Click **LastName.**
➤ Press **enter** to move to the next line. Enter the remaining fields in the address as shown in Figure B.3e. Be sure to add a comma after the **City field** as well as a space.

(e) Inserting Data Fields (step 6)

FIGURE B.3 Hands-on Exercise 1 (continued)

- Delete the word "Sir" in the salutation and replace it with the **Title** and **LastName fields.**
- Delete the words "your company" in the first sentence and replace them with the **Company field.**
- Save the main document.

STEP 7: The Mail Merge Toolbar
- The Mail Merge toolbar enables you to preview the form letters before they are created.
- Click the **<<abc>> button** on the Merge toolbar to display field values rather than field codes; you will see Mr. Jason Frasher instead of <<Title>> <<FirstName>> <<LastName>>, etc.
- The **<<abc>> button** functions as a toggle switch. Click it once and you switch from field codes to field values; click it a second time and you go from field values back to field codes. End with the field values displayed.
- Look at the text box on the Mail Merge toolbar, which displays the number 1 to indicate that the first record is displayed. Click the ▶ **button** to display the form letter for the next record (Ms. Elizabeth Schery in our example).
- Click the ▶ **button** again to display the form letter for the next record (Ms. Lauren Howard). The toolbar indicates you are on the third record. Click the ◀ **button** to return to the previous (second) record.
- Click the I◀ **button** to move directly to the first record (Jason Frasher). Click the ▶I **button** to display the form letter for the last record (Lauren Howard).
- Toggle the **<<abc>> button** to display the field codes.

STEP 8: The Mail Merge Helper
- Click the **Mail Merge Helper button** on the Merge toolbar to display the dialog box in Figure B.3f.
- The Mail Merge Helper shows your progress thus far:
  - The main document has been created and saved as Modified Form Letter.
  - The data source has been created and saved as Names and Addresses.
- Click the **Merge command button** to display the dialog box in Figure B.3g.

EDIT THE DATA SOURCE

Click the Mail Merge Helper button to display a dialog box with information about the mail merge, click the Edit command button under Data Source, then click the file containing the data source. Click the View Source command button to see multiple records in the data source displayed within a table; the first row contains the field names, and each succeeding row contains a data record. Edit the data source, then pull down the Window menu and click the name of the file containing the main document to continue working on the mail merge.

STEP 9: The Merge
- The selected options in Figure B.3g should already be set:
  - If necessary, click the **arrow** in the Merge To list box and select New document.

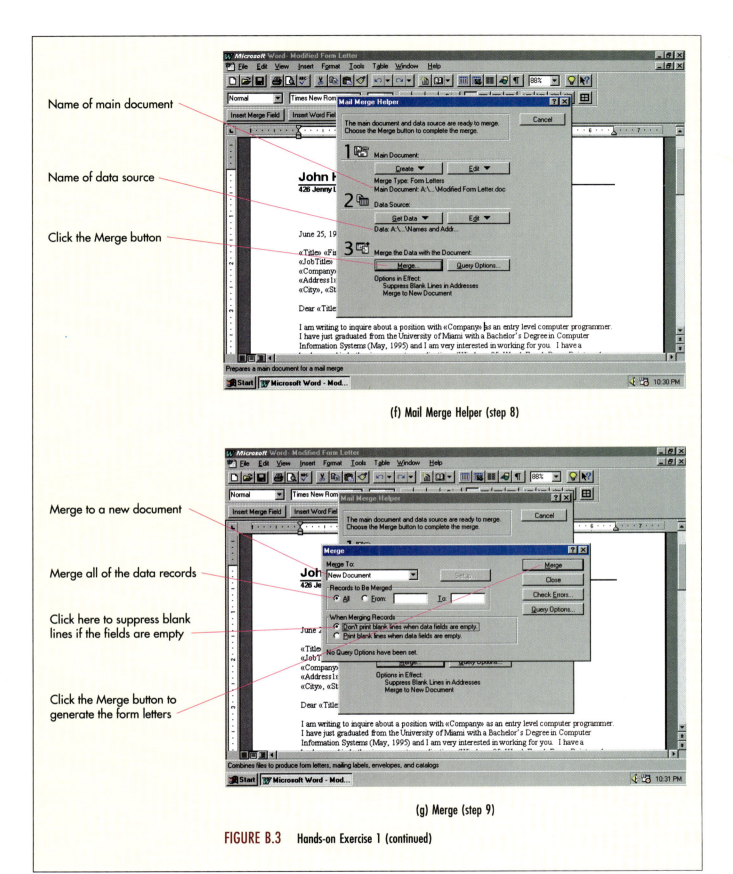

(f) Mail Merge Helper (step 8)

(g) Merge (step 9)

FIGURE B.3 Hands-on Exercise 1 (continued)

- If necessary, click the **All options button** to include all records in the data source.
- If necessary, click the **option button** to suppress blank lines if data fields are empty.

➤ Click the **Merge command button.** Word pauses momentarily, then generates the three form letters in a new document.

STEP 10: The Form Letters

➤ The title bar of the active window changes to Form Letters1. Scroll through the letters to review them individually.

➤ Pull down the **View menu.** Click **Zoom.** Click **Many Pages.** Click the **monitor icon,** then click and drag within the resulting dialog box to display three pages side by side. Click **OK.** You should see the three form letters as shown in Figure B.3h.

➤ Print the letters.

➤ Pull down the **File menu** and click **Exit** to exit Word. Pay close attention to the informational messages that ask whether to save the modified file(s):

- There is no need to save the merged document (Form Letters1) because you can always re-create the merged letters, provided you have saved the main document and data source.
- Save the Modified Form Letter and Names and Addresses documents if you are asked to do so.

➤ Congratulations on a job well done. Good luck in your job hunting!

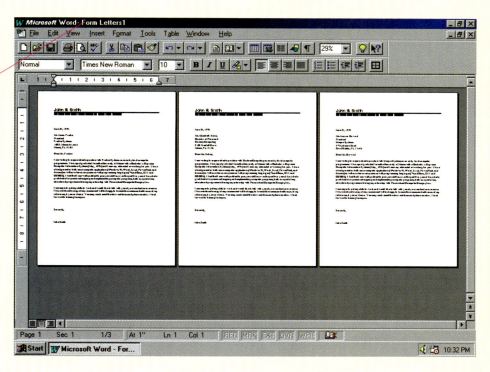

The title bar indicates Form Letters1

(h) The Individual Form Letters (step 10)

FIGURE B.3 Hands-on Exercise 1 (continued)

FINER POINTS OF MAIL MERGE

The hands-on exercise just completed acquaints you with the basics of a mail merge, but there is much more that you can do. You can, for example, sort the data source so that the form letters are printed in a different sequence—for example, by zip code to take advantage of bulk mail. You can also select (filter) the records that are to be included in the mail merge; that is, a letter need not be sent to every record in the data source.

Figure B.4 illustrates both options and is accessed through the Query Options command button in the Mail Merge Helper window. The records in the data source may be sorted on as many as three fields, as indicated in Figure B.4a, which sorts the records by postal code (zip code), and then by last name within the postal code. Both fields are in ascending (low to high) sequence.

The dialog box in Figure B.4b lets you establish selection criteria in order to specify which records from the data source are to be merged. The example in the figure will send letters only to those persons living in California. The implementation is straightforward, and you can impose additional rules or clear an existing rule by clicking the appropriate command button.

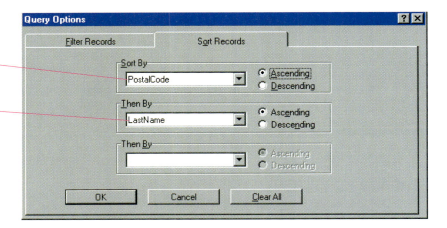

(a) Sorting Records

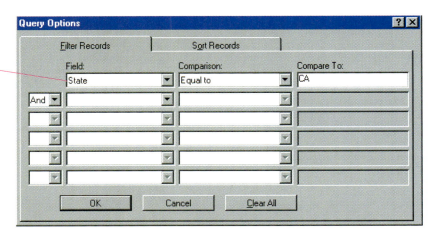

(b) Selecting Records

FIGURE B.4 Finer Points of Mail Merge

SUMMARY

A mail merge creates the same letter many times, changing only the variable data such as the addressee's name and address, from letter to letter. It is performed in conjunction with a main document and a data source, both of which exist as separate documents. The mail merge can be used to create a form letter for selected records, and/or print the form letters in a sequence different from the way the records are stored in the data source.

KEY WORDS AND CONCEPTS

Data source	Filter	Main document
Field	Form letter	Merge field
Field code	Mail merge	Record
Field result	Mail Merge Helper	Sort

APPENDIX C: TOOLBARS

OVERVIEW

Microsoft Word has nine predefined toolbars, which provide access to commonly used commands. The toolbars are displayed in Figure C.1 and are listed here for convenience. They are: the Borders, Database, Drawing, Formatting, Forms, Microsoft, Standard, TipWizard, and Word 2.0 toolbars. The Standard and Formatting toolbars are displayed by default and appear immediately below the menu bar.

In addition to the predefined toolbars, which are displayed continually, seven other toolbars appear only when their corresponding feature is in use. These toolbars appear (and disappear) automatically and are shown in Figure C.2. They are: the Equation Editor, Header/Footer, Macro, Mail Merge, Master Document, Outlining, and Picture toolbars.

The buttons on the toolbars are intended to be indicative of their function. Clicking the Printer button (the fourth button from the left on the Standard toolbar), for example, executes the Print command. If you are unsure of the purpose of any toolbar button, point to it, and a ToolTip will appear that displays its name.

You can display multiple toolbars at one time, move them to new locations on the screen, customize their appearance, or suppress their display.

- To display or hide a toolbar, pull down the View menu and click the Toolbars command. Select (deselect) the toolbar(s) that you want to display (hide). The selected toolbar(s) will be displayed in the same position as when last displayed. You may also point to any toolbar and click with the right mouse button to bring up a shortcut menu, after which you can select the toolbar to be displayed (hidden).
- To change the size of the buttons, display them in monochrome rather than color, suppress the display of the ToolTips or display the associated shortcut key (if available), pull down the View

menu, click Toolbars, and then select (deselect) the appropriate check box. Alternatively, you can click on any toolbar with the right mouse button, select Toolbars, and then select (deselect) the appropriate check box.

- Toolbars may be either docked (along the edge of the window) or left floating (in their own window). A toolbar moved to the edge of the window will dock along that edge. A toolbar moved anywhere else in the window will float in its own window. Docked toolbars are one tool wide (high), whereas floating toolbars can be resized by clicking and dragging a border or corner as you would with any other window.
  - To move a docked toolbar, click anywhere in the gray background area and drag the toolbar to its new location.
  - To move a floating toolbar, drag its title bar to its new location.
- To customize a toolbar, display the toolbar on the screen, pull down the View menu, click Toolbars, click the Customize command button, and select the Toolbars tab. Alternatively, you can click on any toolbar with the right mouse button, select Customize from the shortcut menu, and then click the Toolbars tab.
  - To move a button, drag the button to its new location on that toolbar or any other displayed toolbar.
  - To copy a button, press the Ctrl key as you drag the button to its new location on that toolbar or any other displayed toolbar.
  - To delete a button, drag the button off the toolbar and release the mouse button.
  - To add a button, select the category containing the button from the Categories list box and then drag the button to the desired location on the toolbar. (To see a description of a tool's function prior to adding it to a toolbar, click the tool in the Customize dialog box and read the displayed description.)
  - To restore a predefined toolbar to its default appearance, pull down the View menu, click Toolbars, select (highlight) the desired toolbar, and click the Reset command button.
- Buttons can also be moved, copied, or deleted without displaying the Customize dialog box.
  - To move a button, press the Alt key as you drag the button to the new location.
  - To copy a button, press the Alt and Ctrl keys as you drag the button to the new location.
  - To delete a button, press the Alt key and drag the button off the toolbar.
- To create your own toolbar, pull down the View menu, click Toolbars, and click the New command button. Alternatively, you can click on any toolbar with the right mouse button, select Toolbars from the shortcut menu, and then click the New command button.
  - Enter a name for the toolbar in the dialog box that follows. The name can be any length and can contain spaces.
  - The new toolbar will appear at the top left of the screen. Initially it will be big enough to hold only one button. Add, move, and delete buttons following the same procedures as outlined above. The toolbar will automatically size itself as new buttons are added and deleted.
  - To delete a custom toolbar, pull down the View menu, click Toolbars, and make sure that the custom toolbar to be deleted is the only one selected (highlighted). Click the Delete command button. Click Yes to confirm the deletion. (Note that a predefined toolbar cannot be deleted.)

Borders Toolbar

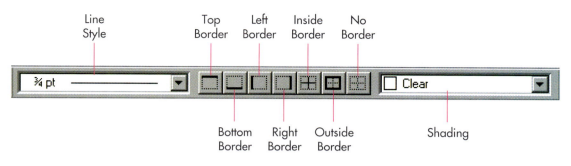

Database Toolbar

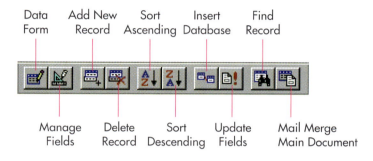

Drawing Toolbar

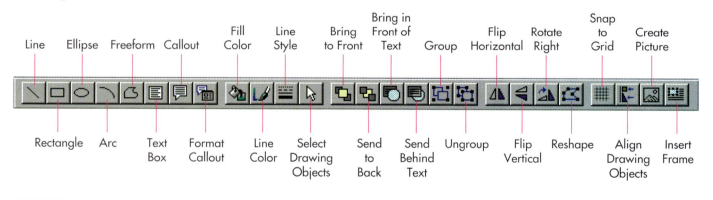

Formatting Toolbar

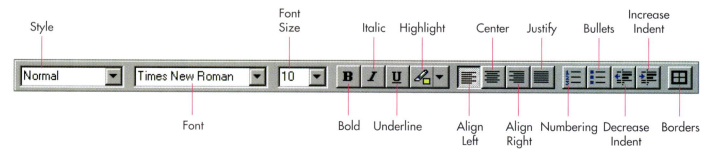

FIGURE C.1 Predefined Toolbars

Forms Toolbar

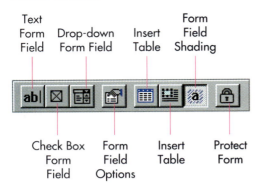

Microsoft Toolbar

Standard Toolbar

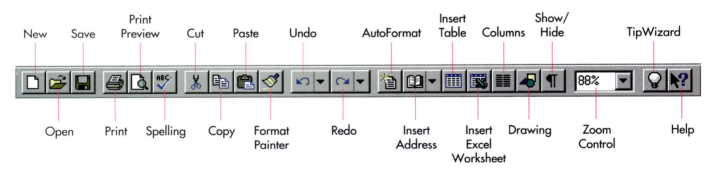

TipWizard Toolbar

FIGURE C.1   Predefined Toolbars (continued)

Word 2.0 Toolbar

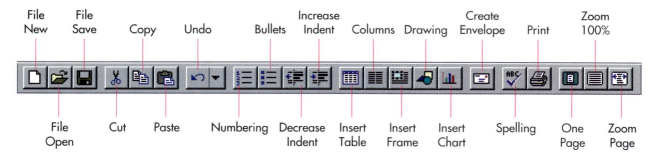

FIGURE C.1 Predefined Toolbars (continued)

Equation Editor Toolbar

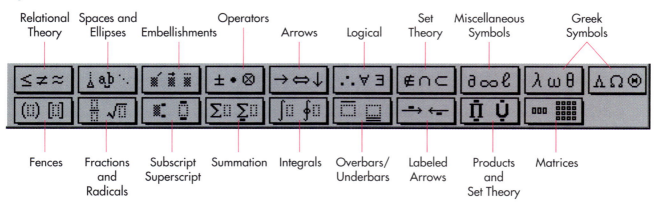

Header/Footer Toolbar

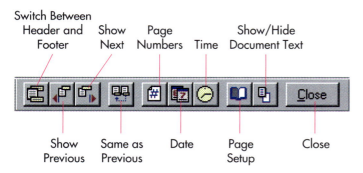

FIGURE C.2 Feature Toolbars

APPENDIX C

Macro Toolbar

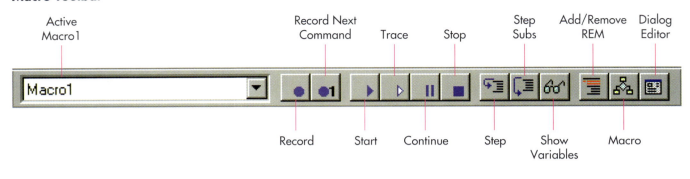

Mail Merge Toolbar

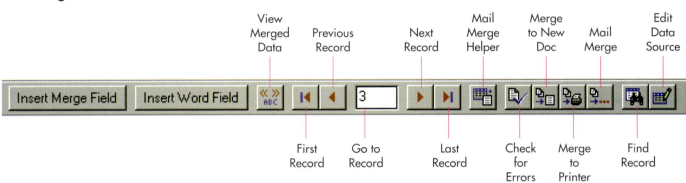

Master Document Toolbar

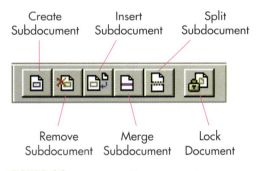

FIGURE C.2 Feature Toolbars (continued)

Outlining Toolbar

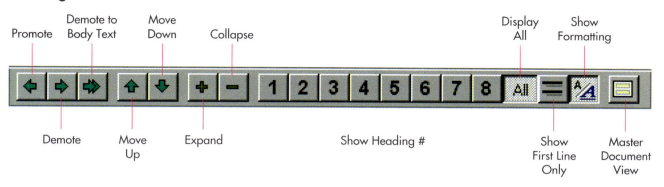

Picture Toolbar

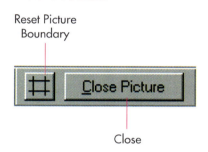

FIGURE C.2 Feature Toolbars (continued)

PREREQUISITES: ESSENTIALS OF WINDOWS 95®

OBJECTIVES

After reading this appendix you will be able to:

1. Describe the objects on the Windows desktop; use the Start button to access the online help.
2. Explain the function of the minimize, maximize, restore, and close buttons; move and size a window.
3. Discuss the function of a dialog box; describe the different types of dialog boxes and the various ways in which information is supplied.
4. Format a floppy disk.
5. Use My Computer to locate a specific file or folder; describe the different views available for My Computer.
6. Describe how folders are used to organize a disk; create a new folder; copy and/or move a file from one folder to another.
7. Delete a file, then recover the deleted file from the Recycle Bin.
8. Describe the document orientation of Windows 95; use the New command to create a document without explicitly opening the associated application.
9. Explain the differences in browsing with My Computer versus browsing with the Windows Explorer.

OVERVIEW

Windows 95 is a computer program (actually many programs) that controls the operation of your computer and its peripherals. One of the most significant benefits of the Windows environment is the common user interface and consistent command structure that are imposed on every Windows application. Once you learn the basic concepts and techniques, you can apply that knowledge to every Windows application. This appendix teaches you those concepts so that you will be able to work productively in the Windows environment. It is written for you, the computer novice, and assumes no previous knowledge about a computer or about Windows. Our goal is to get you "up and running" as quickly as possible so that you can do the work you want to do.

We begin with an introduction to the Windows desktop, the graphical user interface that lets you work in intuitive fashion by pointing at icons and clicking the mouse. We show you how to use the online help facility to look up information when you need it. We identify the basic components of a window and describe how to execute commands and supply information through various types of dialog boxes.

The appendix also shows you how to manage the hundreds (indeed, thousands) of files that are stored on the typical system. We describe the use of My Computer to search the drives on your computer for a specific file or folder. (All files in Windows 95 are stored in folders, which are the electronic equivalent of manila folders in a filing cabinet.) We show you how to create a new folder and how to move or copy a file from one folder to another. We show you how to rename a file, how to delete a file, and how to recover a deleted file from the Recycle Bin.

All file operations are done through My Computer or through the more powerful Windows Explorer. My Computer is intuitive and geared for the novice, as it opens a new window for each folder you open. Explorer, on the other hand, is more sophisticated and provides a hierarchical view of the entire system in a single window. A beginner will prefer My Computer, whereas a more experienced user will most likely opt for the Explorer. This is the same sequence in which we present the material. We start with My Computer, then show you how to accomplish the same result more quickly through the Explorer.

THE DESKTOP

Windows 95 creates a working environment for your computer that parallels the working environment at home or in an office. You work at a desk. Windows operations take place on the ***desktop.***

There are physical objects on a desk such as folders, a dictionary, a calculator, or a phone. The computer equivalent of those objects appear as ***icons*** (pictorial symbols) on the desktop. Each object on a real desk has attributes (properties) such as size, weight, and color. In similar fashion, Windows assigns properties to every object on its desktop. And just as you can move the objects on a real desk, you can rearrange the objects on the Windows desktop.

Figure 1a displays the desktop when Windows is first installed on a new computer. This desktop has only a few objects and is similar to the desk in a new office, just after you move in. Figure 1b displays a different desktop, one with three open windows, and is similar to a desk during the middle of a working day. Do not be concerned if your Windows desktop is different from ours. Your real desk is arranged differently from those of your friends, and so your Windows desktop will also be different.

The simplicity of the desktop in Figure 1a helps you to focus on what's important. The ***Start button,*** as its name suggests, is where you begin. Click the Start button (mouse operations are explained in the next section) and you see a menu that provides access to any program (e.g., Microsoft Word or Microsoft Excel) on your computer. The Start button also gives you access to an online help facility that provides information about every aspect of Windows.

In addition to the Start button, the desktop in Figure 1a contains three objects, each of which has a special purpose. ***My Computer*** enables you to browse the disk drives (and optional CD-ROM drive) that are attached to your computer.

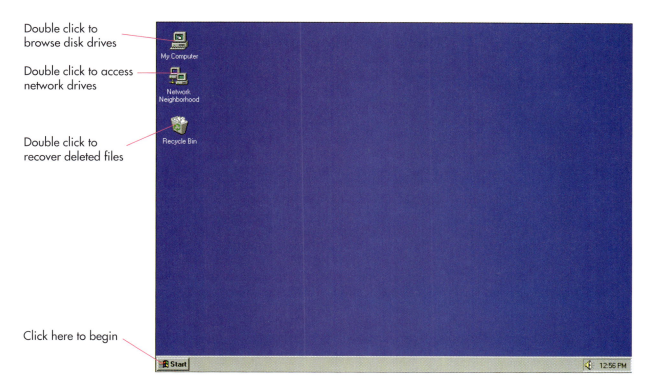

(a) New Desktop

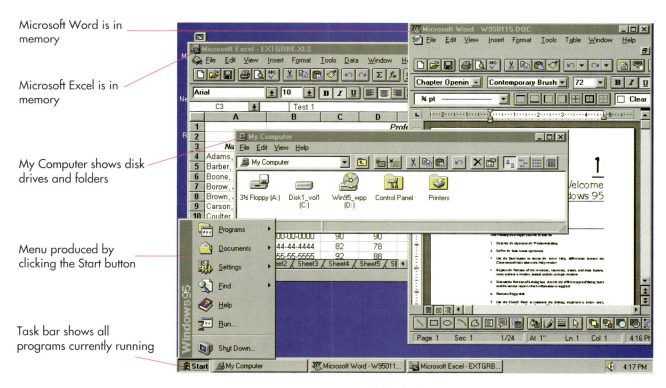

(b) A Working Desk

FIGURE 1 The Windows Desktop

Network Neighborhood extends your view of the computer to include the accessible drives on the network to which your machine is attached, if indeed it is part of a network. (You will not see this icon if you are not connected to a network.) The **Recycle Bin** lets you recover a file that was previously deleted and is illustrated in a hands-on exercise later in the appendix (see page 40).

Each object in Figure 1a contains additional objects that are displayed when you open (double click) the object. Double click My Computer in Figure 1a, for example, and you see the objects contained in the My Computer window of Figure 1b. Double click Network Neighborhood, and you will see all of the drives available on your network.

Two additional windows are open on the desktop in Figure 1b and correspond to programs that are currently in use. Each window has a title bar that displays the name of the program and the associated document. (The Start button was used to open each program, Microsoft Word and Microsoft Excel, in Figure 1b.) You can work in any window as long as you want, then switch to a different window. ***Multitasking,*** the ability to run several programs at the same time, is one of the major benefits of the Windows environment. It lets you run a word processor in one window, a spreadsheet in a second window, communicate online in a third window, run a game in a fourth window, and so on.

The ***taskbar*** at the bottom of the desktop shows all of the programs that are currently running (open in memory). It contains a button for each open program and lets you switch back and forth between those programs, by clicking the appropriate button. The taskbar in Figure 1a does not contain any buttons (other than the Start button) since there are no open applications. The taskbar in Figure 1b, however, contains three additional buttons, one for each open window.

ANATOMY OF A WINDOW

Figure 2 displays a typical window and labels its essential elements. Every window has the same components as every other window, which include a title bar, a Minimize button, a Maximize or Restore button, and a Close button. Other elements, that may or may not be present, include a horizontal and/or vertical scroll bar, a menu bar, a status bar, and a toolbar. Every window also contains additional objects (icons) that pertain specifically to the programs(s) or data associated with that window.

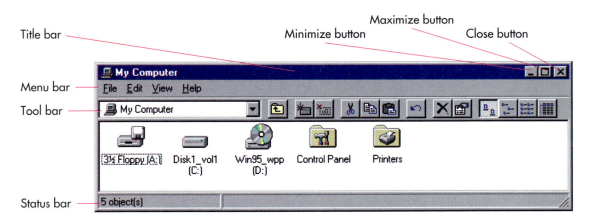

FIGURE 2 Anatomy of a Window

The ***title bar*** appears at the top of the window and displays the name of the window—for example, My Computer in Figure 2. The icon at the extreme left of the title bar provides access to a control menu that lets you select operations relevant to the window. The ***Minimize button*** shrinks the window to a button on the taskbar. The ***Maximize button*** enlarges the window so that it takes up the entire desktop. The ***Restore button*** (which is not shown in Figure 2) appears instead of the Maximize button after a window has been maximized, and restores the window to its previous size. The ***Close button*** closes the window and removes it from the desktop.

The ***menu bar*** appears immediately below the title bar and provides access to pull-down menus as discussed in the next section. A ***toolbar*** appears below the menu bar and lets you execute a command by clicking an icon, as opposed to pulling down a menu. The ***status bar*** is found at the bottom of the window and displays information about the window as a whole or about a selected object within a window.

A ***vertical (horizontal) scroll bar*** appears at the right (bottom) border of a window when its contents are not completely visible and provides access to the unseen areas. Scroll bars do not appear in Figure 2 since all five objects in the window are visible.

MY COMPUTER

My Computer lets you browse the disk drives (and CD-ROM) on your system. It is present on every desktop, but the contents depend on the specific configuration. Our system, for example, has one floppy drive, one hard disk, and a CD-ROM, each of which is represented by an icon within the My Computer window. My Computer is discussed in greater detail later in this appendix, beginning on page 19.

Moving and Sizing a Window

Any window can be sized or moved on the desktop through appropriate actions with the mouse. To ***size a window,*** point to any border (the mouse pointer changes to a double arrow), then drag the border in the direction you want to go: inward to shrink the window or outward to enlarge it. You can also drag a corner (instead of a border) to change both dimensions at the same time. To ***move a window*** while retaining its current size, click and drag the title bar to a new position on the desktop.

Pull-down Menus

The menu bar provides access to ***pull-down menus*** that enable you to execute commands within an application (program). A pull-down menu is accessed by clicking the menu name or by pressing the Alt key plus the underlined letter in the menu name; for example, press Alt+V to pull down the View menu. Three pull-down menus associated with My Computer are shown in Figure 3.

The commands within a menu are executed by clicking the command once the menu has been pulled down, or by typing the underlined letter (for example, C to execute the Close command in the File menu). Alternatively, you can bypass the menu entirely if you know the equivalent keystrokes shown to the right of the command in the menu (e.g., Ctrl+X, Ctrl+C, or Ctrl+V to cut, copy, or paste as

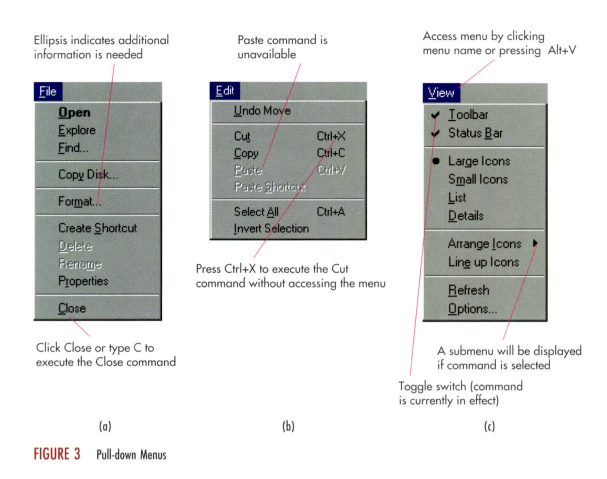

FIGURE 3 Pull-down Menus

shown within the Edit menu). A ***dimmed command*** (e.g., the Paste command in the Edit menu) means the command is not currently executable, and that some additional action has to be taken for the command to become available.

An ***ellipsis*** (...) following a command indicates that additional information is required to execute the command; for example, selection of the Format command in the File menu requires the user to specify additional information about the formatting process. This information is entered into a dialog box (discussed in the next section), which appears immediately after the command has been selected.

A check next to a command indicates a toggle switch, whereby the command is either on or off. There is a check next to the Toolbar command in the View menu of Figure 3, which means the command is in effect (and thus the toolbar will be displayed). Click the Toolbar command and the check disappears, which suppresses the display of the toolbar. Click the command a second time, the check reappears, as does the toolbar in the associated window.

An arrowhead after a command (e.g., the Arrange Icons command in the View menu) indicates a ***submenu*** will follow with additional menu options.

Dialog Boxes

A ***dialog box*** appears when additional information is needed to execute a command. The Format command, for example, requires information about which drive to format and the type of formatting desired.

Option (radio) buttons indicate mutually exclusive choices, one of which must be chosen; for example, one of three Format Type options in Figure 4a. Click a button to select an option, which automatically deselects the previously selected option.

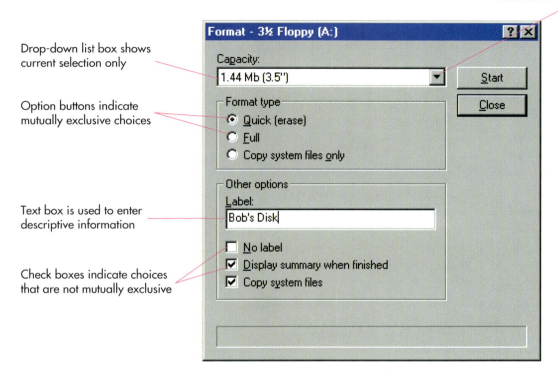

(a) Option Boxes and Check Boxes

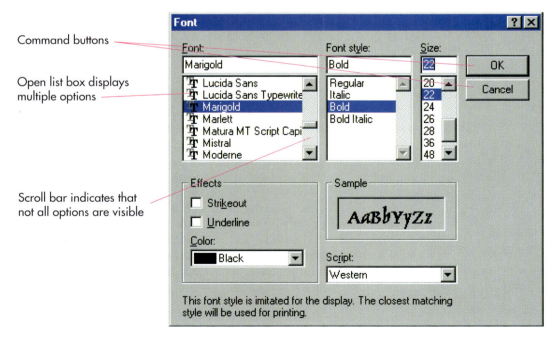

(b) List Boxes

FIGURE 4   Dialog Boxes

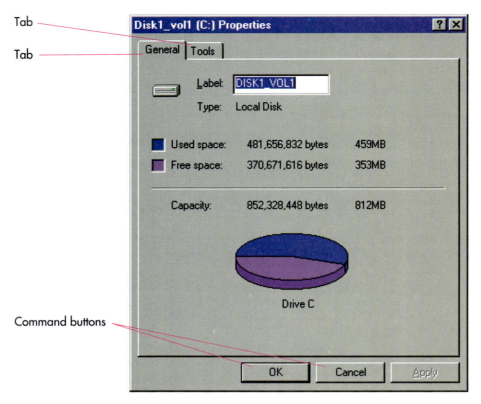

(c) Tabbed Dialog Box

FIGURE 4   Dialog Boxes (continued)

Check boxes are used instead of option buttons if the choices are not mutually exclusive or if an option is not required. Multiple boxes can be checked as in Figure 4a, or no boxes may be checked as in Figure 4b. Individual options are selected (cleared) by clicking on the appropriate check box.

A *text box* is used to enter descriptive information, such as Bob's Disk in Figure 4a. A flashing vertical bar (an I-beam) appears within the text box (when the text box is active) to mark the insertion point for the text you will enter.

A *list box* displays some or all of the available choices, any one of which is selected by clicking the desired item. A *drop-down list box,* such as the Capacity list box in Figure 4a, conserves space by showing only the current selection. Click the arrow of a drop-down list box to produce a list of available options. An *open list box,* such as those in Figure 4b, displays the choices without having to click a down arrow. (A scroll bar appears within an open list box if not all of the choices are visible at one time and provides access to the hidden choices.)

A *tabbed dialog box* provides multiple sets of options. The dialog box in Figure 4c, for example, has two tabs, each with its own set of options. Click either tab (the General tab is currently selected) to display the associated options.

All dialog boxes have a title bar, which contains a What's This button (in the form of a question mark) and a Close button. The *What's This button* provides help for any item in the dialog box; click the button, then click the item in the dialog box for which you want additional information. The Close button at the right of the title bar closes the dialog box.

All dialog boxes also contain one or more *command buttons,* the function of which is generally apparent from the button's name. The Start button, in Figure 4a, for example, initiates the formatting process. The OK Command button in

Figure 4b accepts the settings and closes the dialog box. The Cancel button does just the opposite, and ignores (cancels) the settings, then closes the dialog box without further action.

ONLINE HELP

Windows 95 has an extensive *online help* facility that contains information about virtually every topic in Windows. We believe that the best time to learn about help is as you begin your study of Windows. Help is available at any time, and is accessed most easily by clicking the *Help command* in the Start menu, which produces the help window in Figure 5.

The *Contents tab* in Figure 5a is similar to the table of contents in an ordinary book. The major topics are represented by books, each of which can be opened to display additional topics. Each open book will eventually display one or more specific topics, which may be viewed and/or printed to provide the indicated information.

The *Index tab* in Figure 5b is analogous to the index of an ordinary book. Type the first several letters of the topic to look up, click the topic when it appears in the window, then click the Display button to view the descriptive information as shown in Figure 5c. The help information is task-specific and describes how to accomplish the desired task.

You can print the contents of the Help windows in Figures 5a and 5b by clicking the Print command button at the bottom of a window. You can also print the contents of the display window in Figure 5c by right clicking in the window, then clicking the Print topic command from the shortcut menu.

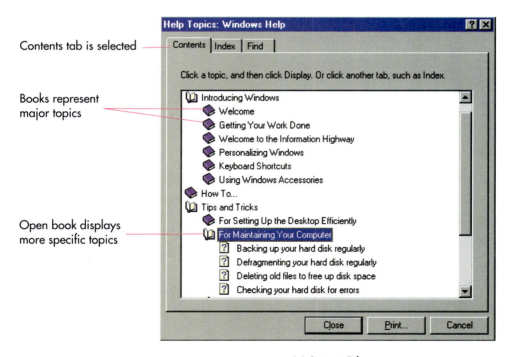

(a) Contents Tab

FIGURE 5   Online Help

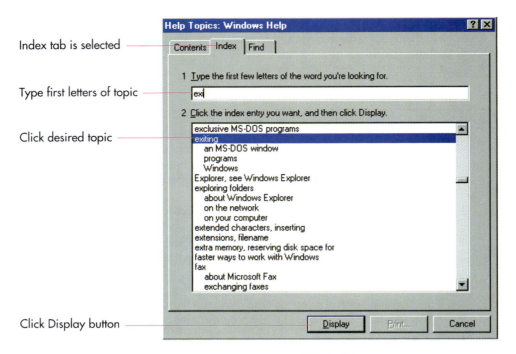

(b) Index Tab

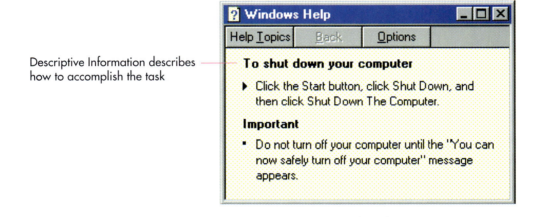

(c) Help Display

FIGURE 5 Online Help (continued)

THE MOUSE

The mouse is indispensable to Windows and is referenced continually in the hands-on exercises throughout the text. There are four basic operations with which you must become familiar:

- To *point* to an object, move the mouse pointer onto the object.
- To *click* an object, point to it, then press and release the left mouse button; to *right click* an object, point to the object, then press and release the right mouse button.

- To ***double click*** an object, point to it, then quickly click the left button twice in succession.
- To ***drag*** an object, move the pointer to the object, then press and hold the left button while you move the mouse to a new position.

The mouse is a pointing device—move the mouse on your desk and the ***mouse pointer,*** typically a small arrowhead, moves on the monitor. The mouse pointer assumes different shapes according to the location of the pointer or the nature of the current action—for example, a double arrow when you change the size of a window, an I-beam to insert text, a hand to jump from one help topic to the next, or a circle with a line through it to indicate that an attempted action is invalid.

The mouse pointer will also change to an hourglass to indicate that Windows is processing your last command, and that no further commands may be issued until the action is completed. The more powerful your computer, the less frequently the hourglass will appear; and conversely, the less powerful your system, the more you see the hourglass.

The Mouse versus the Keyboard

Almost every command in Windows can be executed in different ways, using either the mouse or the keyboard. Most people start with the mouse but add keyboard shortcuts as they become more proficient. There is no right or wrong technique, just different techniques, and the one you choose depends entirely on personal preference in a specific situation. If, for example, your hands are already on the keyboard, it is faster to use the keyboard equivalent. Other times, your hand will be on the mouse and that will be the fastest way. Toolbars provide still other ways to execute common commands.

In the beginning you may wonder why there are so many different ways to do the same thing, but you will eventually recognize the many options as part of Windows' charm. It is not necessary to memorize anything, nor should you even try; just be flexible and willing to experiment. The more you practice, the faster all of this will become second nature to you.

FORMATTING A DISK

All disks have to be formatted before they can hold data. The formatting process divides a disk into concentric circles called tracks, then further divides each track into sectors. You don't have to worry about formatting a hard disk, as that is done at the factory prior to the machine being sold. You do, however, have to format a floppy disk in order for Windows to read from and write to the disk. The procedure to format a floppy disk is described in step 6 of the following exercise.

FORMATTING A DISK

You must format a floppy disk at its rated capacity or else you may be unable to read the disk. There are two types of 3½-inch disks, double-density (720KB) and high-density (1.44MB). The easiest way to determine the type of disk is to look at the disk itself for the labels DD or HD, for double- and high-density, respectively. You can also check the number of square holes in the disk; a double-density disk has one, a high-density has two.

LEARNING BY DOING

Learning is best accomplished by doing, and so we come to the first of four exercises in this appendix. The exercises enable you to apply the concepts you have learned, then extend those concepts to further exploration on your own.

Our first exercise welcomes you to Windows 95, shows you how to open, move, and size a window on the desktop, and how to format a floppy disk.

HANDS-ON EXERCISE 1

Welcome to Windows 95

Objective: To turn on the computer and start Windows 95; to use the help facility and explore the topic "Ten Minutes to Using Windows"; to open, move, and size a window; to format a floppy disk. Use Figure 6 as a guide in the exercise.

STEP 1: Turn the Computer On

➤ The floppy drive should be empty prior to starting your machine. This ensures that the system starts by reading files from the hard disk (which contains the Windows files), as opposed to a floppy disk (which does not).

➤ The number and location of the on/off switches depend on the nature and manufacturer of the devices connected to the computer. The easiest possible setup is when all components of the system are plugged into a surge protector, in which case only a single switch has to be turned on. In any event:

- Turn on the monitor if it has a separate switch.
- Turn on the printer if it has a separate switch.
- Turn on the power switch of the system unit.

➤ Your system will take a minute or so to get started, after which you should see the desktop in Figure 6a (the Start menu is *not* yet visible). Do not be concerned if the appearance of your desktop is different from ours.

➤ You may (or may not) see the Welcome message in Figure 6a. All of the command buttons are interesting and merit further exploration, which we will do at a later time. But for now, we ask that you click the **Close button** if you see the Welcome message.

➤ Click the **Start button** to display the Start menu. Again, do not be concerned if your start menu is different from ours, or if your icons are smaller (or larger) than ours.

➤ Click the **Help command** as shown in Figure 6a.

MASTER THE MOUSE

Moving the mouse pointer is easy, but it takes practice to move it to an exact position on the screen. If you're having trouble, be sure the mouse is perpendicular to the system unit. Move the mouse to the left or right, and the mouse pointer moves left or right on the screen. Move the mouse forward or back, and the pointer moves up or down.

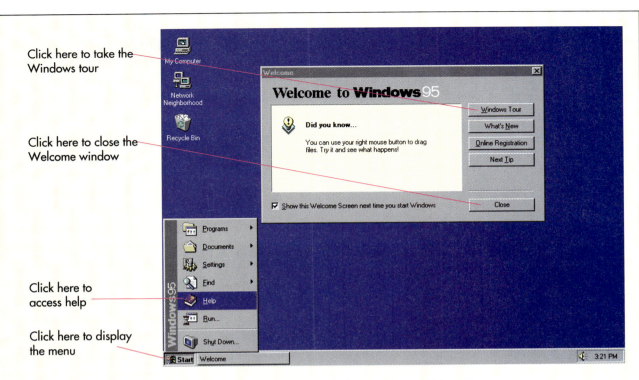

(a) Welcome to Windows 95 (step 1)

FIGURE 6 Hands-on Exercise 1

STEP 2: Ten Minutes to Windows

➤ If necessary, click the **Contents tab** in the Help Topics dialog box. All of the books on your screen will be closed.

➤ Click the topic **Ten Minutes to Using Windows,** then click the **Display button** to begin the Windows tour. (You can double click the topic to avoid having to click the Display button.)

➤ You should see the menu in Figure 6b. Click the **Book icon** next to Using Help to learn about the help facility.

➤ Follow the instructions provided by Windows until you complete the session on help. Click the **Exit button** at the upper right of the screen, then click the **Exit Tour button** to return to the desktop and continue with the exercise.

DOUBLE CLICKING FOR BEGINNERS

If you are having trouble double clicking, it is because you are not clicking quickly enough, or more likely, because you are moving the mouse (however slightly) between clicks. Relax, hold the mouse firmly on your desk, and try again.

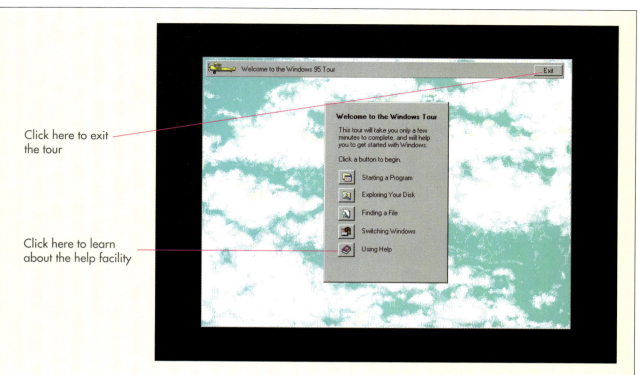

(b) Windows 95 Tour (step 2)

FIGURE 6   Hands-on Exercise 1 (continued)

STEP 3: Open My Computer

➤ Point to the **My Computer icon,** click the **right mouse button,** then click the **Open command** from the shortcut menu. (Alternatively, you can double click the **icon** to open it directly.)

➤ My Computer will open into a window as shown in Figure 6c. (The menus are not yet visible.) Do not be concerned if the contents of your window or its size and position on the desktop are different from ours.

➤ Pull down the **View menu** (point to the menu and click) as shown in Figure 6c. Make or verify the following selections. (You have to pull down the menu each time you choose a different command.)

- The **Toolbar command** should be checked. The Toolbar command functions as a toggle switch. Click the command and the toolbar is displayed; click the command a second time and the toolbar disappears.)

- The **Status Bar command** should be checked. The Status Bar command also functions as a toggle switch.

- **Large Icons** should be selected.

➤ Pull down the **View menu** a final time. Click the **Arrange Icons command** and (if necessary) click the **AutoArrange command** so that a check appears. Click outside the menu (or press the **Esc key**) if the command is already checked.

Drag the title bar to move the window (when menu is closed)

Click and drag a border to size the window (when menu is closed)

(c) My Computer (step 3)

FIGURE 6 Hands-on Exercise 1 (continued)

> **TOOLTIPS**
>
> Point to any button on the toolbar, and Windows displays the name of the button, which is indicative of its function. Point to the clock at the extreme right of the taskbar, and you will see a ToolTip with today's date. Point to the Start button, and you will see a ToolTip telling you to click here to begin.

STEP 4: Move and Size the Window

➤ Move and size the My Computer window on your desk to match the display in Figure 6c. (Press **Esc** to close the open menus.)
 - Click the **Restore button** (which appears only if the window has been maximized) or else you will not be able to move and size the window.
 - To change the width or height of the window, click and drag a border (the mouse pointer changes to a double arrow) in the direction you want to go; drag the border inward to shrink the window or outward to enlarge it.
 - To change the width and height at the same time, click and drag a corner rather than a border.
 - To change the position of the window, click and drag the title bar.

➤ Click the **Maximize button** so that the window expands to fill the entire screen. Click the **Restore button** (which replaces the Maximize button and is not shown in Figure 6c) to return the window to its previous size.

➤ Click the **Minimize button** to shrink the My Computer window to a button on the taskbar. My Computer is still open and remains active in memory.

➤ Click the **My Computer button** on the taskbar to reopen the window.

STEP 5: Scrolling

➤ Pull down the **View menu** and click **Details** (or click the **Details button** on the toolbar). You are now in the Details view as shown in Figure 6d.

➤ Click and drag the bottom border of the window inward so that you see the vertical scroll bar in Figure 6d. The scroll bar indicates that the contents of the window are not completely visible.

- Click the **down arrow** on the scroll bar. The top line (for drive A) disappears from view, and a new line containing the Control Panel comes into view.

- Click the **down arrow** a second time, which brings the Printers folder into view at the bottom of the window as the icon for drive C scrolls off the screen.

➤ Click the **Small Icons button** on the toolbar. Size the window so that the scroll bar disappears when the contents of the window become completely visible.

➤ Click the **Details button** on the toolbar. The scroll bar returns because you can no longer see the complete contents. Move and/or size the window to your personal preference.

(d) Scrolling (step 5)

FIGURE 6 Hands-on Exercise 1 (continued)

THE DETAILS VIEW

The Details view provides information about each object in a folder—for example, the capacity (total size) and amount of free space on a disk. To switch to the Details view, pull down the View menu and click Details. You can also click the Details button on the toolbar, provided the toolbar is displayed.

STEP 6: Format a Floppy Disk

➤ Click the **icon** for **drive A.** Pull down the **File menu** and click **Format.**

➤ You will see the dialog box in Figure 6e. Move the dialog box by clicking and dragging its **title bar** so that your screen matches ours.

➤ Click the **What's This button** (the mouse pointer changes to a question mark). Click the **Full option button** (under Format type) for an explanation. Click anywhere in the dialog box to close the popup window.

➤ Set the formatting parameters as shown in Figure 6e:

- Set the **Capacity** to match the floppy disk you purchased (see boxed tip on page 11).
- Click the **Full option button** to choose a full format. This option is well worth the extra time as it ensures the integrity of your disk.

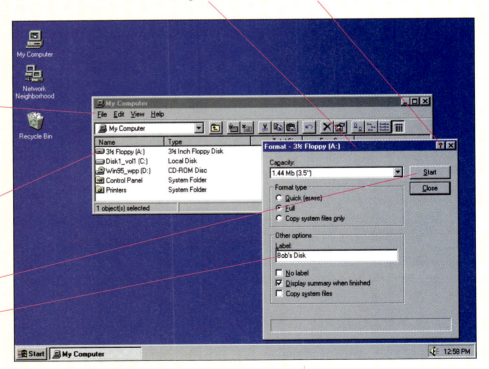

(e) Format a Floppy Disk (step 6)

FIGURE 6 Hands-on Exercise 1 (continued)

- Click the **Label text box** if it's empty, or click and drag over the existing label if there is an entry. Enter a new label such as **Bob's Disk** as shown in Figure 6e.
➤ Click the **Start command button** to begin the formatting operation. This will take about a minute, and you can see the progress of the formatting process at the bottom of the dialog box.
➤ After the formatting process is complete, you will see an informational dialog box with the results of the formatting operation. Read the information, then click the **Close command button** to close the informational dialog box.
➤ Click the **Close button** to close the Format dialog box.

WHAT'S THIS?

The What's This button (a question mark) appears in the title bar of almost every dialog box. Click the question mark, then click the item you want information about, which then appears in a popup window. To print the contents of the popup window, click the right mouse button inside the window, and click Print Topic. Click outside the popup window to close the window and continue working.

STEP 7: Disk Properties

➤ Click the **drive A icon** in the My Computer window, click the **right mouse button** to display a shortcut menu, then click the **Properties command.**
➤ You should see the Properties dialog box in Figure 6f although you may have to move and size the window to match our figure. The pie chart displays the percentage of free and unused space.
➤ Click **OK** to close the Properties dialog box. Click the **Close button** to close My Computer.

PROPERTIES EVERYWHERE

Windows assigns *properties* to every object on the desktop and stores those properties with the object itself. Point to any object on the desktop, including the desktop itself, then click the right mouse button to display the property sheet for that object.

STEP 8: Exit Windows

➤ Click the **Start button,** then click the **Shut Down command.** You will see a dialog box asking whether you're sure that you want to shut down the computer. (The option button to shut down the computer is already selected.)
➤ Click the **Yes command button,** then wait as Windows gets ready to shut down your system. Wait until you see another screen indicating that it is OK to turn off the computer.

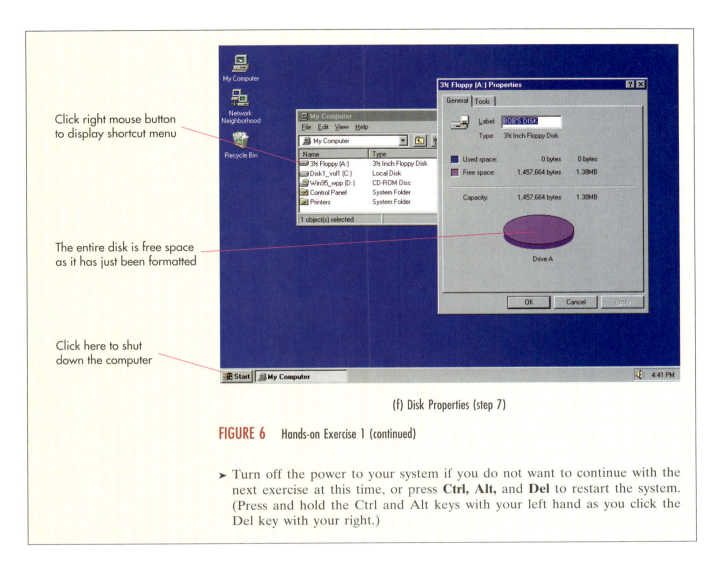

(f) Disk Properties (step 7)

FIGURE 6 Hands-on Exercise 1 (continued)

➤ Turn off the power to your system if you do not want to continue with the next exercise at this time, or press **Ctrl, Alt,** and **Del** to restart the system. (Press and hold the Ctrl and Alt keys with your left hand as you click the Del key with your right.)

MY COMPUTER

My Computer enables you to browse all of the drives (floppy disks, hard disks, and CD-ROM drive) that are attached to your computer. It is present on every desktop, but its contents will vary, depending on the specific configuration. Our system, for example, has one floppy drive, one hard disk, and a CD-ROM as shown in Figure 7. Each drive is represented by an icon and is assigned a letter.

The first (often only) floppy drive is designated as drive A, regardless of whether it is a 3½-inch drive or the older, and now nearly obsolete, 5¼-inch drive. A second floppy drive, if it exists, is drive B. Our system contains a single 3½ floppy drive (note the icon in Figure 7a) and is typical of systems purchased in today's environment.

The first (often only) hard disk on a system is always drive C, whether or not there are one or two floppy drives. A system with one floppy drive and one hard disk (today's most common configuration) will contain icons for drive A and drive C. Additional hard drives (if any) and/or the CD-ROM are labeled from D on.

In addition to an icon for each drive on your system, My Computer contains two other folders. (Folders are discussed in the next section.) The *Control Panel* enables you to configure (set up) all of the devices (mouse, sound, and so on) on your system. The **Printers folder** lets you add a new printer and/or view the progress of a printed document.

The contents of My Computer can be displayed in different views (Large Icons, Small Icons, Details, and List) according to your preference or need. You can switch from one view to the next by choosing the appropriate command from the View menu or by clicking the corresponding button on the toolbar.

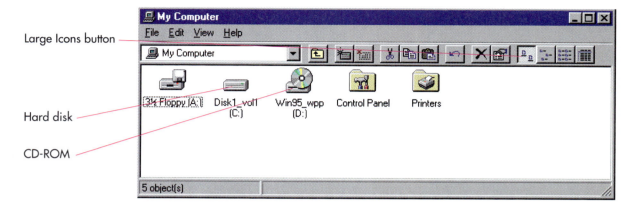

(a) Large Icons

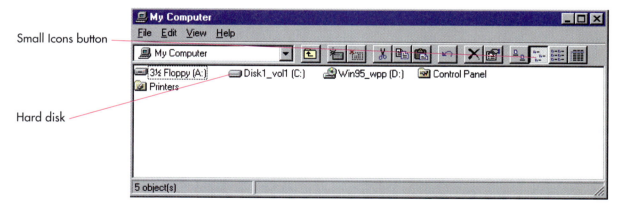

(b) Small Icons

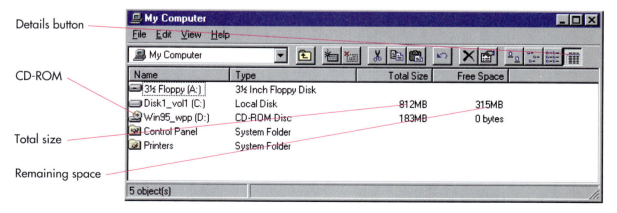

(c) Details View

FIGURE 7 My Computer

The ***Large Icons view*** and ***Small Icons view*** in Figures 7a and 7b, respectively, display each object as a large or small icon. The choice between the two depends on your personal preference. You might, for example, choose large icons if there are only a few objects in the window. Small icons would be preferable if there were many objects and you wanted to see them all. The ***Details view*** in Figure 7c displays additional information about each object. You see the type of object, the total size of the disk, and the remaining space on the disk. (A List view is also available and displays the objects with small icons but without the file details.)

FILES AND FOLDERS

A ***file*** is any data or set of instructions that have been given a name and stored on disk. There are, in general, two types of files, program files and data files. Microsoft Word and Microsoft Excel are program files. The documents and spreadsheets created by these programs are data files. A ***program file*** is executable because it contains instructions that tell the computer what to do. A ***data file*** is not executable and can be used only in conjunction with a specific program.

A file must have a name by which it can be identified. The file name can contain up to 255 characters and may include spaces and other punctuation. (This is very different from the rules that existed under MS-DOS that limited file names to eight characters followed by an optional three-character extension.) Long file names permit descriptive entries such as, *Term Paper for Western Civilization* (as opposed to a more cryptic *TPWCIV* that would be required under MS-DOS).

Files are stored in ***folders*** to better organize the hundreds (often thousands) of files on a hard disk. A Windows folder is similar in concept to a manila folder in a filing cabinet and contains one or more documents (files) that are somehow related to each other. An office worker stores his or her documents in manila folders. In Windows, you store your data files (documents) in electronic folders on disk.

Folders are the key to the Windows storage system. You can create any number of folders to hold your work just as you can place any number of manila folders into a filing cabinet. You can create one folder for your word processing documents and a different folder for your spreadsheets. Alternatively, you can create a folder to hold all of your work for a specific class, which may contain a combination of word processing documents and spreadsheets. The choice is entirely up to you, and you can use any system that makes sense to you. Anything at all can go into a folder—program files, data files, even other folders.

Figure 8 displays two different views of a folder containing six documents. The name of the folder (Homework) appears in the title bar next to the icon of an open folder. The Minimize, Maximize, and Close buttons appear at the right of the title bar. A toolbar appears below the menu bar in each view.

The Details view in Figure 8a displays the name of each file in the folder (note the descriptive file name), the file size, the type of file, and the date and time the file was last modified. Figure 8b shows the Large Icons view, which displays only the file name and an icon representing the application that created the file. The choice between views depends on your personal preference. (A Small Icons view and List view are also available.)

File Type

Every data file has a specific ***file type*** that is determined by the application that created the file initially. One way to recognize the file type is to examine the Type column in the Details view as shown in Figure 8a. The History Term Paper, for

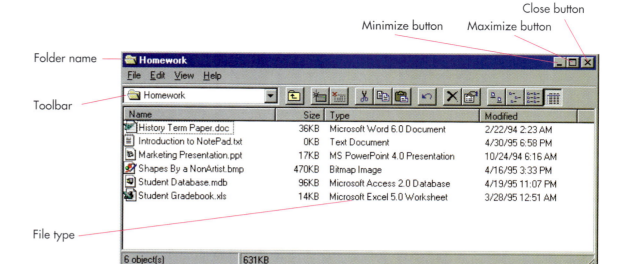

(a) Details View

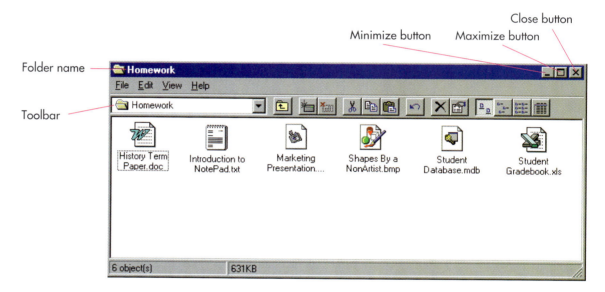

(b) Large Icons View

FIGURE 8 The Homework Folder

example, is a Microsoft Word 6.0 document, and the Student Gradebook is an Excel 5.0 workbook.

You can also determine the file type (or associated application) from any view (not just the Details view) by examining the application icon displayed next to the file name. Look carefully at the icon next to the History Term Paper in Figure 8a, for example, and you will recognize the icon for Microsoft Word. The application icon is recognized more easily in the Large Icons view in Figure 8b.

Still another way to determine the file type is through the three-character extension displayed after the file name. (A period separates the file name from the extension.) Each application has a specific extension, which is automatically assigned to the file name when the file is created. DOC and XLS, for example, are the extensions for Microsoft Word and Excel, respectively. The extension may be suppressed or displayed according to an option in the View menu of My Computer. See step 2 of the hands-on exercise on page 25.

Browsing My Computer

You need to be able to locate a folder and/or its documents quickly so that you can retrieve the documents and go to work. There are several ways to do this, the easiest of which is to browse My Computer. Assume, for example, that you are looking for the Homework folder in Figure 9 in order to work on your term paper for history. Figure 9 shows how easy it is to locate the Homework folder.

You would start by double clicking the My Computer icon on the desktop. This opens the My Computer window and displays all of the drives on your system. Next you would double click the icon for drive C because this is the drive that contains the folder you are looking for. This opens a second window, which displays all of the folders on drive C. And finally you would double click the icon for the Homework folder to open a third window containing the documents in the Homework folder. Once you are in the Homework folder, you would double click the icon of any existing document (which starts the associated application and opens the document), enabling you to begin work.

LEARNING BY DOING

The following exercise has you create a new folder on drive C, then create various files in that folder. The files are created using Notepad and Paint, two accessories that are included in Windows 95. We chose to create the files using these

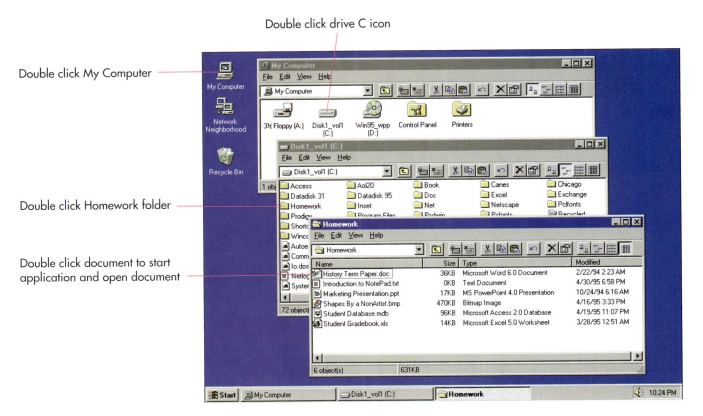

FIGURE 9   Browsing My Computer

simple accessories, rather than more powerful applications such as Word or Excel, because we wanted to create the files quickly and easily. We also wanted to avoid reliance on specific applications that are not part of Windows 95. The emphasis throughout this appendix is the ability to manipulate files within the Windows environment after they have been created.

The exercise also illustrates the document orientation of Windows 95, which enables you to think in terms of the document rather than the application that created it. You simply point to an open folder, click the right mouse button to display a shortcut menu, then select the **New command.** You will be presented with a list of objects (file types) that are recognized by Windows 95 because the associated applications have been previously installed. Choose the file type that you want, and the associated application will be opened automatically. (See step 4 in the following hands-on exercise.)

> **THE NOTEPAD ACCESSORY**
>
> The Notepad accessory is ideal to create "quick and dirty" files that require no formatting and that are smaller than 64K. Notepad opens and saves files in ASCII (text) format only. Use a different editor, e.g., the WordPad accessory or a full-fledged word processor such as Microsoft Word, to create larger files or files that require formatting.

HANDS-ON EXERCISE 2

My Computer

Objective: Open My Computer and create a new folder on drive C. Use the New command to create a Notepad document and a Paint drawing. Use Figure 10 as a guide in the exercise.

STEP 1: Create a Folder

➤ Double click the **My Computer icon** to open My Computer. Double click the **icon** for **drive C** to open a second window as shown in Figure 10a. The size and/or position of your windows will be different from ours.

➤ Make or verify the following selections in each window. (You have to pull down the View menu each time you choose a different command.)
  - The **Toolbar command** should be checked.
  - The **Status Bar command** should be checked.
  - **Large Icons** should be selected.

➤ If necessary, click anywhere within the window for drive C to make it the active window. (The title bar reflects the internal label of your disk, which was assigned when the disk was formatted. Your label will be different from ours.)

➤ Pull down the **File menu,** click (or point to) **New** to display the submenu, then click **Folder** as shown in Figure 10a.

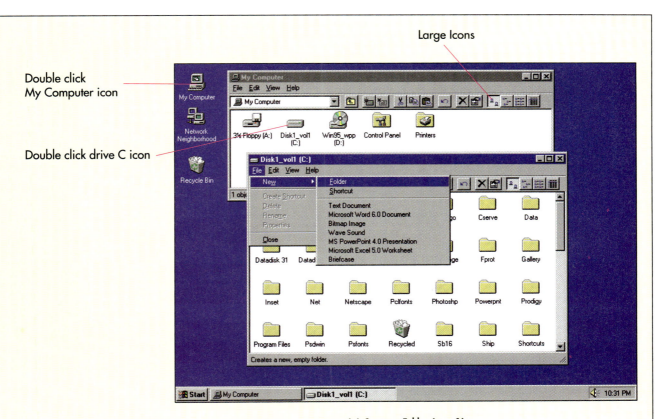

(a) Create a Folder (step 1)

FIGURE 10 Hands-on Exercise 2

> ### ONE WINDOW OR MANY
>
> If opening a window for drive C causes the My Computer window to disappear (and its button to vanish from the taskbar), you need to set an option to open each folder in a separate window. Pull down the View menu, click Options, click the Folder tab, then click the option button to use a separate window for each folder. Click the OK command button to accept this setting and return to the desktop

STEP 2: The View Menu

➤ A new folder has been created within the window for drive C with the name of the folder (New Folder) highlighted. Type **Homework** to change the name of the folder as shown in Figure 10b. Press **enter.**

➤ Pull down the **View menu** and click the **Arrange Icons command.** Click **By Name** to arrange the folders alphabetically within the window for drive C.

➤ Pull down the **View menu** a second time. Click **Options,** then click the **View tab** in the Options dialog box. Check the box (if necessary) to **Hide MS-DOS file extensions.** Click **OK.**

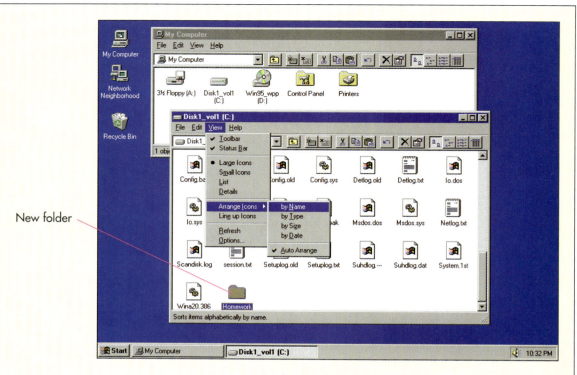

(b) View Menu (step 2)

FIGURE 10 Hands-on Exercise 2 (continued)

RENAME COMMAND

Point to a file or a folder, then click the right mouse button to display a menu with commands pertaining to the object. Click the Rename command. The name of the file or folder will be highlighted with the insertion point (a flashing vertical line) positioned at the end of the name. Type a new name—for example, Homework—to replace the selected name, or click anywhere within the name to change the insertion point and edit the name.

STEP 3: Open the Homework Folder

➤ Click the **Homework folder** to select it. Pull down the **File menu** and click **Open** (or double click the **folder** without pulling down the menu) to open the Homework folder.

➤ The Homework folder opens into a window as shown in Figure 10c. The window is empty because the folder does not contain any documents. If necessary, pull down the **View menu** and check the **Toolbar command** to display the toolbar.

➤ **Right click** a blank position on the taskbar to display the menu in Figure 10c. Click **Tile Vertically** to tile the three open windows.

26 ESSENTIALS OF WINDOWS 95

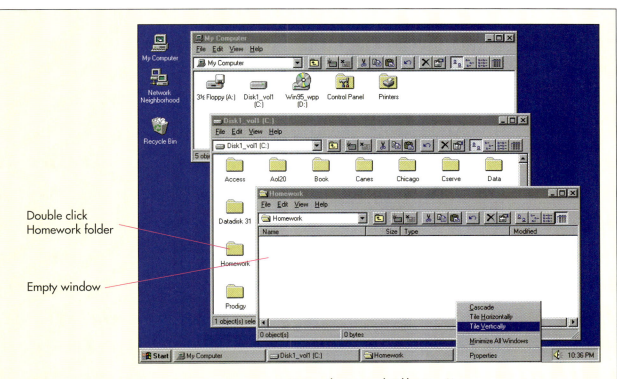

(c) Open the Homework Folder (step 3)

FIGURE 10 Hands-on Exercise 2 (continued)

THE RIGHT MOUSE BUTTON

The right mouse button is the fastest way to change the properties of any object on the desktop or even the desktop itself. Point to a blank area on the desktop, click the right mouse button, then click Properties in the shortcut menu to display the dialog box (property sheet) for the desktop. In similar fashion, you can right click the taskbar to change its properties. You can also right click any icon on the desktop or any icon in a window.

STEP 4: The New Command

➤ The windows on your desktop should be tiled vertically as shown in Figure 10d. Click in the **Homework window.** The title bar for the Homework window should be highlighted, indicating that this is the active window.

➤ Pull down the **File menu** (or point to an empty area in the window and click the right mouse button).

➤ Click (or point to) the **New command** to display a submenu. The document types depend on the installed applications:
  • You may (or may not) see Microsoft Word Document or Microsoft Excel Worksheet, depending on whether or not you have installed these applications.

- You will see Text Document and Bitmap Image, corresponding to the Notepad and Paint accessories that are installed with Windows 95.
➤ Select (click) **Text Document** as the type of file to create as shown below in Figure 10d. The icon for a new document will appear with the name of the document, New Text Document, highlighted.
➤ Type **Files and Folders** to change the name of the document. Press the **enter** key.

> ### THE DOCUMENT, NOT THE APPLICATION
>
> Windows 95 enables you to create a document without first starting the associated application. Select the folder that is to contain the document, pull down the File menu, and click New (or right click an empty space within a folder), then choose the type of document you want to create. Once the document has been created, double click its icon to load the associated application and begin editing the document. In other words, you can think about the document and not the application.

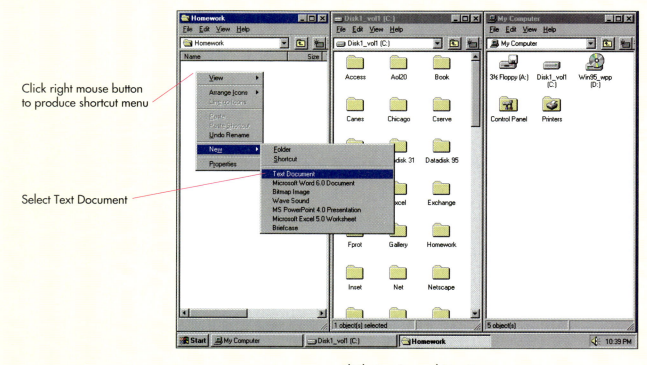

(d) The New Command (step 4)

FIGURE 10   Hands-on Exercise 2 (continued)

STEP 5: Create the Document

➤ If necessary, pull down the **View menu** and change to the **Large Icons view** so that the view in your Homework folder matches the view in Figure 10e.

➤ Select (click) the **Files and Folders document.** Pull down the **File menu.** Click **Open** (or double click the **Files and Folders icon** without pulling down the File menu) to load Notepad and open a Notepad window. The window is empty because the text of the document has not yet been entered.

➤ Pull down the **Edit menu:**
- If there is no check mark next to Word Wrap, click the **Word Wrap** command to enable this feature.
- If there is a check mark next to Word Wrap, click outside the menu to close the menu without changing any settings.

➤ Type the text of the document as shown in Figure 10e. Type just as you would on a regular typewriter with one exception—press the enter key only at the end of a paragraph, not at the end of every line. Since word wrap is in effect, Notepad will automatically start a new line when the word you are typing does not fit at the end of the current line.

➤ Pull down the **File menu** and click **Save** to save the document when you are finished.

➤ Click the **Close button** to close the Notepad accessory.

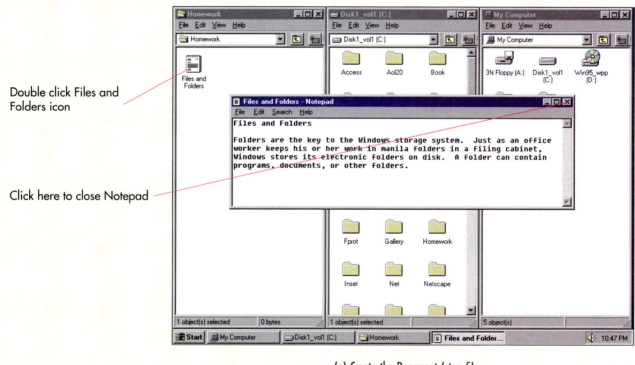

(e) Create the Document (step 5)

FIGURE 10 Hands-on Exercise 2 (continued)

FILE EXTENSIONS

Long-time DOS users will recognize a three-character extension at the end of a file name to indicate the file type; for example, TXT to indicate a text (ASCII) file. The extensions are displayed or hidden according to the option you establish through the View menu of My Computer. Open My Computer, pull down the View menu, and click the Options command. Click the View tab, then check (clear) the box to hide (show) MS-DOS file extensions. Click OK.

STEP 6: Create a Drawing

➤ **Right click** within the Homework folder, click the **New command,** then click **Bitmap Image** as the type of file to create. The icon for a new drawing will appear with the name of the drawing (New Bitmap Image) highlighted.

➤ Type **Rectangles** to change the name of the drawing. Press **enter.**

➤ Pull down the **File menu** and click **Open** (or double click the **Rectangles icon** without pulling down the menu) to open a Paint window. The window is empty because the drawing has not yet been created.

➤ Click the **Maximize button** (if necessary) so that the window takes the entire desktop. Create a drawing of various rectangles as shown in Figure 10f.

➤ To draw a rectangle:
  • Select (click) the rectangle tool.

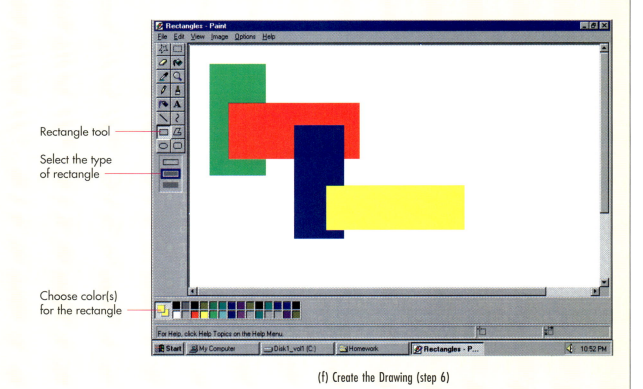

(f) Create the Drawing (step 6)

FIGURE 10 Hands-on Exercise 2 (continued)

- Select (click) the type of rectangle you want (a border only, a filled rectangle with a border, or a filled rectangle with no border).
- Select (click) the colors for the border and fill using the left and right mouse button, respectively.
- Click in the drawing area, then click and drag to create the rectangle.

➤ Pull down the **File menu** and click **Save As** to produce the Save As dialog box. Change the file type to **16-Color Bitmap** (from the default 256-color bitmap) to create a smaller file and conserve space on the floppy disk.

➤ Click **Save.** Click **Yes** to replace the file.

➤ Click the **Close button** to close Paint when you have finished the drawing.

THE PAINT ACCESSORY

The Paint accessory enables you to create simple or (depending on your ability) elaborate drawings. There is a sense of familiarity to the application since it follows the common user interface and consistent command structure common to all Windows applications. The Open, Save, and Print commands, for example, are found in the File menu. The Cut, Copy, Paste, and Undo commands are in the Edit menu. There is also a Help menu, which explains the various Paint commands and which functions identically to the Help menu in all Windows applications.

STEP 7: Edit the Document

➤ Double click the **Files and Folders icon** to reopen the document in a Notepad window. Pull down the **Edit menu** and toggle **Word Wrap on.** Press **Ctrl+End** to move to the end of the document.

➤ Add the additional text as shown in Figure 10g. Do *not* save the document at this time.

➤ Click the **Close button** to exit Notepad. You will see the informational message in Figure 10g, which indicates you have forgotten to save the changes. Click **Yes** to save the changes and exit.

DOS NOTATION

The visually oriented storage system within Windows 95 makes it easy to identify folders and the documents within those folders. DOS, however, was not so simple and used a text-based notation to indicate the drive, folder, and file. For example, C:\HOMEWORK\FILES AND FOLDERS specifies the file FILES AND FOLDERS, in the HOMEWORK folder, on drive C.

STEP 8: Change the View

➤ Right click an empty space on the taskbar, then click the **Tile Horizontally command** to tile the windows as shown in Figure 10h. (The order of your windows may be different from ours.)

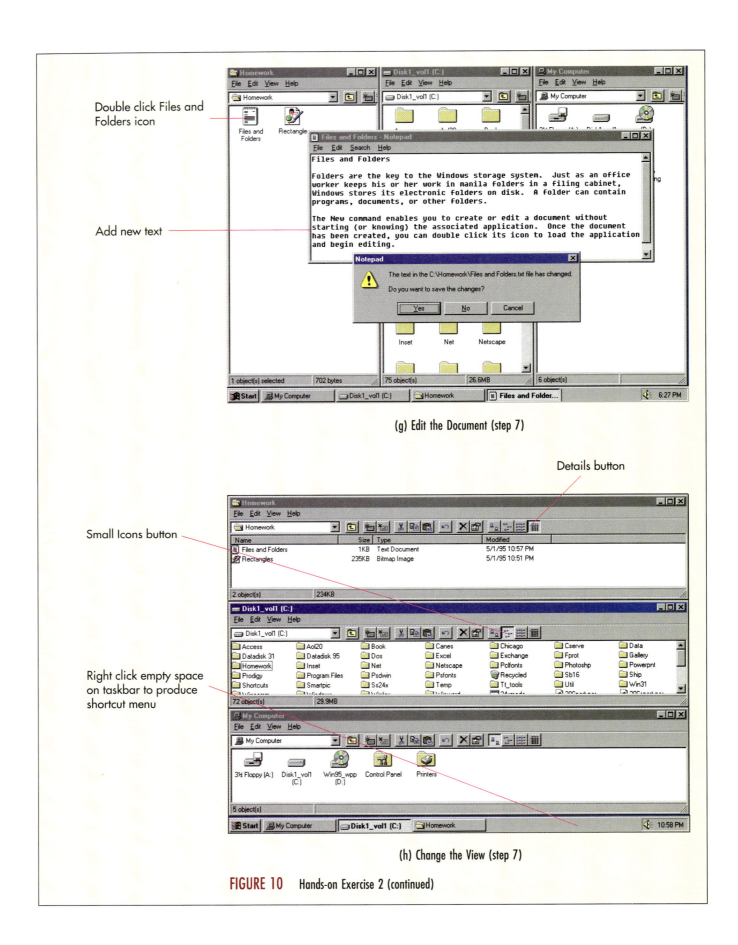

(g) Edit the Document (step 7)

(h) Change the View (step 7)

FIGURE 10 Hands-on Exercise 2 (continued)

> - Click in the window for the **Homework folder,** then click the **Details button** on the toolbar to display the details view.
> - Press the **F5 key** to refresh the window and update the file properties (the file size, type, and the date and time of the last modification).
> - Click in the window for drive C, then click the **List view** or **Small Icons button** on the toolbar to display small icons as shown in Figure 10h.
>
> **STEP 9: Exit Windows**
> - Click the **Close button** in each of the three open windows (My Computer, drive C, and Homework) to close each window.
> - Exit Windows if you do not want to continue with the next exercise at this time.

FILE OPERATIONS

The exercise just completed had you create a folder and place documents in that folder. As you continue to work on the computer, you will create additional folders, as well as files within those folders. Learning how to manage those files is one of the most important skills you can acquire. This section describes the different types of file operations that you will perform on a daily basis.

Moving and Copying a File

There are two basic ways to move or copy a file from one location to another. You can use the ***Cut, Copy,*** and ***Paste commands,*** or you can simply drag and drop the files from one location to the other. Both techniques require you to open the disk or folder containing the source file (the file you are moving or copying) in order to select the file you will move or copy. This is typically done by opening successive windows through My Computer.

Assume, for example, that you want to copy a file from the Homework folder on drive C to a floppy disk in drive A. You would begin by double clicking the My Computer icon to open the My Computer window. Then you would double click the icon for drive C because that is the drive containing the file you want to copy. And then you would double click the icon for the Homework folder (opening a third window) because that is the folder containing the file to be copied.

To copy the file (after the Homework folder has been opened), select the file by clicking its icon, then drag the icon to the drive A icon in the My Computer window. (Alternatively, you could select the file, pull down the Edit menu, and click the Copy command, then click the icon for drive A, pull down the Edit menu, and click the Paste command.) It sounds complicated, but it's not and you will get a chance to practice in the hands-on exercise.

Backup

It's not a question of if it will happen, but when—hard disks die, files are lost, or viruses may infect a system. It has happened to us and it will happen to you, but you can prepare for the inevitable by creating adequate ***backup*** *before* the problem occurs. The essence of a backup strategy is to decide which files to back up, how often to do the backup, and where to keep the backup. Once you decide on a strategy, follow it, and follow it faithfully!

Our strategy is very simple—back up what you can't afford to lose, do so on a daily basis, and store the backup away from your computer. You need not copy every file, every day. Instead copy just the files that changed during the current session. Realize, too, that it is much more important to back up your data files, rather than your program files. You can always reinstall the application from the original disks, or if necessary, go to the vendor for another copy of an application. You, however, are the only one who has a copy of the term paper that is due tomorrow.

Deleting Files

The ***Delete command*** deletes (removes) a file from a disk. If, however, the file was deleted from a hard disk, it is not really gone, but moved instead to the Recycle Bin from where it can be subsequently recovered.

The ***Recycle Bin*** is a special folder that contains all of the files that were previously deleted from any hard disk on your system. Think of the Recycle Bin as similar to the wastebasket in your room. You throw out (delete) a report by tossing it into a wastebasket. The report is gone (deleted) from your desk, but you can still get it back by taking it out of the wastebasket as long as the basket wasn't emptied. The Recycle Bin works the same way. Files are not deleted from the hard disk per se, but are moved instead to the Recycle Bin from where they can be recovered. The Recycle Bin should be emptied periodically, however, or else you will run out of space on the disk. Once a file is removed from the Recycle Bin, it can no longer be recovered.

WRITE-PROTECT YOUR BACKUP DISKS

You can write-protect a floppy disk to ensure that its contents are not accidentally altered or erased. A 3½-inch disk is write-protected by sliding the built-in tab so that the write-protect notch is open. The disk is write-enabled when the notch is covered. The procedure is reversed for a 5¼-inch disk; that is, the disk is write-protected when the notch is covered and write-enabled when the notch is open.

HANDS-ON EXERCISE 3

File Operations

Objective: Copy a file from drive C to drive A, and from drive A back to drive C. Delete a file from drive C, then restore the file using the Recycle Bin. Demonstrate the effects of write-protecting a disk. Use Figure 11 as a guide in the exercise.

STEP 1: Open the Homework Folder

➤ Double click the **icon** for **My Computer** to open My Computer. Double click the **icon** for **drive C** to open a second window showing the contents of drive C. Double click the **Homework folder** to open a third window showing the contents of the Homework folder.

➤ Right click the taskbar to tile the windows vertically as shown in Figure 11a. Your windows may appear in a different order from those in the figure.

➤ Make or verify the following selections in each window. (You have to pull down the View menu each time you choose a different command.)
- The **Toolbar command** should be checked.
- The **Status Bar command** should be checked.
- Choose the **Details view** in the Homework window and the **Large Icons view** in the other windows.

➤ Pull down the **View menu** in any open window. Click **Options,** then click the **View tab** in the Options dialog box. Check the box (if necessary) to **Hide MS-DOS file extensions.** Click **OK** to exit the dialog box.

> **QUICK VIEW**
>
> If you forget what is in a particular document, you can use the Quick View command to preview the document without having to open it. Select (click) the file you want to preview, then pull down the File menu and click Quick View (or right click the file and select the Quick View command) to display the file in a preview window. If you decide to edit the file, pull down the File menu and click Open File for Editing; otherwise click the Close button to close the preview window.

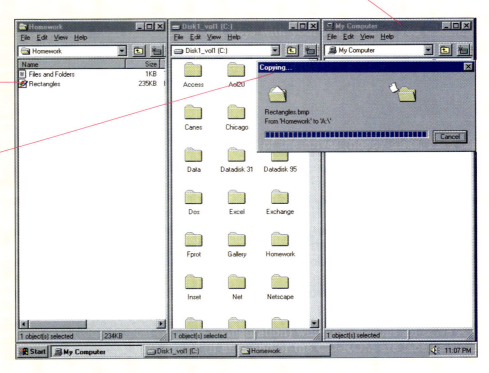

(a) Copy to Drive A (step 1)

FIGURE 11   Hands-on Exercise 3

STEP 2: Backup the Homework Folder

➤ Place a freshly formatted disk in drive A. Be sure that the disk is not write-protected or else you will not be able to copy files to the disk.

➤ Click and drag the icon for the **Rectangles file** from the Homework folder to the icon for **drive A** in the My Computer window.

- You will see the ⊘ symbol as you drag the file until you reach a suitable destination (e.g., until you point to the icon for drive A). The ⊘ symbol will change to a plus sign when the icon for drive A is highlighted, indicating that the file can be copied successfully.

- Release the mouse to complete the copy operation. You will see a popup window as shown in Figure 11a, indicating the progress of the copy operation. This takes several seconds since Rectangles is a large file (235KB).

➤ Click and drag the icon for the **Files and Folders file** from the Homework folder to the icon for drive A. You may or may not see a popup window showing the copy operation since the file is small (1KB) and copies quickly.

USE THE RIGHT MOUSE BUTTON TO MOVE OR COPY A FILE

The result of dragging a file with the left mouse button depends on whether the source and destination folders are on the same or different drives. Dragging a file to a folder on a different drive copies the file. Dragging the file to a folder on the same drive moves the file. If you find this hard to remember, and most people do, click and drag with the right mouse button to produce a shortcut menu asking whether you want to copy or move the file. This simple tip can save you from making a careless (and potentially serious) error. Use it!

STEP 3: View the Contents of Drive A

➤ Double click the **icon** for **drive A** in the My Computer window to open a fourth window.

➤ Right click a blank area on the taskbar. Tile the windows vertically or horizontally (it doesn't matter which) to display the windows as in Figure 11b.

➤ Click in the window for drive A. If necessary, pull down the **View menu,** display the toolbar, and change to the **Details view.**

➤ Compare the file details for each file in the Homework folder and drive A; the details are identical, reflecting the fact that the files have been copied.

CHANGE THE COLUMN WIDTH

Drag the right border of a column heading to the right (left) to increase (decrease) the width of the column in order to see more (less) information in that column. Double click the right border of a column heading to automatically adjust the column width to accommodate the widest entry in that column.

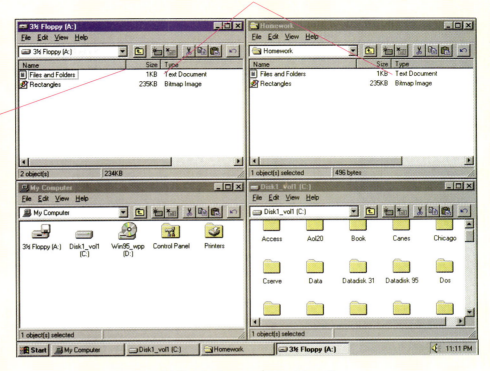

(b) View the Contents of Drive A (step 3)

FIGURE 11 Hands-on Exercise 3 (continued)

STEP 4: Delete a File

➤ Select (click) the **Files and Folders icon** in the Homework folder. Pull down the **File menu.** Click **Delete.**

➤ You will see the dialog box in Figure 11c, asking whether you want to delete the file. Click **Yes** to delete the file.

➤ Right click the **Rectangles icon** in the Homework folder to display a shortcut menu. Click **Delete.**

➤ Click **Yes** when asked whether to delete the Rectangles file. The Homework folder is now empty.

THE UNDO COMMAND

The Undo command pertains not just to application programs such as Notepad or Paint, but to file operations as well. It will, for example, undelete a file if it is executed immediately after the Delete command. Pull down the Edit menu and click Undo to reverse (undo) the last command. Some operations cannot be undone (in which case the command will be dimmed out), but Undo is always worth a try.

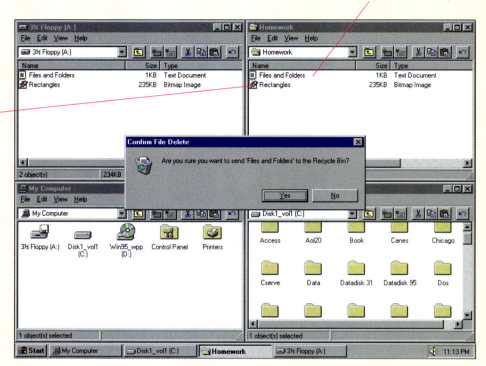

(c) Delete a File (step 4)

FIGURE 11 Hands-on Exercise 3 (continued)

STEP 5: Copy from Drive A to Drive C

➤ The backup you did in step 2 enables you to copy (restore) the Files and Folders file from drive A to drive C. You can do this in one of two ways:
- Select (click) the **Files and Folders icon** in the window for drive A. Pull down the **Edit menu.** Click **Copy.** Click in the **Homework folder.** Pull down the **Edit menu.** Click **Paste** as shown in Figure 11d.
- Click and drag the **icon** for the **Files and Folders file** from drive A to the Homework folder.

➤ Either way, you will see a popup window showing the Files and Folders file being copied from drive A to drive C.

➤ Use whichever technique you prefer to copy the Rectangles file from drive A to drive C.

BACK UP IMPORTANT FILES

We cannot overemphasize the importance of adequate backup and urge you to copy your data files to floppy disks and store those disks away from your computer. It takes only a few minutes, but you will thank us, when (not if) you lose an important file and wish you had another copy.

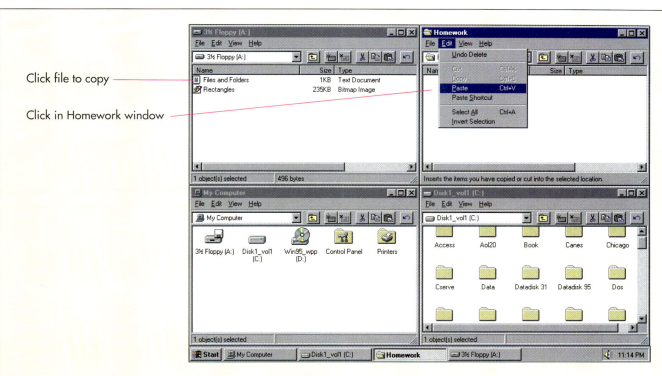

(d) Copy to Drive C (step 5)

FIGURE 11   Hands-on Exercise 3 (continued)

STEP 6: Modify a File

➤ Double click the **Files and Folders icon** in the Homework folder to reopen the file as shown in Figure 11e. Pull down the **Edit menu** and toggle **Word Wrap on.**

➤ Press **Ctrl+End** to move to the end of the document. Add the paragraph shown in Figure 11e.

➤ Pull down the **File menu** and click **Save** to save the modified file. Click the **Close button** to close the file.

➤ The Files and Folders document has been modified and should once again be backed up to drive A. Click and drag the **icon** for **Files and Folders** from the Homework folder to the drive A window.

➤ You will see a message indicating that the folder (drive A) already contains a file called Files and Folders (which was previously copied in step 2) and asking whether you want to replace the existing file with the new file. Click **Yes.**

THE SEND TO COMMAND

The Send To command is an alternative way to copy a file to a floppy disk and has the advantage that the floppy disk icon need not be visible. Select (click) the file to copy, then pull down the File menu (or simply right click the file). Click the Send To command, then select the appropriate floppy drive from the resulting submenu.

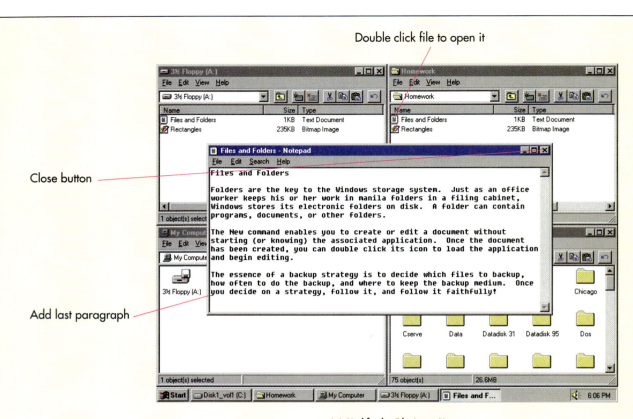

(e) Modify the File (step 6)

FIGURE 11 Hands-on Exercise 3 (continued)

STEP 7: Write-protect a Disk

➤ You can write-protect a floppy disk so that its contents cannot be changed; that is, existing files cannot be modified or erased nor can new files be added.

➤ Remove the floppy disk from drive A and follow the appropriate procedure:
  • To write-protect a 3½ disk, move the built-in tab so that the write-protect notch is open.
  • To write-protect a 5¼ disk, cover the write-protect notch with a piece of opaque tape.

➤ Return the write-protected disk to the floppy drive.

➤ Click the **icon** for the **Rectangles file** on drive A, then press the **Del key** to delete the file.

➤ You will see a warning message asking whether you are sure you want to delete the file. Click **Yes.**

➤ You will see the error message in Figure 11f, indicating that the file cannot be deleted because the disk is write-protected. Click **OK.**

➤ Remove the write-protection by reversing the procedure you followed earlier. Select the **Rectangles file** a second time and delete the file. Click **Yes** in response to the confirmation message, after which the file will be deleted from drive A.

➤ You have just deleted the Rectangles file, but we want it back on drive A for the next exercise. Accordingly, click and drag the **Rectangles icon** in the Homework folder to the icon for **drive A** in the My Computer window.

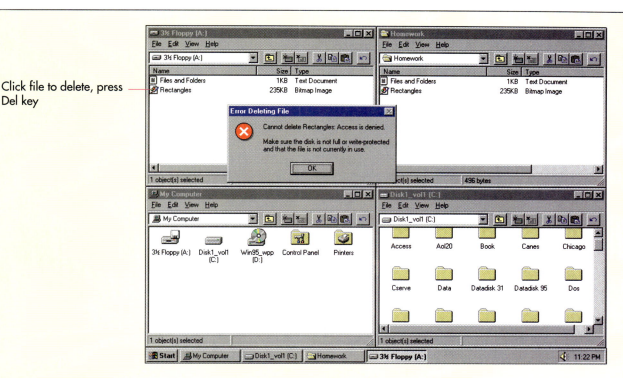

Click file to delete, press Del key

(f) Write-Protect a Disk (step 7)

FIGURE 11 Hands-on Exercise 3 (continued)

➤ Click the **Close button** in the window for drive A.

STEP 8: The Recycle Bin

➤ Select (click) the **Files and Folders icon** in the Homework folder. Pull down the **File menu** and click **Delete.** Click **Yes** in the dialog box asking whether you want to delete the file.

➤ To restore a file, you need to open the Recycle Bin:
  • Double click the **Recycle Bin icon** if you can see the icon on the desktop
    or
  • Double click the **Recycled icon** within the window for drive C. (You may have to scroll in order to see the icon.)

➤ Right click a blank area on the taskbar, then tile the open windows as shown in Figure 11g. The position of your windows may be different from ours. The view in the Recycle Bin may also be different.

➤ Your Recycle Bin contains all files that have been previously deleted from drive C, and hence you may see a different number of files than those displayed in Figure 11g.

➤ Scroll until you can select the (most recent) **Files and Folders icon.** Pull down the **File menu** and click the **Restore command.** The Files and Folders file is returned to the Homework folder.

EMPTY THE RECYCLE BIN

All files that are deleted from a hard drive are automatically moved to the Recycle Bin. This enables you to restore (undelete) a file, but it also prevents you from recovering the space taken up by those files. Accordingly, you should periodically delete files from the Recycle Bin or otherwise you will find yourself running out of space on your hard disk. Be careful, though, because once you delete a file from the Recycle Bin, it is gone for good!

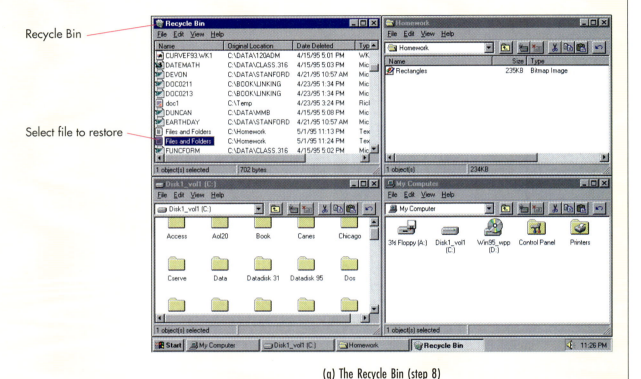

(g) The Recycle Bin (step 8)

FIGURE 11 Hands-on Exercise 3 (continued)

STEP 9: Exit Windows

➤ Click the **Close button** in each of the four open windows (the Recycle Bin, My Computer, drive C, and Homework) to close each window.

➤ Exit Windows if you do not want to continue with the next exercise.

WINDOWS EXPLORER

The *Windows Explorer* enables you to browse through all of the drives, folders, and files on your system. It does not do anything that could not be accomplished through successive windows via My Computer. The Explorer does, however, let you perform a given task more quickly, and for that reason is preferred by more experienced users.

Assume, for example, that you are taking five classes this semester, and that you are using the computer in each course. You've created a separate folder to hold the work for each class and have stored the contents of all five folders on a single floppy disk. Assume further that you need to retrieve your third English assignment so that you can modify the assignment.

You can use My Computer to browse the system as shown in Figure 12a. You would start by opening My Computer, double clicking the icon for drive A to open a second window, then double clicking the icon for the English folder to display its documents. The process is intuitive, but it can quickly lead to a desktop cluttered with open windows. And what if you next needed to work on a paper for Art History? That would require you to open the Art History folder, which produces yet another open window on the desktop.

The Explorer window in Figure 12b offers a more sophisticated way to browse the system as it shows the hierarchy of folders as well as the contents of the selected folder. The Explorer window is divided into two panes. The left pane contains a tree diagram of the entire system, showing all drives and optionally the folders in each drive. One (and only one) object is always selected in the left pane, and its contents are displayed automatically in the right pane.

Look carefully at the tree diagram in Figure 12b and note that the English folder is currently selected. The icon for the selected folder is an open folder to differentiate it from the other folders, which are closed and are not currently selected. The right pane displays the contents of the selected folder (English in Figure 12b) and is seen to contain three documents, Assignments 1, 2, and 3. The right pane is displayed in the Details view, but could just as easily have been displayed in another view (e.g., Large or Small Icons) by clicking the appropriate button on the toolbar.

As indicated, only one folder can be selected (open) at a time in the left pane, and its contents are displayed in the right pane. To see the contents of a different folder (e.g., Accounting), you would select (click) the Accounting folder, which will automatically close the English folder.

The tree diagram in the left pane displays the drives and their folders in hierarchical fashion. The desktop is always at the top of the hierarchy and contains My Computer, which in turn contains various drives, each of which contains folders, which in turn contain documents and/or additional folders. Each object may be expanded or collapsed to display or hide its subordinates.

Look again at the icon next to My Computer in Figure 12b, and you see a minus sign indicating that My Computer has been expanded to show the various drives on the system. There is also a minus sign next to the icon for drive A to indicate that it too has been expanded to show the folders on the disk. Note, however, the plus sign next to drives C and D, indicating that these parts of the tree are currently collapsed and thus their subordinates are not visible.

A folder may contain additional folders, and thus individual folders may also be expanded or collapsed. The minus sign to the left of the Finance folder in Figure 12b, for example, shows that the folder has been expanded and contains two additional folders, for Assignments and Spreadsheets, respectively. The plus sign next to the Accounting folder, however, indicates the opposite; that is, the folder is collapsed and its folders are not currently visible. A folder with neither a plus or minus sign, such as Art History or Marketing, means that the folder does not contain additional folders and cannot be expanded or collapsed.

The advantage of the Windows Explorer over My Computer is the uncluttered screen and ease with which you switch from one folder to the next. If, for example, you wanted to see the contents of the Art History folder, all you would do would be to click its icon in the left pane, which automatically changes the right pane to show the documents in Art History. The Explorer also makes it easy to move or copy a file from one folder or drive to another as you will see in the hands-on exercise that follows shortly.

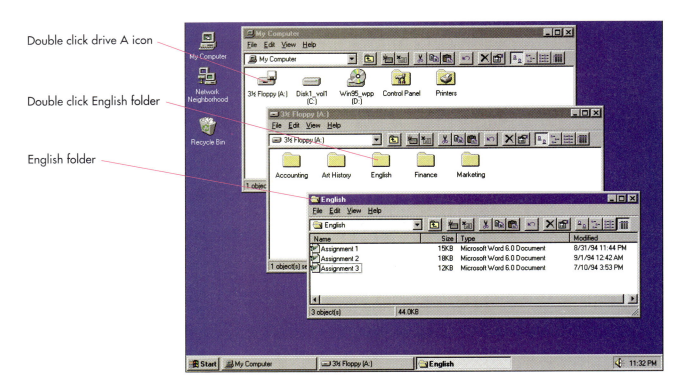

(a) My Computer

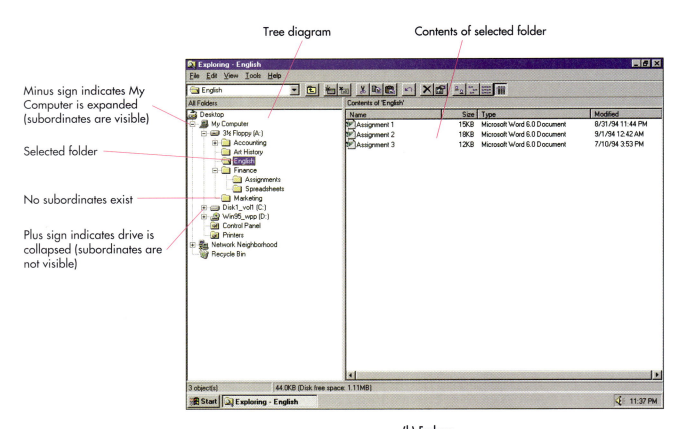

(b) Explorer

FIGURE 12   Browsing a System

44 ESSENTIALS OF WINDOWS 95

> **ORGANIZE YOUR WORK**
>
> A folder may contain anything at all—program files, document files, or even other folders. Organize your folders in ways that make sense to you such as a separate folder for every class you are taking. You can also create folders within a folder; for example, a correspondence folder may contain two folders of its own, one for business correspondence and one for personal letters.

LEARN BY DOING

The Explorer is especially useful for moving or copying files from one folder or drive to another. You simply open the folder that contains the file, use the scroll bar in the left pane (if necessary) so that the destination folder is visible, then drag the file from the right pane to the destination folder. The Explorer is a powerful tool, but it takes practice to master.

The next exercise illustrates the procedure for moving and copying files and uses the floppy disk from the previous exercise. The disk already contains two files—one Notepad document and one Paint drawing. The exercise has you create an additional document of each type so that there are a total of four files on the floppy disk. You then create two folders on the floppy disk, one for drawings and one for documents, and move the respective files into each folder. And finally, you copy the contents of each folder from drive A to a different folder on drive C. By the end of the exercise you will have had considerable practice in both moving and copying files.

HANDS-ON EXERCISE 4

Windows Explorer

Objective: Use the Windows Explorer to copy and move a file from one folder to another. Use Figure 13 as a guide in the exercise.

STEP 1: Open the Windows Explorer

➤ Click the **Start button.** Click (or point to) the **Programs command** to display the Programs menu. Click **Windows Explorer.**

➤ Click the **Maximize button** so that the Explorer takes the entire desktop as shown in Figure 13a. Do not be concerned if your screen is different from ours.

➤ Make or verify the following selections using the **View menu.** (You have to pull down the View menu each time you choose a different command.)

- The **Toolbar command** should be checked.
- The **Status Bar command** should be checked.
- The **Details view** should be selected.

➤ Pull down the **View menu** a second time. Click **Options,** then click the **View tab** in the Options dialog box. Check the box (if necessary) to **Hide MS-DOS file extensions.** Click **OK.**

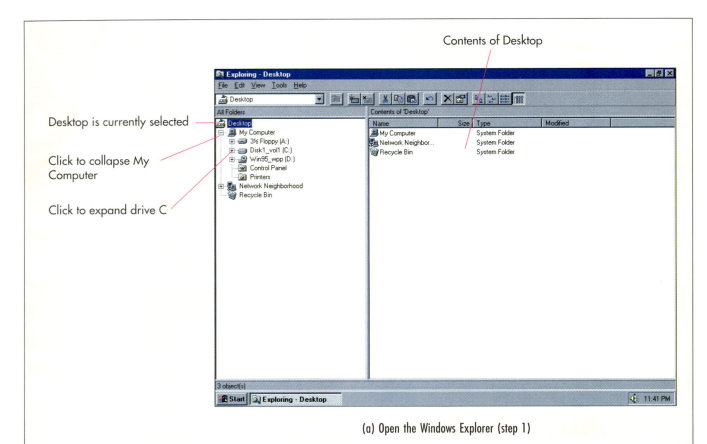

(a) Open the Windows Explorer (step 1)

FIGURE 13 Hands-on Exercise 4

STEP 2: Collapse and Expand My Computer

➤ Click (select) the **Desktop icon** in the left pane to display the contents of the desktop in the right pane. Our desktop contains only the icons for My Computer, Network Neighborhood, and the Recycle Bin. Your desktop may have different icons.

➤ Toggle back and forth between expanding and collapsing My Computer by clicking the plus or minus sign that appears next to the icon for My Computer. Clicking the plus sign expands My Computer, after which a minus sign is displayed. Clicking the minus sign collapses My Computer and changes to a plus sign. End with My Computer expanded and the **minus sign** displayed as shown in Figure 13a.

➤ Place the disk from the previous exercise in drive A. Expand and collapse each drive within My Computer. (Drive A does not have any folders at this time, and hence will have neither a plus nor a minus sign.)

➤ End with a **plus sign** next to drive C so that the hard drive is collapsed as shown in Figure 13a. (The contents of My Computer will depend on your particular configuration.)

STEP 3: Create a Notepad Document

➤ Click the **icon** for **drive A** in the left pane to view the contents of the disk in the right pane. You should see the Files and Folders and Rectangles files that were created in the previous exercise.

➤ Pull down the **File menu.** Click (or point to) **New** to display the submenu. Click **Text Document** as the type of file to create.

➤ The icon for a new document will appear with the name of the document (New Text Document) highlighted. Type **About Explorer** to change the name of the document. Press **enter.** Double click the **file icon** to open the Notepad accessory and create the document.

➤ Move and/or size the Notepad window to your preference. You can also maximize the window so that you have more room in which to work.

➤ Pull down the **Edit menu** and toggle **Word Wrap** on. Enter the text of the document as shown in Figure 13b.

➤ Pull down the **File menu** and click **Save** to save the document when you are finished. Click the **Close button** to close Notepad and return to the Explorer.

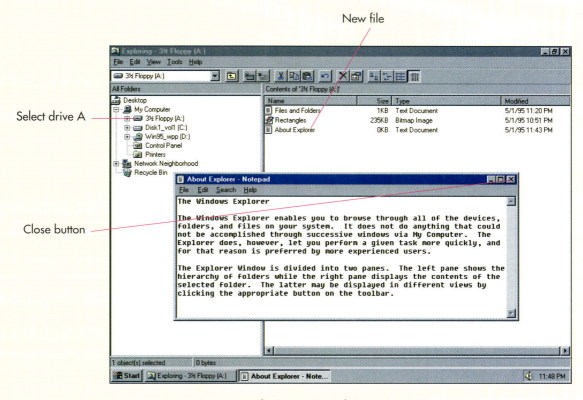

(b) Create a NotePad Document (step 3)

FIGURE 13   Hands-on Exercise 4 (continued)

STEP 4: Create a Paint Drawing

➤ Click the **icon** for **drive A** in the Explorer window, then pull down the **File menu.** (Alternatively, you can click the **right mouse button** in the right pane of the Explorer window when drive A is selected in the left pane.)

➤ Click (or point to) the **New command** to display the submenu. Click **Bitmap Image** as the type of file to create.

➤ The icon for a new drawing will appear with the name of the file (New Bitmap Image) highlighted. Type **Circles** to change the name of the file. Press **enter.** Double click the **file icon** to open the Paint accessory and create the drawing.

➤ Move and/or size the Paint window to your preference. You can also maximize the window so that you have more room in which to work.

- Create a simple drawing consisting of various circles and ellipses as shown in Figure 13c.
- Pull down the **File menu.** Click **Save As** to produce the Save As dialog box. Change the file type to **16-Color Bitmap** (from the default 256-color bitmap) to create a smaller file and conserve space on the floppy disk. Click **Save.** Click **Yes** to replace the file.
- Click the **Close button** to close Paint and return to the Explorer.

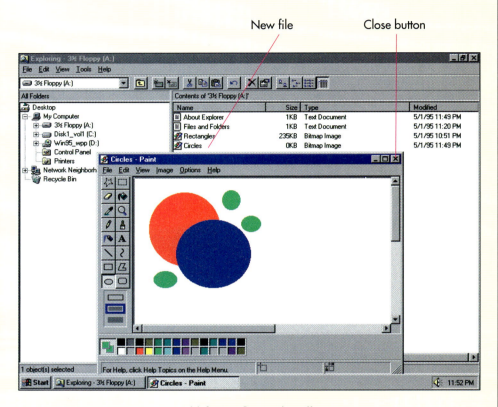

(c) Create a Drawing (step 4)

FIGURE 13   Hands-on Exercise 4 (continued)

STEP 5: Create the Folders

- If necessary, click the **icon** for **drive A** in the left pane of the Explorer window. Drive A should contain four files as shown in Figure 13d (the folders have not yet been created).
- Pull down the **File menu,** click (or point to) the **New command,** then click **Folder** as the type of object to create.
- The icon for a new folder will appear with the name of the folder (New Folder) highlighted. Type **Documents** to change the name of the folder. Press **enter.**
- Click the **icon** for **drive A** in the left pane. Pull down the **File menu.** Click (or point to) the **New command.** Click **Folder** as the type of object to create.
- The icon for a new folder will appear with the name of the folder (New Folder) highlighted. Type **Drawings** to change the name of the folder. Press **enter.** The right pane should now contain four documents and two folders.

➤ Pull down the **View menu.** Click (or point to) the **Arrange Icons command** to display a submenu, then click the **By Name command.**

➤ Click the **plus sign** next to drive A to expand the drive. Your screen should match Figure 13d:

- The left pane shows the subordinate folders on drive A.
- The right pane displays the contents of drive A (the selected object in the left pane). The folders are shown first and appear in alphabetical order. The document names are displayed after the folders and are also in alphabetical order.

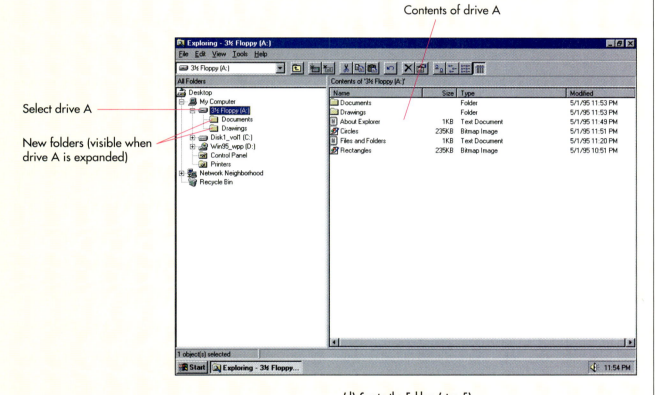

(d) Create the Folders (step 5)

FIGURE 13 Hands-on Exercise 4 (continued)

STEP 6: Move the Files

➤ This step has you move the Notepad documents and Paint drawings to the Documents and Drawings folders, respectively.

➤ To move the About Explorer document:

- Point to the **icon** for **About Explorer** in the right pane. Use the **right mouse button** to click and drag the icon to the Documents folder in the left pane.
- Release the mouse to display the menu shown in Figure 13e. Click **Move Here** to move the file. A popup window will appear briefly as the file is being moved.

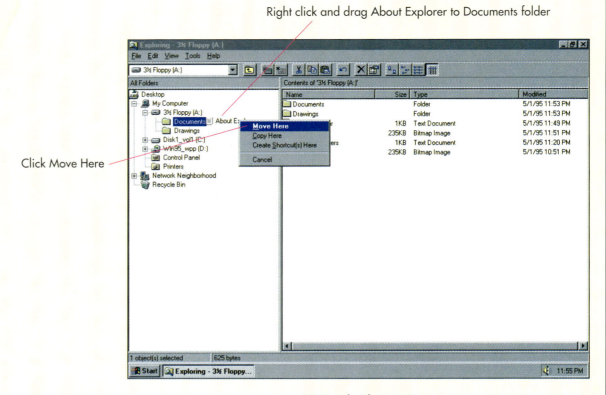

(e) Move the Files (step 6)

FIGURE 13   Hands-on Exercise 4 (continued)

➤ To prove that the file has been moved, you can view the contents of the Documents folder:
- Click the **Documents folder** in the left pane to select the folder. The icon for the Documents folder changes to an open folder and its contents (About Explorer) are displayed in the right pane.

➤ Move the Files and Folders document to the Documents folder:
- Click the **icon** for **drive A** to select the drive and display its contents.
- Point to the **icon** for **Files and Folders.** Use the **right mouse button** to click and drag the icon to the Documents folder in the left pane.
- Release the mouse to display a menu. Click **Move Here** to move the file.

➤ Use the **right mouse button** to move the Circles and Rectangles files to the Drawings folder.

STEP 7: Copy the Contents of the Documents Folder

➤ This step has you copy the contents of the Documents folder on drive A to the Homework folder on drive C. Click (select) the **Documents folder** on drive A to open the folder and display its contents as shown in Figure 13f.

➤ Click the **plus sign** next to the icon for drive C to expand the drive and display its folders. You should see the Homework folder that was created in the first exercise. Do *not* click the folder on drive C as the Documents folder on drive A is to remain open.

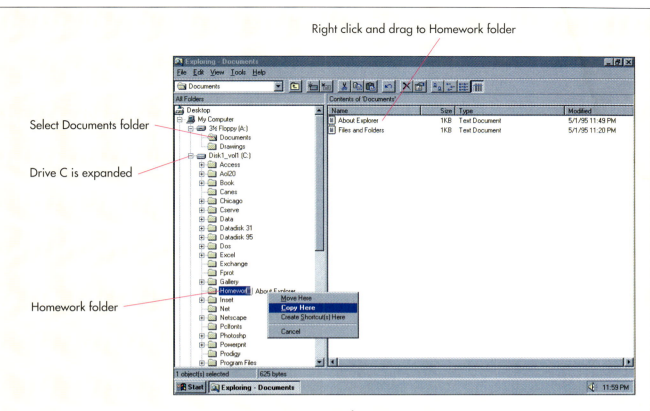

(f) Copy to Drive C (step 7)

FIGURE 13   Hands-on Exercise 4 (continued)

➤ Point to the **About Explorer file** (in the Documents folder on drive A). Use the **right mouse button** to click and drag the icon to the Homework folder on drive C. Release the mouse. Click **Copy Here** to copy the file to the Homework folder.

➤ Point to the **Files and Folders file** (in the Documents folder on drive A). Use the **right mouse button** to click and drag the icon to the Homework folder on drive C. Release the mouse. Click **Copy Here.**

➤ You will see a dialog box asking whether you want to replace the Files and Folders file that is already in the Homework folder (from the previous hands-on exercise). Click **No** since the files are the same.

OPEN FOLDERS QUICKLY

Click in the left pane of the Explorer window, then type any letter to select (open) the first folder whose name begins with that letter. If you type two letters in quick succession—for example, W and O—you will open the first folder beginning with the letters W and O. Pausing between the letters—that is, typing W, then leisurely typing O—will open a folder beginning with W, then open a second folder (while closing the first) whose name begins with O.

STEP 8: Copy the Contents of the Drawings Folder

➤ This step has you copy the contents of the Drawings folder on drive A to the Homework folder on drive C. Click (select) the **Drawings folder** on drive A to open the folder and display its contents. You should see the Circles and Rectangles files that were moved to this folder in the previous step.

➤ Click the **icon** for the **Circles file,** then press and hold the **Ctrl key** as you click the **icon** for the **Rectangles file** to select both files.

➤ Point to either of the selected files, then click the **right mouse button** as you drag both files to the Homework folder on drive C. Release the mouse. Click **Copy Here** to copy the files to the Homework folder.

➤ Explorer will begin to copy both files. You will, however, see a dialog box asking whether you want to replace the Rectangles file that is already in the Homework folder (from the previous hands-on exercise). Click **No** since the files are the same.

SELECT MULTIPLE FILES

You can perform the same operation on multiple files at the same time by selecting the files prior to executing the command. Press and hold the Ctrl key as you click the icon of each additional file you want to select. If the files are adjacent to one another, click the icon of the first file, then press and hold the Shift key as you click the icon of the last file.

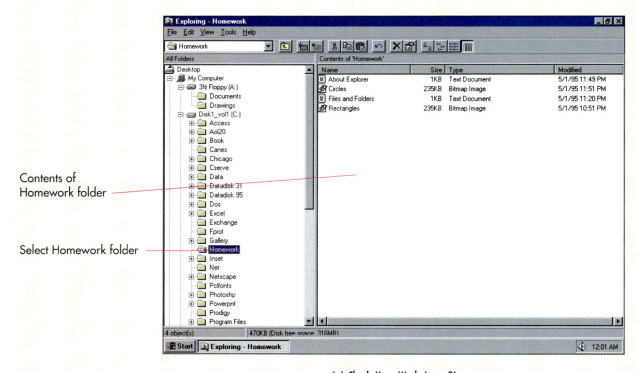

(g) Check Your Work (step 9)

FIGURE 13 Hands-on Exercise 4 (continued)

STEP 9: Check Your Work

➤ Select (click) the **Homework folder** on drive C to display its contents.

➤ The icon changes to an open folder, and you should see the four files in Figure 13g.

➤ Click the **Close button** to close Explorer. Click the **Start button.** Click the **Shut Down** command to exit Windows.

SUMMARY

All Windows operations take place on the desktop. The Start button, as its name suggests, is where you begin. Online help is accessed by clicking the Help command from the Start button. The mouse is essential to Windows and has four basic actions: pointing, clicking (with the left or right button), double clicking, and dragging. The mouse pointer assumes different shapes according to the nature of the current action.

Every window contains the same basic elements, which include a title bar, a Minimize button, a Maximize or Restore button, and a Close button. Other elements that may be present include a menu bar, vertical and/or horizontal scroll bars, a status bar, and a toolbar. All windows may be moved and sized.

A dialog box supplies information needed to execute a command. Option buttons indicate mutually exclusive choices, one of which must be chosen. Check boxes are used if the choices are not mutually exclusive or if an option is not required. A text box supplies descriptive information. A (drop-down or open) list box displays multiple choices, any of which may be selected. A tabbed dialog box provides access to multiple sets of options.

The first (often only) floppy drive on a system is designated as drive A. The first (often only) hard disk is drive C regardless of whether there are one or two floppy drives. Additional hard drives and/or the CD-ROM drive are labeled from D on.

A file name can contain up to 255 characters in length and may include spaces and other punctuation. Files are stored in folders to better organize the hundreds (or thousands) of files on a disk. A folder may contain program files, data files, and/or other folders.

The most basic way to locate a specific file or folder is to use My Computer, which opens a new window for each successive folder. The Windows Explorer is a more sophisticated tool that displays a hierarchical view of the entire system in a single window.

The Delete command deletes (removes) a file from a disk. If, however, the file was deleted from a hard disk, it is not really gone, but moved instead to the Recycle Bin from where it can be subsequently recovered.

The result of dragging a file icon from one folder to another depends on whether the folders are on the same or different drives. Dragging the file to a folder on the same drive moves the file. Dragging the file to a folder on a different drive copies the file. It's easier, therefore, to click and drag with the right mouse button to produce a menu from which you can select the operation.

KEY WORDS AND CONCEPTS

Backup	Click	Command button
Check box	Close button	Contents tab

Control Panel	Index tab	Pull-down menu
Copy command	Large Icons view	Recycle Bin
Cut command	List box	Rename command
Data file	Maximize button	Restore button
Delete command	Menu bar	Right click
Desktop	Minimize button	Size a window
Details view	Mouse pointer	Small Icons View
Dialog box	Move a window	Start button
Dimmed command	My Computer	Status bar
Double click	Network Neighborhood	Submenu
Drag	New command	Tabbed dialog box
Drop-down list box	Online help	Taskbar
Ellipsis	Open list box	Text box
File	Option buttons	Title bar
File type	Paste command	Toolbar
Folder	Point	Vertical scroll bar
Help command	Printers folder	What's This button
Horizontal scroll bar	Program file	Windows Explorer
Icons	Properties	Windows 95

INDEX

Agenda Wizard, 122–123, 127–128
Alignment, 76–77
Answer Wizard, 24
Arial, 63, 64
AutoCorrect, 28–29, 35, 110, 147, 150
AutoFormat, 110, 147, 150, 173–174, 175, 185
Automatic replacement, 50
Award Wizard, 122–123

Backup, 30, 32, 57
Body Text style, 172
Boller, Paul F., 159
Bookmark, 193
Borders and Shading command, 82–83, 87, 214
Borders toolbar, 87, 227, 281
Bulleted list, 154, 156–157
Bullets and Numbering command, 154–155, 215

Calendar Wizard, 122–123
Caps Lock key, 3
   correction of, 28
Case-insensitive replacement, 50
Case-sensitive replacement, 50
Cell, 163
Character style, 172
Client application, 245
Clip art, 129, 217
Clipboard, 49, 59
Close button, 5, 6
Column break, 217
Columns command, 208–209, 228
Common user interface, 256
Compound document, 129, 245
Container, 245
Copy command, 49, 59
   shortcut for, 60
Courier New, 63, 64
Custom dictionary, 26
   deletion from, 115
Cut command, 49
   shortcut for, 60

Data disk, 11
Data record, 265
Data source, 265, 271, 274
Default folder, 31
Default Paragraph Font Style, 172
Deleting text, 5, 22
   caution with, 49
Deselecting text, 5, 22
Desktop publishing, 205–234
Dialog box, shortcuts for, 74
Double clicking, 14
Drag and drop, 61
Drawing toolbar, 220, 281
Drop Cap command, 140, 220, 226
Drop shadow, 83, 140

Embedded object, 245
Embedding, 247–253
Emphasis, as design element, 230
Endnote, 154–156, 162
ENIAC computer, 101
Envelopes and Labels command, 111, 118
Equation Editor toolbar, 283

Facing pages, 233
Fax Cover Sheet Wizard, 122–123
Field, 110
Field code, 113
Field result, 113
File menu, 8
File name, 8
Find command, 50, 59
   with formatting, 71
First line indent, 78
Font, 65
Footer, 181–182
Footnote, 154–156, 159–162
Form letter, 265, 276
Format Font command, 65–67
Format Frame command, 131, 137, 249–250
Format painter, 72, 73
Format Paragraph command, 80–82
Format Style command, 176

Formatting toolbar, 5, 7, 281
Frame, 127, 220–221

Go To command, 184
Grammar check, 104, 106–107
   customization of, 116–117
Graphic design, 229–233
Grid, in desktop publishing, 229–231
Gridline, in a table, 166

Hanging indent, 78
Hard page break, 68
Hard return, 2, 13, 20
Header, 181–182, 189–191
Header/Footer toolbar, 283
Heading 1 style, 172
Help, 24
Horizontal ruler, 6

Indents, 76, 78, 86–87
   increasing and decreasing, 88, 157
Index and Tables command, 184
In-place editing, 139, 246, 250
Insert Date and Time command, 110, 270
Insert Footnote command, 155–156
Insert Frame command, 136, 223
Insert mode, 4, 57
Insert Object command, 129–133, 247–248
Insert Page Numbers command, 181
Insert Picture command, 217–220, 222
Insert Symbol command, 110–111
Insert Table command, 166
Insertion point, 2

Landscape orientation, 67, 166
Leader character, 79
Left indent, 76
Letter Wizard, 269
Line spacing, 79
   shortcut for, 86
Linked object, 245
Linking, 254–262

Mail merge, 265–278
Mail Merge Helper, 268–269, 274
Mail Merge toolbar, 284
Main document, 265, 270
Margins, 73
Masthead, 213–214, 226
Maximize button, 5, 6, 12
Merge field, 265
Microsoft ClipArt Gallery, 129–131, 134–137
Microsoft Fax Accessory, 126
Microsoft toolbar, 282
Microsoft WordArt, 131–133, 138–139

Minimize button, 5, 6
Monospaced typeface, 65
Multitasking, 258

Newsletter Wizard, 209–210
Newspaper-style columns, 208–209, 211–212
Normal style, 172
Normal view, 16–17, 53
Numbered list, 154

Object, 129
Object linking and embedding, (OLE), 133, 245–263
Open command, 8–9, 18–19
Overtype mode, 4, 57

Page break, 67–68
Page Layout view, 16–17, 53–54
Page numbers, 181
Page Setup command, 67–68, 73
Paper, selection of, 101
Paragraph formatting, 76–90
Paragraph style, 172, 173
Paste command, 49, 59
   shortcut for, 60
Paste Special command, 259
Point size, 65
Portrait orientation, 67
Print command, 15
Proportional typeface, 65
Pull quote, 206

Record. *See* Data record
Redo command, 49, 60
Replace command, 50, 58–59
   with formatting, 71
Restore button, 5
Résumé Wizard, 120–121
Reverse, 206
Right indent, 76
Ruler, 6

Sans serif typeface, 63
Save As command, 28–29, 32
Save command, 8–9, 13–14
Scrolling, 51–53
   mouse versus keyboard, 57, 58
Section, 182–183
Section break, 182, 188
Section formatting, 182
Selecting text, with F8 key, 84
Selection bar, 69
Selective replacement, 50
Select-then-do, 48
Serif typeface, 63

Server application, 245
Shortcut menu, 48, 70
Show/Hide ¶ button, 13
Sizing handle, 131, 137, 224–225
Smart quotes, 173
Soft page break, 68
Soft return, 2
Sort, in mail merge, 277
Spell check, 26–28, 32, 34
    customization of, 113
Standard toolbar, 5, 7, 282
Status bar, 6
Style, 172–180
Summary information, 25

Tab key, with tables, 167
Tab stop, 79
Table of contents, 184, 186–187
    updating of, 191
Tables feature, 163–171
Tabs, 79–80
Taskbar, 258
Template, 120
Thesaurus, 104, 105, 115
Times New Roman, 63, 64
Tip of the Day, 17, 20
TipWizard, 17–18, 20
TipWizard toolbar, 282

Toggle switch, 3
Toolbar, 5, 7, 17, 19, 279–285
ToolTip, 21
Type size, 65
Type style, 65
Typeface, 63–64
Typography, 63–67, 206–208

Undo Command, 23, 49, 60

Vertical ruler, 6
View menu, 17, 19, 53–54, 56, 185–186
    effect on columns, 211
    effect on footnotes, 161
    effect on headers and footers, 191

White space, 230, 232
Whole word replacement, 50
Widows and orphans, 81–82
Windows 95, tour of, 10
Wizard, 120–129
Word wrap, 2
WordPerfect, conversion from, 17

Zoom command, 53–54